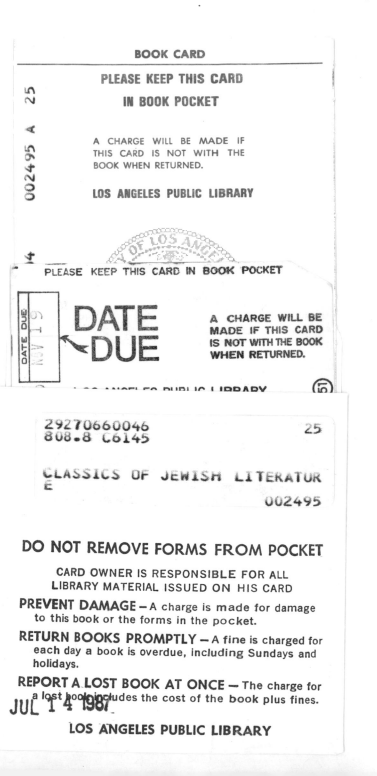

BOOK CARD

PLEASE KEEP THIS CARD
IN BOOK POCKET

25 A 002495

14

A CHARGE WILL BE MADE IF
THIS CARD IS NOT WITH THE
BOOK WHEN RETURNED.

LOS ANGELES PUBLIC LIBRARY

PLEASE KEEP THIS CARD IN BOOK POCKET

DATE DUE: NOV 19

DATE
DUE

A CHARGE WILL BE
MADE IF THIS CARD
IS NOT WITH THE BOOK
WHEN RETURNED.

LOS ANGELES PUBLIC LIBRARY

⑤

29270660046   25
808.8 C6145

CLASSICS OF JEWISH LITERATUR
E
                                002495

DO NOT REMOVE FORMS FROM POCKET

CARD OWNER IS RESPONSIBLE FOR ALL
LIBRARY MATERIAL ISSUED ON HIS CARD

PREVENT DAMAGE – A charge is made for damage
to this book or the forms in the pocket.

RETURN BOOKS PROMPTLY – A fine is charged for
each day a book is overdue, including Sundays and
holidays.

REPORT A LOST BOOK AT ONCE – The charge for
a lost book includes the cost of the book plus fines.

JUL 14 1987

LOS ANGELES PUBLIC LIBRARY

Classics
of
Jewish Literature

C. 004

Classics
of
Jewish Literature

Leo Lieberman, Ph.D.
&
Arthur F. Beringause, Ph.D.

Philosophical Library
New York

Library of Congress Cataloging-in-Publication Data

Classics of Jewish literature.

  1. Jewish literature. 2. Judaism—History—Sources.
I. Lieberman, Leo. II. Beringause, Arthur F.,
1919-
PN6067.C56   1986   808.8'98924   86-8124
ISBN 0-8022-2092-4

Contents

A Note of Gratitude

The editors wish to express their appreciation to Mrs. Evelyn Schweidel, Department Secretary of the English Department at Bronx Community College, for her patience and care in typing the manuscript; to Professor Jeffrey Spielberger of the English Department of Bronx Community College for his assistance with proofreading; to Mrs. Ann Silverman of the Yonkers Library; to Rose Runes for her devotion and suggestions, her interest and commitment and to Ann and Barbara for proving that there are still "women of valor" whose price exceeds rubies.

General Introduction

Until recently, a primary purpose of Jewish literature, which was chiefly religious in inspiration, was to abolish time and obliterate geography—making all the Children of Israel, if not into members of one family, certainly into contemporaries and neighbors despite divisions of historical era and physical barrier. This is not to imply that the development of Jewish thought was either smooth or unanimous. Because of their dispersal to every continent, the Jews have played a role in an array of events almost as diverse as the history of the human race itself. Israel Besht, founder of the Hasidic movement in eighteenth century Russia, said: "Like the soil, everyone treads on the Jews. But God has put into that soil the power to bring forth all kinds of plants and fruits."

Notwithstanding their extraordinary variety, the many Jewish communities and the overwhelming majority of indi-

13

vidual Jews remained unified—one people with one history. Demarcations in the outline of Western history are often neither helpful nor valid for insight into the history of the Jews. There is no Reformation in Jewish history. There are no Dark Ages, although, paradoxically, millions of Jews in Czarist Russia emerged from the medieval era only near the dawn of the twentieth century.

Unique in all history, the Jews—scattered over every continent, speaking a diversity of languages, subject to the pressures of contrasting cultures—endured as one people because Jewish literature, the writings of Jews about themselves and their existence, became their portable homeland. Although hunted and driven, Jews took sustenance from their literature, which they studied and safeguarded through persecution and exile. No wonder that for centuries they have been called *Am ha-Sefer*, People of the Book.

Continuity was not always easy; there were milestones as well as rocky and barren stretches along the way. Jewish writing reflected at first the struggle of the Hebrews to become a religious people; later, their zeal for the Torah, the law of God; still later, their belief in a glorious future to be heralded by the Messiah. Then Jewish literature came to express a settled way of life with stable religious values and a core of regulations unquestioned as to validity. Practice was standardized but broad latitude on questions of belief was allowed. The overriding concern of Jewish writers was instruction of their fellow Jews, sometimes by way of castigation, sometimes by way of interpretation, always by way of coalescing faith and knowledge. Their central theme is that there is divine purpose in everything, including the forces of history. Of these writings, it is often hard to tell where history ends and legend begins.

Seeking to reconcile Greek philosophy with the religion of their fathers, medieval Jewish scholars cross-fertilized Hebrew, Greek, and Arabic ideas, producing an intellectual harvest that has fed the Western mind down to the present day. But Arab civilization declined, and the Jews were besieged by Turkish barbarity in the East and Christian bigotry in the West. Walled in by their literature with its bastions stronger than the strongest medieval battlements—ramparts of ritual, idea, and belief—the Jews survived as a people, and took comfort in legalistic study and mystical writing. The pattern of Jewish life became rigidly fixed as the Jews insulated themselves.

In contrast, having suffered a rupture with the past, modern Jewish writers—more secular than religious, more aesthetic than didactic—have attempted to adjust Jewish values, beliefs, and customs to a rapidly changing world, at the same time that they express nostalgia for family, religious experience, and tradition ever present yet forever left behind. As yet, no one has explained how to be traditionally Jewish and fully modern at the same time. Increasingly, Jewish writers of today regard themselves not so much Children of Israel as citizens of the entire earth.

Nevertheless, the Jewish literary tradition, the world's oldest, remains unbroken, although problems of Jewish identity are complex. The position of the Jew is anomalous, for he has always lived in two worlds—the large external one of the Gentiles, and the small internal one of ancient tradition and belief. Many Jews have found it impossible to lead a hyphenated existence. Throughout history, the pressures of anti-Semitism on those Jews who sought advancement or derived their scale of values from the surrounding Gentile environment have generated feelings of self-hatred which led to assimilation and conversion.

Who is a Jew and what are Jewish writings? In the Diaspora, where Jews live according to societal rules of time, place, and mores, the American Jewish community is as American as the English is English and the German was German. Emma Lazarus does not always defend, Israel Zangwill long for, Moses Mendelsohn commemorate. Jewish literature, whatever and wherever its origin, has always transcended boundaries of epoch and nation to illuminate not only the Jewish reality but the human condition as well.

It is difficult to overestimate the importance of Jewish writings. Not only Jewish history but also the history of humanity has been fundamentally affected. The extent of this influence is neither fully understood nor generally appreciated. Too few Jews as well as Christians are familiar with the values, vitality, and relevance of Jewish creativity during the long sweep of the last 3,000 years. The purpose of this anthology, which is designed for the general reader, Jewish and non-Jewish, is to gather classic writings from all the genres and eras so as to survey the development of the literature of the Children of Israel.

The widest possible definition of classic has been adopted for this book: a work of acknowledged excellence having such intrinsic interest and value, that it is accepted as part of the enduring cultural achievement of all humankind. The works are presented in translation, except for those originally composed in English.

Translation always presents a problem, especially when working with writers whose names have been transcribed by reputable scholars in different ways. The sound *a* or [ei] can be recorded *ay*, *a*, *ei*, and the Hebrew *chet* and *chaf*, which correspond somewhat to the German *ch*, a gutteral sound, has no direct counterpart in English; thus, the pseudonym of Sholem Rabinowitz can be transcribed as Sholem Aleichem or Sholem Aleikhem or even Sholem Alaychem. We have consulted a number of sources and have attempted to use the spelling which is most familiar, in this instance Sholem Aleichem.

A second matter of concern is the arrangement of the authors within each genre. Usage is the guide. An alphabetical arrangement according to the surname of the writer is employed except when the writer is known by a pseudonym. The selection by Sholem Jacob Abramowitch (pen name: Mendele Mokher Sefarim) is placed according to *Mendele*, the name by which he is usually known. Many medieval writers are listed under Ibn, sign of the patronym.

Texts are based on the best editions, and spelling and punctuation are modernized throughout. Organization under broad headings allows coordination of the various writings through allusion and comparison. Alongside soaring works of art, plain writings are given a place in the hope that this book will be not a treasury of the famous but a record of development. No effort has been made to include hitherto unknown documents, but rather we have brought together selections illustrative of the greatness inherent in Jewish literature. Even so, the vast number of diverse Jewish writings precludes any thoroughly adequate representation between the covers of one book. Some omitted works are referred to in the historical or biographical headnotes that attempt to place each composition in its proper setting.

No anthology is complete. For several reasons, among them that of space, the works of many modern writers have been excluded from this volume. In a succeeding book we hope to indicate the vast scope and amazing achievements of contemporary Jewish authors. In the United States alone there are Alfred Kazin in criticism, Arthur Miller in drama, Oscar Handlin in history, Saul Bellow in the novel, Morris Raphael Cohen in philosophy, Karl Shapiro in poetry, Carl Sagan in science, and a host of other fine writers. The situation is similar in England, France, and elsewhere. In Israel, too, especially capable authors like Amos Oz have come to the fore. Obviously, for today's Jews as for their ancestors, life without literature is inconceivable.

The focus of the diversity of Jewish writings is the Bible, with the commentaries on it and the lore that grew around it. Today, many Israeli writers consider themselves fortunate to be writing in a direct line from Biblical, Talmudic, and Midrashic literature. As Hebrew writers in a revitalized language they have access to a built-in symbolic system which, when skillfully handled, can give resonance and reverberation to words, ideas, and feelings across the ages. The many, many volumes of Jewish literature link the generations in an awesome chain of destiny and heritage, revealing how the Jews have turned every crisis, every sounding of the death knell, into rebirth and an instrument of growth.

Jewish history, Jewish literature, is unique.

Chronology

The Bible	Canon closed c. 100 C.E. (The Bible is a composite, a blend of writings reaching all the way back to mist-shrouded antiquity.)
Apocrypha	c. 200 B.C.E.-800 C.E.
Dead Sea Scrolls	c. 100 B.C.E.
Philo	c. 20 B.C.E.-c. 40 C.E.
Josephus	c. 40-100 C.E.
The Midrash	c. 200-c. 1200
The Talmud	Closed c. 500 (The time span is about seven centuries.)
Responsa	c. 550-
Eldad ha-Dani	fl. 800
Rabbenu Gershom Ben Judah	960-1040
Isaac Alfasi	1013-1103
Ahimaaz Ben Paltiel	1020-1060

Solomon Ibn Gabirol	1021-1058
Bahya Ben Joseph Ibn Pakuda	c.1050-c. 1120
Jehudah Halevi	c. 1080-c. 1140
Abraham Ibn Ezra	c. 1090-c. 1165
Berechiah Ben Natronai Ha Nakdan	c. 1200
Maimonides (Moses Ben Maimon)	1135-1205
The Zohar	c. 1300
Eliezer of Maience	d. 1357
Joseph Caro	1488-1575
Baruch Spinoza	1632-1677
Glückel of Hameln	1646-1724
Moses Mendelsohn	1729-1786
Levi Yitzhak of Berditchev	1740-1809
Chelm Folktales	c. 1750
Heinrich Heine	1795-1856
Mendele Mokher Sefarim	c. 1836-1917
Emma Lazarus	1849-1887
Isaac Leib Peretz	1851-1915
Ahad Ha'am	1856-1927
Sholem Aleichem	1859-1916
Theodor Herzl	1860-1904
S. Anski	1863-1920
Israel Zangwill	1864-1926
Yehoash (Solomon Bloomgarden)	1872-1927
David Pinski	1872-1959
Hayyim Nachman Bialik	1873-1934
Saul Tchernichovsky	1875-1943
Martin Buber	1878-1965
Albert Einstein	1879-1955
Peretz Hirschbein	1880-1948
Sholem Asch	1880-1966
Lion Feuchtwanger	1884-1958
H. Leivick	1888-1962
Shmuel Yosef Agnon	1888-1970
Isaac Rosenberg	1890-1918
Rachel	1890-1931
Nellie Sachs	1891-1970
Uri Zevi Greenberg	1894-1981
Isaac Bashevis Singer	1904-
Anne Frank	1929-1945

The Biblical Era
(c. 1500 B.C.E.-500 C.E.)

Just as the Bible is not one book composed at one particular time but a compilation revised and edited by redactors, so the Biblical Era spans several culture periods. Over the centuries Jews produced a miscellany of literary compositions revered in varying degree and differing in attitude, feeling, idea, and style, even idiom. Without doubt, these writings were influenced by the various peoples with whom Hebrews came in contact. The impact of Rome and Greece on Josephus and Philo is obvious. More subtle is Jewish borrowing from Egyptian, Babylonian, Persian, and numerous other sources. This is not to imply that literature of the Biblical Era is a mere composite of diverse influences nor that the Jews took much from their neighbors without returning even more. Jewish writings are fully original and significant in their own right, not only archetypal but central as well.

Beginning about 1500 B.C.E. and ending about 500 C.E., after the collapse of Judea and the dispersion of the Jews, the Biblical Era moved out from chronicles based on folk memory all the way to works of art by sophisticated individual writers. Unfortunately, along the way a host of books were permanently lost. The Bible itself mentions, among others, the *Book of Yashar* and the *Book of the Wars of the Lord*.

The diversity of writings exhibited in the Biblical Era are responses to challenges Jews faced—including war, defeat, and exile. The voluminous but pithy records of the Talmud concentrate on interpretation and formulation of law, both religious and secular, in order to save what is most dear. The poetic fragments of the library of the Essenes indicate a passionate desire to prepare religiously for a better future. Ben Sira and other authors in the Apocrypha assimilate Greek philosophy while they interpret Jewish faith and ideals to the world. Towering above all is the Bible, an immortal epic of a people's striving to live the word of God, a priceless repository of ideals: political as well as ethical, social as well as economic, heaven-sent as well as earth-bound. The Ten Commandments and the moral thunderings of the Prophets have set standards of behavior for all humanity for evermore. The Bible keeps before us the vision of a world democracy governed by altruism and glorifying in God-given life.

Inspired by the quest for more knowledge and better understanding of man and the universe, the Biblical Era abounds in works of genius worthy to be ranked with those of every other great literary period.

The Bible

Although universally acclaimed as "the greatest book ever written" for its theological, cultural, and literary importance, spanning more than fourteen centuries and going back beyond 1300 B.C.E., the Bible is not a book but a collection of books. Christians call the Hebrew Bible the Old Testament, considering it a forerunner of another testament or covenant. For the Jews, the Scriptures remain a collection of twenty-four books divided into three sections: *Torah* (the *Pentateuch*), *Neviim* (Prophets), and *K'tuvim* (Writings).*

Each section has distinct literary appeal and presents special literary problems. The Bible is not easy to fathom. An anthology of ancient literature, it contains almost every genre of writing, among them: history, stories, poems, songs, epics, legends, biographies, riddles, proverbs. More than a mere miscellany haphazardly collected, the Bible is a saga of the struggle of the Jews to become a holy people dedicated to the service of God. As with

---

* Christian Bibles usually tally thirty-four books because they divide Samuel, Kings, and Chronicles into two books each and enter Ezra, Nehemiah, and the twelve minor prophets as individual units.

every other classic, the Bible needs to be reinterpreted by each generation of readers, although the text—which Orthodox Jews regard as literally the word of God—seems to have come down to us through the ages accurate and unchanged from the original.

Despite the fact that only the first section is called the *Torah*, the Five Books of Moses, the word *Torah* (law) is often associated with the Hebrew Bible as a whole. The *Pentateuch* opens with the creation tale and begins the story of man, soon focusing upon the special relationship of God and His people, the Hebrews, a choosing as well as a chosen folk. Development and transmission of a covenant signalling the unique pact between God and Israel becomes a dominant theme of the Five Books of Moses although Moses is not mentioned in Genesis, the first book. Interspersed with historical matters and legal and ritualistic codes in the first section of the *Torah* are many sublime poems. The Song of Moses (Exodus 15) and the *Ha-Azinu* (Deuteronomy 32) are two prime examples. But the prose should not be slighted. It is hard not to react to the story of creation, the revelation at Sinai, the "test" of Abraham in the land of Moriah.

For the most part, the Biblical books have come down to us in Hebrew, which, despite changes in spelling and punctuation, seems faithful to the original text. But most scholars agree that we cannot be certain about the language of the text. No one can be sure of the meaning of every word in the *Torah*. Doubtless there are significant portions that are not in the original form but in veiled translation.

Neviim is filled with great literary moments. Judges depicts in biographical vignettes the great figures of Deborah, Samson, and Gideon; Kings tells in epic form of the ambivalence of Saul in his relationship with David, of David's passion for Bathsheba, of Jonathan's friendship for David. The Prophets loom up in their writings, wedding morality to religion and calling out messages of social justice in words that sear yet cleanse. They speak up fearlessly and unequivocally against empty ritualistic practices, religious abominations, man's inhumanity. In their desire to restore Israel to its covenanted status, the Prophets point an accusing finger at priests and kings alike.

K'tuvim contains literary gems with a universality of appeal, such as the Book of Ruth, the Psalms, the Song of Songs, and the Book of Job. Moving from the praise of God to the complexities of man, from human relationships to meditation on spiritual matters, *K'tuvim* presents great wisdom of the past applicable to the present and the future.

The Bible can be read as a library of books with discrete sections that together form a historical and literary memory at once diverse yet unique. It is not a mere collection of books in one binding but a thrilling, fascinating, and inspiring record of the particular experience of a particular people. The Bible presents Jews—indeed, all humankind—with a memory that is a life force, a construction of the past that gives meaning to the present and importance to the future.

The Book of Job

The Talmud (Avot 4:15) states: "It is beyond our power to understand why the wicked are at ease or why the righteous suffer." The modern reader may also reach this conclusion to the problem of human suffering and divine justice after perusing the Book of Job. The personal name Job (*A-ia-Ab* or "Where is the father?"), which reflects the struggle of man to believe, reinforces the impression that the theme of this great philosophical drama is the attempt to reconcile the undeniable facts of human misery and wretchedness with the unverifiable belief in a beneficent and omnipotent deity.

A literary masterpiece, the Book of Job is a complex, profound dialogue of highly sophisticated poetry set between a prologue and epilogue, both written in a straightforward, folk tale prose. The story of the trial and test of Job is well known. God and Satan enter into a wager concerning Job's devotion. Satan asserts that if Job is made to suffer, if family and property are lost to him, his faith will waver. Agreeing to let Job be tested, God permits a series of dreadful calamities to be visited upon him.

Job in agony asks God for an explanation of his suffering and for insight into the relationship between man and fate. God responds out of the whirlwind (a symbol of the apparent meaninglessness of any individual natural phenomenon) in some of the most beautiful verses that have come down to us. Giving no direct answer to Job's questions, which involve problems that have perplexed the human race for millennia, God rebukes Job by piling one query on another and reminding him that man was not present at creation, that he is incapable of understanding the cosmos, and that if he were to attempt to control the universe the result would be disaster.

For the modern reader of the Book of Job, aware of man's difficulties in harnessing atomic energy, God's warning is not to be taken lightly. The contrast between the vastness of the universe and the insignificance of man is stark. Space stretches on and on, seemingly amoral and indifferent. The cosmos is a mystery, and divine justice is inscrutable. But belief in God's presence imparts meaning to all things, although the meaning remains unknowable.

Chapter 38

Then the Lord answered Job out of the whirlwind and said:
Who is this that darkeneth counsel
By words without knowledge?
Gird up now thy loins like a man;
For I will demand of thee, and declare thou unto Me.

Where wast thou when I laid the foundations of the earth?
Declare, if thou hast the understanding.

Who determined the measures thereof, if thou knowest?
Or who stretched the line upon it?
Whereupon were the foundations thereof fastened?
Or who laid the corner-stone thereof,
When the morning stars sang together,
And all the sons of God shouted for joy?

Or who shut up the sea with doors;
When it broke forth, and issued out of the womb;
When I made the cloud the garment thereof,
And thick darkness a swaddling band for it,
And prescribed for it My decree,
And set bars and doors,
And said: 'Thus far shalt thou come, but no further;
And here shall thy proud waves be stayed'?

Hast thou commanded the morning since thy days began,
And caused the dayspring to know its place,
That it might take hold of the ends of the earth,
And the wicked be shaken out of it?
It is changed as clay under the seal;
And they stand as a garment.
But from the wicked their light is withholden,
And the high arm is broken.

Hast thou entered into the springs of the sea?
Or hast thou walked in the recesses of the deep?
Have the gates of death been revealed unto thee?
Or hast thou seen the gates of the shadow of death?
Hast thou surveyed unto the breadths of the earth?
Declare, if thou knowest it all.

Where is the way to the dwelling of light,
And as for darkness, where is the place thereof;
That thou shouldest take it to the bound thereof,
And that thou shouldest know the paths to the house thereof?

Thou knowest it, for thou wast then born,
And the number of thy days is great!

Hast thou entered the treasuries of the snow,
Or hast thou seen the treasuries of the hail,
Which I have reserved against the time of trouble,
Against the day of battle and war?

By what way is the light parted,
Or the east wind scattered upon the earth?
Who hath cleft a channel for the waterflood,
Or a way for the lightning of the thunder;
To cause it to rain on a land where no man is,
On the wilderness; wherein there is no man;
To satisfy the desolate and waste ground,
And to cause the bud of the tender herb to spring forth?
Hath the rain a father?
Or who hath begotten the drops of dew?
Out of whose womb came the ice?
And the hoar-frost of heaven, who hath gendered it?
The waters are congealed like stone,
And the face of the deep is frozen.
Canst thou bind the chains of the Pleiades,
Or loose the bands of Orion?
Canst thou lead forth the Mazzaroth in their season?
Or canst thou guide the Bear with her sons?
Knowest thou the ordinances of the heavens?
Canst thou establish the dominion thereof in the earth?
Canst thou lift up thy voice to the clouds,
That abundance of waters may cover thee?
Canst thou send forth lightnings, that they may go,
And say unto thee: 'Here we are'?

Who hath put wisdom in the inward parts?
Or who hath given understanding to the mind?
Who can number the clouds by wisdom?
Or who can pour out the bottles of heaven,
When the dust runneth into a mass,
And the clouds cleave fast together?

Wilt thou hunt the prey for the lioness?
Or satisfy the appetite of the young lions,
When they couch in their dens,
And abide in the covert to lie in wait?

Who provideth for the raven his prey,
When his young ones cry unto God,
And wander for lack of food?

Chapter 39

Knowest thou the time when the wild goats of the rock bring
    forth?
Or canst thou mark when the hinds do calve?
Canst thou number the months that they fulfil?
Or knowest thou the time when they bring forth?
They bow themselves, they bring forth their young,
They cast out their fruit.
Their young ones wax strong, they grow up in the open field;
They go forth, and return not again.
Who hath sent out the wild ass free?
Or who hath loosed the bands of the wild ass?
Whose house I have made the wilderness,
And the salt land his dwelling-place.
He scorneth the tumult of the city,
Neither heareth he the shoutings of the driver.
The range of the mountains is his pasture,
And he searcheth after every green thing.

Will the wild-ox be willling to serve thee?
Or will he abide by the crib?
Canst thou bind the wild-ox with his band in the furrow?
Or will he harrow the valleys after thee?
Wilt thou trust him, because his strength is great?
Or wilt thou leave thy labor to him?
Wilt thou rely on him, that he will bring home thy seed,
And gather the corn of thy threshing-floor?

The wing of the ostrich beateth joyously;

But are her pinions and feathers the kindly stork's?
For she leaveth her eggs on the earth,
And warmeth them in the dust,
And forgetteth that the foot may crush them,
Or that the wild beast may trample them.
She is hardened against her young ones, as if they were not
    hers;
Though her labour be in vain, she is without fear;
Because God hath deprived her of wisdom,
Neither hath He imparted to her understanding.
When the time cometh, she raiseth her wings on high,
And scorneth the horse and his rider.

Hast thou given the horse his strength?
Hast thou clothed his neck with fierceness?
Hast thou made him to leap as a locust?
The glory of his snorting is terrible.
He paweth in the valley, and rejoiceth in his strength;
He goeth out to meet the clash of arms.
He mocketh at fear, and is not affrighted;
Neither turneth he back from the sword.
The quiver rattleth upon him,
The glittering spear and the javelin.
He swalloweth the ground with storm and rage;
Neither believeth he that it is the voice of the horn.
As oft as he heareth the horn he saith: 'Ha, ha!'
And he smelleth the battle afar off,
The thunder of the captains, and the shouting.

Doth the hawk soar by thy wisdom,
And stretch her wings toward the south?
Doth the vulture mount up at thy command,
And make her nest on high?
She dwelleth and abideth on the rock,
Upon the crag of the rock, and the stronghold.
From thence she spieth out the prey;
Her eyes behold it afar off.
Her young ones also suck up blood;
And where the slain are, there is she.

Chapter 40

Moreover the Lord answered Job, and said:
Shall he that reproveth contend with the Almighty?
He that argueth with God, let him answer it.

Then Job answered the Lord, and said:
Behold, I am of small account; what shall I answer Thee?
I lay my hand upon my mouth.
Once have I spoken, but I will not answer again;
Yea, twice, but I will proceed no further.

Then the Lord answered Job out of the whirlwind, and said:
Gird up thy loins now like a man;
I will demand of thee, and declare thou unto Me.
Wilt thou even make void My judgment?
Wilt thou condemn Me, that thou mayest be justified?
Or hast thou an arm like God?
And canst thou thunder with a voice like Him?
Deck thyself now with majesty and excellency,
And array thyself with glory and beauty.
Cast abroad the rage of thy wrath;
And look upon every one that is proud, and abase him.
Look on every one that is proud, and bring him low;
And tread down the wicked in their place.
Hide them in the dust together;
Bind their faces in the hidden place.
Then will I also confess unto thee
That thine own right hand can save thee.

Behold now behemoth, which I made with thee;
He eateth grass as an ox.
Lo now, his strength is in his loins,
And his force is in the stays of his body.
He straineth his tail like a cedar;
The sinews of his thighs are knit together.
His bones are as pipes of brass;
His gristles are like bars of iron.

He is the beginning of the ways of God;
He only that made him can make His sword to approach unto
   him.
Surely the mountains bring him forth food,
And all the beasts of the field play there.
He lieth under the lotus-trees,
In the covert of the reed, and fens.
The lotus-trees cover him with their shadow;
The willows of the brook compass him about.
Behold, if a river overflow, he trembleth not;
He is confident, though the Jordan rush forth to his mouth.
Shall any take him by his eyes,
Or pierce through his nose with a snare?

Canst thou draw out leviathan with a fish-hook?
Or press down his tongue with a cord?
Canst thou put a ring into his nose
Or bore his jaw through with a hook?
Will he make many supplications unto thee?
Or will he speak soft words unto thee?
Will he make a covenant with thee,
That thou shouldest take him for a servant forever?
Wilt thou play with him as with a bird?
Or wilt thou bind him for thy maidens?
Will the bands of fishermen make a banquet of him?
Will they part him among the merchants?
Canst thou fill his skin with barbed irons,
Or his head with fish-spears?
Lay thy hand upon him;
Think upon the battle, thou wilt do so no more.

Chapter 41

Behold, the hope of him is in vain;
Shall no one be cast down even at the sight of him?
None is so fierce that dare stir him up;
Who then is able to stand before Me?

Who hath given Me anything beforehand, that I should repay
   him?
Whatsoever is under the whole heaven is Mine.
Would I keep silence concerning his boastings,
Or his proud talk, or his fair array of words?

Who can uncover the face of his garment?
Who shall come within his double bridle?
Who can open the doors of his face?
Round about his teeth is terror.
His scales are his pride,
Shut up together as with a close seal.
One is so near to another,
That no air can come between them.
They are joined one to another;
They stick together, that they cannot be sundered.
His sneezings flash forth light,
And his eyes are like the eyelids of the morning.
Out of his mouth go burning torches,
And sparks of fire leap forth.
Out of his nostrils goeth smoke,
As out of a seething pot and burning rushes.
His breath kindleth coals,
And a flame goeth out of his mouth.
In his neck abideth strength,
And dismay danceth before him.
The flakes of his flesh are joined together;
They are firm upon him; they cannot be moved.

His heart is as firm as a stone;
Yea, firm as the nether millstone.
When he raiseth himself up, the mighty are afraid;
By reason of despair they are beside themselves.
If one lay at him with the sword, it will not hold;
Nor the spear, the dart, nor the pointed shaft.
He esteemeth iron as straw,
And brass as rotten wood.
The arrow cannot make him flee;

Slingstones are turned with him into stubble.
Clubs are accounted as stubble;
He laugheth at the rattling of the javelin.
Sharpest potsherds are under him;
He spreadeth a threshing-sledge upon the mire.
He maketh the deep to boil like a pot;
He maketh the sea like a seething mixture.
He maketh a path to shine after him;
One would think the deep to be hoary.
Upon earth there is not his like,
Who is made to be fearless.
He looketh at all high things;
He is king over all the proud beasts.

The Book of Ruth

A basic aim of the Book of Ruth, one of the five scrolls ascribed by Talmudic tradition to the Hagiographa, is to present the origin of King David. What seems strange, at first, is that for emphasis the book concludes with a genealogical table revealing David as the great-grandson of the Moabite, Ruth, an alien and, what is more, from a people especially disliked by the Hebrews.

Ruth is pictured sympathetically as a righteous convert who leaves her people to follow her mother-in-law to Bethlehem. Despite her mother-in-law's insistence that she remain in her homeland, Ruth vows to return with Naomi and share her fate in Bethlehem. Ruth gleans in the fields of Boaz, a wealthy kinsman of Naomi's deceased husband. Through a levirate marriage, Ruth is wed to Boaz and redeems the land of the dead husband, which Naomi had sold. And through this marriage, Ruth and Boaz become the ancestors of King David.

At once a pastoral idyll and a domestic romance, the Book of Ruth is a short tale of love and devotion and divine reward for goodness. But it is more. Like Jonah and other parts of the Bible, the Book of Ruth appears to have been told (or edited) so that the great moral lessons of the Prophets are implicit in the narrative. After Moses, David is the greatest hero of Israel. And he is the product of a mixed marriage of a Jew and a converted Gentile, a marriage that tied the Messiah—Israel's future redeemer—to the rest of mankind. The Book of Ruth thus presents an argument against the prohibition of intermarriage and for the idea that God is the father of all the people on earth.

Chapter 1

And it came to pass in the days when the judges judged, that there was a famine in the land. And a certain man of Bethlehem in Judah went to sojourn in the field of Moab, he, and his wife, and his two sons. And the name of the man was Elimelech, and the name of his wife Naomi, and the name of his two sons Mahlon and Chilion, Ephrathites of Beth-lehem in Judah. And they came into the field of Moab, and continued there. And Elimelech Naomi's husband died; and she was left, and her two sons. And they took them wives of the women of Moab: the name of the one was Orpah, and the name of the other Ruth; and they dwelt there about ten years. And Mahlon and Chilion died both of them; and the woman was left of her two children and of her husband. Then she arose with her daughters-in-law, that she might return from the field of Moab; for she had heard in the field of Moab how that the Lord had remembered His people in giving them bread. And she went forth out of the place where she was, and her two daughters-in-law with her; and they went on the way to return unto the land of Judah. And Naomi said unto her two daughters-in-law: 'Go, return each of you to her mother's house; the Lord deal kindly with you, as ye have dealt with the dead, and with me. The Lord grant you that ye may find rest, each of you in the house of her husband.' Then she kissed them; and they lifted up their voice, and wept. And they said unto her: 'Nay, but we will return with thee unto thy people.' And Naomi said: 'Turn back, my daughters; why will ye go with me? Have I yet sons in my womb, that they may be your husbands? Turn back, my daughters, go your way; for I am too old to have a husband. If I should say: I have hope, should I even have a husband to-night, and also bear sons? Would ye tarry for them till they were grown? Would ye shut yourselves off for them and have no husbands? Nay, my daughters; for it grieveth me much for your sakes, for the hand of the Lord is gone forth against me.' And they lifted up their voice, and wept again; and Orpah kissed her mother-in-law; but Ruth

cleaved unto her. And she said: 'Behold, thy sister-in-law is
gone back unto her people, and unto her god; return thou after
thy sister-in-law.' And Ruth said: 'Entreat me not to leave
thee, and to return from following after thee; for whither thou
goest, I will go; and where thou lodgest, I will lodge; thy people
shall be my people, and thy God my God; where thou diest, will
I die, and there will I be buried; the Lord do so to me, and more
also, if aught but death part thee and me.' And when she saw
that she was steadfastly minded to go with her, she left off
speaking unto her. So they two went until they came to Beth-
lehem. And it came to pass, when they were come to Beth-
lehem, that all the city was astir concerning them, and the
women said: 'Is this Naomi?' And she said unto them: 'Call me
not Naomi, call me Marah; for the Almighty hath dealt very
bitterly with me. I went out full, and the Lord hath brought me
back home empty; why call ye me Naomi, seeing the Lord
hath testified against me, and the Almighty hath afflicted
me?' So Naomi returned, and Ruth the Moabitess, her
daughter-in-law; with her, who returned out of the field of
Moab—and they came back to Beth-lehem in the beginning of
barley harvest.

Chapter 2

And Naomi had a kinsman of her husband's, a mighty man
of valour, of the family of Elimelech, and his name was Boaz.
And Ruth the Moabitess said unto Naomi: 'Let me now go to
the field, and glean among the ears of corn after him in whose
sight I shall find favour.' And she said unto her: 'Go, my
daughter.' And she went, and came and gleaned in the field
after the reapers; and her hap was to light on the portion of the
field belonging unto Boaz, who was of the family of Elimelech.
And, behold, Boaz came from Beth-lehem, and said unto the
reapers: 'The Lord be with you.' And they answered him: 'The
Lord bless thee.' Then said Boaz unto his servant that was set
over the reapers: 'Whose damsel is this?' And the servant that
was set over the reapers answered and said: 'It is a Moabitish

damsel that came back with Naomi out of the field of Moab; and she said: Let me glean, I pray you, and gather after the reapers among the sheaves; so she came, and hath continued even from the morning until now, save that she tarried a little in the house.' Then said Boaz unto Ruth: 'Hearest thou not, my daughter? Go not to glean in another field, neither pass from hence, but abide here fast by my maidens. Let thine eyes be on the field that they do reap, and go thou after them; have I not charged the young men that they shall not touch thee? And when thou art athirst, go unto the vessels, and drink of that which the young men have drawn.' Then she fell on her face, and bowed down to the ground, and said unto him: 'Why have I found favour in thy sight, that thou shouldest take cognizance of me, seeing I am a foreigner?' And Boaz answered and said unto her: 'It hath fully been told me, all that thou hast done unto thy mother-in-law since the death of thy husband; and how thou hast left thy father and thy mother, and the land of thy nativity, and art come unto a people that thou knewest not heretofore. The Lord recompense thy work, and be thy reward complete from the Lord, the God of Israel, under whose wings thou art come to take refuge.' Then she said: 'Let me find favour in thy sight, my lord; for that thou hast comforted me, and for that thou hast spoken to the heart of thy handmaid, though I be not as one of thy handmaidens.' And Boaz said unto her at meal-time: 'Come hither, and eat of the bread, and dip thy morsel in the vinegar.' And she sat beside the reapers; and they reached her parched corn, and she did eat and was satisfied, and left thereof. And when she was risen up to glean, Boaz commanded his young men, saying: 'Let her glean even among the sheaves, and put her not to shame. And also pull out some for her of purpose from the bundles, and leave it, and let her glean, and rebuke her not.' So she gleaned in the field until even; and she beat out that which she had gleaned, and it was about an ephah of barley. And she took it up and went into the city; and her mother-in-law saw what she had gleaned; and she brought forth and gave to her that which she had left after she was satisfied. And her mother-in-law said unto her: 'Where hast thou gleaned to-day?

And where wroughtest thou? Blessed be he that did take knowledge of thee.' And she told her mother-in-law with whom she had wrought, and said: 'The man's name with whom I wrought to-day is Boaz.' And Naomi said unto her daughter-in-law: 'Blessed be he of the Lord, who hath not left off His kindness to the living and to the dead.' And Naomi said unto her: 'The man is nigh of kin unto us, one of our near kinsmen.' And Ruth the Moabitess said: 'Yea, he said unto me: Thou shalt keep fast by my young men, until they have ended all my harvest.' And Naomi said unto Ruth her daughter-in-law: 'It is good, my daughter, that thou go out with his maidens, and that thou be not met in any other field.' So she kept fast by the maidens of Boaz to glean unto the end of barley harvest and of wheat harvest; and she dwelt with her mother-in-law.

Chapter 3

And Naomi her mother-in-law said unto her: 'My daughter, shall I not seek rest for thee, that it may be well with thee? And now is there not Boaz our kinsman, with whose maidens thou wast? Behold, he winnoweth barley tonight in the threshing-floor. Wash thyself therefore, and anoint thee, and put thy raiment upon thee, and get thee down to the threshing-floor; but make not thyself known unto the man, until he shall have done eating and drinking. And it shall be, when he lieth down, that thou shalt mark the place where he shall lie, and thou shalt go in, and uncover his feet, and lay thee down; and he will tell thee what thou shalt do.' And she said unto her: 'All that thou sayest unto me I will do.

And she went down unto the threshing-floor, and did according to all that her mother-in-law bade her. And when Boaz had eaten and drunk, and his heart was merry, he went to lie down at the end of the heap of corn; and she came softly, and uncovered his feet, and laid her down. And it came to pass at midnight, that the man was startled, and turned himself; and, behold, a woman lay at his feet. And he said: 'Who art thou?' And she answered: 'I am Ruth thy handmaid; spread therefore thy skirt over thy handmaid; for thou art a near kinsman.' And he said: 'Blessed be thou of the Lord, my daughter; thou hast shown more kindness in the end than at the beginning, inasmuch as thou didst not follow the young men, whether poor or rich. And now, my daughter, fear not; I will do to thee all that thou sayest; for all the men in the gate of my people do know that thou art a virtuous woman. And now it is true that I am a near kinsman; howbeit there is kinsman nearer than I. Tarry this night, and it shall be in the morning, that if he will perform unto thee the part of a kinsman, well; let him do the kinsman's part; but if he be not willing to do the part of a kinsman to thee, then will I do the part of a kinsman to thee, as the Lord liveth; lie down until the morning.' And she lay at his feet until the morning; and she rose up before one could discern another. For he said: 'Let it not be known that the woman came to the threshing-floor.' And he said: 'Bring the mantle that is upon thee, and hold it'; and she held it; and he measured six measures of barley, and laid it on her; and he went into the city. And when she came to her mother-in-law, she said: 'Who art thou, my daughter?' And she told her all that the man had done to her. And she said: 'These six measures of barley gave he me for he said to me: Go not empty unto thy mother-in-law.' Then said she: 'Sit still, my daughter, until thou know how the matter will fall; for the man will not rest, until he have finished the thing this day.'

Chapter 4

Now Boaz went up to the gate, and sat him down there; and, behold, the near kinsman of whom Boaz spoke came by; unto whom he said: 'Ho, such a one! turn aside, sit down here.' And he turned aside, and sat down. And he took ten men of the elders of the city, and said: 'Sit ye down here.' And they sat down. And he said unto the near kinsman: 'Naomi, that is come back out of the field of Moab, selleth the parcel of land, which was our brother Elimelech's; and I thought to disclose it unto thee, saying: Buy it before them that sit here, and before the elders of my people. If thou wilt redeem it, redeem it; but if it will not be redeemed, then tell me, that I may know; for there is none to redeem it beside thee; and I am after thee.' And he said: 'I will redeem it.' Then said Boaz: 'What day thou buyest the field of the hand of Naomi—hast thou also bought of Ruth the Moabitess, the wife of the dead, to raise up the name of the dead upon his inheritance?' And the near kinsman said: 'I cannot redeem it for myself, lest I mar mine own inheritance: take thou my right of redemption on thee; for I cannot redeem it.'

Now this was the custom in former times in Israel concerning redeeming and concerning exchanging, to confirm all things a man drew off his shoe, and gave it to his neighbour; and this was the attestation in Israel.—So the near kinsman said unto Boaz: 'Buy it for thyself.' And he drew off his shoe. And Boaz said unto the elders, and unto all the people: 'Ye are witnesses this day, that I have bought all that was Elimelech's, and all that was Chilion's and Mahlon's, of the hand of Naomi. Moreover, Ruth the Moabitess, the wife of Mahlon, have I acquired to be my wife, to raise up the name of the dead upon his inheritance, that the name of the dead be not cut off from among his brethren, and from the gate of his place; ye are witnesses this day.' And all the people that were in the gate, and the elders, said: 'We are witnesses. The Lord make the woman that is come into thy house like Rachel and like Leah, which two did build the house of Israel; and do thou worthily in Ephrath, and be famous in Beth-lehem; and let thy house be like the house of Perez, whom Tamar bore unto Judah, of the seed which the Lord shall give thee of this young woman.'

So Boaz took Ruth, and she became his wife; and he went in unto her, and the Lord gave her conception, and she bore a son. And the women said unto Naomi: 'Blessed be the Lord, who hath not left thee this day without a near kinsman, and let his name be famous in Israel. And he shall be unto thee a restorer of life, and a nourisher of thine old age; for thy daughter-in-law, who loveth thee, who is better to thee than seven sons, hath borne him.' And Naomi took the child, and laid it on her bosom, and became nurse unto it. And the women her neighbours gave it a name, saying: 'There is a son born to Naomi'; and they called his name Obed; he is the father of Jesse, the father of David.

Now these are the generations of Perez: Perez begot Hezron; and Hezron begot Ram, and Ram begot Amminadab; and Amminadab begot Nahshon, and Nahshon begot Salmon; and Salmon begot Boaz, and Boaz begot Obed; and Obed begot Jesse, and Jesse begot David.

Apocrypha

Highly valued today because they are among the very few writings extant showing the way Jews lived, thought, and felt during the period from 200 B.C.E. to 800 C.E., the fourteen books of the Apocrypha have always been popular. The literature, art, and music of all succeeding eras, including our own, have been enriched by material from the Apocrypha.

Although written by Jews for Jews and much like the writings of the Bible, the Apocrypha were excluded from the Biblical canon for several possible reasons. They reflect Hellenist conceptions of the deity, the world, and man. They are occasionally in direct opposition to such rabbinic teachings as immortality of the soul. They were composed after the closing of the Bible to new writings. But the Apocrypha were incorporated in the Septuagint, the Greek translation of the Hebrew Bible about 250 B.C.E. and from there canonized by the Catholic Church in the Latin version for Christians, some five hundred years later. Today, the Apocrypha is found in Roman Catholic versions of the Bible but not in Jewish or Protestant editions.

41

The term Apocrypha (from the Greek for writings of hidden lore) is applied only to non-canonical books incorporated in the Septuagint. (Other non-canonical works are called Pseudipigrapha.) The Apocrypha have been preserved only in translation, and next to nothing is known of the authors, although most of the books were originally ascribed to ancient Hebrew worthies, such as Enoch. The Wisdom of Ben Sirach (called Ecclesiasticus in Latin) is unique in that it is the work of a single author and it bears his name. During Talmudic times the Rabbis spoke out against reading portions of the Apocrypha as scripture in the synagogue adding that, since the Apocrypha contain many references to God, they should not be destroyed but stored away. Thus the term Apocrypha may reflect the Hebrew *genuzim* (hidden). The Rabbis of the Talmud themselves, however, refer to the Apocrypha as *sefarim hizonim* (extraneous books).

Among the fourteen books of the Apocrypha are diverse types of literature:

1. religious poetry: The Song of the Three Children;
2. history: The Books of the Maccabees;
3. wisdom literature: The Wisdom of Ben Sirach;
4. fictional narrative with a moral: The Story of Susanna and the Elders;
5. chronicle-romance: Judith;
6. revelation: Esdras;
7. folktale: Tobit;
8. prophecy: Baruch.

Tobit

The story of Tobit, written about 200-165 B.C.E., is a charming narrative reflecting for Jews outside Israel Jewish mores and morals. Outwardly, the plot revolves about Tobit, a pious Jew in Nineveh, and the travels and adventures of his son, Tobias. But the story is more than simple entertainment; it contains traditional religious and ethical teaching, as for example, Tobit's advice to his son: "What you hate, do not do to any one."

I Tobit have walked all the days of my life in the way of truth and justice, and I did many almsdeeds to my brethren, and my nation, who came with me to Nineveh, into the land of the Assyrians. And when I was in my own country, in the land of Israel, being but young, I alone went often to Jerusalem at the feasts, as it was ordained unto all the people of Israel by an everlasting decree, having the first fruits and tenths of increase, with that which was first shorn; and them gave I at the altar to the priests, the children of Aaron. The first tenth part of all increase I gave to the sons of Aaron, who ministered at Jerusalem: another tenth part I sold away, and went, and spent it every year at Jerusalem: and the third I gave unto them to whom it was meet, as Debora my father's mother had commanded me, because I was left an orphan by my father. Furthermore, when I was come to the age of a man, I married Anna of mine own kindred, and of her I begot Tobias. And when we were carried away captives to Nineveh, all my brethren and those that were of my kindred did eat of the bread of the Gentiles. But I kept myself from eating because I remembered God with all my heart. My wife Anna was restored unto me, with my son Tobias, in the feast of Pentecost, which is the holy feast of the seven weeks. There was a good dinner prepared me, in the which I sat down to eat. And when I saw abundance of meat, I said to my son, "Go and bring what poor man, soever thou shalt find out of our brethren, who is mindful of the Lord; and, lo, I tarry for thee."

But he came again, and said, "Father, one of our nation is strangled, and is cast out in the marketplace."

After the going down of the sun I went and made a grave, and buried him. But my neighbours mocked me, and said, "This man is not yet afraid to be put to death for this matter: who fled away; and yet, lo, he burieth the dead again."

The same night also I returned from the burial, and slept by the wall of my courtyard, being polluted, and my face was uncovered: and I knew not that there were sparrows in the wall, and mine eyes being open, the sparrows muted warm dung into mine eyes, and a whiteness came in mine eyes; and I went to the physicians, but they helped me not.

It came to pass the same day, that in Ecbatana, a city of Media, Sara the daughter of Raguel was reproached by her father's maids. Because that she had been married to seven husbands, whom Asmodeus the evil spirit had killed, before they had lain with her, she prayed toward the window, and said, "Blessed art thou, O Lord my God, and thine holy and glorious name is blessed and honourable for ever: let all thy works praise thee for ever. And now, O Lord, I set mine eyes and my face toward thee, and say, 'If it please not thee that I should die, command some regard to be had of me, and pity taken of me, that I hear no more reproach.' "

So the prayers of them both were heard before the majesty of the great God. And Raphael was sent to heal them both, that is, to scale away the whiteness of Tobit's eyes, and to give Sara the daughter of Raguel for a wife to Tobias the son of Tobit; and to bind Asmodeus the evil spirit.

In that day Tobit remembered the money which he had committed to Gabael in Rages of Media, and said with himself, "I have wished for death; wherefore do I not call for my son Tobias, that I may signify to him of the money before I die?" And when he had called him, he said:

"My son, when I am dead, bury me; and despise not thy mother, but honour her all the days of thy life, and do that which shall please her, and grieve her not. Beware of all whoredom, my son, and chiefly take a wife of the seed of thy fathers, and take not a strange woman to wife, which is not of thy father's tribe: for we are the children of the prophets, Noah, Abraham, Isaac, and Jacob: remember, my son, that our fathers from the beginning, even that they all married wives of their own kindred, and were blessed in their children, and their seed shall inherit the land. Let not the wages of any man, which hath wrought for thee, tarry with thee, but give him it out of hand: for if thou serve God, He will also repay thee. Bless the Lord thy God always, and desire of Him that thy ways may be directed, and that all thy paths and counsels may prosper. What you hate, do not do to anyone.

"And now I signify this to thee, that I committed ten talents to Gabael the son of Gabrias at Rages in Media. And fear not, my son, that we are made poor: for thou hast much wealth, if thou fear God, and depart from all sin, and do that which is pleasing in His sight."

Tobias then answered and said, "Father, I will do all things which thou hast commanded me: but how can I receive the money, seeing I know him not?"

Then he gave him the handwriting, and said unto him, "Seek thee a man which may go with thee, while I yet live, and I will give him wages: and go and receive the money."

Therefore when he went to seek a man, he found Raphael that was an angel. But he knew not; and he said unto him, "Canst thou go with me to Rages? And knowest thou those places well?"

To whom the angel said, "I will go with thee, and I know the way well: for I have lodged with our brother Gabael."

And as they went on their journey, they came in the evening to the river Tigris, and they lodged there. And when the young man went down to wash himself, a fish leaped out of the river, and would have devoured him.

Then the angel said unto him, "Take the fish." And the young man laid hold of the fish, and drew it to the land.

To whom the angel said, "Open the fish, and take the heart and the liver and the gall, and put them up safely."

So the young man did as the angel commanded him; and when they had roasted the fish, they did eat it: then they both went on their way, till they drew near to Ecbatana. Then the young man said to the angel, "Brother Azarias, to what use is the heart and the liver and the gall of the fish?"

And he said unto him, "Touching the heart and the liver, if a devil or an evil spirit trouble any, we must make a smoke thereof before the man or the woman, and the party shall be no more vexed. As for the gall, it is good to anoint a man that hath whiteness in his eyes, and he shall be healed."

And when they were come near to Rages, the angel said to the young man, "Brother, to-day we shall lodge with Raguel, who is thy cousin; he also hath one only daughter, named Sara; I will speak for her, that she may be given thee for a wife. For to thee doth the right of her appertain, seeing thou only art of her kindred. And the maid is fair and wise: now therefore hear me, and I will speak to her father; and when we return from Rages we will celebrate the marriage: for I know that

Raguel cannot marry her to another according to the law of Moses, but he shall be guilty of death, because the right of inheritance doth rather appertain to thee than to any other."

Now when Tobias had heard these things, he loved her, and his heart was effectually joined to her.

And when they were come to Ecbatana, they came to the house of Raguel, and Sara met them: and after they had saluted one another, she brought them into the house. Then said Raguel to Edna his wife, "How like is this young man to Tobit my cousin!" And Raguel asked them, "From whence are ye, brethren?" To whom they said, "We are of the sons of Nephthalim, which are captives in Nineveh." Then he said to them, "Do ye know Tobit our kinsman?" And they said, "We know him." Then said he, "Is he in good health?" And they said, "He is both alive, and in good health": and Tobias said, "He is my father."

Then Raguel leaped up, and kissed him, and wept, and blessed him, and said unto him," "Thou art the son of an honest and good man." But when he had heard that Tobit was blind, he was sorrowful, and wept. And likewise Edna his wife and Sara his daughter wept. Moreover they entertained them cheerfully; and after that they had killed a ram of the flock, they set store of meat on the table.

Then said Tobias to Raphael, "Brother Azarias, speak of those things of which thou didst talk in the way, and let this business be dispatched."

So he communicated the matter with Raguel: and Raguel said to Tobias, "Eat and drink, and make merry: for it is meet that thou shouldest marry my daughter: nevertheless I will declare unto thee the truth. I have given my daughter in marriage to seven men, who died that night they came in unto her: nevertheless for the present be merry."

But Tobias said, "I will eat nothing here, till we agree and swear to one another."

Raguel said, "Then take her from henceforth according to the manner, for thou art her cousin, and she is thine, and the merciful God give you good success in all things."

Then he called his daughter Sara, and she came to her

father, and he took her by the hand, and gave her to be wife to Tobias, saying, "Behold, take her after the law of Moses, and lead her away to thy father." And he blessed them; and called Edna his wife, and took paper, and did write an instrument of covenants, and sealed it.

And when they had supped, they brought Tobias in unto her. And as he went, he remembered the words of Raphael, and took the ashes of the perfumes, and put the heart and the liver of the fish thereupon, and made a smoke therewith. When the evil spirit had smelled the smoke, he fled into the utmost parts of Egypt, and the angel bound him.

And after that they were both shut in together, Tobias rose out of the bed, and said, "Sister, arise, and let us pray that God would have pity on us."

Then began Tobias to say, "Blessed art thou, O God of our fathers, and blessed is thy holy and glorious name for ever; let the heavens bless thee, and all thy creatures." And she said with him, "Amen." So they slept both that night.

And Raguel arose, and went and made a grave, saying, "I fear lest he also be dead." But when Raguel was come into his house he said unto his wife Edna, "Send one of the maids, and let her see whether he be alive: if he be not, that we may bury him, and no man know it."

So the maid opened the door, and went in, and found them both asleep, and came forth, and told them that he was alive.

Then Raguel bade his servants to fill the grave. And he kept the wedding feast fourteen days. For before the days of the marriage were finished, Raguel had said unto him by an oath, that he should not depart till the fourteen days of the marriage were expired; and then he should take the half of his goods, and go in safety to his father; and should have the rest when he and his wife be dead.

Then Tobias called Raphael, and said unto him, "Brother Azarias, take with thee a servant and two camels, and go to Rages of Media to Gabael, and bring me the money, and bring him to the wedding. For Raguel hath sworn that I shall not depart. But my father counteth the days; and if I tarry long, he will be very sorry."

So Raphael went out, and lodged with Gabael, and gave him the handwriting: who brought forth bags which were sealed up, and gave them to him. And early in the morning they went forth both together, and came to the wedding: and Tobias blessed his wife.

Then Raguel arose, and gave him Sara his wife, and half his goods, servants, and cattle, and money: And he blessed them, and sent them away, saying, "The God of heaven give you a prosperous journey, my children." And he said to his daughter, "Honour thy father and thy mother-in-law, which are now thy parents, that I may hear good reports of thee." And he kissed her. Edna also said to Tobias, "The Lord of heaven restore thee, my dear brother, and grant that I may see thy children of my daughter Sara before I die, that I may rejoice before the Lord: behold, I commit my daughter unto thee of special trust; wherefore do not entreat her evil."

After these things Tobias went his way, praising God that he had given him a prosperous journey, and blessed Raguel and Edna his wife, and went on his way till they drew near unto Nineveh.

Then Raphael said to Tobias, "Thou knowest, brother, how thou didst leave thy father: let us haste before thy wife, and prepare the house. And take in thine hand the gall of the fish."

Now Anna sat looking toward the way for her son. And when she espied him coming, she said to his father, "Behold, thy son cometh, and the man that went with him."

Then said Raphael, "I know, Tobias, that thy father will open his eyes. Therefore anoint thou his eyes with the gall, and being pricked therewith, he shall rub, and the whiteness shall fall away, and he shall see thee."

Then Anna ran forth, and fell upon the neck of her son, and said unto him, "Seeing I have seen thee, my son, from henceforth I am content to die." And they wept both.

Tobit also went forth toward the door, and stumbled: but his son ran unto him, and took hold of his father: and he stroked of the gall on his father's eyes, saying, "Be of good hope my father."

And when his eyes began to smart, he rubbed them; and the

whiteness peeled away from the corners of his eyes: and when he saw his son, he fell upon his neck. And he wept, and said, "Blessed art thou, O God, and blessed is thy name forever; and blessed are all thine holy angels: for thou hast scourged, and hast taken pity on me: for, behold, I see my son Tobias."

Then Tobit went out to meet his daughter-in-law at the gate of Nineveh, rejoicing, and praising God: and they which saw him go marvelled, because he had received his sight. When he came near to Sara his daughter-in-law, he blessed her, saying, "Thou art welcome, daughter: God be blessed, which hath brought thee unto us, and blessed be thy father and thy mother."

Then Tobit called his son Tobias, and said unto him, "My son, see that the man have his wages, which went with thee, and thou must give him more."

So Raphael called the angel, and he said unto him, "Take half of all that ye have brought, and go away in safety."

Then Raphael took them both apart, and said unto them, "Bless God, praise Him and magnify Him, and praise Him for the things which He hath done unto you in the sight of all that live. It is good to praise God, and exalt His name, and honourably to show forth the works of God; therefore be not slack to praise Him. It is good to keep close the secret of a king, but it is honourable to reveal the works of God. Do that which is good, and no evil shall touch you. Prayer is good with fasting and alms and righteousness. A little with righteousness is better than much with unrighteousness. It is better to give alms than to lay up gold: for alms doth deliver from death, and shall purge away all sin. Those that exercise alms and righteousness shall be filled with life: but they that sin are enemies to their own life. Now therefore give God thanks: for I go up to Him that sent me; but write all things which are done in a book."

And when they arose, they saw him no more. Then they confessed the great and wonderful works of God, and how the angel of the Lord had appeared unto them.

—Edited and adapted by A.F.B.

The Wisdom of Jesus Ben Sirach

The wonderful treatise called Ecclesiasticus or The Wisdom of Jesus Ben Sirach was written in Hebrew in the second century B.C.E. Part of the wisdom literature, it has been compared with the Book of Proverbs, which was attributed to Solomon. Both works deal with everday concerns as well as with ethics, but throughout the two books there is the feeling that human behavior is governed by divine law. Ben Sirach emphasizes religion of the heart, not of form and ritual; he holds the belief that piety can not be separated from social ethics. He believes in free will, the redemption of Israel and in a close relationship of God and man, seeing in natural wonders the manifestation of the greatness of God.

Wise Counsel Concerning Men

Do not quarrel with a powerful man,
Or you may fall into his hands.

Do not contend with a rich man,
Or he may outweigh you.
Gold has been the destruction of many,
And has perverted the minds of kings.
Do not quarrel with a garrulous man,
And do not add fuel to the fire.
Do not make sport of an uneducated man,
Or you may dishonor your own forefathers.
Do not reproach a man when he turns from his sin;
Remember that we are all liable to punishment.

Do not treat a man with disrespect when he is old,
For all of us are growing old.
Do not exult over a man who is dead;
Remember that we are all going to die.
Do not neglect the discourse of wise men,
But busy yourself with their proverbs,

For from them you will gain instruction,
And learn to serve great men.
Do not miss the discourse of old men,
For they learned it from their fathers.
From them you will gain understanding,
And learn to return an answer in your time of need.
Do not kindle the coals of a sinner,
Or you may be burned with the flame of his fire....

Do not lend to a man who is stronger than you,
Or if you do, act as though you had lost it.
Do not give surety beyond your means,
And if you give surety, regard it as something you will
     have to pay.

Do not go to law with a judge,
For in view of his dignity they will decide for him.
Do not travel with a reckless man,
So that he may not overburden you.
For he will do just as he pleases,
And you will perish through his folly.

Do not fight with a hot-tempered man,
And do not travel across the desert with him,
For bloodshed is as nothing in his eyes,
And where there is no help, he will strike you down.
Do not take counsel with a fool,
For he will not be able to keep the matter secret.
Do not do a secret thing before a stranger,
For you do not know what he will bring forth....

Wisdom Concerning Wise Men and Fools

The man who keeps the Law controls his thoughts,
And wisdom is the consummation of the fear of the Lord.
The man who is not shrewd will not be instructed,
But there is a shrewdness that spreads bitterness.
A wise man's knowledge abounds like a flood,
And his counsel is like a living spring.
The heart of a fool is like a broken dish;
It will hold no knowledge.
If a man of understanding hears a wise saying,
He commends it, and adds to it;
A self-indulgent man hears it, and it displeases him,
And he throws it behind his back.

The discourse of a fool is like a burden on a journey;
But enjoyment is found on the lips of a man of
     understanding.

The utterance of a sensible man will be asked for in an
     assembly,
And what he says they will think over in their minds.
To a fool wisdom is like a ruined house,
And the knowledge of a man without understanding is
     stuff that will not bear investigation.
To the foolish man, instruction is fetters on his feet,
And handcuffs on his right hand.
A fool raises his voice when he laughs,
But a shrewd man will smile quietly.
To a sensible man instruction is like a gold ornament,
And like a bracelet on his right arm.

Sharp Counsel Concerning Women

Do not be jealous about the wife of your bosom,
And do not teach her an evil lesson, to your own hurt.
Do not give your soul to a woman,
So that she will trample on your strength.
Do not greet a prostitute,
Or you may fall into her snares.
Do not associate with a woman singer,
Or you may be caught by her wiles.
Do not look closely at a girl,
Or you may be entrapped in penalties on her account.

Do not give yourself to prostitutes,
So that you may not lose your inheritance.
Do not look around in the streets of the city,
And do not wander in the unfrequented parts of it.
Avert your eyes from a beautiful woman,
And do not look closely at beauty that belongs to someone
    else.
Many have been led astray by a woman's beauty,
And love is kindled by it like a fire.
Do not ever sit at table with a married woman,
And do not feast and drink with her,
Or your heart may turn away to her,
And you may slip into spiritual ruin.

Dead Sea Scrolls

The discovery of the Dead Sea Scrolls in 1947 and subsequent years near Khirbet Qumran on the western shore of the Dead Sea is undoubtedly one of the greatest archaeological finds of all time. Now housed in the Shrine of the Book of Jerusalem, the Scrolls, which were written on leather and papyrus some 2,000 years ago, are invaluable for linguistic and geographic study, analysis of Biblical texts, and religious history. They include two complete copies of Isaiah and portions from almost every other book of the Bible, as well as commentaries of the Community of the Covenant, a Jewish sect that withdrew from Jerusalem to a monastic existence at the Dead Sea.

While exact dating of the Scrolls remains a matter of controversy, they must have been written before 70 C.E., by which time the site at Qumran had been destroyed in the Jewish revolt against Rome. Before the discovery of the Scrolls, the oldest known copies of the Bible were those that date from the Middle Ages. Since the Scrolls are very close to the Masoretic text, the implication is that the Jews have accurately preserved the Bible for 2,000 years—no mean feat when it is realized that for more than 1,500 of those years the text was copied only by hand.

Of the non-Biblical material among the Scrolls, the most significant historically is the Manual of Discipline, which gives beliefs and practices of a religious sect akin to or identical with the Essenes in religious views and social structure. The purposes of this Community of the Covenant were to lead a life dedicated to the purity of body and soul and to prepare for the Day of Judgment with its victory of "Sons of Light" over "Sons of Darkness." The Community expected a "Teacher of Righteousness" to be followed by a Messiah who would bring salvation. While not a direct link to the origins of Christianity, inferentially the Scrolls do provide information as to the Jewish background of the earliest Christian communities.

The Hymn of the Initiants

[Day and night will I offer my praise]*
and at all the appointed times which God has prescribed.

When daylight begins its rule,
    when it reaches its turning-point,
    and when it again withdraws to its appointed abode;

When the watches of darkness begin,
    when God opens the storehouse thereof,
    when He sets that darkness against the light,
    when it reaches its turning-point,
    and when it again withdraws in face of the light;

When sun and moon shine forth from the holy Height,
and when they again withdraw to the glorious Abode,

When the formal seasons come on the days of new moon,
    when they reach their turning-points,
    and when they yield place to one another,
    as each comes round anew;

When the natural seasons come, at whatever time may
    be;
when, too, the months begin;
    on their feasts and on holy days,
    as they come in order due,
    each as a memorial in its season

---

* Brackets indicate lack of scholarly agreement concerning enclosed words.

I shall hold it as one of the laws
engraven of old on the tablets
to render to God as my tribute
   —the blessings of my lips.

When the [natural] years begin;
   at the turning-points of their seasons
   and when each completes its term
   on its natural day,
   yielding each to each—
   reaping-time to summer,
   sowing-time to verdure;

In the [formal] years of weeks,
   in the several seasons thereof,
   and when, at the jubilee,
   the series of weeks begins—

I shall hold it as one of the laws
engraven of old on the tablets to offer to God as my
fruits—
   the praises of my tongue,
and to cull for Him as my tithe
   —the skilled music of my lips.

With the coming of day and night
   I shall come ever anew
   into God's covenant;
and when evening and morning depart,
   shall observe how He sets their bounds.

Only where God sets bounds
—the unchangeable bounds of His Law—
will I too set my domain.

I shall hold it as one of the laws
engraven to fold on the tablets
to face my sin and transgression
and avouch the justice of God.

I shall say unto God:
'Thou, for me, art the Right!'
and unto the Most High:
'For me Thou art cause of all good!'

Fountain of all knowledge,
Spring of holiness,
Zenith of all glory,
Might omnipotent,
Beauty that never fades,
   I will choose the path He shows me,
   and be content with His judgments.

Whenever I first put forth my hand or foot,
I will bless His name;
when first I go or come,
when I sit and when I rise,
when I lie down on my couch,
I will sing unto Him.
   At the common board,
or ever I raise my hand
to enjoy the rich fruits of the earth,
with that which flows from my lips
   I will bless Him as with an oblation.

At the onset of fear and alarm,
or when trouble and stress are at hand,
I will bless Him with special thanksgiving
and muse upon His power,
and rely on His mercies always,
and come thereby to know
that in His hand lies the judgment of all living,
and that all His works are truth.

Whenever distress breaks out,
   I still will praise Him;
and when His salvation comes,
   join the chorus of praise.

I will heap no evil on any,
but pursue all men with good,
knowing that only with God
lies the judgment of all living,
and He it is will award
each man his deserts.

I will not be envious
of the profit of wickedness;
    for wealth unrighteously gotten my soul shall not lust.

I will not engage in strife
with reprobate men,
    forestalling the Day of Requital.

I will not turn back my wrath
from froward men,
    nor rest content until justice be affirmed.

I will harbor no angry grudge
against those that indeed repent,
but neither will I show compassion
    to any that turn from the way.

I will not console the smitten
until they amend their course.

I will cherish no baseness in my heart,
nor shall there be heard in my mouth
coarseness or wanton deceit;
neither shall there be found upon my lips
    deception and lies.
The fruit of holiness shall be on my tongue,
and no heathen filth be found thereon.
    I will open my mouth with thanksgiving,
and my tongue shall ever relate
the bounteousness of God
and the perfidy of men
until men's transgression be ended.

Empty words will I banish from my lips;
filth and perverseness from my mind.

I will shelter knowledge with sound counsel,
and protect [it] with shrewdness of mind.

I will [set] a sober limit
to all defending of faith
and exacting of justice by force.
  I will bound God's righteousness
by the measuring-line of occasion.
  [I will temper] justice [with mercy],
will show kindness to men downtrodden,
bring firmness to fearful hearts,
discernment to spirits that stray,
enlighten the bowed with sound doctrine,
reply to the proud with meekness,
with humility answer the base
—men rich in worldly goods,
who point the finger of scorn
and utter iniquitous thoughts.

To God I commit my cause.
It is His to perfect my way,
His to make straight my heart.
He, in His charity,
  will wipe away my trangression.

For He from the Wellspring of Knowledge
has made His light to burst forth,
and mine eye has gazed on His wonders;
and the light that is in my heart
has pierced the deep things of existence.

He is ever the stay of my right hand.
The path beneath my feet
is set on a mighty rock
unshaken before all things

For that rock beneath my feet
is the truth of God,
and His power is the stay of my right hand;
from the fount of His charity
my vindication goes forth.

Through His mysterious wonder
light is come into my heart;
mine eye has set its gaze
on everlasting things.
A virtue hidden from man,
a knowledge and subtle lore
concealed from human kind;
a fount of righteousness,
a reservoir of strength,
a wellspring of all glory
wherewith no flesh His converse—
these has God bestowed
on them that He has chosen,
to possess them for ever.
He has given them an inheritance
in the lot of the Holy Beings,
and joined them in communion with the Sons of Heaven,
to form one congregation,
one single communion,
a fabric of holiness,
a plant of evergreen,
   for all time to come.

But I—I belong to wicked mankind,
to the communion of sinful flesh.
   My trangressions, my iniquities and sins,
and the waywardness of my heart
condemn me to communion with the worm
and with all that walk in darkness.
   For a mortal's way is [not] of himself,
neither can a man direct his own steps.
The judgment lies with God,
and 'tis His to perfect man's way.

Only through His knowledge
have all things come to be,
and all that is, is ordained by High thought;
and apart from Him is nothing wrought.

Behold, if I should totter,
God's mercies will be my salvation.
If I stumble in the error of the flesh,
I shall be set aright
through God's righteousness ever-enduring.
If distress break out,
He will snatch my soul from perdition,
and set my foot on the path.
    For He, in His compassion,
has drawn me near unto Him,
and His judgment upon me shall be rendered in His
mercy.
    In His bounteous truth He has judged me,
and in His abundant goodness
will shrive my iniquities,
and in His righteousness cleanse me
from all the pollution of man
and the sin of human kind,
that I may acknowledge unto God His righteousness,
and unto the Most High His majestic splendor.

    Blessed art Thou, O my God, Who hast opened the
heart of Thy servant unto knowledge.
Direct all his works in righteousness,
and vouchsafe unto the son of Thine handmaid
the favor which Thou hast assured to all the mortal elect,
to stand in Thy presence for ever.
    For apart from Thee no man's way can be perfect,
and without Thy will is nothing wrought.

Though it is that hath taught all knowledge,
and all things exist by Thy will;
and there is none beside Thee
to controvert Thy plan;

none to understand all Thy holy thought,
none to gaze into the depth of Thy secrets,
none to perceive all Thy wonders and the might of Thy
    power.

Who can compass the sum of Thy glory?
And what is mere mortal man
amid Thy wondrous works?
And what the child of woman
to sit in Thy presence?
For, behold he is kneaded of dust,
and His [flesh]* is the food of worms.
He is but a molded shape,
a thing nipped out of the clay,
whose attachment is but to the dust.
    What can such clay reply,
    or that which is molded by hand?
    What thought can it comprehend?

---

* Scholars have disagreed as to the correct translation since the original
Hebrew was not clear.

Josephus (c. 40-100 C.E.)

Just as nothing is known of Josephus save what he tells of himself in his writings, much of what is known of Jewish history from 73 B.C.E. to 37 C.E. (from the rise of the Maccabees to the fall of Masada) is derived from the books of Josephus. Joseph Ben Mattathias, better known by his Latin name, Flavius Josephus, states that he is of priestly and Hasmonean descent. He attempts in *Vita*, his autobiography, to justify his betrayal of his country to save his life and win the favor of the Romans. Ironically, a conscienceless Romanophile in Jerusalem, he became a proud Judeophile in Rome. He wrote *The Jewish War* to praise the Romans and their cause and, later, *Against Apion* and *Antiquities of the Jews* to defend the worth of the Jews and Judaism.

Following the tradition of Greco-Roman historiography by asserting as his goal historical truth, Josephus in effect sets his work apart from Biblical authors before him and Jewish writers for centuries after him who regarded the purpose of history as providing proof that God controls the destiny of humankind. His writings do contain erroneous statements, owing to faulty sources, bias, outright fabrication, rhetorical embellishment, and the inclusion as fact of legend and folklore. Yet Josephus is probably as accurate as other Hellenic historians. Although he omits reference to such great leaders as Hillel, Josephus is the chief authority on the everyday life of Judea as well as on its politics, agriculture, and geography.

An important sourcebook for a period of which little is known, two of the most critical centuries of recorded history, *Jewish War* is a magnificent literary achievement that tears at the emotions, spurs the imagination, and haunts the memory.

El'Azar's Oration

"My loyal followers, long ago we resolved to serve neither the Romans nor anyone else but only God, who alone is the true and righteous Lord of men: now the time has come that bids us prove our determination by our deeds. At such a time we must not disgrace ourselves: hitherto we have never submitted to slavery, even when it brought no danger with it: we must not choose slavery now, and with it penalties that will mean the end of everything if we fall alive into the hands of the Romans. For we were the first of all to revolt, and shall be the last to break off the struggle. And I think it is God who has given us this privilege, that we can die nobly and as free men, unlike others who were unexpectedly defeated. In our case it is evident that daybreak will end our resistance, but we are free to choose an honourable death with our loved ones. This our enemies cannot prevent, however earnestly they may pray to take us alive; nor can we defeat them in battle.

"Let our wives die unabused, our children without knowledge of slavery: after that, let us do each other an ungrudging kindness, preserving our freedom as a glorious winding-sheet. But first let our possessions and the whole fortress go up in flames: it will be a bitter blow to the Romans, that I know, to find our persons beyond their reach and nothing left for them to loot. One thing only let us spare—our store of food: it will bear witness when we are dead to the fact that we perished, not through want but because, as we resolved at the beginning, we chose death rather than slavery.

"If only we had all died before seeing the Sacred City utterly destroyed by enemy hands, the Holy Sanctuary so impiously uprooted! But since an honourable ambition deluded us into thinking that perhaps we should succeed in avenging her of her enemies, and now all hope has fled, abandoning us to our fate, let us at once choose death with honour and do the kindest thing we can for ourselves, our wives and children, while it is still possible to show ourselves any kindness. After all, we were born to die, we and those we brought into the world: this even the luckiest must face. But outrage, slavery, and the sight of our wives led away to shame with our children—these are not evils to which man is subject by the laws of nature: men undergo them through their own cowardice if they have a chance to forestall them by death and will not take it. We are very proud of our courage, so we revolted from Rome: now in the final stages they have offered to spare our lives and we have turned the offer down. Is anyone too blind to see how furious they will be if they take us alive? Pity the young whose bodies are strong enough to survive prolonged torture; pity the not-so-young whose old frames would break under such ill-usage. A man will see his wife violently carried off; he will hear the voice of his child crying 'Daddy!' when his own hands are fettered. Come! While our hands are free and can hold a sword, let them do a noble service! Let us die unenslaved by our enemies, and leave this world as free men in company with our wives and children."

(Tr. L.L.)

Philo (c. 20 B.C.E.-c. 40 C.E.)

The antithetical processes of thought of Greece and Judea converged in Egypt by way of Hellenistic Judaism in the person of Philo of Alexandria. While Philo's attempted synthesis of Greek philosophy and Jewish religion was not considered important by contemporary Greek and Jewish thinkers, it became of such significance to Christian and Islamic theologians that it remained the single most dominant force in Western philosophy until superseded sixteen centuries later by the conceptions of Spinoza, another Jewish savant. Ironically, the works of Philo, a devout Jew, were placed under ban by the Rabbinic Sages even as Philo was revered in Rome as a Father of the Church, which preserved his works under the misapprehension that they were among the earliest of Christian writings.

The scion of a distinguished and wealthy Alexandrian family. Philo was better educated in Greek literature than in Hebrew. All his writings were composed in Greek. He accepted Platonic-Stoic doctrines and terminology. From the Stoics, he borrowed the method of allegorical interpretation to correlate Jewish scripture with Greek concepts. He transformed the Stoic notion of *logos*, imparting several different meanings to it, referring to it as an image of God, as a spiritual power which mediates between the world and God, and as the first-born son of God that links the finite and the infinite. Philo adapted the number symbolism of the Pythagoreans, and he accepted the Platonic idea of Natural Law, insisting that the Patriarchs were living embodiments of it and that the *Torah* contains its principles. Philo tried to find a middle way between the Jewish God of creation and the perfect Platonic deity who never comes into contact with matter, and also to harmonize the Jewish conception of truth through revelation with Greek apprehension of wisdom.

What resulted from Philo's attempted synthesis of Greek conceptions and Jewish tenets was not a new philosophy. Like other Jewish Hellenists of his day, Philo tried to show that the major ideas and ethical principles of Greek philosophy, if not drawn from the Bible, were inherent in it. His essential emphasis is mystical-moralistic in the Hellenistic fashion, although he insists that the literal meaning of the *Torah* not be discarded despite what its underlying signficance as determined by allegory might be. For Philo, man's ultimate goal is union with the Divine. The *Torah*, he believes, embodies an allegorical way for that union, as does mystic meditation.

Several of Philo's chief works, such as *Questions and Answers to Genesis and Exodus* and *Commentary on the Five Books of Moses*, interpreted the Bible for his Grecized fellow Jews and for the increasing number of proselytes to Judaism. In these writings, Philo upholds the glory of Judaism and lays bare the perversion and unreason of heathen religions.

Disciplined in philosophical argument, Philo was a great literary artist— though a poet manqué—who wrote about religion in prose as sensitive as it is thoughtful.

Of God and Man

It is a tenet of the lawgiver also that the perfect man seeks for quietude. For the words addressed to the Sage with God as the speaker, "stand thou here with Me" (*Deut.* 5:31), show most plainly how unbending, unwavering and broad-based is his will. Wonderful indeed is the soul of the Sage, how he sets it, like a lyre, to harmony not with a scale of notes low and high, but with the knowledge of moral opposites, and the practice of such of them as are better; how he does not strain it to excessive heights, nor yet relax it and weaken the concord of virtues and things naturally beautiful, but keeps it ever at an equal tension and plays it with hand or bow in melody. Such a soul is the most perfect instrument fashioned by nature, the pattern of those which are the work of our hands. And if it be well adjusted, it will produce a symphony the most beautiful in the world, one which has its consummation not in the cadences and tones of melodious sound, but in the consistencies of our life's actions. Oh! if the soul of man, when it feels the soft breeze of wisdom and knowledge, can dismiss the stormy surge which the fierce burst of the gale of wickedness has suddenly stirred, and levelling the billowy swell can rest in unruffled calm under a bright clear sky, can you doubt that He, the Imperishable Blessed One, who has taken as His own the sovereignty of the virtues, of perfection itself and beatitude, knows no change of will, but ever holds fast to what He purposed from the first without any alteration?

With men then it must needs be that they are ready to change through instability whether it be in themselves or outside them. So for example often when we have chosen our friends and been familiar with them for a short time, we turn from them, though we have no charge to bring against them, and count them amongst our enemies, or at best as strangers. Such action proves the facile levity of ourselves, how little capacity we have for stoutly holding to our original judgments. But God has no such fickleness. Or again, sometimes we are minded to hold to the standards we have taken but we find ourselves with others who have not remained constant, and thus our judgments perforce change with theirs. For a mere man cannot foresee the course of future events, or the judgments of others, but to God as in pure sunlight all things are manifest. For already He has pierced into the recesses of our soul, and what is invisible to others is clear as daylight to His eyes. He employs the forethought and foreknowledge which are virtues peculiarly His own, and suffers nothing to escape His control or pass outside His comprehension. For not even about the future can uncertainty be found with Him, since nothing is uncertain or future to God. No one doubts that the parent must have knowledge of his offspring, the craftsman of his handiwork, the steward of things entrusted to his stewardship. But God is in very truth the father and craftsman and steward of the heaven and the universe and all that is therein. Future events lie shrouded in the darkness of the time that is yet to be at different distances, some near, some far.

But God is the maker of time also, for He is the father to time's father, that is of the universe, and has caused the movements of the one to be the source of the generation of the other. Thus time stands to God in the relation of a grandson. For this universe, since we perceive it by our senses is the younger son of God. To the elder son, I mean the intelligible universe, He assigned the place of firstborn, and purposed that it should remain in His own keeping. So this younger son, the world of our senses, when set in motion, brought that entity we call time to the brightness of its rising. And thus with God there is no future, since He has made the boundaries of the ages subject to Himself. For God's life is not a time, but eternity, which is the archetype and pattern of time; and in eternity there is no past nor future, but only present existence.

Let us flee, then, without a backward glance from the unions which are unions for sin, but hold fast to our alliance with the comrades of good sense and knowledge. And therefore when I hear those who say, "We are all sons of one man, we are peaceful" (*Gen.* 43:II), I am filled with admiration for the harmonious concert which their words reveal. "Ah! my friends," I would say, "how should you not hate war and love peace—you who have enrolled yourselves as children of one and the same Father, who is not mortal but immortal—God's man, who being the Word of the Eternal must needs himself be imperishable?" Those whose system includes many origins for the family of the soul, who affiliate themselves to that evil thing called polytheism, who take in hand to render homage some to this deity, some to that, are the authors of tumult and strife at home and abroad, and fill the whole of life from birth to death with internecine wars.

But those who rejoice in the oneness of their blood and honour one father, right reason, reverence that concert of virtues, which is full of harmony and melody, and live a life of calmness and fair weather. And yet that life is not, as some suppose, an idle and ignoble life, but one of high courage, and the edge of its spirit is exceeding sharp to fight against those who attempt to break treaties and ever practice the violations of the vows they have sworn. For it is the nature of men of peace that they prove to be men of war, when they take the field and resist those who would subvert the stability of the soul.

The truth of my words is attested first by the consciousness of every virtue-lover, which feels what I have described, and secondly by a chorister of the prophetic company, who possessed by divine inspiration spoke thus: "O my mother, how great didst thou bear me, a man of combat and a man of displeasure in all the earth! I did not owe, nor did they owe to me, nor did my strength fail from their curses" (*Jer.* 15:10). Yes, is not every wise man the mortal foe of every fool, a foe who is equipped not with triremes or engines, or body-armour or soldiers for his defense, but with reasonings only?

For who, when he sees that war, which amid the fullest peace is waged among all men continuously, phase ever succeeding phase, in private and public life, a war in which the combatants are not just nations and countries, or cities and villages, but also house against house and each particular man against himself, who, I say, does not exhort, reproach, admonish, correct by day and night alike, since his soul cannot rest, because its nature is to hate evil? For all the deeds of war are done in peace. Men plunder, rob, kidnap, spoil, sack, outrage, maltreat, violate, dishonour and commit murder sometimes by treachery, or if they be stronger without disguise. Every man sets before him money or reputation as his aim, and at this he directs all the actions of his life like arrows against a target. He takes no heed of equality, but pursues inequality. He eschews thoughts of fellowship, and his eager desire is that the wealth of all should be gathered in his single purse. He hates others, whether his hate be returned or not. His benevolence is hypocrisy. He is hand and glove with canting flattery, at open war with genuine friendship; an enemy to truth, a defender of falsehood, slow to help, quick to harm, ever forward to slander, backward to champion the accused, skillful to cozen, false to his oath, faithless to his promise, a slave to anger, a thrall to pleasure, protector of the bad, corrupter of the good.

These and the like are the much-coveted treasures of the peace which men admire and praise so loudly—treasures enshrined in the mind of every fool with wonder and veneration. But to every wise man they are, as they should be, a source of pain, and often will he say to his mother and nurse, wisdom, "O mother, how great didst thou bear me!" Great, not in power of body, but in strength to hate evil, a man of displeasure and combat, by nature a man of peace, but for this very cause also a man of war against those who dishonour the much-prized loveliness of peace. "I did not owe nor did they owe to me," for neither did they use the good I have to give, nor I their evil, but, as Moses wrote, "I received from none of them what they desired" (*Num.* 16:15). For all that comes under the head of their desire they kept as treasure to themselves, believing that to be the greatest blessing which was the supreme mischief. "Nor did my strength fail from the curses which they laid upon me," but with all my might and main I clung to the divine truths: I did not bend under their ill-treatment, but used my strength to reproach those who refused to effect their own purification. For "God has set us up for a contradiction to our neighbours," as is said in a verse of the Psalms: us, that is all who desire right judgment. Yes, surely they are by nature men of contradiction, all who have ever been zealous for knowledge and virtue, who contend jealously with the "neighbors" of the soul; who test the pleasures which share our home, the desires which live at our side, our fears and faintings of heart, and put to shame the tribe of passions and vices. Further, they test also every sense, the eyes on what they see, the ears on what they hear, the sense of smell on its perfumes, the taste on its flavours, the touch on the characteristics which mark the qualities of substances as they come in contact with it. And lastly they test the utterance on the statements which it has been led to make.

For what our senses perceive, or our speech expresses, or our emotion causes us to feel, and how or why each result is attained, are matters which we should scrutinize carefully and expose every error that we find. He who contradicts none of these, but assents to all as they come before him, is unconsciously deceiving himself and raising up a stronghold of dangerous neighbours to menace the soul, neighbours who should be dealt with as subjects, not as rulers. For if they have the mastery since folly is their king, the mischief they work will be great and manifold; but as subjects they will render due service and obey the rein, and chafe no more against the yoke.

And, when these have thus learnt the lesson of obedience, and those have assumed the command which not only knowledge but power has given them, all the thoughts that attend and guard the soul will be one in purpose and approaching Him that ranks highest among them will speak thus: "Thy servants have taken the sum of the men of war who were with us, and there is no discordant voice" (*Num.* 31:49). "We," they will continue, "like instruments of music where all the notes are in perfect tune, echo with our voices all the lessons we have received. We speak no word and do no deed that is harsh or grating, and thus we have made a laughing stock of all that other dead and voiceless choir, the choir of those who know not the muse, the choir which hymns Midian, the nurse of things bodily, and her offspring, the heavy leathern weight whose name is Baal-Peor. For we are the race of the Chosen ones of that Israel who sees God, 'and there is none amongst us of discordant voice' " (*Ex.* 24:II), that so the whole world, which is the instrument of the All, may be filled with the sweet melody of its undiscording harmonies.

And therefore too Moses tells us how peace was assigned as the prize of that most warlike reason, called Phinehas (*Num.* 25:12), because, inspired with zeal for virtue and waging war against vice, he ripped open all created being; how in their turn that prize is given to those who, after diligent and careful scrutiny, following the more certain testimony of sight, rather than hearing, have the will to accept the faith that mortality is full of unfaith and clings only to the seeming.

Wonderful then indeed is the symphony of voices here described, but most wonderful of all, exceeding every harmony, is that united universal symphony in which we find the whole people declaring with one heart, "All that God hath said we will do and hear" (*Ex.* 19:8). Here the precentor whom they follow is no longer the Word, but God the Sovereign of all, for whose sake they become quicker to meet the call to action than the call of words. For other men act after they have heard, but these under the divine inspiration say—strange inversion—that they will act first and hear afterwards, that so they may be seen to go forward to deeds of excellence, not led by teaching or instruction, but through the self-acting, self-dictated instinct of their own hearts. And when they have *done*, then, as they say, they will *hear*, that so they may judge their actions, whether they chime with the divine words and the sacred admonitions.

הבית והעלייה פרק עשירי בבא מציעא

Sample Babylonian Talmud page from tractate Baba M'ziha. To the left of the tractate text is Rashi's commentary; to the right is Tosafot. Marginal notations carry emendations and page numbers of other tractates quoted in the text. This format was established in Venice in the 1520s, and all subsequent editions have followed the Venice edition format and pagination.

The Talmud

The *Talmud* (from the Hebrew, to study) remains the most important work of Jewish literature after the Bible. It has been studied and re-studied through the ages by millions and millions of Jews, in the process molding Jewish culture and shaping religious, social, economic, and political attitudes of the people. Today, without some acquaintance with the main thrust of Judaism and the circumstances of Jewish history that brought about the writings of The *Talmud*, it is impossible even to begin to understand this remarkable book. (In reality, The *Talmud* is not a book: it is a series of a dozen volumes totalling more than 6,000 folio pages with the commentary of more than 2,000 scholars and sages.)

Judaism regards as the purpose of life the fulfillment of the Covenant with God. Every Jew must try to the utmost to obey God's commandments, both as an individual and as a member of the Jewish people, in order to create a perfect society on Earth. Jews of ancient Israel, therefore, as individuals and in groups studied the Bible. Their interpretations took two forms:

1. Haggadah (from the Hebrew, to relate, tell): basically narrative interpretations in the forms of folklore, parables, anecdotes, meditations—including speculative inquiry of all kinds, even of dreams.

2. Halakhah (from the Hebrew, to go; by extension, the rule by which to go—the law); basically legal interpretation of the Bible in the form of laws, principles, and obligatory practices as a result of decisions in religious, civil, and criminal cases.

After canonization of the Bible, no religious book could be added, so the custom arose of keeping all succeeding religious teachings unwritten. Each oral interpretation became known as a Midrash. These along with the Haggadah and Halakhah, grew enormously, until Judah Ha-Nasi had a compilation made, the *Mishnah*. But scholars and rabbis became anxious about Jews scattered over the known world without a viable political center. How could they remain faithful to Judaism by obeying the law, since changing circumstances require changing decisions? As discussions and debates continued in the academies of Jerusalem and Babylon, the centers of Jewish learning, the amount of oral lore and law became too vast for memorization. Notes were taken for internal purposes but not for publication. Then the decision to put everything into writing publicly was taken at the two academies. Two *Talmuds* resulted, the Babylonian and the Jerusalem, each an amplification and explication of the *Mishnah*, with the Babylonian the more popular.

The *Talmud* consists of the *Mishnah* and its interpretation the *Gemara* (from the Aramaic, completion), made during the three centuries or so following the original compilation by Judah Ha-Nasi. Midrashim produced later on appear as separate writings or in exegetical collections dating from the sixth century. (Rabbis of the *Mishnah* are known as Tannaim teachers; those of the *Gemara* as Amoraim, interpreters.) Although there are some Hebrew passages, the *Talmud* is mainly Aramaic—the lingua franca of the time. The earliest surviving manuscript of the entire *Talmud* dates from 1343 C.E. With the first printing in Venice, 1520 C.E., the arrangement became fixed: an excerpt from the *Mishnah* is followed by a much longer discussion (Halakhah and/or Haggadah) in the *Gemara*. References to particular sections are by tractate and folio page.

The *Talmud* is not easy to understand. It is not a legal document with a beginning, middle, and end arranged logically for the sake of clarity. It is an anthology of opinions and facts on topics related to the cases under consideration. The wording is probably from shorthand notes taken down verbatim at the academies. The result is a kind of transcript of many voices. Variant views are recorded, and nothing is presented as dogma. There is little or no background information as to time and date. Often, names of participants are not given. A statement is made or quoted, and the rabbis plunge into discussion, one rabbi reacting to the words of another. Cases and problems are stated, arguments given, hypothetical examples or actual illustrations adduced, and reflections on even the minutest details developed. Many diverse subjects are introduced without explicit clarification of ideas unifying them. Connections between remarks are often tenuous as the conversation opens out.

While the purpose of the rabbis is to arrive at authoritative norms, problems are not conclusively disposed of in the *Talmud*, as Jews who study the Tractates soon perceive. The Jew who would live according to the law must analyze the reasoning of the Talmudic rabbis and himself try to arrive at a suitable outcome. The rabbis and scholars of the *Talmud* thus insured the unification of Jewish spiritual life; by securing a continual exchange of teaching between the generations they fused together the past, present, and future of the Jewish people.

Gemara

Comments on Charity

Rabbi Assi said: Charity is equal to all Mitzvot.

Rabbi Eleazar said: Greater is he who persuades others to give than him who gives.

Rabba said to the people of Mehuza: Perform charity among yourselves so that you will enjoy peace.

Rabbi Eleazar said: Give charity now, for if you do not, it will be forcibly taken from you by officials.

Said R. Eleazar: He who gives charity in secret is as great as Moses. *Baba Batra, 8-9*

R. Eleazar ben Jose said: Kind deeds and charity achieve peace between Israel and their Father in Heaven.

R. Judah said: Great is charity for it brings Redemption nearer.

R. Judah said: Come and see how great is charity. Ten strong things exist in the world: a mountain is strong, but iron breaks it; iron is strong, but fire softens it; fire is strong, but water extinguishes it; water is strong, but clouds bear it along; clouds are strong, but the wind spreads them out; the wind is strong, but the body of man withstands it; the body is strong, but fear breaks it; fear is strong, but wine overcomes it; wine is strong, but sleep dispels it; sleep is strong, but death is stronger still. But charity rescueth even from death.

If a man gives with a sullen face, it is as if he gave nothing; but he who receives the needy person with a cheerful countenance, even if he was not able to give him anything, it is as if he gave him a good gift.   *Abot de-R. Nathan, 13*

R. Eleazar of Bertota said: Give unto Him of what is His, seeing that thou and what thou hast are His; this is found expressed in David who said: "For all things come from Thee, and of Thine own have we given Thee." (I Chronicles 29:14)

Abot, 3, 8

Charity knows neither race nor creed.   *Gittin, 61a*

If a poor man comes to thee for aid in the morning, give it to him. If he comes again in the evening, give it to him once more.   *Bereshit Rabbah, 61, 3*

He who gives charity serves the Holy One daily, and sanctifies His name.   *Zohar, iii, 113b*

Greater is he who practices charity than all the sacrifices.

Sukkah, 49b

Mishnah

The Hebrew word *mishnah*, which means "repetition" or "review" with the connotation of "learning," is applied to the first compilation of Jewish law after the canonization of the Bible. Tradition holds that under the leadership of Rabbi Judah Ha-Nasi a group of scholars sometime before 200 C.E. organized and systematized a vast amount of tradition and legal material gathered in discussion of the oral law during the previous two centuries. No one knows exactly when this authoritative corpus of the oral law was first put into written form and called the *Mishnah*. The first printed edition was not published until near the end of the fifteenth century.

This *Mishnah* is divided into six orders, as follows:

1. "Seeds," matters of importance to an agricultural society.
2. "Festivals," matters dealing with the celebration of holidays, with the first subdivision of twenty-four chapters devoted to celebration of the Sabbath.
3. "Women," matters dealing with marriage and divorce as well as with family life.
4. "Damages" or "Torts," legal matters including courts, injuries, and buying and selling.
5. "Sacred Matters," sacrificial rites, dietary matters, and matters referring to the temple service.
6. "Purifications," ritual matters concerning purities and impurities.

The *Mishnah* is not rigid in structure. The rabbis and sages saw themselves, not as theologians who develop a definitive creed and dogma, but as God-conscious Jews concerned that their people act in accordance with the will of God as revealed in the Bible. Aware that most Jews after the destruction of the Temple in 70 C.E. were living outside Israel under constantly changing conditions, they tried to insure that precedents would be remembered and new ordinances, statutes, and practices would be in accord with Jewish principles. Again and again a problem is stated and a rich variety of assorted materials given in answer. Laws are cited, traditions mentioned, principles explored, and ideas elucidated, not because they pertain exactly to the problem at hand, but because in one way or another they relate to it by association. The third order, for example, in its consideration of divorce suddenly introduces ideas and ordinances related to peace, seemingly because, like bills of divorcement, they deal with maintaining proper order in society.

There is as yet no definitive text of the *Mishnah* with all the variant readings. Nevertheless, extant texts are of inestimable historical value, for the *Mishnah* is a rich repository of ethical discussions which shed light on rabbinic thinking in early centuries of the Common Era and on the evolution of Halakhah (Jewish law) and of Judaism in general.

Pirke Avot

Although *Pirke Avot* (Ethics of the Fathers) is a short treatise added to the section *Nezikim* (Damages) in the *Mishnah*, it contains many aphorisms, maxims, and epigrams—morally profound as well as worldly wise—that have stirred the imagination for centuries. So important do Jews consider *Pirke Avot* that they call it "The Small Talmud" and continue the tradition of reflective reading of its pithy wisdom and gentle humanity on the Sabbath from Passover to *Shevuot*.

Concerned with religio-ethical teachings, *Pirke Avot* emphasizes man's relationship to his fellow man and the need to emulate the Divine by choosing the path of righteous conduct and true piety. Much of Pirke Avot, seemingly modeled on Ecclesiastes and Proverbs but with a folkloristic overlay (unlike the other sixty-two treatises of the *Talmud*, *Pirke Avot* concerns itself solely with Haggadah), is in direct line with central postulates of the Bible, which the prophet Micah summed up as: "to seek justice, to love mercy, and to walk humbly before God." This may be why the rabbis, hoping to quicken the religiosity of their congregation by preoccupying them with problems of ethical conduct, inserted the text of *Pirke Avot* into the *Siddur* (Prayer Book).

Pirke Avot (Ethics of the Fathers)

1.   1. Moses received the Law from Sinai and committed it to Joshua, and Joshua to the elders, and the elders to the Prophets; and the Prophets committed it to the men of the Great Synagogue. They said three things: Be deliberate in judgment, raise up many disciples, and make a fence around the Law.

2. Simeon the Just was of the remnants of the Great Synagogue. He used to say: By three things is the world sustained: by the Law, by the [Temple-]service, and by deeds of loving-kindness.

3. Antigonus of Soko received [the Law] from Simeon the Just. He used to say: Be not like slaves that minister to the master for the sake of receiving a bounty, but be like slaves that minister to the master not for the sake of receiving a bounty; and let the fear of Heaven be upon you.

4. Jose b. Joezer of Zeredah and Jose b. Johanan of Jerusalem received [the Law] from them. Jose b. Joezer of Zeredah said: Let thy house be a meeting-house for the Sages, and sit amid the dust of their feet and drink in their words with thirst.

5. Jose b. Johanan of Jerusalem said: Let thy house be opened wide and let the needy be members of thy household; and talk not much with womankind. They said this of a man's own wife, how much more of his fellow's wife! Hence the Sages have said: He that talks much with womankind brings evil upon himself and neglects the study of the Law and at the last will inherit Gehenna.

6. Joshua b. Perahyah and Nittai the Arbelite received [the Law] from them. Joshua b. Perahyah said: Provide thyself with a teacher and get thee a fellow [-disciple]; and when thou judgest any man incline the balance in his favour.

7. Nittai the Arbelite said: Keep thee far from an evil neighbour and consort not with the wicked and lose not belief in retribution.

8. Judah b. Tabbai and Simeon b. Shetah received [the Law] from them. Judah b. Tabbai said: Make not thyself like them that would influence the judges; and when the suitors stand before thee let them be in thine eyes as wicked men, and

when they have departed from before thee let them be in thine eyes as innocent, so soon as they have accepted the judgment.

9. Simeon b. Shetah said: Examine the witnesses diligently and be cautious in thy words lest from them they learn to swear falsely.

10. Shemaiah and Abtalion received [the Law] from them. Shemaiah said: Love labour and hate mastery and seek not acquaintance with the ruling power.

11. Abtalion said: Ye Sages, give heed to your words lest ye incur the penalty of exile and ye be exiled to a place of evil waters, and the disciples that come after you drink [of them] and die, and the name of Heaven be profaned.

12. Hillel and Shammai received [the Law] from them. Hillel said: Be of the disciples of Aaron, loving peace and pursuing peace, loving mankind and bringing them nigh to the Law.

13. He used to say: A name made great is a name destroyed, and he that increases not decreases, and he that learns not is worthy of death, and he that makes worldly use of the crown shall perish.

14. He used to say: If I am not for myself who is for me? And being for mine own self what am I? And if not now, when?

15. Shammai said: Make thy [study of the] Law a fixed habit; say little and do much, and receive all men with a cheerful countenance.

16. Rabban Gamaliel said: Provide thyself with a teacher and remove thyself from doubt, and tithe not overmuch by guesswork.

17. Simeon his son said: All my days have I grown up among the Sages and I have found naught better for a man than silence; and not the expounding [of the Law] is the chief thing but the doing [of it]; and he that multiplies words occasions sin.

18. Rabban Simeon b. Gamaliel said: By three things is the world sustained: by truth, by judgment, and by peace, as it is written, *Execute the judgment of truth and peace* [Zech. 8:16].

4. 1. Ben Zoma said: Who is wise? He that learns from all men, as it is written, *From all my teachers have I got under-*

standing [Ps. 119:99]. Who is mighty? He that subdues his [evil] nature, as it is written, *He that is slow to anger is better than the mighty, and he that ruleth his spirit than he that taketh a city* [Prov. 16:32]. Who is rich? He that rejoices in his portion, as it is written, *When thou eatest the labour of thy hands happy shalt thou be, and it shall be well with thee* [Ps. 128:2]. *Happy shalt thou be*—in this world; *and it shall be well with thee*—in the world to come. Who is honored? He that honors mankind, as it is written, *For them that honor me I will honor, and they that despise me shall be lightly esteemed* [I Sam. 2:30].

2. Ben Azzai said: Run to fulfil the lightest duty even as the weightiest, and flee from transgression; for one duty draws another duty in its train, and one transgression draws another transgression in its train; for the reward of a duty [done] is a duty [to be done], and the reward of one transgression is [another] transgression.

3. He used to say: Despise no man and deem nothing impossible, for there is not a man that has not his hour and there is not a thing that has not its place.

4. Levitas of Jabneth said: Be exceeding lowly of spirit, for the hope of man is but the worm. R. Johanan b. Baroka said: He that profanes the name of Heaven in secret shall be requited openly: in profaning the Name it is all one whether it be done unwittingly or wantonly.

5. R. Ishmael his son said: He that learns in order to teach is granted the means to learn and to teach; but he that learns in order to perform is granted the means to learn and to teach, to observe and to perform. R. Zadok says: Keep not aloof from the congregation, and make not thyself like them that seek to influence the judges. Make them not a crown wherewith to magnify thyself or spade wherewith to dig. And thus used Hillel to say: He that makes worldly use of the crown shall perish. Thus thou mayest learn that he that makes profit out of the words of the Law removes his life from the world.

6. R. Jose said: He that honours the Law is himself by mankind; and he that dishonours the Law shall himself be dishonoured by mankind.

7. R. Ishmael his son said: He that shuns the office of judge

rids himself of enmity and theft and false swearing; and he that is forward in giving a decision is foolish, wicked, and arrogant.

8. He used to say: Judge not alone, for none may judge alone save One. And say not, 'Receive ye my opinion,' for it is for them to choose, and not for thee.

9. R. Jonathan said: He that fulfils the Law in poverty shall in the end fulfil it in wealth; and he that neglects the Law in wealth shall in the end neglect it in poverty.

10. R. Meir said: Engage not overmuch in business but occupy thyself with the Law; and be lowly in spirit before all men. If thou neglectest the Law many things neglected shall rise against thee; but if thou laborest in the Law He has abundant reward to give thee.

11. R. Eliezer b. Jacob says: He that performs one precept gets for himself one advocate; but he that commits one transgression gets for himself one accuser. Repentance and good works are as a shield against retribution. R. Johanan the Sandal-maker said: Any assembling together that is for the sake of Heaven shall in the end be established, but any that is not for the sake of Heaven shall not in the end be established.

12. R. Eleazar b. Shammua said: Let the honor of thy disciple be as dear to thee as thine own and as the honor of thy companion, and the honour of thy companion as the fear of thy teacher, and the fear of thy teacher as the fear of Heaven.

13. R. Judah said: Be heedful in study, for an unwitting error in study is accounted wanton transgression. R. Simeon said: There are three crowns: the crown of the Law, the crown of the priesthood, and the crown of kingship; but the crown of a good name excels them all.

14. R. Nehorai said: Wander afar to a place of the Law; and say not that it will follow after thee or that thy companions will establish it in thy possession; and lean not upon thine own understanding.

15. R. Yannai said: It is not in our power to explain the well-being of the wicked or the sorrows of the righteous. R. Mattithiah b. Heresh said: Be first in greeting every man; and be a tail to lions and be not a head to jackals.

16. R. Jacob said: This world is like a vestibule before the

world to come: prepare thyself in the vestibule that thou mayest enter into the banqueting hall.

17. He used to say: Better is one hour of repentance and good works in this world than the whole life of the world to come; and better is one hour of bliss in the world to come than the whole life of this world.

18. R. Simeon b. Eleazar said: Appease not thy fellow in the hour of his anger, and comfort him not while his dead lies before him, and question him not in the hour of his vow, and strive not to see him in the hour of his disgrace.

19. Samuel the Younger said: *Rejoice not when thine enemy falleth, and let not thine heart be glad when he is overthrown, lest the Lord see it and it displease him, and he turn away his wrath from him* [Prov. 24:17-18].

20. Elisha b. Abuyah said: He that learns as a child, to what is he like? To ink written on new paper. He that learns as an old man, to what is he like? To ink written on paper that has been blotted out. R. Jose b. Judah of Kefar ha-Babli said: He that learns from the young, to what is he like? To one that eats unripe grapes and drinks wine from his winepress. And he that learns from the aged, to what is he like? To one that eats ripe grapes and drinks old wine. R. Meir said: Look not on the jar but on what is in it; there may be a new jar that is full of old wine and an old one in which is not even new wine.

21. R. Eleazar ha-Kappar said: Jealousy, lust, and ambition put a man out of the world.

22. He used to say: They that have been born [are destined] to die, and they that are dead [are destined] to be made alive, and they that live [after death are destined] to be judged, that men may know and make known and understand that he is God, he is the Maker, he is the Creator, he is the Discerner, he is the Judge, he is the Witness, he is the Complainant, and it is he that shall judge, blessed is he, in whose presence is neither guile nor forgetfulness nor respect of persons nor taking of bribes; for all is his. And know that everything is according to the reckoning. And let not thy [evil] nature promise thee that the grave will be thy refuge: for despite thyself wast thou

fashioned, and despite thyself wast thou born, and despite thyself thou livest, and despite thyself thou diest, and despite thyself thou hereafter give account and reckoning before the King of kings, the Holy One, blessed is he.

Drama

Drama, inhibited by religious tradition, was until recently one of the least developed forms of Jewish literature. Opposition to theater as a form of public entertainment was discernible in Biblical times and became conspicuous during the Augustan era, when obscenity and lewdness were as popular in Latin plays as bestiality and cruelty were in Roman arenas. Even today the prayer book in many synagogues quotes the *Talmud*: "I give thanks, Lord God of my Fathers, that you placed my portion among those in the House of Study and in the House of Prayers, and that you did not cast my lot among those who frequent theaters and circuses."

Ironically, religious practice inspired and spurred production of Jewish plays. Dramas on Biblical themes composed in imitation of Christian miracle plays were produced in Yiddish early in the fifteenth century. *Purim* plays, utilizing satire and burlesque, appeared soon after. Sporadic and isolated Hebrew productions followed in Italy and Holland during the sixteenth, seventeenth, and eighteenth centuries. But the increasing secularization of Jewish life failed to stimulate either dramatic composition or the establishment of independent Jewish theaters until near the end of the nineteenth century. Until then, Purim plays were virtually the only dramas performed in the ghettos.

But Yiddish and Hebrew acting companies began to emerge in Europe and Palestine, gaining a particularly high reputation in Russia and the United States during the early part of the twentieth century. At present original Jewish drama, primarily in Hebrew, is linked to Israel and its developing society.

S. Anski (1863-1920)

The Dybbuk by S. Anski (pseudonym of Shloyme Fanul Rappoport) is the most famous Yiddish play. Sadly, its author died before its first performance. None of his other writings published in his lifetime achieved popularity. Produced in many languages and many lands, *The Dybbuk* has also been seen as a film and opera. Today in the Hebrew translation of Bialik, it is a *force majeure* in the repertoire of Habimah, the national theatre of Israel.

A byproduct of Anski's interest in Jewish folklore, *The Dybbuk* is set in the mystical milieu of Hassidic pietism, which was pervaded by faith in magic and in the immediacy of the divine. The plot is simple: A rejected suitor dies. His spirit enters the girl he was to marry, refuses to leave, and speaks through her. The exorcism of the dybbuk and the strange lawsuit between a disembodied soul and a living human defendant, although grotesque, are thrilling episodes. But it is neither the occult nor the revelation of recondite Jewish lore that gives the play significance.

Although melodramatic, *The Dybbuk* is a meticulously constructed play with a complex and intricate framework whose dramatic exposition acts out the themes and motifs expressed in speeches of deliberate ambiguity with overtones of meaning. Its basic theme is the soul's strength, with the spirit-

89

ual triumphing over the physical. Supporting themes include the interdependence of all mankind, for each of us is responsible for others, and the power of good men "to compel," in Martin Buber's words, "the upper world," since the righteous can enlist the aid of higher powers. Motifs repeated over and over include the ever-present possibility of man's self-redemption and the certainty of God's justice amidst the interplay of the natural and supernatural in the universe.

The Dybbuk

The Dybbuk has as its setting the universe of Hassidism, peopled by characters who have a firm and unshakable belief in man, God, Torah, and justice. Khonnon, the kindly and scholarly youth, feels that he legally is entitled to claim the gentle and lovely Leye as his wife because of a former vow made by both Nissen and Sender. Khonnon's belief in the justice of this vow enables him to return after his death as a dybbuk to invade the being of Leye and to prevent her marriage to Menashe. The third act is filled with tension revolving around Reb Azrielke of Miropolye, a holy and revered sage.

Act III

(In Miropolye, at the home of Reb Azrielke, *the Tzaddik of Miropolye. A large room. Right, a door leading to other rooms. In the middle of the rear wall, a door leading to the street. Benches on either side of the door, extending almost the whole length of the wall left, a wide table covered with a white cloth. On the table, pieces of* challah *piled up to be used for reciting the blessing that begins a meal. At the head of the table, an armchair. In the right wall, past the door, a small Ark and reading stand. In front of these, a table, a sofa, several chairs. Saturday evening, soon after sundown, Hassidim in the room.* Mikhol, *the Rabbi's aid, stands at the table and prepares the piles of* challah. The Messenger *is seated near the Ark, surrounded by a group of Hassidim. Others are seated by themselves studying.* First *and* Second Hassid *are standing in the middle of the room near the small table. From the rooms within, quiet singing:* "God of Abraham, Isaac, and Jacob.")*

FIRST HASSID. The stranger's tales of wonder are positively frightening. It scares me to listen to them.

SECOND HASSID. What's the matter?

FIRST HASSID. They're full of subtleties beyond my understanding. They sound like the mystic teachings of Rabbi Nakhman of Bratslav. Who knows....

SECOND HASSID. If the older Hassidim are listening, there's probably nothing to worry about. (*They join the group around* THE MESSENGER.)

THIRD HASSID. Tell us another!

MESSENGER. It's late. The time is short.

FOURTH HASSID. Don't worry. The Reb won't be out so soon.

MESSENGER. (*narrates*). At the edge of the world stands a tall mountain, and on the mountain lies a great rock, and from the rock flows a clear spring. And at the other edge of the world, there is the heart of the world; for each thing in the world has a heart and the world as a whole has a great heart of its own. And the heart of the world gazes always at the clear spring and cannot have its fill of looking; and it longs and yearns and thirsts for the clear spring, but it cannot take even the slightest step toward it. For as soon as the heart of the world stirs from its place, it loses sight of the mountain top with the clear spring; and if the heart of the world cannot see the clear spring even for a single instant, it loses its life. And at that very moment the world begins to die. And the clear spring has no time of its own, and it lives with the time that the heart of the world grants it. And the heart grants it only one day. And when the day wanes, the clear spring begins to sing to the heart of the world. And the heart of the world sings to the clear spring. And their singing spreads over the world and from it issue gleaming threads that reach to the hearts of all things in the world and from one heart to another. And there is a man of righteousness and grace who walks about over the world and gathers the gleaming threads from the hearts and out of them weaves time. And when he weaves an entire day, he gives it to the heart of the world, and the heart of the world gives it to the clear spring. and the spring lives yet another day.

THIRD HASSID. The Rebbe is coming! (*All are silent. They rise.* REB AZRIELKE *enters from the door right, a very old man in a white kaftan and a* shtraymel.*)

REB AZRIELKE (*weary and deep in thought, he walks slowly to the table, sinks heavily into the sofa.* MIKHOL *stands at his right hand. The Hassidim seat themselves around the table. The older ones sit on the benches; the younger ones stand behind them.* MIKHOL *hands out the* challah *to the Hassidim.* REB AZRIELKE *raises his hand and in a soft quavering voice begins to chant).* "Here is the feast of King David the Messiah." *(All respond and each says grace over a piece of* challah. *They begin singing softly a melody without words, mystic and sad. Pause.* REB AZRIELKE *sighs deeply, rests his head on both hands, and sits a while deep in meditation. Apprehension pervades the silence.* REB AZRIELKE *raises his head and begins softly in a quavering voice.)* They tell about the holy Baal Shem, may his merits protect us. (*Brief pause.*) Once there came to Mezhibuzh some fellows, acrobats they were, that do their tricks in the streets. They stretch a rope across the river and one of them walked on the rope. And people came running from all parts of the city to see this marvelous feat. The Baal Shem also went down to the river and stood there along with everyone else, watching the man who walked upon the rope. His students were astonished at his presence and they asked him why he had come to watch the tricks. The holy Baal Shem replied: "I came to watch so that I might see how a man crosses a deep abyss. And as I watched, I thought: If Man were to develop his soul as carefully as he has developed his body, what deep abysses might his soul not cross on the slender cord of life!" (*He sighs deeply. Pause. The Hassidim exchange enraptured glances.*)

FIRST HASSID. How lofty!

SECOND HASSID. Wonder of wonders!

THIRD HASSID. How beautiful!

REB AZRIELKE (*softly to* MIKHOL, *who bends down to him*). There is a stranger present.

---

*A fur-timmed hat.

MIKHOL (*looks around*). He is a messenger and apparently a student of Cabal too.

REB AZRIELKE. What is his mission here?

MIKHOL. I don't know. Shall I ask him to leave?

REB AZRIELKE. Heaven forbid! Quite the contrary, a stranger should be received with honor. Give him a chair. (MIKHOL, *somewhat surprised, gives* THE MESSENGER *a chair. No one takes note of it.* REB AZRIELKE *glances at one of the Hassidim who is singing a mystic melody without words. Pause.* REB AZRIELKE *as before.*) God's world is great and holy. The holiest land in the world is the Land of Israel. In the Land of Israel the holiest city is Jerusalem. In Jerusalem the holiest place was the Temple, and in the Temple the holiest spot was the Holy of Holies. (*Brief pause.*) There are seventy peoples in the world. The holiest among these is the People of Israel. The holiest of the People of Israel is the tribe of Levi. In the tribe of Levi the holiest are the priests. Among the priests the holiest was the High Priest. (*Brief pause.*) There are 354 days in the year. Among these the holidays are holy. Higher than these is the holiness of the Sabbath. Among Sabbaths, the holiest is the Day of Atonement, the Sabbath of Sabbaths. (*Brief pause.*) There are seventy languages in the world. The holiest is Hebrew. Holier than all else in this language is the holy Torah, and in the Torah the holiest part is the Ten Commandments. In the Ten Commandments the holiest of all words is the name of God. (*Brief pause.*) And once during the year, at a certain hour, these four supreme sanctities of the world were joined with one another. That was on the Day of Atonement, when the High Priest would enter the Holy of Holies and there utter the name of God. And because this hour was beyond measure holy and awesome, it was the time of utmost peril, not only for the High Priest, but for the whole of Israel. For if in this hour there had, God forbid, entered the mind of the High Priest a false or sinful thought, the entire world would have been destroyed. (*Pause.*) Every spot where a man raises his eyes to heaven, is a Holy of Holies. Every man, having been created by God in His own image and likeness, is a High Priest. Every day of a man's life is a Day of Atonement, and every word that a man speaks with sincerity is the name of the Lord. Therefore it is that every sin and every wrong that a man commits brings the destruction of the world. (*In a trembling voice.*) Human souls, through great anguish and pain, through many an incarnation, strive, like a child reaching for its mother's breast to reach their source, the Throne of Glory on high. But it sometimes happens, even after a soul has reached exalted heights, that evil suddenly overwhelms it, God forbid, and the soul stumbles and falls. And the more exalted it was, the deeper is the abyss into which it falls. And when such a soul falls, a world is destroyed, and darkness descends on all the holy places, and the ten Sephiroth* mourn. (*Pause, as though awakening.*) My children! Today we will cut short our repast of farewell to the Sabbath.

(*All except* MIKHOL *leave silently, deeply impressed by what they have heard. Brief pause.*)

MIKHOL (*approaches the table with uncertainty*). Rebbe!

(REB AZRIELKE *looks up at him wearily and sadly.*) Rebbe, Sender of Brinnits has come.

REB AZRIELKE (*as if repeating*). Sender of Brinnits. I know.

MIKHOL. A great misfortune has befallen him. His daughter is possessed by a dybbuk, God have mercy on us.

REB AZRIELKE. Possessed by a dybbuk. I know.

MIKHOL. He has brought her to you.

REB AZRIELKE (*as if to himself*). To me? To me? How could he have come to me if the "me" in me is not here.

MIKHOL. Rebbe, all the world comes to you.

REB AZRIELKE. All the world. A blind world. Blind sheep following a blind shepherd. If they were not blind they would come not to me but to Him who say "I," to the only "I" in the world.

MIKHOL. Rebbe, you are His messenger.

REB AZRIELKE. So says the world, but I do not know that. For forty years I have occupied a rebbe's seat, and I am not

---

* According to Cabalistic doctrine, the emanations of God.

sure to this very day whether I am a messenger of God, blessed be He. There are times when I feel my closeness to the All. Then I have no doubts. Then I am firm and I have influence in the worlds above. But there are times when I do not feel sure within. And then I am small and weak as a child. Then I need help myself.

MIKHOL. Rebbe, I remember, once you came at midnight and asked me to recite the Psalms with you. And then we recited them and wept together the whole night through.

REB AZRIELKE. That was once. Now it is even worse. (*With a trembling voice.*) What do they want of me? I am old and weak. My body needs rest; my spirit thirsts for solitude. Yet the misery and the anguish of the world reach out to me. Every plea pierces me as a needle does the flesh. And I have no more strength. I cannot!

MIKHOL (*frightened*). Rebbe! Rebbe!

REB AZRIELKE (*sobbing*). I can go no further! I cannot go on!

MIKHOL. Rebbe! You must not forget that behind you stand long generations of tsaddikim and holy men. Your father, Reb Itchele of blessed memory, your grandfather the renowned scholar Reb Velve the Great, who was a pupil of the Baal Shem....

REB AZRIELKE (*recovers*). My forebears...My saintly father, who three times had a revelation from Elijah; my uncle Reb Meyer Ber, who used to ascend to heaven in his prayers; my grandfather, the great Reb Velevel, who resurrected the dead.

(*Turns to* MIKHOL, *his spirits restored.*) Do you know, Mikhol, that my grandfather, the great Reb Velvele, used to exorcise a dybbuk without either holy names of incantations, with merely a command. With a single command! In my times of need I turn to him and he sustains me. He will not forsake me now. Call in Sender.

(MIKHOL *leaves and returns with* SENDER.)

SENDER (*stretching out his arms imploringly*). Rebbe, have pity! Help me! Save my only child!

REB AZRIELKE. How did the misfortune occur?

SENDER. In the midst of veiling the bride, just as...

REB AZRIELKE (*interrupts him*). That's not what I'm asking. What could have caused this misfortune? A worm can penetrate a fruit only when it begins to rot.

SENDER. Rebbe! My child is a God-fearing Jewish daughter. She is modest and obedient.

REB AZRIELKE. Children are sometimes punished for the sins of their parents.

SENDER. If I knew of any sin of mine, I would do penance.

REB AZRIELKE. Has the dybbuk been asked who he is and why he has taken possession of your daughter?

SENDER. He does not answer. But by his voice he was recognized as a student of our yeshiva who some months ago died quite suddenly in the synagogue. He was meddling with Cabala and came to grief.

REB AZRIELKE. By what powers?

SENDER. They say, by evil spirits. Some hours before his death he told a fellow student that one should not wage war against sin and that in evil, heaven protect us, there is a spark of holiness. He even wanted to use magic to get two barrels of gold.

REB AZRIELKE. You knew him?

SENDER. Yes, he ate regularly at my house.

REB AZRIELKE (*looks attentively at* SENDER.) Did you perhaps in any way cause him grief or shame? Try to remember.

SENDER. I don't know. I don't remember. (*In despair.*) Rebbe, I'm only human, after all. (*Pause.*)

REB AZRIELKE. Bring in the girl.

(SENDER *leaves and returns immediately with* FRADE, *both leading* LEYE *by the hand. She stops stubbornly at the threshold and refuses to enter.*)

SENDER (*tearfully*). Leye dearest, have pity. Don't shame me before the Rebbe. Go in.

FRADE. Go in, Leyele. Go in, my dove.

LEYE. I want to enter but I cannot!

REB AZRIELKE. Maiden! I command you to enter. (LEYE *crosses the threshold and goes to the table.*) Sit down.

LEYE (*sits down obediently. Suddenly she springs up and begins to shout in a voice not hers*). Let me go! I refuse! (*She tries to run,* SENDER *and* FRADE *restrain her.*)

REB AZRIELKE. Dybbuk, I command you to say who you are.

LEYE (DYBBUK). Rebbe of Miropolye! You know who I am, but I do not wish to reveal my name before others.

REB AZRIELKE. I do not ask your name. I ask, who are you?

LEYE (DYBBUK) (*softly*). I am one of those who sought new roads.

REB AZRIELKE. Only he seeks new roads who has lost the right one.

LEYE (DYBBUK). That road is too narrow.

REB AZRIELKE. That was said by one who did not return. (*Pause.*) Why did you enter into this maiden?

LEYE (DYBBUK). I am her destined bridegroom.

REB AZRIELKE. Our holy Torah forbids the dead to abide among the living.

LEYE (DYBBUK). I am not dead.

REB AZRIELKE. You departed from our world and you are forbidden to return to it until the great ram's horn is sounded. Therefore, I command you to leave the body of this girl so that a living branch of the eternal tree of Israel may not wither and die.

LEYE (DYBBUK) (*shouting*). Rebbe of Miropolye, I know how powerful, how invincible you are. I know that you can command the angels and the seraphim, but you cannot sway me. I have nowhere to go! For me every road is blocked, every gate is shut, and everywhere evil spirits lie in wait to consume me. (*With a trembling voice.*) There are heaven and earth, there are worlds without number, but not in a single one is there a place for me. And now that my anguished and harried soul has found a haven, you wish to drive me forth. Have pity. Do not conjure or compel me.

REB AZRIELKE. Wandering soul, I feel great pity for you, and I will try to release you from the destroying angels. But you must leave the body of this girl.

LEYE (DYBBUK) (*with firmness*). I will not leave.

REB AZRIELKE. Mikhol, summon a *minyan* from the synagogue. (MIKHOL, *leaves and soon returns followed by ten Jews, who take their places at one side of the room.*) Sacred congregation, do you give me the authority in your name and with your power to expel from the body of a Jewish maiden a spirit who refuses to leave of his own free will?

ALL TEN MEN. Rebbe, we give you the authority in our name and with our power to expel from the body of a Jewish maiden a spirit who refuses to leave of his own free will.

REB AZRIELKE. (*rising*). Dybbuk! Soul of one who left our world, in the name and with the authority of a holy congregation of Jews, I, Azrielke ben Hadas, command you to leave the body of the maiden Leye bas Khanne and in leaving not to harm her nor any other living creature. If you do not obey my command, I will proceed against you with anathema and excommunication, with all the powers of exorcism and with the whole might of my outstretched arm. If, however, you obey my command, I will do all in my power to reclaim your soul and drive off the spirits of evil and destruction that surround you.

LEYE (DYBBUK) (*shouting*). I do not fear your anathemas and excommunications and I do not believe in your assurances! There is no power in the world that can help me! There is no more exalted height than my present refuge and there is no darker abyss than that which awaits me. I will not leave!

REB AZRIELKE. In the name of Almighty God I charge you for the last time and command you to leave. If you do not, I excommunicate you and give you over into the hands of the destroying angels.

(*A fearful pause.*)

LEYE (DYBBUK). In the name of Almighty God, I am joined with my destined bride and I will not part from her forever.

REB AZRIELKE. Mikhol, have white robes brought in for all those present. Bring seven rams' horns and seven black candles. Then take from the Holy Ark seven Sacred Scrolls. (*Awesome pause while MIKHOL goes out and returns with the ram's horns and black candles. He is followed by* THE MESSENGER *carrying the white robes.*)

MESSENGER (*counts the robes*). There is one extra robe. (*Looks around.*) Perhaps someone is missing here?

REB AZRIELKE (*worried as though reminding himself*). In order to excommunicate a Jewish soul, permission must be obtained from the rabbi of the city. Mikhol, for the present put away the horns, the candles, and the robes. Take my staff, go to Rabbi Shimshon and ask him to come here as quickly as possible. (MIKHOL *gathers up the horns and candles and leaves with* THE MESSENGER, *who is carrying the robes. To the ten men.*) You may go, for the present. (*They leave. Pause.* REB AZRIELKE *raises his head.*) Sender! Where are the groom and his party staying?

SENDER. They remained at my house in Brinnits for the Sabbath.

REB AZRIELKE. Send a rider to inform them in my name that they are to stay there and await my command.

SENDER. I'll send a rider at once.

REB AZRIELKE. In the meantime you may go out and take the girl into the next room.

LEYE (*awakens, in her own voice, trembling*). Granny! I am afraid. What will they do to him? What will they do to me?

FRADE. Don't be afraid, my child. The Rebbe knows what he is doing. He won't harm anyone. The Rebbe cannot do any harm. (*She and* SENDER *lead* LEYE *into the next room.*)

REB AZRIELKE (*sits sunk deep in meditation. As though awakening*). And even if it has been otherwise decided in the world above, I will reverse that decision.

(REB SHIMSHON *enters.*)

REB SHIMSHON. May the week ahead be a good one, Rebbe.*

REB AZRIELKE. A good week to you, too, Rabbi, and a good year.* Please sit down (REB SHIMSHON *sits down.*) I have troubled you because of a most important matter. A Jewish girl has been possessed by a dybbuk, may God have

---

* Exchange of greetings, customary at the end of the Sabbath.

mercy, and nothing will induce him to leave. There remains only the last resort, to expel him by excommunication. I therefore ask your consent, and the good deed of saving a soul will be yours.

REB SHIMSHON. Excommunication is a bitter enough punishment for the living. How much more terrible for the dead. But as long as there is no other way and so godly a man as you consider it necessary, I delegate to you my authority. But I must first reveal to you, Rebbe, a secret that has a bearing on the matter.

REB AZRIELKE. Please do.

REB SHIMSHON. You may remember, Rebbe, a young man from Brinnits, Nissen Ben Rivke, a student of Cabala, who was a Hassid of yours about twenty years ago.

REB AZRIELKE. He left from some distant place and died there.

REB SHIMSHON. Yes, Well this very Nissen ben Rivke came to me in my dreams three times last night and demanded that I summon Sender of Brinnits to a trial before a rabbinical court.

REB AZRIELKE. What claims has he against Sender ?

REB SHIMSHON. He did not say. He only charged that Sender had spilled his blood.

REB AZRIELKE. If a Jew has a case against another and demands a trial, a rabbi cannot, of course, refuse. Especially when the accuser is deceased and can therefore appeal to the Throne of Glory itself. But does this have a bearing on the matter of the dybbuk?

REB SHIMSHON. It does. I have heard that the deceased young man who entered as a dybbuk into Sender's daughter was the son of Nissen ben Rivke. There is also talk of an obligation that Sender had to Nissen which he did not fulfill.

REB AZRIELKE (*thoughtful a while*). In that case I will postpone the exorcism of the dybbuk until tomorrow noon. In the morning, God willing, right after the prayers we will ensure that your dreams are for good, and you will summon the deceased to a trial. Afterwards, with your authority I will drive out the dybbuk.

REB SHIMSHON. Inasmuch as a trial between the living and the dead is difficult and unusual. I would ask you, Rebbe, to consent to be the chief judge and to conduct the trial.

REB AZRIELKE. I accept. Mikhol! (MIKHOL *enters*.) Have the girl brought in. (SENDER *and* FRADE *bring in* LEYE, *who sits with eyes shut tight*.) Dybbuk, I give you half a day's time till tomorrow noon. If you will not leave within the designated time and of your own free will, I will, with the authority of the rabbi of the city, expel you by the bitter force of excommunication. (*Pause.* SENDER *and* FRADE *start to lead* LEYE *out*.) Sender! Remain here a while. (FRADE *leads* LEYE *out*.) Sender! Do you remember your friend of years ago, Nissen ben Rivke?

SENDER (*frightened*), Nissen ben Rivke? He died....

REB AZRIELKE. Know, then, that last night he appeared three times in dreams before the Rabbi of the City. (*Points to* REB SHIMSHON.) And he demanded that you be summoned to trial to answer his charges.

SENDER (*staggered*), Me? A trial? Heaven help me! What does he want of me? What should I do, Rebbe?

REB AZRIELKE. I do not know what his accusations are, but you must accept the summons.

SENDER. I will do as you say.

REB AZRIELKE (*with a different tone*). Send the swiftest horses to Brinnits immediately and instruct the bridegroom and his party to be here before noon tomorrow, so that the marriage can take place as soon as the dybbuk leaves.

SENDER. Rebbe, what if they no longer approve of the match and refuse to come?

(THE MESSENGER *appears in the doorway*.)

REB AZRIELKE (*with authority*). Let them be told that I have commanded it. But see that the bridegroom is here in time.

MESSENGER. The bridegroom will be here in time.

(*The clock strikes twelve*.)

Sholem Asch (1880-1966)

God of Vengeance

   Although best known to English readers as a novelist, Sholem Asch is the author of some twenty plays, all written before the end of the second decade of the twentieth century. His drama, *The God of Vengeance*, was regarded as a classic by the outstanding directors of the day, Stanislavsky and Reinhardt among them. As successful on the non-Yiddish as on the Yiddish stage, it appeared in German in Vienna and in English on Broadway, where it caused a scandal. Harshly realistic, the play pictures a brothel as a symbol of the world of business, implying that no one can remain moral while accepting the mores and morality of the marketplace. Yankel, the protagonist, owner of a whorehouse, deludes himself into thinking not only that he can remain loyal to Jewish ideals while trafficking in human flesh but also that he can keep his daughter innocent in the midst of the evil from which he earns a living. In the third act Yankel's illusions shatter, he recognizes the loss of his ideals, and he rages agonizingly just before his final downfall.

Act III

(*The same room as in Act I. Closets and chests of drawers are open and clothes and underwear lie in disorder all over the floor. The door to* RIVKELE'S *room is open and the light of a candle can be seen through the open door.* SORE, *her hair dishevelled, her clothes in disarray, keeps picking up the scattered garments and piling them together as though preparing to leave, but she puts most of them back where they were. A gray morning. The gray light seeps in through the closed shutters.*)

SORE (*picking up the clothing*). Yankel, what's the matter with you? Yankel! (*Goes over to the open door to* RIVKELE'S *room and looks in.*) Why do you keep sitting there? (*Turns back, picking up some more things.*) What a misfortune! He's fallen apart completely. He's trying to ruin the whole house. (*Goes to the door again.*) Yankel, why do you sit there without a word? What's the matter with you? (*Turns back, with tears.*) The man just sits there in front of the Torah Scroll, thinking and thinking. What's there to think about? If you're in trouble, go down to the police station and talk to the captain. Find the scoundrel by hook or by crook, while there is still time. (*Turns to the door.*) Why don't you say something? Say something! (*She sits down on a bundle near the door, covers her face with her hands, and bursts into tears.*) He sits there all by himself like a madman, looking at the Torah Scroll and muttering to himself; he hears nothing and he sees nothing. What's wrong with him? (*Rises from the bundle, to* UNCLE *from the door.*) It's all the same to me. If you want me to leave, I'll leave. The devil won't take me. I'll manage to earn my bread. (*Begins to pack her things in silence. Pause.*)

UNCLE (*comes in from the next room, without a head covering, without his coat, his hair dishevelled. His eyes have a wild look. His voice is hoarse. His speech is slow.*) I'll go...you'll go...Rivkele will go...everything will go. (*Points to the cellar.*) Everything will go down to the house. God does not want....

SORE. Yankel, what is the matter with you! Have you gone out of your mind? (*Goes over to him.*) Consider what you're doing. Misfortune has struck us, But who doesn't suffer misfortune? Come, let's find Shloyme. Give him two or three hundred rubles. Let him give our child back to us. He'll do it. Why do you sit around doing nothing? What's wrong with you?

UNCLE (*in the same voice, walking aimlessly about the room.*) It doesn't matter. I gave my soul to the devil. Nothing will help. God is against it. (*He stops at the window and looks through the slats of the shutters.*)

SORE. God's against it. You're kidding yourself. You're against it. Do you really love your child? Yankel, Yankel (*she pulls him*), what has come over you? Think carefully while there is still time. He might take her away somewhere while you hesitate. Let's go over to his place. The girl must have taken her there. Why do you just stand there? (*Abruptly.*) I sent for Reb Elye. Let's hear what he has to say! (*Pause. UNCLE keeps looking though the window.*) What are you looking at? (*Pause.*) Why don't you answer me? Good heavens, you can go out of your mind. (*Turns away from him weeping audibly.*)

UNCLE (*as before, walking aimlessly*). No more home. No more wife. No more daughter. To the house! Back to the house! We don't need a daughter. We don't need anything. A whore, like her mother. God is against it. Back to the house! Back to the house!

SORE. You want to move down to the house? Go ahead. See if I care! (*Starts packing again.*) Why must he destroy our home? What's the matter with him? (*Thoughtful awhile.*) If you're going to sit on your hands, I'm going to do something. (*She removes her diamond earrings from her ears.*) I'm going over to Shloyme's. I'll give him the diamond earrings (*she searches in a package and pulls out a gold chain*), and this gold chain, and if he still doesn't want to, I'll throw in a hundred. (*She puts her hands into* UNCLE'S *pockets looking for his wallet. He lets himself be searched.*) And in fifteen minutes Rivkele will be back. (*She throws a shawl around her shoulders and starts to leave.*) He'll do it for me. (*She slams the door behind her.*)

UNCLE (*wanders about the house, his head bowed low*). It's all the same to me. Everything's gone to hell. No more daughter...no more Torah Scroll...down to the house...to the house...God says no.

(*A long interval.* REYZL *appears at the door, pokes her head in. Slides into the house and remains standing at the door.* UNCLE *notices her. He looks at her.*)

REYZL (*stammering*). I've been to Reb Elye's. The mistress sent me. He'll be here soon.

UNCLE (*stares at her for a while*). Gone to the devil anyway. God says no.

REYZL. She was such a good girl. What a shame!

(UNCLE *looks at her in surprise.*)

REYZL (*apologetically*). The mistress asked me to wait here till she comes back.

UNCLE. Don't be afraid. I haven't gone mad yet. Not yet. God has punished me.

REYZL. Who would have thought of it. Such a good girl, she was. It's a shame, so help me!

REB ELYE (*comes in, carrying a lantern*). What happened here anyway? Did you have to call me before daybreak? (*He comes inside, looks out through the shutter.*) Almost time for prayers.

UNCLE (*not looking at* REB ELYE). The Torah Scroll has been defiled, defiled unto death.

REB ELYE (*alarmed*). What are you saying, man? Has anything, heaven forbid, happened to the Torah Scroll? Was it dropped to the ground? The whole city will have to fast....

UNCLE. Worse than that, Reb Eyle.

REB ELYE (*angered*). What are you saying! The whole city can be held responsible, heaven forbid! What happened? Say something, man, in heaven's name!

UNCLE. Down into the house. (*Points to the floor and then to* REYZL.) Downstairs with them...into the house...no more Torah Scroll.

REB ELYE. Man, what are you saying? What's going on

here? Talk!

REYZL (*at the door, calms* REB ELYE). No, Rebbe, no, the Torah Scroll, the daughter. Rivkele. The Torah Scroll is unharmed. (*Points to* RIVKELE'S *room.*) In there.

REB ELYE (*takes a breath of relief*). The Lord be praised! But the Torah Scroll is unharmed?

REYZL. Yes, Rebbe.

REB ELYE (*more calmly; spits*). Thank God it was only a scare. (*To* UNCLE.) What kind of nonsense were you talking? (*Motioning to* REYZL *without looking at her.*) Leave. Isn't she here yet? (*To* UNCLE.) Has anyone gone to look for her?

UNCLE. To me my daughter is holier than a Torah Scroll.

REB ELYE. Stop talking nonsense. Just keep quiet. Just don't make any commotion. Has anyone gone to look for her? To bring her back? Of course not! Why are you standing around?

REYZL. The mistress went after her.

REB ELYE. Does anyone know where she went?

REYZL. Yes, the mistress will bring her home soon.

REB ELYE. Then everything is fine. So why all the noise and excitement? Do you want the whole world to find out? Such things are kept quiet. It's not decent. Let a young man's father find out about it, and it will cost you a couple of hundred extra right off.

UNCLE. It's all the same to me. Let everybody know. No more daughter. No more Torah Scroll. Down to the house! Everything down to the house!

REB ELYE. Say, you're really out of your mind. Supposing misfortune does strike. People do have troubles. May God protect us. Never mind the details. God helps. Troubles pass. The main thing is: nobody knows. Nobody hears anything; nobody sees anything. You wipe your lips and make believe nothing happened. (*To* REYZL.) You've got to watch what you say so that, heaven forbid, it does not get around. Do you hear? (*Turns to* UNCLE *whose gaze is lost in some distant nowhere.*) I saw.... (*Looks around to see whether* REYZL *is still present. Noticing her, he stops. After a pause he starts again, more quietly, motioning to* REYZL *to leave. Slowly.*) I saw....(*He looks at* REYZL. REYZL *understands and leaves the room.*) I saw the young man's father in the synagogue between afternoon and evening prayers. I spoke with him. He was close to agreeing. I even gave him to understand, in passing, that the bride did not come from the best of families. Well, another hundred added to the dowry—these days such matters are less important. Saturday, God willing, I'll bring the man up here; then we'll go over and have the rabbi test the young man's learning. But the most important thing is that no one should know; no one must find out about the matter. Heaven forbid. It could do a lot of harm. The man comes from a good family and the son is a fine scholar. Come, come, calm yourself, trust God, and with His help all will turn out for the best. I'm going home to prepare for prayers, and when the girl is back, let me know immediately, you hear? (*Leaving.*) But immediately, without fail. (*Starts to leave.*)

UNCLE (*arises, catches* REB ELYE *by the hand*). Listen, Reb Elye: you take your Torah Scroll with you. I don't need it any more.

REB ELYE (*surprised*). What are you talking about? What do you want? Have you gone crazy? Have you lost your senses?

UNCLE. My daughter went to the house. The Torah Scroll was defiled. God punished me.

REB ELYE (*tries to interrupt him*). What are you talking about?

UNCLE. I am a sinful man. I know that well enough. He should have broken my legs, ruined me, sent me to an early grave.... But what did He want of my child, of my poor child?

REB ELYE. Listen, that's no way to talk. You mustn't talk against God.

UNCLE (*angry*). You can say anything, if it's the truth. I may be Yankel Chapchovich, uncle of a house, but I can tell even God the truth. I'm not afraid at all. I came to you in the synagogue. I told you everything. You advised me to have a Torah Scroll copied. I put it in there, in her room. Night after night I stood before it and I said to it: you are a God. You know everything that I do. If you want to punish me, then punish me. Punish my wife. We have sinned. But not my innocent child. Have pity on my poor child.

REB ELYE. But she has suffered no harm. She'll come back. She'll turn out to be a fine Jewish wife.

UNCLE. It makes no difference. She's gone to the devil. She'll be hankering. Once she's made a beginning, she won't rest. If it isn't today, it will be tomorrow. She's given her soul to the devil. I know that. Oh, how I know that.

REB ELYE. You stop talking nonsense. Calm yourself. Ask God's forgiveness in your heart. Give up your business. With God's help, your daughter will still get married like any other Jewish girl, and you will still have much joy in her.

UNCLE. Lost, Rebbe, all is lost. Had she died young, Rebbe, I would have said nothing. Had she died, I would have known that I buried a chaste child, an honorable child. But now what am I worth in this world? You're sinful yourself and you leave behind a sinful generation. And so sin goes on from generation to generation.

REB ELYE. Don't you talk that way; a Jew must not talk that way. You better trust to God and say to yourself: what was done cannot be undone.

UNCLE (interrupts him). Don't try to persuade me, Rebbe. I know that it's too late. Sin lies upon me and upon my house like a rope about the neck. God was against it. But I ask you, Rebbe, why was God against it? Why should it have bothered Him if you Yankel Chapchovich, save yourself from the swamp into which you're sinking? (Goes into RIVKELE'S room, returns with the Torah Scroll, holds it aloft, and addresses it.) You, Torah Scroll! I know—you are a mighty God! And you are our God. I, Yankel Chapchovich, have sinned. (Beats his breast with his fist.) The sins are mine! Mine! Go ahead and perform a miracle. Send down a fire to consume me on the spot. Open the earth and let me be swallowed up. But protect my child. Send her back to me as pure, as innocent as she was. I know...for you everything is possible. Perform a miracle. You are a mighty God, aren't you? And if you don't—you are no God at all. I, Yankel Chapchovich, say to you, you are no God at all. You are vengeful! You are like a man!

REB ELYE (rouses himself with a start and tears the Torah

Scroll from UNCLE'S *arms*). Do you know whom you are talking to? (*Stares at him, then goes into* RIVKELE'S *room with the Torah Scroll.*) Beg the Torah Scroll's forgiveness!

UNCLE. God Himself can be told the truth to His very face. (*Follows* REB ELYE.) If He is a God, let Him here and now perform His miracle.

SORE (*runs in quickly. She is excited. She runs over to the mirror straightens her hair with her hand, calling*). Come in, Shloyme. Why stand outside?

SHLOYME (*in the doorway*). Where is Yankel? (*Coming in.*) Let him know that I'll do anything for a pal, even though he did insult me.

SORE (*meanwhile she runs over to* RIVKELE'S *door and locks it behind* UNCLE *and* REB ELYE). Let him alone in there. Lately, you know, he's got religion, Hangs around with pious Jews. (*Runs over and locks the door behind* SHLOYME.) You sure pick your brides! She's such a pest. you can't shake her off. Chases after you as though you belonged to her already. I'll bet she comes running after you here. (*Smiling.*) Oh, Shloyme, Shloyme, what a bargain you picked up! (*She goes over to the window, opens the shutters with a bang. The room lights up.*) What did they shut themselves in for?

SHLOYME. Don't worry, I tell you. If I promise you I'll do it, I'll do it. I wouldn't do it for everybody, but for you I'll do it, even though you haven't been nice to me lately. But I don't mind. She can drop dead if she wants to; it won't do her a bit of good.

SORE (*walks over to him, takes him by the hand, looks straight into his eyes*). A fellow like you—why do you have to take a girl like that? Who is she, anyway? She's been tossing about from house to house. A fellow like you—you can pick up a pretty penny now; why do you need her? A fellow with a couple of hundred rubles, why can't you take a decent girl? Why not? Aren't you as young as the next fellow? (*Slaps him on the back.*) You talk it over with me, Shloyme. You know I was never mean to you. Even if I did act like that a little lately, still I was always Sore. Wasn't I? Tell me. (*Looks him in the eye.*)

SHLOYME (*brushing his mustache*). Aw, hell. I let that

broad turn my head, the devil knows why. It was just temporary, To pick up some change. You didn't think I really intended....My mother would have cursed every bone in my body. My mother is a decent woman. Not to mention my sister.

SORE. Didn't you have anything better to do than to get involved with a nobody like that and set up a house? For the kind of income that you get from a house these days, it certainly doesn't pay to get mixed up with no-goods like that. (*Goes over to him, presses the earrings into his hand.*) Here, you take this, and here's a hundred besides, and you tell me where Rivkele is.

SHLOYME. What's true is true. You were once a good woman. (*Winks to her.*) Lately you got spoiled. But one thing has nothing to do with another. Let me tell you, Shloyme is a pal. (*Takes the earrings and puts them into his pocket.*)

SORE. Tell me, Shloyme, where is she now? You can tell me everything even though I am her mother. You know, these things don't scare me. Tell me, have you taken her away somewhere—to a....

SHLOYME. She's very near here. If I tell you I'm gonna bring her to you, I'll bring her. But I tell you, what a tart she could be, so help me. Her looks, her class, she's one well-stacked broad, I can tell you that.

SORE. Hey, Sore still knows! Tell me, Shloyme, where have you got her? You can tell me everything. (*She puts one arm around him, slapping him on the back with her other hand and looking him roguishly in the eye.*) Come on, tell me, buddy boy.

SHLOYME. Not far from here, not far. (*The sound of fists pounding on the outside of the door is heard.*)

HINDL (*offstage*). You don't know anything about her! You don't know a thing.

SORE. Let her go jump in the lake. She's really got him in her grimy little paws! Ha ha, he's not even allowed to budge without her! (*Looks at him roguishly.*) Shame on you, running around the girls! (SHLOYME *is thoughtful.* SORE *grabs him by the hand, pulls him aside.*) Talk it over with me. Why do you need her? I'll give you a girl. You'll see. (*Winks at him.*)

HINDL (*bursts open the door, rushes in*). What in blazes have they latched onto him for? The devil take them—their daughter runs off...(*Grabs* SHLOYME *by the hand.*) You don't know where she is. What do they want from you?

SORE (*sits down on a chair, looks roguishly at* SHLOYME, *indicates* HINDL). So that's the dog, eh? Ha, ha, ha.

HINDL (*turns around*). Listen to that vicious cackle. (*To* SHLOYME.) You don't know a thing about her. (*Draws him aside. Quietly.*) We'll go to Lodz, get married there, rent a place. With two tarts like that—think of what you're doing. (*Loud.*) What are they pestering you for? You don't know where she is. (*Draws him by the hand.*) Come, Shloyme. (SHLOYME *is undecided.*)

SORE (*out loud, with a flattering smile.*) Well, why don't you go with her, Shloyme? She came for you, didn't she? To go off to Lodz, get married, rent a place. (*Approaches* SHLOYME, *draws him away from* HINDL.) A young fellow like you, with a decent Jewish mother. Your father was a pious man. What does she want from you? Why does she stick to you like a leech?

SHLOYME (*calls*). Come, Sore, let's get Rivkele up here.

HINDL (*clasps her hand over his mouth*). You won't tell! You don't know where she is! (*She runs over to the door, closes it and stands blocking it.*) I won't let you out. (*Rushes to* SHLOYME, *grabs his hand.*) Think, Shloyme, is it all right for them and not for us? Come, Shloyme. Let's go away. We could earn such a good living!

SHLOYME. I've heard all that before. (*Pushes her away.*) We'll talk later. I'm busy now. (*Leaves with* SORE.)

SORE (*comes running back in, bursts open the door to* RIVKELE'S *room, calling.*) Rivkele is back!

HINDL (*in the hall*). I won't let you! You won't tell!

SHLOYME (*at the door*). Come, Sore.

SORE (*running out after* SHLOYME). I'm coming, Shloyme. (SORE, SHLOYME, HINDL *leave.*)

REB ELYE (*coming in with* UNCLE). God be praised! God be praised! (*To* UNCLE *who is pacing up and down the room.* REB ELYE *follows him.*) And you see, God did help you. He punishes but he also sends the cure for our ills. Even though you sinned, even though you spoke so blasphemously. (*Warning him.*) From now on you must be careful not to speak such words. You should be respectful. You should know what a Torah Scroll means and what the learning of a Jewish scholar means. You'll have to go to the synagogue, you will. You'll have to make a substantial contribution for the support of aged scholars. And you'll fast in penance. And God will forgive you. (*Pause. He watches* UNCLE *who is pacing up and down absorbed in other matters.*) Don't you hear me? With God's help, everything will turn out right. I'll go over for the bridegroom's father soon, and we'll talk the matter over in all the details. But don't haggle. A hundred more, a hundred less—remember who you are and who he is. And pay the dowry right away and don't hem and haw about the wedding so that we don't run into any obstacles, heaven forbid. Such things shouldn't be postponed. (*He looks at* UNCLE.) Don't you hear me? I'm talking to you.

UNCLE (*to himself*). I want to ask her one thing, just one thing. And let her tell me the truth...the whole truth—yes or no.

REB ELYE. Don't you multiply your sins. Just thank God that he helped as much as he did.

UNCLE (*as before*). I won't do a thing to her. Just the truth: yes or no.

REB ELYE. The truth, the truth. God will help and everything will turn out well. I'm going over to see the groom's father. He's in the synagogue, probably waiting for me. (*Looks around.*) Tell your wife to tidy the place up in the meantime. And as for you—shake hands on the matter right away. Don't give him a chance to find out about anything and change his mind. Agree on the wedding arrangements and send the bride off to the groom's family. Just don't jabber. Keep everything quiet. Don't let anyone find one thing. (*Starts to leave.*) And forget about all that nonsense. Look to God for help. And cheer up a little. Don't let him suspect anything. (*Leaving.*) Tell your wife to put the place in order. (*He leaves.*)

UNCLE (*resuming his pacing*). Just let her tell me the truth, just the truth. (*A long pause.*)

SORE (*at the door*). Come in, come on in. Your father won't beat you. (*Pause*). Go on in, I tell you. (*Pushes* RIVKELE *in. RIVKELE is wrapped in a shawl over her head. She stands at the door, looks in with eyes unabashed and lips set defiantly. She says nothing and does not move from the spot.*)

SORE. Well, why don't you move, darling daughter? All the joy you've given us...for our toil...for our effort. We'll settle accounts later. (*Stops abruptly*). Go on in. Comb your hair. Put on a dress. There's something coming. (*To* UNCLE.) I met Reb Elye. He went for the groom's father. (*Looks around the room.*) Looks like a tornado hit it. (*Begins to clean up hastily.*)

UNCLE (*notices* RIVKELE, *looks at her, approaches her, takes her gently by the hand and leads her to the table*). Don't be afraid. I won't hit you. (*He sits down.*) Sit down here next to me. (*Pushes a chair over for her.*) Sit down.

RIVKELE. I can stand just as well.

UNCLE. Sit down. (*He sits her down.*) Don't be afraid.

RIVKELE (*from behind the shawl*). Why should I be afraid?

UNCLE (*stammering*). Rivkele, tell me, Rivkele...you are my daughter and I am your father..(*Points to* SORE.) There's your mother. Tell me, child, but tell me the whole truth. Don't be afraid of me. And don't be ashamed before me. I know that it was not for your sins, not for your sins but for mine, for mine and your mother's, for our sins. Tell me, child.

SORE. Look at him, sitting down for a heart to heart talk with her. What does he want from her? He could hardly wait! Let her go in and get dressed. People will be here any minute. (*She goes over to take* RIVKELE *away from* UNCLE.)

UNCLE. Let her go, I tell you. (*He pushes* SORE *away from* RIVKELE.)

SORE. He's gone stark raving mad today! What's the matter with him? (*Starts to clean up once more.*)

UNCLE (*seats* RIVKELE *near him.*) I won't hit you. (*Puts his fingers around her slender throat.*) Had I twisted your neck off like this before you grew up, it would have been better for you and better for me. But don't be afraid. I won't harm you. It wasn't for your sins that God punished us but for ours. I protected you as one protects the very eyes of his head. I had a Torah Scroll copied for your sake.I put it into your room and I prayed to God the long nights through: Protect my child from evil. Punish me, punish her mother, but protect my child. When you grew up, I thought, I'll make a fine match for you. I'll get you an honorable young man for a husband; I'll support you both; you'll live together....

RIVKELE (*from behind the shawl*). I've got plenty of time to get married. I'm not that old.

SORE. She's got the nerve to talk back!

RIVKELE. Trying to make a rabbi's wife out of me! Why didn't Mama marry as young?

SORE. Shut your trap or I'll shut it for you! She sure learned a lot in one night!

RIVKELE (*misinterpreting*). Yes, now I know....

UNCLE. Let her alone! (*Hastily.*) I just want to ask her one thing, just one thing. And tell me the truth. I won't hit you. I won't touch you. You're not the guilty one. (*Can't get himself to say the word.*) Tell it to me...straight. Tell me...the truth. I want...the truth....

SORE. What's this that you want? What do you want from her?

UNCLE. I'm not asking you. (*Rises, takes* RIVKELE *by the hand.*) Don't be embarrassed before me. I'm your father. You can tell me everything. Tell me plainly, are you still...are you still as pure as when you left here? Are you still a chaste Jewish girl?

SORE (*pulls* RIVKELE *from* UNCLE'S *grasp*). What do you want from her? The child has done nothing wrong. Let her alone.

UNCLE (*holds fast to* RIVKELE'S *hand, tries to look her in the eye*). Tell me the truth. I'll believe you. Look me in the eye, straight in the eye. Are you still a chaste Jewish girl? Look me in the eye, straight in the eye! (*He tries to look into her eyes.* RIVKELE *hides her face in the shawl.*)

SORE. Why don't you take the shawl off your head? Do you need a shawl in the house? (*She pulls the shawl off her head.* RIVKELE *resists, hides her face in her coat.*)

UNCLE (*shouting*). Tell me now. Don't be bashful. I won't hurt you. (*He takes her firmly by the hands, draws her towards him, and looks into her eyes.*) Are you still a chaste Jewish girl? Tell me now.

RIVKELE (*tries to hide her face in the coat*). I don't know....

UNCLE (*shouting*). You don't know? You don't know? Well then who does know? You don't know! Tell me the truth: are you still....

RIVKELE (*tearing herself out of her father's grasp*). Was it all right for my mother? Was it all right for my father? Now I know everything. (*She holds her arms up to protect her face.*) Hit me! Go ahead and hit me!

(SORE *runs towards her with hands raised to strike her.* UNCLE *pushes her off with a single blow. He sits down on his chair, pale, breathing heavily.* RIVKELE *drops to the floor weeping loud. A long pause of silence.* SORE *walks about the room. It is clear that she doesn't know where to begin. After a while she picks up the broom and starts to sweep up silently, almost stealthily. Then she goes over to* RIVKELE, *pulls her by the hand, and leads her into her room. She does all this in silence.* UNCLE *does not move.* RIVKELE *exits.*)

SORE (*coming back from* RIVKELE'S *room, runs over to* UNCLE, *grasps his hand, pleading.*) Yankel, consider what you're doing! Remember God! Why does anyone have to know? (*Pause*). Calm yourself. (*Pause.*) Rivkele will get married; we'll be proud of her yet.

(UNCLE *says nothing.*)

SORE. Put on your jacket. They'll be here soon. (*Looks at* UNCLE. *Abruptly.*) Why must anyone know?

(UNCLE *says nothing. Stares at the same spot.*)

SORE (*brings* UNCLE'S *jacket in. She helps him into it. He lets her*). What a calamity! What a calamity! Who could have expected it? (*She finishes dressing* UNCLE *and begins to straighten her own clothes. She tidies up, runs into* RIV-KELE'S *room. Sounds of her hiding something. Returns quickly.*) We'll settle with you later. (*Looks around the room to see whether everything is in place, straightens up here and there.*) Raise children these days! (*Sighs audibly.*)

(*Sounds of footsteps coming up the stairs.*)

SORE (*runs over to* UNCLE, *pulling him by the sleeve*). They're coming. Remember God! Yankel...it can still turn out right.

(REB ELYE *comes in with a stranger.* SORE *pushes her stray hair underneath her wig, stands near the door to receive the guests.*)

REB ELYE. Good morning.

SORE. Good morning and a good year. Welcome. (*Somewhat confused. She offers them each a chair.*)

REB ELYE (*gaily*). Where's the father of the bride? (*Looks around for* UNCLE.)

SORE (*smiling, to* UNCLE). Yankel, why don't you show yourself? (*She pushes a chair closer to* UNCLE.)

(*The men shake hands with* UNCLE *and sit down.*)

REB ELYE (*gesticulating*). Let's get right down to the matter at hand. (*To the stranger, indicating* UNCLE.) This man wants to arrange a match with you. His daughter is a chaste Jewish maiden and he wants to give her a scholar for a husband, and he'll support them both for the rest of their lives.

THE STRANGER. Good.

UNCLE (*rising*). Yes, my friend, a chaste Jewish maiden, a chaste....

REB ELYE (*to* THE STRANGER). He'll pay five hundred rubles cash at the engagement, support for him to study for the rest of his days; he'll treat him as if he were his own child.

THE STRANGER. There's no need for me to boast about what I've got. Two more years of study and he'll be a rabbi.

REB ELYE. We know that. This man will watch over him as he would the eye of his head. He'll have everything of the best here. And he'll be able to sit and study day and night.

UNCLE (*pointing to* RIVKELE'S *room*). Yes, in there, he can sit and study the holy Torah...I have a chaste Jewish daughter. (*He goes into* RIVKELE'S *room and drags her out forcibly by the arm. She is still half undressed, her hair dishevelled. Points to her.*) A chaste Jewish maiden will be marrying your son. She'll bear chaste Jewish children, like any other Jewish girl. (*To* SORE.) Isn't that so? (*Laughs wildly to* THE STRANGER.) Yes, indeed, my friend, she'll be a chaste

Jewish wife...My wife will lead her to the wedding canopy....
Down to the whore house! Downstairs! (*Points to the base-
ment.*) To the house! (*He drags* RIVKELE *by the hair to the
door.*) Down to the house!

SORE (*runs over wildly.*) Help, everybody, he's gone crazy!
(*She tries to pull* RIVKELE *away.* UNCLE *pushes her off and
continues to pull* RIVKELE *out by the hair.*)

UNCLE. Down to the house! (*Exits with* RIVKELE. RIV-
KELE'S *crying can be heard offstage.*)

THE STRANGER (*astounded and alarmed*). What's this?
(REB ELYE *draws him toward the door. They leave. Pause.*)

UNCLE (*returns pulling* REB ELYE *by the arm, having
caught him on the stairs*). Take the Torah Scroll with you. I
don't need it any more!

Peretz Hirschbein (1880-1948)

A producer and director as well as playwright of high literary caliber, Hirschbein wrote more than fifty plays, full-length and one-act. At first he wrote in Hebrew, later in Yiddish. Disillusionment with Communist Russia led him to Vienna, then to London and New York. But he could not get his plays produced in the U.S., and so he went to Argentina. During World War I, he wrote *In the Shadow of Generations*, which subsequently became part of the repertoire of the Yiddish theater in New York.

Although Hirschbein wrote many plays about the lower classes—such as *In the Dark*, the story of a girl who commits suicide because of poverty—he is famous for his folk comedy, *Green Fields*. It is tender without sentimentality, moral without didacticism, Jewish without chauvinism. A celebration of the *mentshlekayt* (Yiddish for decency, morality, gentleness), which Hirschbein perceived in Jewish farmers, *Green Fields* is also a paean of praise for traditional Jewish values. The play is an idyll—naive, whimsical, earthy—despite its humorous dialogue.

Green Fields

Green Fields takes us to the idyllic world of the country, of farm and field. Here within the surroundings of nature there is a purity of life, a rediscovery of values, and rededication to one's faith and one's roots. The humanity of the characters with their special dignity, their sense of morality, and religious ethics becomes apparent as the drama unfolds. In Act III of *Green Fields* the charming and simple—though certainly not simplistic—Tsine, daughter of Dovid-Noyakh and Rokkel, and the object of her love, the gentle and scholarly youth Levi-Yitskhok, cause us to realize that Jewish tradition with its dependence on learning, wisdom, and morality can flourish "even in the country."

Act III

(*In front of* DOVID-NOYAKH'S *house. It is late summer. Evening.* LEVI-YITSKHOK'S *voice is heard from inside the house. He is studying.*)

(TSINE *seated in front of the door churning butter. Every now and then she pauses and listens to the chanting from the house. She reminds herself of something and runs off into the garden.* LEVI-YITSKHOK *comes out. Examines the butter churn. Tries to work the rod. He notices the globules of butter stuck to the rod. From the garden.* TSINE'S *anxious outcry is heard, followed by a noise among the branches of a tree. He stops for a moment, frightened. He takes several steps toward the garden, climbs quickly over the fence but soon returns and hurries back into the house.* TSINE *enters. She is pale and holds her side. She climbs over the fence and approaches her previous place near the door. She examines a bleeding scratch on her arm.*)

LEVI-YITSKHOK (*comes out, carrying a dipper of water*). Here's a drink of water. Did you hurt yourself?

(TSINE *takes the dipper from his hand and drinks.*)

LEVI-YITSKHOK. You gave me a start.

TSINE. I fell down from the top of the tree.

LEVI-YITSKHOK. You should thank the Lord.

TSINE. I got frightened and I fell.

LEVI-YITSKHOK. There's blood on your hand.

TSINE. My heart is really pounding.

LEVI-YITSKHOK. Did you really have to go climbing trees?

TSINE. I heard you studying and I went to pick some apples for you.

LEVI-YITSKHOK. For whom?

TSINE. For you. Do you think I didn't pick any? (*Takes two red apples out of her apron pocket.*) You see, as red as the apples for Simchas Torah. It was on account of you that I fell out of the tree. I could have gotten killed.

LEVI-YITSKHOK. God forbid.

TSINE. Why should you care if I get killed?

LEVI-YITSKHOK. I have a Jewish heart, don't I?

TSINE. Take the two apples.

LEVI-YITSKHOK. To recite the blessing just before Rosh Hashonna—it's not proper.

TSINE. What if you want an apple and can't resist?

LEVI-YITSKHOK. One must be able to conquer the *yetser hara*, the inclination to do wrong.

TSINE. But the apples grow in summertime. How can one resist so long? I eat about ten apples every day, and nothing happens. I didn't even know you weren't allowed to eat them.

LEVI-YITSKHOK. Well, I just told you that you're not allowed to.

TSINE. Who is the *yetser hara*?

LEVI-YITSKHOK. He lurks within people. You see how he just sent you to climb the tall tree for apples, and you were quickly punished.

TSINE. Oh, you don't know why I fell out of the tree.

LEVI-YITSKHOK. What makes you think I don't know?

TSINE. You don't know. You really don't know at all. If you only knew how I've become a new Tsine....Well, why did I fall out of the tree?

LEVI-YITSKHOK. Certainly not on purpose. Nobody cuts his hand up on purpose.

TSINE. I want to show you something. (*She runs into the house.*)

(LEVI-YITSKHOK *examines the two apples that are lying on the ground near him. He smells them.* TSINE *comes out. She brings a board with letters written in chalk.*)

LEVI-YITSKHOK. What's that?

TSINE. Read what's written here.

LEVI-YITSKHOK. But it's not Avrom-Yankev's hand-writing.

TSINE. It's mine.

LEVI-YITSKHOK (*looks at the letters with surprise. He reads*). "Tsine, daughter of Reb Noyakh."

TSINE. Well, who wrote it?

LEVI-YITSKHOK. Not Avrom-Yankev.

TSINE. Erase it.

LEVI-YITSKHOK. Why do you want me to do that? It's not good to erase a name.

TSINE. Please erase it. Wipe it off, like this...

LEVI-YITSKHOK. He—ho—so childish. Well, there, I've erased.

TSINE. Now close your eyes.

(LEVI-YITSKHOK *does so.* TSINE *takes a piece of chalk out of her pocket and writes.*)

LEVI-YITSKHOK. Now?

TSINE. Keep them closed just a little longer. There we are. Now, what does it say?

LEVI-YITSKHOK. My name..."Levi-Yitskhok"...Who wrote it?

TSINE. I did.

LEVI-YITSKHOK. That's impossible.

TSINE. It certainly is possible.

LEVI-YITSKHOK. I'll erase it and you write it again.

TSINE. Then close your eyes again.

(LEVI-YITSKHOK *closes his eyes.* TSINE *writes his name again in large letters, and as he stands there with his eyes shut, she steals close to him and gives him a kiss. Then she runs into the house.* LEVI-YITSKHOK *is surprised by what has happened. He starts to go into the house but at the door he realizes that he should not go in. He takes the board, wipes his name off, and throws it away. He sits down on the same bench where he sat before. He sits thoughtfully with his head bent.*)

ELKONE (*enters*). God bless you, Rebbe. Alone, are you?

(LEVI-YITSKHOK *looks at him, very upset.*)

ELKONE. What's this? Have you been put to work churning butter? That's a fine state of affairs.

(LEVI-YITSKHOK *looks at him uncomprehending.*)

ELKONE. Are you churning butter?

LEVI-YITSKHOK. There's no reason why I can't churn butter too. What's so remarkable?

ELKONE. I came to ask you to resolve a problem of religious procedure.

LEVI-YITSKHOK. I have no authority to deal with such problems.

ELKONE. What's the difference. As long as we know. Besides, this sort of question is one you can answer for me.

LEVI-YITSKHOK. For instance?

ELKONE. My older daughter took something into her head, and nothing helps.

LEVI-YITSKHOK. Maybe she's right.

ELKONE. What do you mean, a child being right if her father says no?

LEVI-YITSKHOK. It sometimes happens that an older person is wrong, too.

ELKONE. But supposing one is impudent enough to defy a father? That's what I'm asking.

LEVI-YITSKHOK. Sometimes a parent should hear what the older child has to say.

ELKONE. No, there I disagree with you. The Torah says that one should honor one's parents. It does say so, doesn't it?

LEVI-YITSKHOK. Who doesn't know that?

ELKONE. That's why I say, a girl ought to obey her father. Say, isn't Dovid-Noyakh here?

LEVI-YITSKHOK. No, he's not.

ELKONE. I can't stand an ignoramus. What's the use of kidding myself? I may not be educated myself, but I can still tell the difference between a man and a swine.

LEVI-YITSKHOK. One must not talk that way about a Jew.

ELKONE. Why be ashamed to say so? Dovid-Noyakh is a nobody and his son is a nobody.

LEVI-YITSKHOK. They're fine people. I have nothing against them.

ELKONE. It's you that I'm really talking about. They don't show you enough respect. This is no way to treat a stranger.

LEVI-YITSKHOK. They certainly don't treat me with disrespect.

ELKONE. The boy doesn't really take after him, that's true. I mean Avrom-Yankev. But he himself is a nobody. Lets his daughter run wild. I wouldn't let her run around like a hussy.

LEVI-YITSKHOK. That's not my business. That's gossip.

ELKONE. You may be learned and pious, but you don't see what they're doing with you.

LEVI-YITSKHOK. What is there to see? They're Jews like any other Jews.

ELKONE. Well, what am I to do if my daughter latches on to that oaf of a son of his? If I beat her, she talks back to me. That's what I came to talk to you about.

LEVI-YITSKHOK. He's a decent fellow. He'll be a pious Jew.

ELKONE. Ha-ha, I really wanted you to stay at my house. They'd have looked after you better at my place. Maybe the children would have learned something. Well, they got to you first. That's luck.

LEVI-YITSKHOK. You're angry, Reb Elkone, and that's why you're saying things you'll regret. You're a fine man. Dovid-Noyakh wishes you no ill; and the children get along well together. Why do you do such a thing?

ELKONE. Perhaps you're right. A Jew should not act this way. But what can I do? My heart aches. And just because I am an ignoramus. My sons—they'll be nobodies. Well, then, why shouldn't I try to get for my daughter someone, an outsider who can bring honor to a house? There are the holidays. There is the Sabbath. And especially when you come into town for the High Holy Days. What's the use of talking? I wouldn't care about the cost—down to my last shirt.

LEVI-YITSKHOK. Well, what's the problem? All you need to do is ride into town and make inquiries. There are many fine young scholars in town.

ELKONE. Who knows how? Who can turn the trick? Who even thought of it? My eyes were just recently opened.

LEVI-YITSKHOK. I don't know what you mean.

ELKONE. You don't follow me? I say, you be my son-in-law. My Stere, the older one; with a good heart. I wanted to hit her today, but I felt sorry for her. It isn't even my idea; it's my wife. She sent me over here. Why deny it, ha-ha. If you tell me where your parents live, I wouldn't mind hitching up and taking a ride over to see them. Maybe you can tell me where they live?

LEVI-YITSKHOK. They're dead.

ELKONE. Really?

LEVI-YITSKHOK. Died long ago.

ELKONE. An orphan! Isn't that something! It would be a pity if I let you get away.

DOVID-NOYAKH (enters). God bless you, Elkone. What brings you here at this hour?

ELKONE. Nothing much. Just chatting.

DOVID-NOYAKH. Who's churning the butter? My wife is at home I see.

ELKONE. I thought you people had given the Rebbe the honor of churning the butter.

DOVID-NOYAKH. Ha, ha. My wife still knows how to treat someone with respect.

(LEVI-YITSKHOK goes off behind the house.)

DOVID-NOYAKH. Isn't there anyone in the house? Let me have a look. (He looks through the window.)

ELKONE. I think your girl is inside.

DOVID-NOYAKH. Come on in. Why stand outside?

ELKONE. I'll be getting ready to leave.

DOVID-NOYAKH. Where were you going, anyway?

ELKONE. I was coming here. I wanted to talk to the teacher.

DOVID-NOYAKH. What's the trouble? Don't the children listen to him?

ELKONE. I had something else in mind. You know, he's a full orphan. Now you tell me, who needs parents?

DOVID-NOYAKH. In town, everything is possible.

ELKONE. He might get the idea that I was trying to malign you.

DOVID-NOYAKH. What might give him that idea?

ELKONE. Where did he go? He's a big fool. I was talking with him and he probably misunderstood me.

ROKHEL (*enters*). A guest. It's nearly a week since we saw you last. How is Gittl?

ELKONE. She's a little under the weather.

ROKHEL Does she still have pains in her side? She ought to see someone in town! She works too hard.

(GITTL *enters*.)

ROKHEL. Ah, we have a guest. We were just talking about you.

GITTL. As my mother always says, if God's in His heaven, why should I worry. Did my daughter give me a hard time!

ROKHEL. Nothing wrong, heaven forbid.

GITTL. Nothing wrong, you say.

ELKONE. Too bad I wasn't home. She'd have caught it from me.

ROKHEL. She's as fine a child as anyone would want.

GITTL. I know you like her.

ROKHEL. Of course I like her. If Tsine has at least three sisters like Stere, what more could I ask for?

DOVID-NOYAKH. A real handy girl; what's there to complain about? She's a year younger than Tsine and, bless her, she's twice as big.

GITTL (*to* ELKONE). What, are you afraid to talk? I don't know what there is to be afraid of. I left the house to come over here because I don't want it to drag out.

ROKHEL. Gittl, I really don't understand what you're talking about.

GITTL. I want Hersh-Ber to stop annoying her.

DOVID-NOYAKH. What do you mean *annoying* her? What have you got against him anyway—I mean Hersh-Ber?

ELKONE. I've got nothing against him. To you, he's your son. You like him. I don't.

ROKHEL. And I don't care if you don't like him. Did you ever?

GITTL. Then let him stop putting ideas into Stere's head.

DOVID-NOYAKH. What's the matter, Elkone? Is it beneath you to be related to me?

ELKONE. It's beneath me for your son to be my son-in-law.

DOVID-NOYAKH. Then why come to tell me about it? I don't know a thing. You can keep Hersh-Ber out of your house. It's your blessing.

ROKHEL. I don't even see that he's running after her. I don't know what you have against my child.

ELKONE. I'll speak plainly.

GITTL. What have you got to be ashamed of?

ELKONE. I want the stranger, the children's teacher. Y'understand, he's right for Stere.

GITTL. And you packed him off to your house.

ELKONE. Your daughter is spoiling him.

DOVID-NOYAKH. What do you mean?

ELKONE. I found him sitting outside.

ROKHEL. What outside? When outside? Whatever I dreamt this night and the other night....What do you want here? Why did you come here to malign my children?

DOVID-NOYAKH. Take it easy. Don't shout. We can discuss it calmly, like reasonable people. I still don't understand the whole thing. He's talking about Hersh-Ber, I thought, not about the girl. What in the world can he have against her?

ROKHEL. Don't you hear what they're saying? I have a good mind to ask....Tsinele? Come on out here for a minute!

(TSINE *comes out, a little confused.*)

ELKONE. Aw, what are you making a fuss about? Go, back into the house, Tsine. It won't do you a bit of harm even if I did, heaven forbid, say something against you. Your mother won't put up with it.

TSINE. What do you want me for?

ROKHEL. Where were you when Elkone arrived?

TSINE. In the house.

ROKHEL. I wouldn't have believed it of you, Elkone.

GITTL. So what ? Who cares?

DOVID-NOYAKH. But what is there to quarrel about? I say, let's ask the children.

ELKONE. I have nothing to ask anybody. My daughter will do as I say.

DOVID-NOYAKH. Have it your own way.

ROKHEL. Go, child, go into the house.

TSINE. What did you want me for?

GITTL. Tell me, Tsine, what does Stere talk to you about?

TSINE. She talks to me about—she talks to me about everything. How can I keep track?

ELKONE. Do you hear, my wife, how clever some people are? That's the one that's misleading my little one. I'll teach her to come here. I'm going home and I'll give her a piece of my mind. (*Starts off.*)

DOVID-NOYAKH. That's not right, Elkone. I thought you were a better father. Where did he run off to?

TSINE. Do go home, Gittl. Don't let him do anything to her, because she hasn't done anything wrong.

GITTL. I'd rather not say anything to you, Tsinele, since your mother is present, but if she weren't....

ROKHEL. Feel free to leave any time. I didn't send for you. I really thought you were our good friends. Come inside, Dovid-Noyakh; I have nothing to say to her. (*Both go into the house.*)

GITTL. Listen to me, Tsine. Your mother thinks that I wish her ill. I'm not an enemy of yours. I only want to tell you, without your mother's hearing it, that I know everything you spoke about to Stere.

TSINE. I'm not afraid. I said nothing to be afraid about.

GITTL. Here comes Hersh-Ber. I want to talk to him plainly.

HERSH-BER (*enters*). What's Elkone mad about? I called him, but he wouldn't turn around.

GITTL. He knows why he's angry.

HERSH-BER. What are you in a huff about? I didn't throw any rocks into your garden.

GITTL. Let me tell you, you certainly are throwing rocks.

HERSH-BER. What are you making a fuss about? Let me ask you, have you got a better husband for Stere? Why did you start making trouble? What do you want me to do, pay you for her? I love Stere and Stere loves me. So why are you mixing in, tell me?

GITTL. So that's how it is? Has it gone that far?

TSINE. Yes, of course.

GITTL. Look at them, will you! What sort of plague is this?

HERSH-BER. If you don't want to, that's all right with me too. Whatever you say. and tell Elkone that if he raises a hand to her, I'll show him how to be a father.

GITTL. Listen to him! Listen to him, will you!

HERSH-BER. Then don't listen if you don't want to. Come on inside, Tsine. (*He goes inside.*)

GITTL. I can't believe my ears! I must tell this to Elkone. (*She leaves.*)

(AVROM-YANKEV *enters.*)

TSINE. Good thing you came, Avrom-Yankev. I've been looking for you everywhere. Here's a kiss and don't tell the Rebbe that you taught me to write his name and my name.

AVROM-YANKEV. What? What did you say.

TSINE. Please, here's another kiss; all right? Here he comes. Don't tell him anything. (*She runs into the house.*)

LEVI-YITSKHOK (*enters*). Where have you been, Avrom-Yankev?

AVROM-YANKEV. I went to check whether the horse didn't wander off into the mire.

LEVI-YITSKHOK. Why did your sister learn to write my name?

AVROM-YANKEV. Ha-ha—she told me she envied my studying with you. She says she wants to study, too.

LEVI-YITSKHOK. So you taught her, it seems.

AVROM-YANKEV. Is it forbidden? She wanted me to teach her how to say the prayers, but I was afraid. Maybe you're not allowed to.

LEVI-YITSKHOK.Women are allowed to study the prayers. Women have to know how to pray, too.

AVROM-YANKEV. I'll tell her.

LEVI-YITSKHOK. Wait a bit.

AVROM-YANKEV. She'll be very happy. (*Runs into the house.*)

HERSH-BER. (*Comes out*). Good you're here, Rebbe. I want to ask you something. Don't take offense.

LEVI-YITSKHOK. Of course.

HERSH-BER. You know the Torah; tell me, what does the law say, if I've picked a wife for myself and her parents get ideas and refuse?

LEVI-YITSKHOK. What do you mean, they refuse? There must be a reason.

HERSH-BER. They don't want to, that's all. What can you do?

LEVI-YITSKHOK. You have to do things so that they are pleased.

HERSH-BER. They've gone daffy and there's nothing you can do.

LEVI-YITSKHOK. Jews can talk things over. There's probably a reason for their actions.

HERSH-BER. What do you mean a reason? There's no reason at all. Her father is a stubborn mule and her mother is a jackass and that's all. There's no reason at all. Just plain stubbornness.

LEVI-YITSKHOK. You ought to approach them with kindliness. Explain things to them.

HERSH-BER. Maybe you're right, there. Maybe my words were a little rough. But how can you know what you're doing? Maybe you'd like to mix in, Rebbe; maybe he'd have respect for you, Rebbe. I mean Elkone. I want to take his daughter for my wife. So he messed things up.

LEVI-YITSKHOK. How could I be of any help?

HERSH-BER. He'll respect you. You know her. You've seen her. Grew up together. I want to take her just as she is. But how can you do anything with them?

LEVI-YITSKHOK. It's best to do it yourself. You should speak for yourself; and be kindly and reasonable.

HERSH-BER. I could manage with him. But her mother has turned up her nose.

LEVI-YITSKHOK. Let your mother speak with her.

HERSH-BER. The mothers have quarreled.

LEVI-YITSKHOK. Wait till Rosh Hashonna; they'll make up, as the custom is. During the ten days of penitence, people regret any wrongs they've done.

HERSH-BER. Rebbe, you talk like a tsaddik. But I can't wait that long. I want to go to their house, but they told me not to. I know why, Rebbe; I know the real reason, but I can't tell you. It doesn't matter if you don't know.

LEVI-YITSKHOK. What could I know?

HERSH-BER. I know. Rebbe, that you don't know a thing about it. That's why I say that she doesn't know anything about it either. They're the ones that are after her. She won't hear of it. You can mix in.

LEVI-YITSKHOK. I really don't see how I can be of any help.

HERSH-BER. I wouldn't want my father to hear this. You know, he wants you for a son-in-law.

LEVI-YITSKHOK. Whom?

HERSH-BER. Elkone wants you for his son-in-law.

LEVI-YITSKHOK. What do you mean?

HERSH-BER. He's got a daughter Stere, doesn't he? You know her, Rebbe.

LEVI-YITSKHOK. I don't understand it.

HERSH-BER. So you don't. He comes here to hang around you. Why do you think he manages to come just when there's no one else around? That's the whole story.

LEVI-YITSKHOK. He probably has something else in mind.

HERSH-BER. You tell him that you don't want his daughter.

LEVI-YITSKHOK. The whole thing comes as a complete surprise to me.

HERSH-BER. I told my father and mother that you didn't know the first thing about it.

LEVI-YITSKHOK. I'm simply amazed.

(TSINE *appears in the doorway and listens quietly to the conversation.*)

HERSH-BER. I agree that something like that shouldn't be

done without the parents. But what's the use? What can you do with them?

LEVI-YITSKOHK. Simply amazing!

HERSH-BER. Don't take it amiss, Rebbe....

(DOVID-NOYAKH *comes out. He catches* TSINE *eavesdropping. She is embarrassed and hides behind the door.* HERSH-BER *would like to say something more, but gives up and with a gesture of his hand goes into the house.*)

DOVID-NOYAKH. An obstinate man, this Elkone. It's hard to believe that a man can be so stubborn. We've had many a quarrel. The wives too. If not for Yom Kippur, we'd never talk to each other. My question is: why? Isn't it possible to live together in peace? Why should Jews quarrel for no good reason at all? What do you say, Rebbe?

LEVI-YITSKHOK. The world rests only on unity and peace.

DOVID-NOYAKH. I heard that once. The Rabbi in town said it in a sermon. But, thank God, I don't have to be reminded of it. I'm a man who knows how little value one has in the world. My wife does feel like kicking over the traces every now and again, but I don't let her. If you live way out in the country, what does it take to become, heaven forbid, like the Gentiles? Gentiles quarrel and Jews—quarrel....I know what I mean.

LEVI-YITSKHOK. Any town should be glad to have Jews like you.

DOVID-NOYAKH. He-he, you get a little uncouth in the country. But when it comes to wronging someone—you remind yourself. Thank the Lord, we know up from down. Although in town they don't have too much respect for country people. Well, after all, we can't compare ourselves to city folk. The town Jew is really a Jew. He can exchange a few words with a rabbi, attend a synagogue when he's supposed to, and he can donate to charity, if heaven helps him.

LEVI-YITSKHOK. You are a fine Jew. No one need be ashamed of Jews like you.

DOVID-NOYAKH. My father, may he rest in heaven, was a farmer too. Didn't know how to teach his children. What could you do? Barely managed to teach us to read. He died right here in my house. I brought him to town, and when I got there, I didn't feel like leaving. Well, I suppose the Lord wants us to live far from Jews and at least to find Jewish burial among Jews. What can you do? As far as my older one is concerned, it's too late. But the younger one could still amount to something. I figured, if Elkone were willing to chip in....So I hear that his boys get out of hand. Still, let me say this to you: don't leave us. Let things be as they are.

LEVI-YITSKHOK. I'm not leaving, Reb Dovid-Noyakh. I was going to ask you to think it over, maybe....

DOVID-NOYAKH. Let's not discuss it any further. If Elkone won't, I'll do it myself— with everything in my power. After all....

LEVI-YITSKHOK. I mean, I want to be your son-in-law. That's what I mean.

DOVID-NOYAKH (*somewhat confused*). Wha...?

LEVI-YITSKHOK. My parents are dead, or I would have had them speak for me.

DOVID-NOYAKH. Yes, Tsine. My child.

LEVI-YITSKHOK. You understand...that if...you have to agree.

DOVID-NOYAKH. Agreed! Agreed! We don't have to ask her anything.

LEVI-YITSKHOK. Her mother must be asked.

DOVID-NOYAKH. I mean, ask her mother, he-he...I mean, my child will obey, a fine girl....Rokhel! Rokhel! Come out here for a moment!

LEVI-YITSKHOK. Still....

DOVID-NOYAKH (*calls*). Rokhel, Rokhel, if you please.

ROKHEL (*coming out*). We have a God in heaven. What's all the excitement about?

DOVID-NOYAKH. Here's her mother. He wants to know whether you agree.

ROKHEL. God in heaven, what more could I ask for my child? (*Wipes her tears.*)

DOVID-NOYAKH. You don't understand what we're talking about....

ROKHEL. You think I don't know? How could a mother not know? I know everything....(*Embraces* LEVI-YITSKHOK *and kisses him.*) I'll be like a mother to you. What more could I ask God to bless me with? How should I tell her? Dear me, she may faint when she hears it.

(ELKONE, GITTL, STERE *arrive.*)

ELKONE. Where's your son, Dovid-Noyakh?

DOVID-NOYAKH. I beg you, Elkone, don't quarrel with me now.

ELKONE. Where is your son? I want Stere to tell him in my presence that she doesn't want to know him.

STERE (*with eyes red from weeping*). I wish I knew what you want of me.

(HERSH-BER *comes out.*)

GITTL. There he is in person.

ROKHEL. Don't spoil my happiness, Gittlshe.

GITTL. You're rejoicing but we're suffering.

HERSH-BER. Stere, I'm glad you came. Tell the truth!

ELKONE. She has nothing to say.

HERSH-BER. Let the whole world hear the truth, Stere! I'm not afraid!

ROKHEL. Hush, child, don't shout so loud.

HERSH-BER. Now I'm mad! I laugh at such parents. Stere and I grew up together right here! We grew up in the same field, and she's mine! Say it, Stere. Say it. Don't be afraid.

ELKONE. How do you like that head on him. Gittl? He couldn't put two and two together, but what a tongue he's got now! Listen to him talk! Ha-ha-ha.

HERSH-BER. I don't know whether I'm talking properly or not. I asked the Rebbe. I told him I didn't want to oppose her parents. The Rebbe advised kindliness. I wanted to do it tonight, so why did you come now, dragging her here with her eyes full of tears. Why do you want to make her cry, anyway, for no good reason?

ROKHEL. So help me, he's right.

HERSH-BER (*choking back the tears*). You have no reason to make her life miserable. I can't stand to see her cry....

(STERE *bursts out in loud crying.*)

GITTL. Hush, foolish child. He delivered a speech and she....

ELKONE. Ha-ha-ha. Look at me, just standing and listening. What's the matter with you, Elkone?

HERSH-BER. We grew up in the same field. Why do you want to stand in our way? Why? I'll take her as she is. What more do you want? Let's get it over with, once and for all.

ELKONE. I'll give you a dowry, too, Hersh-Ber. When you talk like that, I like you. I thought, maybe....But that's out. Treat her well. Enough, stop crying. Who would have dreamed that Hersh-Ber could shed a tear? It's even made me....(*All wipe their eyes.*) Give me you hand, Dovid-Noyakh. (*They embrace, sobbing. The women weep out loud.*)

(TSINE *and* AVROM-YANKEV *come out, look around in surprise, and start to wipe their eyes, too.*)

ROKHEL (*embraces* TSINE. *Kisses her*). My child, you've become a bride.

(TSINE *and* STERE *throw their arms around each other and kiss repeatedly.*)

ELKONE (*goes over to* LEVI-YITSKHOK *and takes his hand*). The best of luck to you. You'll have a fine Jewish girl, even though she did grow up among the peasants, out in the fields.

GITTL. You see, even in the country, God provides....(*She embraces* ROKHEL.)

H. Leivick (1888-1962)

Leivick Halper, known almost exclusively by his pseudonym, H. Leivick, is famous today only for the first of his plays to be published, *The Golem* (1920), although he is one of the best poets in Yiddish literature. Perhaps his long struggle with tuberculosis can account for his preoccupation with the problem of human suffering, suffering he could neither understand nor justify—as *The Golem* reveals.

Leivick found the subject for his powerful poetic drama in medieval Jewish legends about Kabbalist-like theurgists who, because of their skill at combining letters of the divine name, achieve power to create a *golem*— a huge robot, not a machine but a creature of earth, clumsy and crudely shaped in the image of man. The folktales center on golem who defend Jewish communities and frustrate plots against them. In Leivick's drama the old tales become a symbolic story rich in allusion, a political parable, and a philosophical morality play about ends and means, the ineffectiveness of force in solving human problems, and the impossibility of separating the ideal from the real. Pervading all the ideas of the play is the feeling that life is replete with pain, inexplicable pain—as the *golem* learns when, because he has life foisted on him, he must leave the peace of non-being.

135

The Golem

In Leivick's play, the Maharal, Rabbi of Prague, forms the Golem and gives the creature life—and with life come all the emotions and yearnings, desires and suffering. But *The Golem* is also a parable about ends and means and the use of force to solve human problems.

Scene I: Clay

(*A deserted place on the bank of the river outside of Prague. Daybreak. All is dark and silent. Reb Levi Bar Bezalel, or* THE MAHARAL, *an old man of seventy, stands over an outlined mound of clay, kneading the figure of a man. He finishes.* ABRAHAM THE SHAMMES *stands near him, helping with the work.* THE MAHARAL *straightens up from his work and addresses* THE SHAMMES.)

MAHARAL.
    It's done. All done. Now hurry to the synagogue,
    To Isaac and to Jacob and bid them come.
SHAMMES.
    And should I stay there, Rabbi?
MAHARAL.
    Stay in the synagogue. But Abraham,
    Remember, lock forever in your heart
    The secret you were privileged to know.
    Let no one ever hear of it from you.
SHAMMES.
    Forever, Rabbi.
MAHARAL.
    And do not tell them yet that all is done.
    They must see it for themselves.
    The day begins to dawn. Hurry.
    (*Exit* SHAMMES.)
MAHARAL (*bends over the figure*).
    Yes, all is done and darkness covers all.

The hour of wonder comes with the day,
And as I look upon this great frame
That has been shaped and kneaded by my hands,
I can descry his shadow striding here,
The shadow of a being breathing life.
(*Raises his head to the sky.*)
But who am I to say: "My hands have shaped?"
Blind was I until You gave me sight—
A puff from heaven's height upon my brows—
And showed me where the slumbering body lay.
How many generations has he slept
While somewhere else his soul in longing wanders?
Or has the soul forgot, in age-long wandering,
The road's return to where the body sleeps?
Or does it, too, somewhere lonely slumber,
Waiting like its frame for You again
To free my eyes, reveal again....
I hear the rush of wings about my head.
The night around is filled with flutter.
Expectantly the figure lies outstretched.
His head, uncovered, looks aloft to heaven.
And from within his lips a prayer seeks release.
(*He covers his face with his hands. Remains in this position
a long while. Steps back in fright.*)
Who was it flew across my eyes?
Who touched my brow with something sharp?
Who pierced my ear with screeching shriek?
Whence comes the blunted echo that I hear?
(*Looks around and listens.*)
I see no one. Silence. The river flows.
The stars go out, each after the other.
The eastern sky should have grown light.
And yet it darkens. O give me strength, Creator.
In the midst of joy and pride I saw
A second shadow of this great frame.
(*A distant rustle is suddenly heard and something com-
pletely black strides across the river, sways and revolves.*)
Who walks upon the surface of the river?

Approaches me yet comes no nearer;
Withdraws from me yet is no further?
(*A* FIGURE *appears before* The MAHARAL.)
MAHARAL,
Who are you, dark presence?
FIGURE.
You do not know me?
MAHARAL.
I cannot see your face.
FIGURE.
You do not recognize my voice?
MAHARAL.
Your voice is like a cold wind
That blows in a deep pit
Without entrance, without exit.
FIGURE.
I have a voice that is not yet a voice.
I have a heart that is not yet a heart.
MAHARAL.
Who are you? Speak. What is your name?
FIGURE.
Not till later will I be known by name.
I am not yet among mankind.
I am as yet a shadow's shadow.
MAHARAL.
Whence do you come?
FIGURE.
I have come to warn you: create me not.
Do not dislodge me from my rest.
MAHARAL.
Vanish. I order you.
FIGURE.
I tell you once again; again I warn:
Create me not!
You see: the stars go out, each one.
So will the light go out
In every eye that looks on me;
And where my foot will tread,

A blight will grow upon that place;
And what my hand will touch,
To dust and ashes will it crumble.
Do not exchange my darkness and my stillness
For the tumult of the streets and for the noise of men.
MAHARAL.
Oh, help me in this heaviest hour, God.
FIGURE.
I know you will not hear my plea.
Therefore I come to give you warning—
And let my warning be a plea.
The whole night through you kneaded me;
With coldness and with cruelty you shaped me.
How good it was to be mere clay,
To lie, lifeless and calm,
Among the sands and stones of earth
Between eternities.
MAHARAL.
Now vanish to your refuge, Figure,
And take your fear of life,
Your sorrow, with you to your lair.
When the hour of wonders comes
As soon as night retreats before the eastern sun,
Then, too, will your despair retreat.
For I was sent by God to knead you,
Disjoin you from the stony earth
And with the first ray that lights the sky
Breathe into you the breath of life.
FIGURE.
I do not want it.
MAHARAL.
Your days and nights and all your deeds
Have been decreed.
You are created for more than merely life.
In silence and concealment you will do
Great wonders, but your deeds will be in secret.
No one will know the hero. You will seem
A hewer of water, a cutter of wood.

FIGURE.
  A Golem, a thing of clay.
MAHARAL.
  A people's champion, a man of might.
FIGURE.
  A servant—to be ruled, commanded.
MAHARAL.
  A living man.
FIGURE.
  A living man? Why do you stand and wait?
  Where is the soul that will be breathed in me?
  Why do you leave my eyes still shut?
  Why is a heart not given me?
  Where is the tongue, the teeth, where is the blood
  That must be poured to flow in me?
  How would you have me? Blind or mute?
  Or lame? Or deaf, perhaps?
  Or all at once? Speak. The night departs;
  The day arrives. O darkness, darkness!
  One moment more conceal me in your depths!
  One moment more what I have been till now:
  A lifeless mound of arid clay.
  (*The* FIGURE *dissolves into the darkness.*)
MAHARAL.
  A darkness has invaded the desire
  I strove so hard to render holy, pure.
  With words of fear I have myself
  Produced a flaw within the heart to be.
  O, I did not surmount temptation
  Nor did I guard my heart from sorrow,
  From anguish and from pity. Great and greater
  Grows the weight of every frightening word.
  My own hands have turned his fate
  Into the road of pain, confusion, and dismay.
  How many weeks, how many days and nights
  I strove to purify my heart and mind,
  To shed entirely self and world

And be transformed into a single thought—Yours!
I saw but one within my mind, but one.
I saw him come and open wide his eyes,
A covert smile upon his lips,
And iron strength within his arms.
He sees, yet no one knows he sees;
He walks, yet no one knows his ways.
His life, his death—one silent breath,
One act of secret faith serene.
He comes to none; he speaks to none.
A corner somewhere is his waiting place
Until the moment that his summons comes.
What is there now to do? Doubt and fear,
The bitter and the angry loneliness
Have placed their taint upon the living word.
I see I am unworthy in Your eyes;
Perhaps I was ambitious, proud,
Too eager to descry what no man yet
Has seen before. I see, I see—
Before You what am I? A crawling worm,
A lump of earth, a grain of dust.
(*A long silence.* THE FIGURE OF THADDEUS *the priest
appears. It approaches* THE MAHARAL *at once.*)
MAHARAL.
    Thaddeus. Yes, it's he. He comes this way.
    My mind just spoke his name—
    Is this a second sign from God?
FIGURE (*collides with* THE MAHARAL. *Steps back*).
    What brings you here this middle of the night?
MAHARAL.
    It is not night but break of day.
FIGURE.
    What brings you here at break of day?
MAHARAL.
    I do at break of day what God commands.
FIGURE.
    And what did God command you do

That I should have to be there too?
MAHARAL.
You need not stay. Go freely on your way.
FIGURE.
That I can go my way is widely known.
Thaddeus can manage well.
But what causes that strange look within your eyes?
They flare with murder and black strength.
Murder in a rabbi's eyes? I have seen
In dungeons, at the stakes of holy courts
So many faces of so many Jews,
So many eyes of every sort, but I
Have never chanced to see two Jewish eyes
That looked upon me with true fury,
With murderous rage and hate, as yours do now.
They seem the eyes of some Golem run wild.
(THE MAHARAL *covers his face with his hands. His shoulders heave.*)
FIGURE.
Why have you suddenly concealed your face?
Grown silent? What is this? Who lies upon the ground
A corpse? Or what? I've stood here all this while
And did not see it.
(*Bends down and looks at the clay figure.*)
What do my eyes discern?
What is this? A figure fashioned out of clay
Lies full length upon the ground!
(*Steps back and crosses himself.*)
O holy Jesus!
MAHARAL.
Until the time that he is fit for life,
To raise his arm, to stand upon his feet,
I bear the look that lives within his eyes.
FIGURE.
Protect me from the Evil One, from all
Who are unbaptised, cursed, and damned, O Christ.
(*Disappears.*)
MAHARAL (*is silent a long while. Awakens as from a trance. Looks around.*)

Is this a second sign that has been sent?
I see that it must be. The hand of God
Has ringed us round within a single ring
And paired me with this little mound of clay.
And all that I conceive, I see;
And everything I see, will be
It will; it must!
And now my heart is light and glad. For I—
What am I? Your portents speak the truth.
It must be! And it will!
(*From the road leading to the city,* THE MAHARAL'S *two
students arrive,* ISAAC *the Kohen and* JACOB *the Levite.
JACOB carries a bundle of clothes in his hands. They come
quietly and seem scarcely to touch the ground.*)
MAHARAL (*going to meet them*).
  You come in time.
ISAAC.
  The day breaks, Rabbi.
MAHARAL.
  Did anyone observe you coming here?
JACOB.
  We walked beside the road and were concealed.
MAHARAL.
  Were you in the synagogue till now?
ISAAC.
  Yes, Rabbi. Apart from one another
  We stood in prayer, and loud we prayed and lit
  No candle till the night was half-way gone.
  The dark surrounded us like a thick wall
  And cut off each from each. So far we seemed,
  We could not hear each other's prayer or speech.
  At first the distance frightened me, as though
  I sought a path in some dark wood
  And finding none, into its dark recesses
  I ran more swiftly. But suddenly I grew
  Quite calm, and felt the distance growing greater.
JACOB.
  And Rabbi, hear what happened after that:
  We stood, we thought, far from one another.

It was so dark, and neither of us moved,
As though we each were fastened to the floor,
And each one thought that in the synagogue
He stood alone. And then at midnight, as you
Bid us, we lit the candles we had each
Prepared, and when we did, behold the wonder:
We stood together, side by side,
And each one's candle lit the other's face.

ISAAC.
A great marvel, Rabbi.

MAHARAL.
A favorable sign. Your hearts
Have cleansed themselves in prayer
And grown worthy to speak the blessing
Which your lips must soon recite.

ISAAC.
Rabbi, may one look at him?

MAHARAL.
You may. Go close and look.
(*Both bend over the figure and look at it.*)

JACOB.
As yet there is not much to see. Clay.

ISAAC.
The clay is moving now; its eyes open.

JACOB.
It moves its legs.

ISAAC.
Its face contorts. It laughs.
(*He recoils in fright.*)

MAHARAL.
What ails you, Isaac?

ISAAC.
I looked at him and then was seized by fright,
Reminded of a dream that I once had.

MAHARAL.
A dream? When?

ISAAC.
Forgive me, Rabbi, I have sinned.
At midnight, when we lit the candles and took

A Torah Scroll out from the Ark as you
Instructed, and when to Genesis we rolled
It open, and each one called the other up
To read the Book, and seven times we each
Had read its early verses, no one disturbed
The reading. We returned the Torah to the Ark,
And silently we each began the Psalms.
And as I stood there, face to wall, reciting,
Suddenly my lids began to stick.
I struggled hard to keep from dozing, raised
My voice to chant aloud. All at once
I heard a clamor. Despairing cries came nearer
And nearer. Doors and windows then flew open.
The synagogue was filled with Jews in panic,
Who threw themselves in every corner, fell
And, breathless, crawled to hide beneath the tables
And as they lay in silence, a man rushed in.
His face was strange, his head was large, his body
Tall, arms long, and eyes of piercing green.
He held a sword and thrust it everywhere.
Up and down he slashed and right and left.
And soon they all lay, gashed and slaughtered;
The darkness covering their bloody dying.
And then he raised his arm to me and would
Have brought it down upon my head—when you
Arrived, Rabbi.

MAHARAL.

I?

ISAAC.

As soon as he perceived you, he appeared
Discouraged. He dropped his sword and to the door
He rushed. But you were there to bar his way.
You seized the sword from him and aimed a blow
Across his face, but woe!
You failed.

MAHARAL (*beside himself*).

I failed?

AAC.

You struck the air.

MAHARAL.
  He ran away?
ISAAC.
  Like a shadow, he dissolved and vanished.
  That shape of clay reminded me of him.
MAHARAL (*to himself*).
  So many signs! So many adverse omens!
  Will not a single ray of hope shine through?
  Lead me, O God, along whatever roads You choose,
  But let your brightness gleam through all
  That is concealed from me.
JACOB.
  In the synagogue they spoke of evil times
  Of old and of the rumors that now thrive
  In Prague about a savage tyrant who
  Has slaughtered multitudes of Jewish folk—
  And so he dreamt this dream, Rabbi.
MAHARAL.
  Yes, my students, evil times will come,
  And with evil times come great ones too.
  We must be ready to receive those days.
  As you see, God has brought us now
  To the dawn of great and trying times.
ISAAC.
  My hands are trembling with fear, Rabbi,
  Shall I lay the bundle down?
MAHARAL.
  Is everything contained in it?
ISACC.
  Everything, Rabbi.
JACOB.
  Where will he stay? In the synagogue?
MAHARAL.
  An end to questions now. Contain your fears.
  Secrete them in your hearts, and with your fears
  Hide all that you will see and hear.
  And now come to the water. We wash our hands.
  (*They go to the river.*)

David Pinski (1872-1959)

Born in Mogilev, Russia, where he received the customary religious train-
ing, Pinski moved to Moscow, where he became interested in secular subjects, then to Poland to work with famed writer and editor Peretz. He came to
the United States in 1899, and in 1950 settled in Haifa, Israel. The street on
which he lived was later named after him in honor of his work as a Labor
Zionist leader and a pioneer in Yiddish literature. Always interested in
scholarship, Pinski studied at Columbia University in New York, completing all requirements for the Ph.D. except the doctoral examination.

Pinski was the first major Yiddish writer to become widely known
through translation in America and Europe. He turned out more than sixty
plays as well as many short stories and novels. He wrote historical plays
such as *Rabbi Akiba and Bar Kochba*, grim contemporary dramas, such as
The Family Tzvi, and comedies such as *The Treasure*. All were problem
plays, dramas of ideas, the total body of his work being conceived with a
broad philosophical base. In the five scenes of *King David and His Wives*,
Pinski traces the ways power changes and corrupts David the leader. The
theme of the play arises out of conflicts among desire, morality, and self-
gratification. Pinski makes clear that the true victories of life occur not in
the attainment of goals but in their pursuit.

King David and His Wives

Pinski turned to the Bible to create a drama which had as its central character the complex poet-king David. The character of David provides the playwright with rich material to explore one of the leading figures of Jewish tradition and love, the shepherd-ruler capable of singing the sweetest lyrics in the Bible and so consumed by lust for a married woman that he violated one of the Torah's statutes. *King David and His Wives* is organized around five discrete yet interrelated scenes. Each scene represents an important aspect in the life of David and can be treated as a self-contained unit, but taken together the five vignettes add up to the discovery of a complex, rich, and highly exciting character. The "Bathsheba" segment (based on II Samuel 11-12) presents the fascinating secondary characters of Nathan, the Prophet; Uriah, husband of Bathsheba; and Bathsheba herself for whom the King was willing to commit a breach of morality even though it would separate him from the God he loved.

Bathsheba

(*The roof of the king's palace. Right foreground, the king's bed. A table set with wine stands before the bed. Several treetops are visible, some level with the roof, some higher. Far in the distance, the misty mountains of Judea.* KING DAVID, *right rear, is half-sitting on the balustrade that rings the roof. His arms are folded across his breast. Before him stands* NATHAN THE PROPHET. *Guards at the stairway leading to the roof.*)

NATHAN. And he will not withdraw his favor from you as he withdrew it from Saul, whom he cleared from your path. (DAVID *leans over and scrutinizes something below among the trees.*) Your house and your kingdom will endure forever, your throne will....You are not listening to me, my King. What have your eyes perceived down there? (DAVID *slowly raises his left hand in a defensive gesture but remains as if transfixed.* NATHAN *looks down in the same direction and is suddenly horrified.*) A woman bathing! Do not look at her, my King!

DAVID (*without shifting his glance*). How lovely she is!

NATHAN. My King, you must not look!

DAVID. Who is that beauty?

NATHAN. She is Bathsheba, the daughter of Eliam, the wife of Uriah the Hittite. She is a married woman. You must not behold her in her nakedness. You sin with your eyes.

DAVID. I accept that responsibility quite willingly.

NATHAN. Turn your eyes to me. I have come to you bearing God's word.

DAVID. But I have seen God's work. Do not disturb me now, Prophet. Let me admire God's handiwork.

NATHAN. King, you blaspheme!

DAVID. How glorious she is! Never have I seen such a figure, such a body!

NATHAN. Restrain yourself, my King. Avert your eyes and thoughts....

DAVID. Should her husband be richer than I? I must be first in Judah and in Israel.

NATHAN. And now sinful desires are born in your breast. Close your eyes and....

DAVID. I close my eyes and still I see her. Ho, guards, go fetch me Bathsheba, the daughter of Eliam, the wife of Uriah the Hittite. She is bathing in the river down below.

NATHAN (*springing up*). King!

DAVID (*to the guards*). Go do as I told you. (*To* NATHAN.) You may leave too.

NATHAN. Do not drive God away from you!

DAVID (*looking down, signals him with his hand*). Go, Nathan, go!

NATHAN. My King!

DAVID. You see I'm impatient.

NATHAN (*raises his voice*). My King, hear me out. Two men once lived in a city, one rich, the other poor. The rich man had sheep and cattle in great numbers and the poor man had only one ewe, that he had bought and raised and that had grown up together with his children. It ate of his bread and drank of his cup and lay in his lap and was a child to him. A visitor came to the rich man, who was loathe to take of his own sheep and cattle for the guest that had come to him. And he took the poor man's lamb and dressed it for his guest.

DAVID (*not removing his glance, angrily*). Fie on such a man! Fie on him! He must die!

NATHAN (*thundering*). You are that man!

DAVID (*gleefully*). They have her! They have taken her! How frightened she is! How she struggles! How quickly she covers herself. Ha-ha-ha. That covering will easily be ripped off. Ho-ho! They're bringing her! They're coming with her! (*Turns to* NATHAN.) Now go! Now go! (*Suddenly remembering*.) Wait. What were you telling me about that man? I believe I have sentenced myself to death!

NATHAN. And your sentence was just. Hear me! Thus saith the Lord God of Israel: I annointed thee king over Israel, and I delivered thee out of the hand of Saul. And I gave thee thy master's house and thy master's wives....

DAVID (*raging*). I will hear no more! I know all that you can tell me and more than you can tell me. Spare yourself the effort.

NATHAN. Thus saith the Lord, I will raise up evil against thee out of thine own house....

DAVID. Do not bring me to greater sin! Go!

NATHAN. And he will take your wives....

DAVID. My sword! My sword! (*Rushes at* NATHAN *with clenched fists*.) Go!

NATHAN (*avoiding him*). So far have you forgotten yourself? (*Covers his head with his cloak, wrings his hands over his head, and walks out with slow steps*.)

DAVID. Ahh, at last! Rid of him! (*Throws himself on his bed*.) Well, why don't they come? Why are they dragging their heels? Are they crawling? Have they forgotten how to walk? (*Listens*.) Come on! Ah, they're coming! They're coming!

(BATHSHEBA *is dragged in by the soldiers. She pulls free of them and runs half-way across the roof. DAVID signals the guard to leave*.)

DAVID (*scrutinzes her*). Ha-ha-ha! Head proudly erect, eyes full of hatred, not the slightest sign of fear. The beauty! Bathsheba, the king desires you.

BATHSHEBA. I am married.

DAVID. Ha-ha-ha!

BATHSHEBA. And I love my husband.

DAVID. What does that mean?

BATHSHEBA. I will not satisfy the king's desire.

DAVID. You will not yield?

BATHSHEBA. I will not yield.

DAVID. Your king?

BATHSHEBA. I kneel before my king and bow to him, but as a woman I belong only to the man I love.

DAVID. Oh, you rouse my blood as when I wrestled with the lion and the bear. Woman, you stand before the eternal conqueror!

BATHSHEBA. You slew when you conquered. Only through death will you conquer me too.

DAVID. I didn't conquer women so. King's daughters gave me their love with rejoicing.

BATHSHEBA. I love my husband. My love burns for him alone. For him my bosom breathes with passion. For him my soul melts in song.

DAVID. You must be mine.

BATHSHEBA. That I will never be.

DAVID. Woman, you forget you are in my power.

BATHSHEBA. You are used to having women offer you their love. You will not use force.

DAVID. Shall I teach you to love me. I am impatient. You have lit a fire within me. How shall I win your love quickly? Tell me, what virtues has Uriah that I do not. (BATHSHEBA *bursts out laughing, then, in fright, stifles her laugh with her hand.*) Well, is Uriah so much more than I?

BATHSHEBA (*trembling*). I do not know, my King.

DAVID. Then describe him to me.

BATHSHEBA. I can only sing of him. Tall is he like the cedar of Lebanon, and like the crown of the tree his black hair lies across the white of his neck. His eyes are brighter than stars. His face is woven of sunbeams. He is as young and as glorious as Adam in the Garden of Eden.

DAVID. Open your eyes and look upon your king.

BATHSHEBA. I see only Uriah.

DAVID. In all things I am like him, only I am not so young any more. Still, I am the king; I am David.

BATHSHEBA. Though you were much more, I would still love Uriah.

DAVID (*gesturing impatiently*). Don't say that to me again!

BATHSHEBA. My King, let me go.

DAVID. Go? Ha-ha! Come sit beside me. Here is wine; let's drink it. I am drunk with you and I want to get drunker still. And you, drink and fill yourself with a fire that will make you forget Uriah. Come, glorious woman! David the strong shepherd and the stronger king, invites you! Come, my sweet, the poet and the singer languishes in his love for you! (*He drinks.*)

BATHSHEBA (*raises her eyes to heaven and joins her hands in prayer*). "The Lord is my rock, my fortress, my deliverer; my God, my strength in whom I trust; my buckler, and the horn of my salvation, and my high tower. I will call upon the Lord, who is worthy to be praised; so shall I be saved from mine enemies."

DAVID (*looks at her wide-eyed and astonished*). My words—my prayer—my psalm of praise to God—

BATHSHEBA. "The sorrows of death compassed me and the flood of ungodly men made me afraid...."

DAVID. Stop, woman, stop! This will not help you. You want to remind me of God and of my gratitude to Him, but it will do you no good. I am ready to break His word. His commandment, His law. I am drunk with you. Let Him punish me. Let His hand rest hard and heavy upon me. But I must have you. My blood boils. I want no master now. Come, glorious woman, come to my arms! For your sake King David has broken with his God. Do not tremble. Be proud! Cry out with rejoicing! (*He advances toward her.*)

BATHSHEBA. Uriah! Uriah!

(URIAH *enters. Grasping the situation, he looks thunderstruck. When he meets the king's glance, however, he falls to his knees before* DAVID.)

BATHSHEBA (*looks around, sees* URIAH *kneeling, and cries out*). Oh, Uriah, my Uriah! My beloved! My deliverer!

DAVID. Is this Uriah? Stand up. (*Grasps his sword.*)

(URIAH *gets up.* BATHSHEBA *embraces him.* URIAH *frees himself from her arms and stands at attention before the king.*)

DAVID (*rebukes him*). Who sent for you? Why did you come to me?

URIAH. Nathan sent me. He said you wanted me.

DAVID. Your blood be on his head.

URIAH. What does my lord want of me?

DAVID. What I want of you? What I—oh, yes. Wait here I have a mission for you.

URIAH. Your servant will carry it out faithfully.

DAVID (*looks at him penetratingly and bursts out laughing.*) This is just a worm. (*Exits.*)

BATHSHEBA (*clings to* URIAH, *trembling and tearful*). Uriah! (URIAH *stands motionless.*) You are angry with me. Your heart is turned to stone against me. But I have not sinned, neither against God nor against you, Uriah. I did not come here willingly. Uriah, do you hear me? The king's will brought me here. He saw me naked while I bathed, and his soldiers drove me, dragged me here. But I withstood him, and the king did not touch me. I spoke to him of my love for you and I called to God and to you. And you came in my greatest need. Uriah, believe me. I am telling you the truth, Uriah, why do you stand like that? Uriah, look at me! Uriah, save me and save yourself!

URIAH. The king desires you. Let the king's will be done.

BATHSHEBA (*cries out*). Uriah! you cannot be serious! Recover you senses. Wake up! You are strong; you are powerful. You must help us both!

URIAH. Against the king?

BATHSHEBA. Kill the king!

URIAH. Bathsheba!

BATHSHEBA. You have your sword with you. Punish him.

URIAH. The king?

BATHSHEBA. The transgressor! The ravisher of your wife! The defiler of your name! The sinner against God! Oh, how could you have kept from punishing him before? How could you have fallen on your knees before him?

URIAH. He is my king!

BATHSHEBA. Uriah? How can you say that? Are you not man enough? The king wishes to take my love from you. Don't you care about my love? Don't you love me any more? Uriah, speak! Have I lost your love?

URIAH. I do love you, Bathsheba.

BATHSHEBA. You love me—you surrender me to the king without a battle?

URIAH. I cannot do battle with my king. (*Breaks out in a wild cry of pain.*) Oh, if it were another man—another man, even one of the king's best warriors! My fingers would coil around his throat like heavy rope and squeeze the breath of life from him. He would become a post, and with the iron of my fists I would hammer him into the earth. Oh, no one has yet died such a death as this defiler would die under the mighty hands of Uriah the Hittite, and long would people marvel at their strength—if it were another man.

BATHSHEBA. But you fear the king? You tremble at his strength? You feel weaker?

URIAH. My hand will never rise against my king.

BATHSHEBA. Uriah! Uriah! Listen! I spoke of God to this lust-king of yours. His own prayer that he sang when he was saved from Saul's hand I here sent up to God. Yet he did not restrain his lust and openly defied God and His commandments, Uriah! Uriah! In his sinful lust, the king forgot his fear of God. Cannot your honorable love raise you against the king?

URIAH. I cannot, Bathsheba!

BATHSHEBA. In the name of our great love, Uriah!

URIAH. I cannot, Bathsheba!

BATHSHEBA. If you cannot punish the sinner against your wife, against yourself, then punish the sinner against God! (URIAH *stands motionless.*) In the name of God, Uriah! Nathan sent you here so that you might punish the blasphemer and adulterer. (URIAH *remains silent.*) Are you so afraid of death? Then I'll die with you, Uriah. I would rather die than survive my shame. Take your sword and run me through. How sweet death will be at your hands! And if you die together with me, then death will be a dance to me! Why do you stand so? Have you turned to stone? Uriah, I want to die with you!

URIAH (*breathes heavily, starts to draw his sword, and suddenly thrusts it back.*) My king needs me.

BATHSHEBA. What! Uriah! Uriah! Stop talking like that! You will be guilty of murder! You will kill my soul! You will kill my love! Has the king so robbed you of your will? Are you so much a slave? Uriah, you were my pride. Everything in me cried out in pride that I love you and am loved by you. And must all this be destroyed in me? I shall become a worm, Uriah! I shall despise myself, Uriah! Uriah, my soul implores you. Help yourself and help me! Help us both in our twofold trial!...You are silent, Uriah! You....

A SERVANT (*enters with a letter in his hand and gives it to* URIAH). The king sends you back to embattled Joab with this and bids you leave at once. (*Exits.*)

URIAH (*takes the message, hides it in his clothing, and starts to leave. With a quiver in his voice*). Farewell, Bathsheba!

BATHSHEBA. You are going? You are going off, leaving me here in the hands of that ravisher? Is this the measure of your love for me?

URIAH. I can do nothing else, Bathsheba.

BATHSHEBA. You can do nothing else!

URIAH. I can die only one death—for my king.

BATHSHEBA. Am I nothing to you? Is the king so much dearer to you than I? Do you know where the king is sending you?

URIAH. To Joab, who is now besieging the city of Rabbah.

BATHSHEBA. Do you know why he is sending you there?

URIAH. I do not need to know why, nor do I care to know.

BATHSHEBA. He is sending you to your death! He wants to get rid of you! He wants to crush you like a worm! Don't you realize that? Can't you see that yourself?

URIAH. I must leave on the king's mission. Don't stand in my way.

BATHSHEBA (*struggles with him*). Uriah! Uriah! You will not go! You will not leave me alone! (*Tears the message away from him.*)

URIAH. How dare you! Give that message back to me!

BATHSHEBA (*escapes behind the bed, breaks open the king's seal, and panting reads the message as she continues to evade* URIAH). "Set Uriah in the forefront of the hottest battle and retire from him, that he may be smitten and die." Uriah!

(URIAH *stops. He is pale and breathing heavily. He shudders.*)

BATHSHEBA. Did you hear? Uriah, you are going to your death. Is it not far better to die here with me? Wake up, Uriah! Be brave! Rouse your fury! Become my champion again!

URIAH (*furious*). Give me that message!

BATHSHEBA. What? Are you turning on me? Are you venting your wrath on me? Oh! (*Tears the message.*)

URIAH. Bathsheba!

BATHSHEBA. (*throws the scraps into his face*). Go ahead! Fulfill the king's mission!

URIAH (*picks up the pieces*). I know it by heart. I am going into battle to die for my king, and dearly will the Ammonites pay for my death! (*Leaves.*)

BATHSHEBA. Uriah! He is leaving. He is gone! (*Furious.*) I spit on you! I send after you the venom of my scorn! I despise you! You dead worm! Ugh, to think that I once loved you! Out, out of my heart and my soul! Out, out! I will tear out my heart where love once nested! I will bite away the lips that once kissed him! And David asked to be compared with him, and I found David wanting! Ha-ha-ha! I laugh at myself in mockery! I loved a slave. Ha-ha-ha. Now I must go to the king. He shall cleanse me of my stain. He shall make me chaste. Oh, I loved a slave. Now I shall love a king! (*She walks toward the steps.*)

(DAVID *meets her triumphantly with open arms.*)

Non-Fiction

For the most part, Jewish non-fiction is in the form of an essay, although there are many books of travel, history, geography, grammar, and theology. An essay is a prose composition on a specific subject. When informal, the essay reflects the author's personality; when formal, the essay is impersonal.

Before the nineteenth century, the vast majority of Jewish essays were formal and with a religious coloring, although they had been continually produced for more than 3,000 years in a multitude of different countries in many languages on diverse themes. Essays were not written for entertainment. Whether polemic or propagandistic in purpose, lexicographic or philosophic, the typical Jewish essay combined exegesis with religious interpretation and homily.

The sharp rise of Zionism in the nineteenth century modified attitudes of Jewish writers and readers. The essay, now

157

regarded as a means of fostering national spirit, widened its horizons, and essayists took as subjects all areas of life—artistic, economic, political, and social. Jewish socialism, Russian pogroms, and attempts in Germany to modernize Judaism while retaining its essence made for lively debate. The number of Jewish periodicals increased markedly and gave authors opportunities to analyze and discuss such problems as the rescue and resettlement of Jews caught in the anti-Semitism of Eastern Europe. Especially popular was the feuilleton, an essay much like an American newspaper column. As writers became more sophisticated, writing itself became a subject for discussion. Appreciation and critical analyses appeared in abundance. These trends have continued during the twentieth century both in the Diaspora and in Israel.

Ahad Ha'am (1856-1927)

Critics refer to Ahad Ha'am (pen name of Asher Ginsberg, in Hebrew meaning "one of the people") as an ironic name to choose because the man was so unusual: a born leader, a talented writer, and an autodidact. But Ginsberg's choice of the name was deliberate, for he was ever proud of his Jewishness. Born in the small town of Shvina in the Ukraine, he moved to Odessa in 1886 and helped make it a Hebrew literary center. In 1908 he went to London, and in 1922 he settled in Tel Aviv.

Called the father of the modern Hebrew essay, Ahad Ha'am dominated the ideological outlook of Hebrew literature from publication of his first article, "This Is Not the Way," in 1899 until the 1920s. As an editor, influenced by John Stuart Mill and other liberal philosophers of the nineteenth century, Ahad Ha'am argued for didacticism, conceiving the function of literature to be close to propaganda—rejecting for publication even superlative writings such as the poems of Bialik, if he felt they did not heighten the national consciousness of Jews.

But Ahad Ha'am's insistence on each author's expressing the truth as he saw it in concise and vigorous writing beneficially influenced a whole generation of Hebrew writers and more than offset any of his didactic tendencies as editor. His own lucid, balanced prose set a high standard for Hebrew writers. He was careful also to buttress points with ideas from the great philosophers and with examples from the natural sciences. Each of his essays is sober, well balanced, logically developed, and thematically unified.

Because he believed the ingathering of the Jews impossible in his time, Ahad Ha'am opposed Herzl's political Zionism. In "Truth from Palestine," Ahad Ha'am argued that colonization was a failure in the 1890s, despite massive financial support from Baron Edmond de Rothschild, because of insufficient idealism on the part of Jews. He thought that, to reestablish Israel as a nation, Jewish leaders had to work first for the rehabilitation of their people through a spiritual and cultural renaissance. He recommended the building of Israel as a center that would incorporate both the religious and secularist factions of Zionism, counter the disintegration of Jewish life in the Diaspora, and serve as a focal point for an indigenous Hebrew culture in harmony with the highest aspirations of Judaism through the ages. Ahad Ha'am hoped in time for the substitution of a national, collective moral sense in place of traditional Orthodoxy, which he believed was holding Judaism captive to the past, unable to change. He wanted, not a radical break with the past, but ongoing modification balanced by continuity.

Semi-Consolation

Among all the calamities that have been renewed against us of late, what will make a particularly saddening impression on the heart of every Jew is the resumption of the "blood libel!" This abominable libel, although old, has been and always will be like new in our eyes, and from the Middle Ages until now has distinguished itself in its strong impact on the spirit of our people not only at the scene of the incident but also in far-off countries which the news has reached.

I have said, "on the spirit of our people," for indeed I see the source of this phenomenon not in external causes but deep in the spirit of the people. In the Middle Ages the Community of Israel in incidents like these was accustomed to think of itself as standing in judgment together with those unfortunate persons whom fate had fixed upon for sacrifice. It may, indeed, be appropriate to perceive in this attitude only a result of the great physical danger to the whole community, which in fact was then involved after every such libel. Even fifty years ago, in a time of calm and peace, the Damascus libel stirred up so very great a noise in countries of the West, that it is still appropriate to say that there was in this just the opposite cause, a force stemming from the extreme jealousy for their honor and privileges that dominated the hearts of our Western brothers who so recently had emerged from slavery to freedom. But in this our time, from one point of view the physical danger is no longer very great, especially in far-off communities. From another point of view we have already become accustomed to hearing with equanimity ourselves slandered, and jealousy for our honor no longer consumes us. Nevertheless, even now we are still aroused and shaken by the force of a report of the "blood libel," and community tumult breaks out on all sides to throw this abomination off us—a sign that neither fear nor dignity has set this reaction in motion, for if the spirit of the people feels dishonor here, that is what is being aroused that in turn arouses us. Yet matters in every other respect have already brought our troubles to a state about which the wise prince in ancient times said, "The corpse does not feel the scalpel." Indeed, here the "scalpel" cuts not flesh alone but may reach to the soul....

But "there is no evil without good," that is to say without a beneficial lesson. Even this great evil with which we are concerned is not devoid of a moral. We who are not masters of our fate and who receive both good and evil from without—which is not to our benefit—for us it is fitting always to seek in our evils the hidden educational advantage. For us this has been, at least, semi-consolation.

One of the greatest forces in our social life is "convention." There was a time that even philosophers saw in this convention certain proof of any subject universally agreed upon, and gave it a place among the rest of their proofs for the existence of the deity. Now, indeed, philosophers know that there is no lie and there is no nonsense on which "universal agreement" cannot be reached, if only conditions of life are suitable. But ony philosophers know this. In the eyes of the masses there is still even now no authority greater than "convention." If "all the world" believes that any thing is so, of course it is so; and if I do not understand it, others understand; and if I see an apparent contradiction of it, why "all" see too and yet believe; and am I wiser than all the world? This is approximately the course of thought of the simple man, with or without clear knowledge, and because of this he agrees also with the universally accepted point of view and himself becomes part of convention.

So very great a force is "convention" that, in general, man may not be able to save his soul from its influence even when he himself is "the subject upon, which there is agreement." If "all the world" say of a certain person that he is great in wisdom or in piety, that there is in him a certain quality, good or bad, even he himself will end by agreeing to this, although at first he did not find in himself that virtue or that defect which others attribute to him. Not only this but approval from the point of view of "the agreed upon" itself influences him little by little in the quality of his being until it brings him near in fact (or, at least, gives birth in him a tendency to draw near) to that state which "all the world" see in him. Therefore, teachers correctly warn us not to awaken children at the beginning of their moral development to their moral faults, and still more not to attribute to them faults which are not in them, for by such means it is possible that we may strengthen the first in their mind and even beget a tendency to the latter.

Of course, the phrase understood as "all the world" does not mean just one thing to everybody. Man sees "his world" only in that society of which he thinks himself a part and in whose people he sees men who are near to him from some point of view. But no one reflects whatsoever on the conventional belief of men whose spirit is completely foreign to him, so that he does not feel in his soul any inner connection between him and them. Thus our Orthodox and Maskilim do not pay attention at all, the one to the conventional belief of the other, even in matters that do not touch faith and religion. Their ridicule and scorn do not make any impression on the mind of either because each of the two sects views the other's society as if it does not exist. Of course when conditions of life compel members of the different sects to find themselves in constant intercourse, one with the other, and they grow accustomed above all to seeing the human being in one another—then "their world' is broadened and their outlooks suffer many changes in accord with the conventional belief of "the world" in its new meaning.

In past generations, therefore, when our forefathers believed in the simple meaning of "You have chosen us," the shame that other peoples visited upon them did not at all influence the purity of their inner soul. They knew their value and were not affected to any degree by "the conventional beliefs" of the outside world, as part of an entire body of "conventions," considered in their eyes as products of a peculiar type of beings foreign to them and differing from them in an essential way—with no relationship and no resemblance between them. Then the Jew was able calmly to listen to all the moral faults and sins of conduct that the conventional beliefs of other peoples attributed to him, without feeling in his soul any inner shame or humiliation. Of what matter to him were the ideas of "foreigner" about him and his value? If only they would let him dwell in peace! But in this generation the matter is not so. Now "our world" has been much broadened, and European convention affects us strongly in all branches of life. Since we no longer regard "everyone" as an exception, we have been influenced against our will by the fact that "everyone" regards us an exception. Recently one Russian writer asked naively: since all the world hates the Jews, is it possible to say that all the world is guilty and the Jews are innocent? A question like this steals even now into the heart of many of our brothers: is it possible to say that all those corrupt characteristics and evil practices which the whole world attributes to the Jews are but "inventions"?

This doubt, once it has been aroused, easily finds sustenance in those misleading inferences "from the particular to the general" that are very common among the masses of mankind. There is a well-known story about a traveler who came to a town and chanced upon an inn where the servant was a stammerer. He wrote in his notebook: in a certain town servants at the inns are stammerers. This story is a wry illustration of the use of logic by the masses in most of their general judgments. All phenomena that seems to belong with some customary particular thing, the crowd is accustomed to attribute to the class to which that thing may be thought of as belonging, so far as its regular name is concerned, without observing that one "particular" can be thought of as in many "classes" jointly, that is to say, to be an associate in one quality with particulars of one class and in another quality with particulars of another class, while the name by which it has been called indicates only its relationship to one of the classes in one of its aspects, not in all of them. On propositions of this kind can lean, and in fact will lean, a universally accepted idea in its relationship to us: A and B are Jews according to their name and swindlers according to their nature; ergo, Jews according to their nature are swindlers. True logic will indeed reply to this that, even if in fact all the Jews in our generation were swindlers, there is not in this more evidence that Jews are swindlers—that is to say, that the characteristic of dishonesty that exists in every Jew exists in him because of his belonging to the class "Jew" and not because of any other class (for example, a class of "merchants") to which the Jew also belongs as an individual, together with others having nothing in common with the class "Jews." In order to explain the matter, it is necessary to examine first those "others" who are participants together with the Jews in other classes. Only after it is found by means of this examination that the characteristic of dishonesty does not exist in any other group that is associated with Jews and non-Jews—only then will it be right for us to pronounce the judgment that Judaism is the mother of dishonesty. But, as I have said, it is not the way of mankind to enter deeply into logic, and we cannot demand such also from the masses of our People. They hear the judgment of convention pronounced and they see from this that many among us are actually so, even as convention says, and this is enough for them and indeed they themselves also begin to agree. And so "Jewish characteristics" pass like a valued coin from hand to hand, for the external convention of other peoples to the internal convention among our people, only with this difference, that other peoples enumerate our bad characteristics one by one with a shout of victory and the mockery of the self-assured. We answer after them word by word in a still small voice and feeble self-justification. They compare us to a vessel of clay which there is no way of repairing but by breaking, and we compare ourselves to a vessel of metal which can be purified by scalding water or white-hot fire....

This state, if it continues for some time, can cause us great moral damage. There is nothing so dangerous to a nation and to a man as admission to sins that are not in them. For him who has sinned in fact, the gates of repentance have not been locked, and with good will he can remove the dire from himself. But he whom others have brought to suspect himself of what is not in him, how will he be able to purify himself in his own eyes? On the one hand he trusts the words of those who tell him: remove the beam from your eyes. On the other hand he feels he cannot remove the beam from his eyes since it is in fact imaginary. Indeed, he is in the position of certain monomaniacs who for some reason have come to believe that a heavy weight is hanging from their nose without their being able to remove it. Not only that, sometimes this trust will bring the individual to share in that disgraceful characteristic which according to his belief is the property of his entire society, although he himself from the point of view of his own individuality is not at all inclined to this. For example, there is no doubt that among that People from whom emerged men like the Rambam there are found even now wise men with systematic minds, lovers of order and method in everything, who by taking part in the work of the community have been able to impart their spirit to it and to influence the workers in the rest of its activities. But what has happened is that "convention" has already decreed that hatred of order is a Jewish characteristic, and by now we agree with this convention (although it is still not clear whether this characteristic that exists in fact among a great part of our people refers to the "Jewish" community or perhaps, what is more acceptable to the mind, to the community of those trained in the Heder). Therefore, the hands of lovers of order will be weakened in the belief that there is neither wisdom nor understanding in opposing the will of the People. And if they are patriots, they will actually uproot from their hearts the love of order that opposes the spirit of the People. They will even behave as they imagine befits true Jews.

It is necessary, therefore to seek some means of freeing ourselves from the influence of "convention" as regards the characteristics and moral worth of Jews, so that we will not be despised in our own eyes and not think that in fact we are inferior to all mankind under the sun, so that we do not by means of this come in the course of time to be in reality what we are now only in imagination.

"Convention" itself affords us this means through the agency of "the blood libel." This libel is the single case in which convention cannot cause us to doubt that "all the world is guilty and we are innocent" because it is founded, all of it, on an absolute lie, and it has no support in some misleading inference "from the particular to the general." Every Jew who was brought up among his people knows with complete certainty that there is not in all Jewry even one individual who drinks human blood in the name of religion. This clear awareness of a mistake by "convention," which is renewed in our hearts from time to time through resumption of the blood libel, we must preserve always in our memory. It will help us uproot from our hearts the tendency to yield to the authority of "all the world" in other matters also. Let all the world say what it will about our moral inferiority. We know that this "convention" rests only on crowd logic with no true scientific basis. For who has come into the secret depths of our soul and seen the "Jew" as he is from his own point of view? For who has weighed this person against that one, Jews and non-Jews who resemble one another in all other "categories": merchants against merchants, persecuted against persecuted, hungry against hungry, and so on? For who has weighed all these on the scales of true wisdom and found the scale tip to one side?

"Is it possible that the whole world is guilty and the Jews are innocent?"

Very possible, as the blood libel proves. Here, indeed, the Jews are innocent and pure as ministering angels. A Jew and blood! Are there two greater contradictions than these? And yet....

(Tr. A. F. B.)

Ahimaaz Ben Paltiel (1020-1060)

A poet of Capua, Italy, Ahimaaz wrote *Megilla Yuhasin* (*Scroll of Descent*) in 1054 C.E. It is known today as the *Chronicle of Ahimaaz* (and translated as a historical essay). Incorporating the genealogy and accomplishments of his distinguished family for a period of two centuries, like other early medieval historical writing the account of Ahimaaz is deficient in a critical sense and so includes miracles and folklore at the same time it weaves fact and fantasy into legend. Yet it is important because, as one of the few firsthand sources of the Jewish history of the time, it is virtually the only means for readers today to learn about the Jewish people in southern Italy. In addition, since the family participated in non-Jewish affairs, Ahimaaz occasionally provides glimpses of them as well. Ahimaaz says that the Jews had judicial autonomy, and he writes of Jewish courts dealing with criminal cases. He records persecution of Jews by the emperor of Byzantium, and he tells of the invasion of Calabria by the Saracens.

A Book of Genealogies

In the name of the Lord, we will begin and finish [our task]. My help [cometh] from the Lord.

In the name of the Lord of Lords that doeth wonders I will write a book of genealogies.

In the name of Him that dwelleth in the heavens of splendor, I will begin to tell the story diligently to investigate, arrange and present a collection of the traditions of my forefathers, to unfold them in proper order, to explain them with notes, to trace without confusion the genealogy whose parts must be collected like stubble.

With praise, I will glorify Him that dwelleth in heaven; that, in His grace and justice, safely guided my ancestors who came forth with the exiles that were spared in Jerusalem, and delivered them from destruction, children and elders, young and old, for the sake of His great mercy and the merits of the fathers of old. At all times they were protected by the God of heaven; shield and buckler has He ever been to my forefathers, and so may He continue to be to their children to the last generation.

Now, with great care, I will set down in order the traditions of my fathers, who were brought on a ship over the Pishon [Euphrates or Po], the first river of Eden, with the captives that Titus took from the Holy City, crowned with beauty. They came to Oria; they settled there and prospered through remarkable achievements; they grew in number and in strength and continued to thrive. Among their descendants there arose a man eminent in learning, a liturgical poet and scholar, master of the knowledge of God's law, distinguished for wisdom among his people. His name was Rabbi Amittai. And he had a number of amiable and worthy sons, intelligent and learned men....The first of them was R. Shephatiah, zealous in the pursuit of wisdom; the second, R. Hananeel, engaged in the study of the Law of God which Jekutiel [Moses] delivered; the third, Elezar who was devoted to [the Law] given in the third [month]. In the days of these good men there came from Bagdad, from our beloved ones, an esteemed man of distinguished family, an illustrious scholar, warding off wrath from the descendants of those that sleep in Hebron; he was as of the [favored] flock unto the Almighty King.

Before Aaron left his native land, his father had a mill by which he supported himself. It was turned by a mule. A lion fell upon the mule and killed it while Aaron was out of the room. When he returned he could not find the mule, so he put the lion in its place, and fastened him to the mill to turn the grinding stones. When his father saw what he had done, he approached him and exclaimed, "What hast thou done? Thou hast put in the lion: thou hast humiliated him and broken his strength. God made him king and intended him to walk erect, and thou hast forced him into thy service, to work for thee. Now, as God liveth, thou shalt not remain with me, thou shalt go into exile, wandering by day and by night, for three years thou shalt suffer punishment for this offense. At the end of that time return to thy native land, and thy Lord thy God will accept thee."

He came to Jaffa. There he found ships on every hand. He said to the sailors, "Comrades and friends, in the name of God I come to you. I will go with you, and, with the favor of Him that dwelleth in light, will control fate, so that by the help of the awe-inspiring God, the ship on which we sail may not be overtaken by enemies or storm wind."

He went in and took his place among them. At the hour for sleep they reached the city of Gaeta. There Aaron came upon a Jew, a Sephardi, who befriended him and proffered the hospitality of his home. At mealtime the Sephardi did not eat, though the day was the Sabbath, sacred unto God. The master, surprised at his conduct, said:

"Today is the Sabbath unto the awe-inspiring One. Why dost thou not delight thyself with that which is called a delight?"

The unhappy man answered, "Oh my master, do not urge me, for I am very sad, I am grieving for my son who has been taken from me for my many sins; I do not really know whether he is alive or dead."

The master then said to him in words of tenderness, "Observe the Sabbath properly, then show me the streets and lanes in which he used to come and go. If he be still alive, I will restore him to thee, and if dead, I will surely tell thee." The next day he did not delay. Together they went to the house of friends that his son had frequently visited, and there they found a woman, an accursed sorceress, practicing her sorcery. She had changed the boy into a mule and had bound him to the mill stones, to make him grind as long as he lived.

When the sage saw him, he recognized him and understood, and said to the father, "See, thy son, whom thou hast thought dead, is restored to thee." He then spoke to the woman, and rebuking her, said, "Why art thou not overwhelmed with shame, since thou art caught in the net? Give back to the father his son, his own flesh."

The wicked woman was crestfallen; she did not give heed to his words and did not answer him either gently or harshly. Thereupon the good man took hold of the mule, led him out, transformed him, gave him his original form, and restored him to his father. The master turned in praise to his Maker. Together they uttered praise to their God, their Creator....

From that city Aaron journeyed onward and went to Oria. There he found tents [of study], set up by the rivers, planted and thriving like trees by the waters, schools established, rooted like cedars growing at the side of flowing streams. There contending and flourishing in the pursuit of study, masters in public discourse and of learned discussion of the Law, the sons of R. Amittai, R. Shephatiah and R. Hananeel, both of them true servants of God, zealously extolling the God of Israel, fervently invoking Him, declaring His praise and holiness; like the company of angels acknowledging the might and dominion of the King of kings. Among them Aaron established his home. His wisdom streamed forth, his learning flourished there. He revealed great powers, and gave decisions of the law like those which were given when the Urim were in use, when the Sanhedrin held court, and the law of Sota was valid [cf. Numbers 5:11-31]. He extended his influence; he founded a seat of learning to take the place of that which had been on the ground of the temple, where the foundations of the ark had been laid....

By the grace of Him that hath formed the earth by His power, that forgiveth iniquity and sin, I will make mention of the incident that occurred at Venosa. There was a man who had come from the land of Israel, profoundly learned in the law of God, a master of wisdom. He remained in Venosa for some time. Every Sabbath he would give instruction and expound the Law before the community of the people of God. The master would lead with a discourse on the selected portion of the law, and R. Silanus would follow with his elucidation.

One day, the men of the villages came in wagons to the city; they began to quarrel among themselves. Some women came out of their houses, with the long staves used for raking the oven and charred by the fire; with these the men and women beat one another. R. Silanus, in a mistaken spirit of levity, resolved to make use of the incident, and committed a great wrong. He sought out the passage of the scriptural portion that the sage was to expound on that Sabbath, erased two lines of it and, in their stead, wrote the above story. This is what R. Silanus inserted, "The men came [to the city] in wagons; the women came from their houses, and beat the men with staves."

On the Sabbath, as the sage came upon the words, he stopped reading and all speech failed him. He looked at the letters and studied, examined and pondered and went over them several times and finally, in his simplicity, read them, and gave as part of the instruction the words that he found written there.

Then R. Silanus, in mocking laughter, said to all assembled there, "Listen to the discourse of the master on the quarrel that occurred among you yesterday, when the women beat the men, when they struck them with oxen staves and drove them off on every hand." When the master realized what had been done he became very faint and pale; he hurried to his associates who were in the school engaged in study, and told them of the sorrowful experience he had just had. All of them were deeply pained and distressed, and they denounced R. Silanus the wise.

He remained in ban a number of years, until R. Ahimaaz arrived there on his pilgrimage, and, in his wisdom, annulled the ban. This is what the wise man did. When he arrived, they were observing the ten days of penitence. The teachers and head of the school urged him to stand before the ark, and, with ardent devotion, lead them in prayer to Him that is revered in the great assembly of the righteous.

In his modesty, he complied with their request. With the fear of God in his heart, he began with the penitential prayers, then melodiously chanted a poem of R. Silanus to show that he was a man of sound faith; that, although he was at first false and sinful and godless. When he remembered the former teachers, he followed them as his masters, who shattered the power of heretical teachings over him, so that he turned away from the heretics. When the sages had finished the prayers, they asked him who that lover of the great teachers was, so consecrated with power to utter prayer, who loved and honored the masters, and turned away and shunned the heretics. He answered, "That beloved one is R. Silanus, who has been denounced as unworthy among you." They immediately arose and annulled the ban which they had declared against him, and, invoking upon him abundant, enduring and substantial good, all of them said, "May R. Silanus ever be blessed."

In those days a king reigned over the Romans, a wicked man, elevated to the throne through treachery and murder, who determined to make an end of the acknowledgment of God whose work is perfect, among the descendants of the upright and holy.

In the 800th year after the destruction of the Holy City and of the Temple, the seat of glory, and of the exile of the people of Judah and of Israel, there arose a king whose name was Basil, a worshipper of images, seeking to destroy the people of Israel

ever under God's protection, to lead them astray, to extermi-
nate the remnant of Israel root and branch, to compel them to
abandon the Law and to accept the worthless doctrine [of
Jesus]. He sent couriers and horsemen to the provinces and all
parts of his kingdom, to force the Jews out of their religion,
and make them adopt his senseless faith.

The agents of the king went through the land as far as the
harbor of Otranto; there they embarked and passed over into
the province of Apulia. When the report of their coming
reached the inhabitants, the people were thrown into conster-
nation. They traversed the province from end to end. Finally,
they came to the city of Irai, bringing a letter, officially
stamped with the royal seal—the seal was the bulla of gold—
that the king had sent to R. Shephatiah.

And these are the words that were written in the letter, "I,
King Basil, send word to thee R. Shephatiah, to have thee
come to visit me. Come to me, do not refuse, for I have heard of
thy wisdom and thy vast learning. I long to see thee; I swear
by my life and by the crown on my head, that thy coming shall
be in peace, and that I will send thee back safe to thy home. I
will receive thee with honor, as I would one of my own kin, and
any boon thou mayest ask of me, I will grant in grateful
affection."

R. Shephatiah then embarked to go to Constantinople,
which Constantine had built—may God shatter its splendor
and the power of all its people. And God let him find favor in
the presence of the king and of his court.

The king led him into a discussion of the Law, and then
questioned him regarding the building of the Temple, and
that of the church called Sophia, asking him to tell in which
structure the greater wealth had been used. The king firmly
contended that it was Sophia, for in its construction uncounted
treasure had been used.

But R. Shephatiah answered, in well-chosen words, "Let the
King command that the Scriptures be brought to him. There
thou wilt find the truth as to which structure is the more
costly." He immediately did so and he found that the quantity
used by David and Solomon was in excess of the amount

counted out for Sophia, by 120 talents of gold and 500 talents of silver.

Thereupon the king exclaimed, "R. Shephatiah, by his wisdom, has prevailed against me."

But R. Shephatiah answered, "My Lord, not I, but the Scriptures have prevailed against thee."

Then the king asked him to be seated with him at the royal table, to partake of refreshing delicacies and fruits. Golden dishes were placed before him that he might eat in the cleanliness required by the Law. The dishes were drawn up and down by costly chains of silver, but no one could see the plane from which they were let down before him.

And Basil had a daughter whom he loved as the apple of his eye. An evil spirit tormented her. He could not find a cure for her. He spoke to Shephatiah in secret and with earnest entreaty said, "Help me, Shephatiah, and cure my daughter of her affliction."

And Shephatiah answered, "With the help of the Almighty, I will surely do so." He then asked the king, "Hast thou any secluded place in which there is no uncleanness?"

The king answered: "I have the beautiful garden of the Bukoleon." After looking about in it, he agreed to make use of the Bukoleon, which literally means the mouth of the lion. He took the maiden into it and exorcised the evil spirit in the name of Him that dwelleth on high, the Creator of height and depth, that founded the earth in His wisdom, the Maker of the mountains and seas, that hangeth the world over nothing.

The evil spirit cried out, "Why dost thou help the daughter of the man who rules in wickedness and heaps affliction upon the people of the redeemed. She has been delivered to me by God, that I should humble and crush her. Therefore, let me be, for I will not come forth from my place."

But Shephatiah answered the evil spirit, "I will not heed thy words; come forth in the name of God, that he may know there is a God in Israel."

It came forth at once and tried to escape; but he seized it and put it into a leaden chest; he then covered the chest on all sides and sealed it in the name of his Maker, dropped it into the sea, and let it sink into the depth of the mighty waters. The maiden, quieted and cured, then returned to the king and queen.

Shephatiah now went to the king for his dismissal. The king came forth to meet him, placed his arm about his neck, brought him into his chamber, and began to tempt him to abandon his religion, and, with the promise of large reward, to induce him to accept the senseless error of the heathen belief. He walked about with him, and insistently urged him; he approached him with a bribe and appointed companions for him.

When Shephatiah, the master, noticed the fanatic zeal and presumption, he exclaimed in a loud voice, "Mighty Master, Thou overwhelmest me with violence." Thereupon the king arouse from his throne, took him from among the people, and gave him permission to go. He sent him to the queen that she might give him her gift and blessing. And the queen questioned him about his affairs saying, "Hast thou any daughters or sons?" He accordingly answered, "Thy servant has one son and two daughters." She then gave him the rings in her ears and the girdle on her loins, and urged them upon him, saying, "As my tribute to thy learning, give them to thy two daughters; in costliness there are none to be compared to them." The weight of the rings was a litra of gold and the girdle was of equal value.

When he was about to go, the king again called him and said to him, "Shephatiah, ask a boon of me and I will give it to thee from my treasures; and if thou dost not desire money I will give thee an inheritance of towns and cities, for I said in my letter to thee, that I would grant thy wish."

He answered in sorrow and bitter weeping, "If thou, my lord, wouldst favor Shephatiah, let there be peace for those engaged in the study of Law. Do not force them to abandon the Law of God, and do not crush them in sorrow and affliction. But if thou be unwilling thus to fulfill my wish, grant for my sake that there be no persecution in my city."

The king exclaimed in anger, "Had I not sent a letter with my seal, and taken an oath, I would this very instant punish thee. But how can I harm thee, since I have bound myself in writing to thee, and cannot retract what I have said in my letter." So he issued for him an edict, sealed with a costly seal of gold, commanding that no persecution take place in the city of Oria, and therewith sent him in peace and honor to his home and people.

Then the wicked king continued to send emissaries into all the provinces and ordered his agents to fall upon them; to force them out of their religion and convert them to the errors and folly of his faith. The sun and moon were darkened for twenty-five years, until the day of his death. Cursed be his end. May his guilt and wickedness be remembered, and his sin not be forgotten. May the recompense of his vileness and cruelty be visited upon the kingdom of Rome, that his royal power may be cast down from its high places and his dominion be removed from the earth, to bring cheer to the afflicted and comfort to the mourners, that, in mercy, we may soon see the time of fulfillment.

After his reign, his own son, Leo, came to the throne; the Lord of God had chosen him. May his memory be blessed. He annulled the cruel edict that had been enacted in the days of his father, and permitted the Jews to return to the laws and statutes of their religion, to observe their Sabbaths, and all the requirements of their commandments, and the ordinances of their covenant, as of old. Praised be the name of their Rock that did not abandon them in the hands of their enemies, that saved them from their despoilers, and delivered them from their oppressors. Praised be the name of God from the heights forever and ever.

Bahya Ben Joseph ibn Pakuda
(c. 1050-c. 1120)

Nothing is known of the personal life of Bahya Ben Joseph Pakuda save that he was a *dayyan* (Hebrew for judge) in the rabbinical court of Saragossa, Spain. He wrote a number of sacred poems distinguished by depth of thought and beauty of expression. But he is famous for *Duties of the Heart*, written originally in Arabic and later translated into Hebrew by other hands. A systematic study of Jewish ethics following the Aristotelian rationalistic philosophy of his day, *Duties of the Heart* is characterized by logical exposition and deep piety. Although an ascetic and mystic Pakuda recommends full participation in life's activities, control of passion by reason and humility, and readiness to sacrifice one's wealth and life for love of God. He insists that conscience is superior in authority to moral doctrine. Long studied as a practical guide of conduct in daily life, the book also influenced Jewish mystics for generations.

Duties of the Heart

Third Treatise

On the service of God, expounding various grounds for the obligation to assume the service of God, blessed be He.

Introduction

Having, in the previous treatises, expounded the obligation of wholeheartedly acknowledging the unity of God and the obligation of examining the various modes of His benefits to mankind, we have next to indicate what a human being's conduct should be, once the foregoing has become clear to him—and that is to assume the obligation of the service of God, as reason would require from a beneficiary to his benefactor. It is proper to open this treatise with an exposition of the various kinds of benefits human beings render each other, and the corresponding obligations of gratitude. We shall then ascend to the consideration of what we owe to the exalted Creator in praise and thanksgiving for His abounding kindness and great goodness to us.

We assert, as a truth generally recognized, that if anyone benefits us, we are under an obligation of gratitude to him in accordance with his intent to help us. Even if he actually falls short, owing to some mishap which prevents his benefiting us, we are still bound to be grateful to him, since we are convinced that he has a benevolent disposition towards us and his intention is to be of use to us. On the other hand, should we obtain any benefit through one who had no such intention, the duties of gratitude to that person would cease and we are under no such obligation.

When we consider the benefits human beings render each other, we find that these fall into five classes: (1) a father's beneficence to his child; (2) a master's to his servant; (3) a wealthy man's beneficence to the poor for the sake of heavenly reward; (4) the beneficence rendered by human beings to each other in order to gain a good name, honor, and temporal reward; and (5) the powerful man's beneficence to the weak, induced by pity for the latter and sympathy with his condition.

Let us now consider the motive in each of the classes mentioned: Is it disinterested, the sole aim being to help the beneficiary, or is it not so? First, a father's beneficence to his child. It is obvious that the father's motive in this is to further his own interest. For the child is a part of the father, whose chief hope is centered in his offspring. Do you not observe that in regard to its food, drink, clothing, and in warding off all hurt from it, a father is more sensitive about his child than about himself? To secure ease for it, the burden of toil and weariness is lightly borne by him—the feelings of tenderness and pity for their offspring being naturally implanted in parents. Nevertheless, the Torah and reason impose upon children the duty of serving, honoring, and revering their parents, as Scripture saith: "Ye shall, everyone, revere his father and his mother" [Lev. 19:3]; "Hear, O my son, the instruction of thy father and forsake not the law of thy mother" [Prov. 1:8]; further, "A son honoreth his father, and a servant his master" [Malachai 1:6]. And these duties are enjoined, notwithstanding that the father is impelled by a natural instinct and the benefaction comes from God, while the parent is only the agent.

The kindness of a master to his servant: It is obvious that the master's intent is to improve his property by an outlay of capital, since he needs his servant's work, and his sole motive is to further his own interest. Nevertheless, the Creator, blessed be He, imposes upon the servant the duties of service and gratitude, as it is said, "A son honoreth his father and a servant his master" [Malachai 1:6].

The rich man's beneficence to the poor man for the sake of a heavenly reward: he is like a merchant who acquires a great and enduring pleasure which he will enjoy at the end of a definite time by means of a small, perishable, and inconsiderable gift which he takes immediately. So the rich man only intends to win glory for his soul at the close of his earthly existence by the benefaction which God entrusted to him, in order to bestow it upon anyone who will be worthy of it. Yet it is generally recognized that it is proper to thank and laud a benefactor. Even though the latter's motive was to gain spiritual glory hereafter, gratitude is, nevertheless, due to him, as Job said: "The blessing of him that was ready to perish came upon me" [Job 29:13]; and further, "If his loins have not blessed me, when he warmed himself with the fleece of my sheep" [Job 31:20].

Kindness men show each other for the sake of praise, honor, and temporal rewards: This is as if one were to deposit an article in another's care or entrust him with money, because of the depositor's apprehension that he may need it later on. Although, in benefiting another person, the aim is to further his own interests, the benefactor is nevertheless entitled to praise and gratitude for his kindness, as the wise king said, "Many court the generous man, and everyone is a friend to him that giveth gifts" [Prov. 19:6]; and he also said, "A man's gift maketh room for him and bringeth him before great men" [Prov. 18:16].

The kindness of one who has compassion on a poor man for whom he is sorry: the benefactor's motive is to get rid of his own distress that results from depression and grief for the one he pities. He is like one who cures a pain which has attacked him by means of the bounties that the Lord bestowed upon him. Nevertheless, he is not to be without due praise, as Job said, "Could I see any perish for want of clothing or any poor without covering? Did not his loins bless me, when he warmed himself with the fleece of my sheep?" [Job 31:19-20].

From what has here been advanced, it is clear that anyone who bestows benefits on others has first his own interest in mind—either to secure an honorable distinction in this world, or hereafter, or relieve himself of pain, or improve his material substance. Yet all these considerations do not absolve the beneficiaries of their duty of praising, thanking, respecting and loving their benefactors and making them some return. And this, despite that the benefit was only loaned to the benefactors; that they were obliged to dispense it, as we have pointed out; and that their beneficence is not permanent, their generosity not prolonged, and their benevolence is mixed with the intent either to further their own interest or ward off injury. How much more, then, does a human being owe service, praise, and gratitude to Him who created the benefit and the benefactor, whose beneficence is unlimited, permanent, perpetual, without any motive of self-interest, or purpose of warding off injury, but only an expression of grace and loving-kindness emanating from Him towards all human beings.

We should furthermore bear in mind that a human being who renders a kindness to another in any of the modes above specified is not superior to the person whom he benefits, except in some casual detail, while in their humanity and essential characteristics they are alike and akin to one another, in substance and form, in physical conformation and figure (or mentality—Gen. 1:26) in their natures and in a larger part of what happens to them.

Nevertheless, the beneficiary, as we have set forth, is under an obligation of service to his benefactor. And if we thought that the beneficiary was extremely defective and imperfect in his physical conformation, figure, and appearance, [we would conclude that] the obligation of service on his part would be so much the greater. So, also, if we should deem the benefactor the best and most perfect of all beings, while the beneficiary was the most defective of all things and the weakest of all creatures, reason would require that the service to the benefactor should be increased to an infinite degree.

Following this analogy, when we investigate the relation of the Creator, blessed be He, to human beings, we will find that the Creator, blessed be He, is infinite exalted and glorified above everything existing, above all that can be apprehended by the senses or conceived by the intellectual as has been expounded in the first treatise of this book; and that a human being, in comparison with other species of animals, is the most defective and this can be demonstrated in three respects:

(1) In respect to his infancy and early childhood: For we find

that other species of living creatures are stronger than he is, better able to endure pain and move independently, and do not trouble their progenitors in their periods of growth to the same extent as a human being does.

(2) In respect to the filth and foulness within the human body and the similar appearances of exudations on its external surface when one has neglected to wash and cleanse himself for a length of time, as also in respect to the state of the body after death—the effluvium of a human corpse being more noisome than that of the carcasses of other creatures, and a human being's ordure more offensive than that of other creatures.

(3) In respect to a human being's helplessness resulting from an injury to his brain, when he loses the rational faculty which God bestowed upon him and which constitutes his superiority to the other creatures that are irrational. For at such times he is stupider and more senseless than other animals. He may inflict serious injuries on himself and even kill himself. Most animals, too, we find, possess an apprehension of what will be to their advantage, and show an ingenuity in obtaining their food, while many intellectual men fall short in this regard, not to speak of one who has lost his senses.

When we concentrate our thoughts on the greatness of the Creator, exalted be He, on His infinite might, wisdom, and plenitude of resources and then turn our attention to a man's weakness and deficiency, and that he never attains perfection; when we consider his poverty and lack of what he needs to supply his wants and then investigate the numerous bounties and favors which the Creator has bestowed on him; when we reflect that the Creator has created man as he is with deficiencies in his very being—poor and needing for his development all requisites which he can only obtain by exerting himself—this too proceeding from the Creator's mercy to him, so that he may know himself, study his conditions and cleave, under all circumstances, to the service of God, and so receive for it a recompense in the world to come, for the attainment of which he was created, as we have already set forth in the second treatise of this book—how much indeed then does a human being owe to the blessed Creator, in service, thanksgiving and continuous praise, in view of the demonstration already given to the obligation of praise and gratitude that human beings owe to each other for favors rendered them.

Should anyone be so foolish as to contest this obligation of a human being towards the Creator—when he examines and closely studies the surely awake, the negligent will be aroused, the ignorant will investigate, the intelligent will comprehend the demonstration of the obligatory character of the service of God, the proofs for which are so clear, the evidence of which is so manifest, and the indications are so true; as the prophet (peace be unto him) said concerning one who neglects to reflect upon the obligation of the service of God, "Do ye thus requite the Lord, O foolish people and unwise?" (Deut. 32:6).

Thus the obligation to assume the service of God, incumbent on human beings in view of the bounties He continually bestows on them, has been demonstrated.

Martin Buber (1878-1965)

Recognized by Christians as well as Jews as one of the profoundest twentieth century religious philosophers, Martin Buber is the one Jewish thinker in whom Christianity can meet Judaism, not by virtue of canonical compromise on his part, but because of his striving after unity and his search for the essentials of all faith.

Born in Vienna, Buber studied at a number of German universities. After joining the Zionist movement in 1898, he became editor of several of its German periodicals—like Ahad Ha'am advocating spiritual rather than political action but encouraging Jewish pioneering in Palestine. Buber's translation of the Bible into German was well received, and in 1924 he was appointed professor of the sociology of Jewish religion in Frankfurt. In 1933, he fled Nazi persecution, settling five years later in Israel, where he was made professor of sociology at the Hebrew University.

Like Ahad Ha'am, who also did not observe precepts and practices of traditional Judaism, Buber advocated a form of national revival in order to exalt and ennoble the life of the individual Jew. Unlike Ahad Ha'am, Buber did not develop his ideas systematically or by way of logical reasoning. He describes religious faith as an interaction between man and God, expressed in the form of dialogue. Putting aside the superstition and anti-intellectualism of Hasidism, and painting a romantic portrait of the sect, Buber deduces from its concepts that man, because he is always in the presence of God, must act so that God will always be present to him.

Buber emphasizes in *Ich und Du*, a metaphysical study of ethical behavior, that when man is intuitively involved with the outer world, it will react on his inner world, the soul, in a similar way. Man, when he behaves properly, sanctifies the material aspect of living, which, in turn enables him to raise human existence to a higher level and thus to sanctify it. The *Tzaddik* (Hebrew for righteous man), the leader whom the Hasidim follow, stands as an example of a sanctified life and as a mediator between God and man. For Buber, Hasidism demonstrates that every Jew can receive religious influences and enhance them in every aspect of daily living by the deep religious intensity of his own behavior.

I and Thou

The extended lines of relations meet in the eternal *Thou*.

Every particular *Thou* is a glimpse through to the eternal *Thou*; by means of every particular *Thou* the primary word addresses the eternal *Thou*. Through this mediation of the *Thou* of all beings fulfillment, and non-fulfillment, of relations comes to them; the inborn *Thou* is realized in each relation and consummated in none. It is consummated only in the direct relation with the *Thou* that by its nature cannot become *It*.

Men have addressed their eternal *Thou* with many names. In singing of Him who was thus named they always had the *Thou* in mind: the first myths were hymns of praise. Then the names took refuge in the language of *It*; men were more and more strongly moved to think of and to address their eternal *Thou* as an *It*. But all God's name are hallowed, for in them He is not merely spoken about, but also spoken to.

Many men wish to reject the word God as a legitimate usage, because it is so misused. It is indeed the most heavily laden of all the words used by men. For that very reason it is the most imperishable and most indispensable. What does all mistaken talk about God's being and works (though there has been, and can be, no other talk about these) matter in comparison with the one truth that all men who have addressed God had God himself in mind? For he who speaks the word God and really has *Thou* in mind (whatever the illusion by which he is held), addresses the true *Thou* of his life, which cannot be limited by another *Thou*, and to which he stands in a relation that gathers up and includes all other.

But when he, too, who abhors the name, and believes himself to be godless, gives his whole being to addressing the *Thou* of his life, as a *Thou* that cannot be limited by another, he addresses God.

If we go on our way and meet a man who has advanced towards us and has also gone on *his* way, we know only our part of the way, not his—his we experience only in the meeting.

Of the complete relational event we know, with the knowledge of life lived, our going out to the relation, our part of the way. The other part only comes upon us, we do not know it; it comes upon us in the meeting. But we strain ourselves on it if we speak of it as though it were some thing beyond the meeting.

We have to be concerned, to be troubled, not about the other side but about our own side, not about grace but about will. Grace concerns us insofar as we go out to it and persist in its presence; but it is not our object.

The *Thou* confronts me. But I step into direct relation with it. Hence the relation means being chosen and choosing, suffering and action in one; just as any action of the whole being which means the suspension of all partial actions, and consequently of all sensations of action grounded only in their particular limitation, is bound to resemble suffering.

This is the activity of the man who has become a whole being, an activity that has been termed doing nothing: nothing separate or partial stirs in the man any more, thus he makes no intervention in the world; it is the whole man, enclosed and at rest in his wholeness, that is effective—he has become an effective whole. To have won stability in this state is to be able to go out to the supreme meeting.

To this end the world of sense does not need to be laid aside as though it were illusory. There is no illusory world, there is only the world—which appears to us as twofold in accordance with our twofold attitude. Only the barrier of separation has to be destroyed. Further, no "going beyond sense-experience" is necessary; for every experience, even the most spiritual, could yield us only an *It*. Nor is any recourse necessary to a world of ideas and values; for they cannot become presentness for us. None of these things is necessary. Can it be said what really is necessary?—Not in the sense of a precept. For everything that has ever been devised and contrived in the time of the human spirit as precept, alleged preparation, practice, or meditation, has nothing to do with the primal, simple fact of the meeting. Whatever the advantages in knowledge or the wielding of power for which we have to thank this or that practice, none of this affects the meeting of which we are speaking; it all has its place in the world of *It* and does not lead one step, does not take *the* step, out of it. Going out to the relation cannot be taught in the sense of precepts being given. It can only be indicated by the drawing of a circle which excludes everything that is not this going out. Then the one thing that matters is visible, full acceptance of the present.

To be sure, this acceptance presupposes that the further a man has wandered in separated being the more difficult is the venture and the more elemental the turning. This does not mean a giving up of, say, the *I*, as mystical writings usually suppose; the *I* is as indispensable to this, the supreme, as to every relation, since relation is only possible between *I* and *Thou*. It is not the *I*, then, that is given up, but that false self-asserting instinct that makes a man flee to the possessing of things before the unreliable, perilous world of relation which has neither density nor duration and cannot be surveyed.

Every real relation with a being or life in the world is exclusive. Its *Thou* is freed, steps forth, is single, and confronts you.

It fills the heavens. This does not mean that nothing else exists; but all else lives in *its* light. As long as the presence of the relation continues, this cosmic range is inviolable. But as soon as a *Thou* becomes *It*, the cosmic range of the relation appears as an offense to the world, its exclusiveness as an exclusion of the universe.

In the relation with God unconditioned exclusiveness and unconditional inclusiveness are one. He who enters on the absolute relation is concerned with nothing isolated any more, neither this nor beings, neither earth nor heaven; but everything is gathered up in the relation. For to step into pure relation is not to disregard everything but to see everything in the *Thou*, not to renounce the world but to establish it on its true basis. To look away from the world, or to stare at it, does not help a man to reach God; but he who sees the world in Him stands in His presence. "Here world, there God" is the language of *It*; "God in the world" is another language of *It*; but to eliminate or leave behind nothing at all, to include the whole world in the *Thou*, to give the world its due and its truth, to include nothing besides God but everything in him—this is full and complete relation.

Men do not find God if they stay in the world. They do not find Him if they leave the world. He who goes out with his whole being to meet his *Thou* and carries to it all being that is in the world, finds Him who cannot be sought.

Of course God is the "wholly Other"; but He is also the wholly Same, the wholly Present. Of course He is the *Mysterium Tremendum* that appears and overthrows; but He is also the mystery of the self-evident, nearer to me than my *I*.

If you explore the life of things and of conditional being you come to the unfathomable, if you deny the life things and of conditioned being you stand before nothingness, if you hallow this life you meet the living God.

Joseph Caro (1488-1575)

The biography of Rabbi Joseph ben Ephraim Caro, compiler of the *Shulhan Arukh*, the last great code of Jewish law, is as scanty as those of other great Jewish scholars in that century. Exiled when a child from the Iberian peninsula, he went with his family to Bulgaria, thence to Turkey, where he headed an academy, and finally to Safed, Palestine, where a galaxy of scholars devoted to Talmudic and Kabbalist learning had gathered. In Safed, Caro completed *Bet Yoseph*, a monumental study of Rabbinic law that attempts to reveal the derivation of all Jewish laws up to and including the Talmud, to present pertinent opinions, and to give authoritative decisions. Later, Caro composed the *Shulhan Arukh*, a digest of *Bet Yoseph*, as a manual for study by younger students.

For his title, Caro probably had in mind a phrase from Psalm 23, "You prepare a table for me," which is also found in early Rabbinic exegeses. It seems clear from the title—*shulhan arukh* in Hebrew means "set table"—that Caro's intention was to set forth spiritual food in such a way that it could readily be consumed. The *Shulhan Arukh* gives decisions—almost always without mention of sources or differences of opinions—in plain, direct, concise statements. Caro divides each chapter into paragraphs, each paragraph treating a specific point of law. His style of Hebrew is so light and clear that it appears transparent, nowhere coming between reader and content.

Yet the *Shulhan Arukh* was unacceptable to French, German, and Polish Jewry because Caro, relying on Sephardic commentaries, had almost totally ignored their authorities. Only after many glosses satisfactory to Ashkenazi scholars, particularly regarding customs and traditions, were added by Rabbi Moses Isserles (c. 1520-1572) did the *Shulhan Arukh* gain acceptance as the standard handbook of Rabbinic law. In succeeding centuries, it had a normative influence, winning unqualified approval from Jewish communities throughout the world as the sole authoritative source. Even today it is still recognized by Orthodox Jews as standard and is found in most observant homes.

The basic text of the *Shulhan Arukh*, that of Caro, is called the "prepared table" in printed editions, and the notes of Isserles are called the "table-cloth" (*mappah* in Hebrew). Beginning with rituals at dawn and ending with rituals at night, the *Shulhan Arukh* presents the obligations necessary throughout each of the twenty-four hours to achieve the sanctification of life. (It omits laws relating to animal sacrifice that are no longer pertinent after destruction of the Temple.) The volume is divided into four parts that try to deal with all phases of life, religious and secular:

1. Daily duties of prayer, Sabbaths, and holidays.
2. Various subjects, such as dietary regulations, charity, mourning.
3. Domestic relations, such as marriage and divorce.
4. Civil and criminal law.

The Law of Honoring Teachers and Learned Men

Chapter 242

1.   It is the duty of a man to honor and respect his teacher. Honor to the teacher comes before honor to the parents, when the parents are ignorant, because the parents support the children materially in this world and the teacher supports them spiritually and prepares them for the future world.

2.   He who strives with his teacher is like one striving with the Lord and he who complains of his teacher is like one complaining of the Lord.

3.   It is forbidden for a scholar to answer questions of law

in the presence of his teacher without the teacher's permission, and he who violates the law is liable to punishment.

4.   It is forbidden to call the teacher by the first name even after his death. He must only be addressed as "My dear teacher."

5.   It is forbidden to occupy the teacher's seat.

6.   If a teacher dies the scholar is bound to tear his coat as he is bound to tear his coat when his father dies.

7.   If the father and the teacher lose anything, and it is impossible to look for both of them at once, the preference belongs to the teacher.

8.   If the father and the teacher carry a heavy load, and need some assistance, and it is impossible to help them both at once, the preference of assistance belongs to the teacher.

9.   If the teacher and the father are in captivity or detention the preference in helping to release them is given to the teacher.

10.   The above rules of preference for the teacher hold good only when the scholar has received the majority of his education from the teacher; if, however, he has not received so much learning from the teacher, then the preference belongs to the father.

11.   If the scholar and the teacher each lose an article and it is impossible to look for both at the same time, then the preference belongs to the scholar.

12.   The teacher is bound to honor the scholar as the scholar is bound to honor him.

13.   It is the duty of the scholar to stand up as soon as he sees the teacher.

Chapter 243

The judges thou shalt not revile; and a ruler among the people thou shalt not curse.

1.   It is the duty of the people to honor and to fear the ruler and the judges and all the learned men.

2.   Clergymen are free from all kinds of taxation.

3.   It is the duty of the people to provide funds to support the

judges and the learned men, that they may have enough to live in a good manner.

4. It is a great sin to slander and to hate learned men. He who does so has no part in the world to come.

5. It is forbidden to ask a service of a learned man.

6. The court has the authority to punish the man who slanders a learned man.

7. The learned man has a right to excuse the slanderer.

Chapter 244

Before the hoary head shalt thou rise up, and honor the face of the old man; and thou shalt be afraid of thy God: I am the Lord.   (Lev. 20)

1. One must rise in the presence of a learned man, even if he is not an old man, and stand up in the presence of an old man, seventy years of age, even if he is not learned, providing he is less than four yards away. It is forbidden to close one's eyes and pretend not to see him.

2. A working man, when he is on duty, is not bound to stand up in the presence of a learned man because his work must not be hindered.

3. It is the duty of the learned man to go in a different way, if he can, to avoid troubling the people to stand up for him.

Chapter 245

1. It is the duty of every man to teach his son and his grandchildren the learning of the Torah; and if the father did not teach them, the children are bound to obtain learning themselves.

2. If the father and the son desire to learn and the father cannot afford the expenditure for both, the father comes first; however, if the son is clever in learning, and he can make quicker progress, then the son comes first.

3. The residents of each city can compel one another to cover the expenses of a school for children.

4. A teacher is supposed to teach not more than 25 chil-

dren, and if there are from 25 to 40, he must have an assistant; if there are 50, the need is for two teachers.

5.   The teacher is not allowed to whip his students with a rod or with a stick, only with a little strap.

6.   Each neighborhood must have a school so that the child will not have to go a great distance to reach the school, and shall not have to pass bridges, rivers, or dangerous places.

7.   If a teacher leaves his scholars alone during school hours and goes out to look for other business, or if he neglects the children and is lazy in the teaching, he is cursed by the Lord and can be discharged without notification.

8.   It is forbidden for the teacher to be up at night, and attend the school in the day time, or to fast at the time of teaching, or to overeat because these things impair his health and result in neglect in the teaching of the children.

Albert Einstein (1879-1955)

Albert Einstein, winner of the Nobel Prize in physics for 1921, was a humanist as well as a scientist.

Although Einstein suggested to President Franklin D. Roosevelt the possibility of an atom bomb, he recognized the terrible dangers of such a weapon. After World War II, Einstein insisted that "the objective of avoiding total destruction must have priority over every other objective," so that the only safe way "to solve conflicts between nations [is] by judicial decision."

Einstein empathized greatly with Jewish concerns, believing that "Jews should be and remain the carriers and patrons of spiritual values." He felt deeply the tragedy of the Holocaust, speaking of "the irreparable loss our martyred Jewish nation has suffered." Einstein viewed Israel as a homeland, a vision fulfilled, and he called on Jews everywhere to take an active part in the wonderful task "of creating in Israel a community which conforms as closely as possible to the ethical ideals of our people as they have been formed in the course of a long history."

The Jews of Israel

There is no problem of such overwhelming importance to us Jews as consolidating that which has been accomplished in Israel with amazing energy and an unequalled willingness for sacrifice. May the joy and admiration that fill us when we think of all that this small group of energetic and thoughtful people has achieved give us the strength to accept the great responsibility which the present situation has placed upon us.

When appraising the achievement, however, let us not lose sight of the cause to be served by this achievement: rescue of our endangered brethren, dispersed in many lands, by uniting them in Israel; creation of a community which conforms as closely as possible to the ethical ideals of our people as they have been formed in the course of a long history.

One of these ideals is peace, based on understanding and self-restraint, and not on violence. If we are imbued with this ideal, our joy becomes somewhat mingled with sadness because our relations with the Arabs are far from this ideal at the present time. It may well be that we would have reached this ideal, had we been permitted to work out, undisturbed by others, our relations with our neighbors, for we *want* peace and we realize that our future development depends on peace.

It was much less our own fault or that of our neighbors than of the Mandatory Power, that we did not achieve an undivided Palestine in which Jews and Arabs would live as equals, free, in peace. If one nation dominates other nations, as was the case in the British Mandate over Palestine, she can hardly avoid following the notorious device of Divide et Impera. In plain language this means: create discord among the governed people so they will not unite in order to shake off the yoke imposed upon them. Well, the yoke has been removed, but the seed of dissension has borne fruit and may still do harm for some time to come—let us hope not for too long.

The Jews of Palestine did not fight for political independence for its own sake, but they fought to achieve free immigration for the Jews of many countries where their very existence was in danger, free immigration also for all those who were longing for a life among their own. It is no exaggeration to say that they fought to make possible a sacrifice perhaps unique in history.

I do not speak of the loss in lives and property fighting an opponent who was numerically far superior, nor do I mean the exhausting toil which is the pioneer's lot in a neglected arid country. I am thinking of the additional sacrifice that a population living under such conditions has to make in order to receive, in the course of eighteen months, an influx of immigrants which comprise more than one third of the total Jewish population of the country. In order to realize what this means you have only to visualize a comparable feat of the American Jews. Let us assume there were no laws limiting the immigration into the United States; imagine that the Jews of this country volunteered to receive more than one million Jews from other countries in the course of one year and a half, to take care of them, and to integrate them into the economy of this country. This would be a tremendous achievement, but still very far from the achievement of our brethren in Israel. For the United States is a big, fertile country, sparsely populated with a high living standard and a highly developed productive capacity, not to compare with small Jewish Palestine whose inhabitants, even without the additional burden of mass immigration, lead a hard and frugal life, still threatened by enemy attacks. Think of the privations and personal sacrifices which this voluntary act of brotherly love means for the Jews of Israel.

The economic means of the Jewish Community in Israel do not suffice to bring this tremendous enterprise to a successful end. For a hundred thousand out of more than three hundred thousand persons who immigrated to Israel since May 1948 no homes or work could be made available. They had to be concentrated in improvised camps under conditions which are a disgrace to all of us.

It must not happen that this magnificent work breaks down because the Jews of this country do not help sufficiently or quickly enough. Here, to my mind, is a precious gift with which all Jews have been presented: the opportunity to take an active part in this wonderful task.

Eldad ha-Dani (fl. 9th century)

The earliest Jewish travel volume extant is *The Travels of Eldad the Danite*, written not by Eldad but by others who heard him recount his adventures. Eldad's origin is a riddle. From the Arabicisms and exotic words intermixed with Hebrew, scholars think that Eldad may have come from among Jews who lived as an independent tribe near the southern tip of the Arabian peninsula.

A merchant traveler, Eldad took the name ha-Dani, claiming to have come from the tribe of Dan. He visited Jewish communities in Babylonia, North Africa, and Spain, thrilling them with strange stories of Dan and other Lost Tribes, which he said had built sovereign states in Eastern Africa, Persia, Arabia, and Khazariah. The tales spread like wildfire despite their romantic and fictitious base (and the fact that many had appeared in Haggadic literature), and they remained popular for more than a thousand years—continuing among oppressed Jewish communities throughout the world to renew the hope of Hebrew empires successfully resisting their neighbors and leading the life their forefathers had lived in Israel centuries before.

The Travels of Eldad the Danite

In the name of the Lord God of Israel! May the name of our Lord, the King of kings, be praised who chose Israel from all the nations and gave us the law of truth and planted eternal life in our midst, the law of the upright to live thereby. Our brethren, sons of the captivity, be of good courage and strengthen your hearts to perform the law of our God in due season, for whensoever Israel doeth the law of the Omnipotent, no nation and no tongue can rule over them. Peace be with you our brethren, sons of the captivity, and peace to Jerusalem, the city of our glory, the place of the Temple of our God which has been destroyed and the place of the kingdom of the house of David and Judah, who wrought justice and righteousness, and the place of the Holy of Holies. Peace to all the elders of Israel, and to the faithful in the law of God and to its interpreters, its priests and Levites and all the tribes of Israel and Judah great and small. May the Lord strengthen your hearts in the Law and in the true prophet Moses, our teacher, the servant of the Lord!

And now we shall tell our brethren, the tribes of Jethrun, of Eldad the Danite, who relates all this, how he went forth in all the countries after being separated from the tribe of Dan and the Lord miraculously saved him in many places and from many troubles, which passed over him, till he came to this land, so that he might go and tell all the children of Israel, who are scattered in Israel, matters concerning him, that he might bring you good tidings of comfort and speak good words to your heart.

And this was my going forth from the other side of the rivers of Ethiopia.

I and a Jew of the tribe of Asher entered a small ship to trade with the shipmen and behold, at midnight, the Lord caused a great and strong wind to arise and the ship was wrecked. Now the Lord had prepared a box and I took hold of it and my companion seeing this also took hold of that box, and we went up and down with it, until the sea cast us among a people called Romranos who are black Ethiopians, tall, without garment or clothing upon them, cannibals, like unto the beasts of the field.

And when we came to their country they took hold of us and, seeing that my companion was fat and healthy and pleasing, slaughtered and ate him, and he cried, "Alas for me that I have been brought to this people and the Ethiopians will eat my flesh," but me they took, for I was sick on board ship, and they put me in chains until I should get fat and well, and they brought before me all kinds of good but forbidden food, but I ate nothing and I hid the food, and when they asked me if I had eaten I answered, yes I had eaten.

And I was with them a long time until the Lord, blessed be He, performed a miracle with me, for a great army came upon them from another place, who took me captive, but they despoiled and killed them and took me along with the captives.

And those wicked men were fire worshippers and I dwelt with them four years, and behold, every morning they made a great fire and bowed down and worshipped it. And they brought me to the province of Azania.

And a Jew, a merchant of the tribe of Issachar, found me and bought me for thirty-two gold pieces and brought me back with him to his country. They live in the mountains of the seacoast and belong to the land of the Medes and Persians. They fulfill the command "the book of this law shall not depart from thy mouth." The yoke of sovereignty is not upon them but only the yoke of law. Among them are leaders of hosts but they fight with no man. They only dispute as to the law and they live in peace and comfort and there is no disturber and no evil chance. They dwell in a country ten days journey by ten days, and they have great flocks and camels and asses and slaves, but they do not rear horses.

They carry no weapons, except the slaughterer's knife, and there is not among them any oppression or robbery and, even if they should find on the road garments or money, they would not stretch forth their hand to take it. But near them are wicked men, fire worshippers, who take their own mothers and sisters to wife, but them they do not hurt. They have a

Judge, and I asked about him and they said his name was Nachshon, and they practice the four death penalties according to the law, and they speak Hebrew and Persian.

And the sons of Zebulun are encamped in the hills of Paron and reach to their [i.e., Issachar's] neighborhood and pitch tents made of hairy skins which come to them from the land of Armenia, and they reach up to the Euphrates, and they practice business and they observe the four death penalties inflicted by the court.

And the tribe of Reuben is over against them behind Mount Paron, and there is peace and brotherhood and companionship between them, and they go together toward and make roads and divide the spoils amongst themselves, and they go on the highroads of the Kings of Media and Persia and they speak Hebrew and Persian, and they possess scripture and *Mishnah*, *Talmud*, and *Haggadah*. Every Sabbath they read the law with accents, the text in Hebrew and the interpretation [*Targum*] thereof in Persian.

And the tribe of Ephraim and the half tribe of Manasseh are there in the mountains over against the city of Mecca, the stumbling block of the Ishmaelites. They are strong of body and of iron heart. They are horsemen, and take the road and have no pity on their enemies, and their only livelihood comes of spoil. They are mighty men of war. One is match for a thousand.

And the tribe of Simeon and the half tribe of Manasseh live in the country of the Babylonians six months' journey away, and they are the most numerous of all of them, and they take tribute from five and twenty kingdoms and some Ishmaelites pay them tribute.

And in our country we say that it is a tradition among us that ye are the sons of the captivity, the tribe of Judah and the tribe of Benjamin under the dominion of the heathen in an unclean land, who were scattered under the Romans who destroyed the Temple of our God, and under the Greeks and the Ishmaelites, may their sword pierce their heart and may their bones be broken!

We have a tradition from father to son that we, the sons of

Dan, were aforetime in the land of Israel dwellers in tents and among all the tribes of Israel there were none like us men of war and mighty of valour. And, when Jeroboam, the son of Nebat, who caused Israel to sin and made two golden calves, arose over them, the kingdom of the house of David was divided and the tribes gathered together and said, "Come and fight against Rehoboam and against Jerusalem." They answered, "Why should we fight with our brothers and with the son of our Lord David, King of Israel and Judah? God forbid!" Then said the elders of Israel, "You have not in all the tribe of Israel mighty ones like the tribe of Dan." At once they said to the children of Dan, "Arise and fight with the children of Judah." They answered, "By the life of Dan our father, we will not make war with our brothers and we will not shed blood."

At once we children of Dan took swords and lances and bow, and devoted ourselves to death to go forth from the land of Israel, for we saw we could not stay, "Let us go hence and find a resting place, but if we wait until the end they will take us away." So we took heart and counsel to go to Egypt to destroy it and to kill all its inhabitants. Our prince said to us, "Is it not written, ye shall not continue to see it again for ever? How will you prosper?" They said, "Let us go against Amalek or against Edom or against Ammon and Moab to destroy them and let us dwell in their place." Our princes said, "It is written in the law that the Holy One, blessed be He, has prevented Israel from crossing their border."

Finally we took counsel to go to Egypt, but not by the way that our fathers went and not to destroy it, but only to go there to cross the River Pishon [Lower Nile] to the land of Ethiopia and behold, when we came near to Egypt, all Egypt was afraid and sent to us asking, "Is it war or peace?" and we said, "For peace; we will cross your country to the River Pishon, and there we will find a resting place,"and behold, they did not believe us, but all Egypt stood on guard until we crossed their country and arrived in the land of Ethiopia.

We found it a good and fat land, and, in it, fields, enclosures, and gardens. They could not restrain the children of Dan from dwelling with them, for they took the land by might and, behold, though they wished to kill them all, they had to pay tribute to Israel, and we dwelt with them many years, and increased and multiplied greatly and held great riches.

Afterwards Sennacherib, King of Assyria, arose and took the Reubenites and the Gadites and the half tribe of Manasseh captive, and took them to Halah and Habor and the River Goazan, and the cities of Media. And Sennacherib arose a second time and took captive the tribe of Asher and the tribe of Naphtali and led them to the land of Assyria, and, after the death of Sennacherib, three tribes of Israel, being Naphtali, Gad, and Asher, journeyed on their own to the land of Ethiopia and encamped in the wilderness until they came to their border, a twenty days' journey, and they slew the men of Ethiopia, and unto this very day, they fight with the children of the kingdoms of Ethiopia.

Eliezer of Maience (died 1357)

Unlike the Christian concept of a last will and testament which deals with money and material concerns, the ethical will still being written in some Jewish communities centers on the spiritual and religious heritage of parents to children. Spiritual deathbed statements appear as early in the Bible as Jacob's blessing of his sons. They also occur in the Apocrypha and the Talmud. Written ethical wills become common in the medieval period from the eleventh century on.

Like the *Responsa* and the *Midrash*, ethical wills are primary sources of history, giving insight not only into social and familial conventions, but also into the habits and amusements of individuals as well as their moral aspirations and the details of daily life. Consider the simple, modest statement of Eliezer of Maience, an ordinary Jew, who in his will entreats his children to avoid gambling and mixed bathing and dancing. Can there be any doubt of the popularity of these activities? Eliezer's instructions for his burial depict the funeral practices of the fourteenth century. His ethical admonitions, undoubtedly illustrative of the ideals of Jewish conduct, indicate why the Jews, although confined to crowded ghettos, were able to survive the plagues and the violent acts of anti-Semitism so common during the Middle Ages.

204

An Ethical Will

My grandfather's Testament to his children; and as it is a rule good for every God-fearer, I write it here, that all men may follow it.

A worthy Testament, whose ways are ways of pleasantness, proved and seemly for publishing to all the people.

These are the things which my sons and daughters shall do at my present request. They shall go to the house of prayer morning and evening, and shall pay special regard to the Tephillah and the Shema. So soon as the service is over, they shall occupy themselves a little with the Torah, the Psalms, or with works of charity. Their business must be conducted honestly in their dealings both with Jew and Gentile.

They must be gentle in their manners, and prompt to accede to ever honorable request. They must not talk more than is necessary; by this they will be saved from slander, falsehood, and frivolity. They shall give an exact tithe of all their possessions; they shall never turn away a poor man empty-handed, but must give him what they can, be it much or little. If he beg a lodging overnight, and they know him not, let them provide him with the wherewithal to pay an innkeeper. Thus shall they satisfy the needs of the poor in every possible way.

My daughters must obey scrupulously the rules applying to women; modesty, sanctity, reverence, should mark their married lives. They should carefully watch for the signs of the beginning of their periods and keep separate from their husbands at such times. Marital intercourse must be modest and holy, with a spirit of restraint and delicacy, in reverence and silence. They shall be very punctilious and careful with their ritual bathing, taking with them women friends of worthy character. They shall cover their eyes until they reach their home, on returning from the bath, in order not to behold anything of unclean nature. They must respect their husbands, and must be invariably amiable to them. Husbands, on their part, must honor their wives more than themselves, and treat them with tender consideration.

If they can by any means contrive it, my sons and daughters should live in communities, and not isolated from other Jews, so that their sons and daughters may learn the ways of Judaism. Even if compelled to solicit from others the money to pay a teacher, they must not let the young, of both sexes, go without instruction in the Torah. Marry your children, O my sons and daughters, as soon as their age is ripe, to members of respectable families. Let no child of mine hunt after money by making a low match for that object; but if the family is undistinguished only on the mother's side, it does not matter, for all Israel counts descent from the father's side.

Every Friday morning, they shall put themselves in careful trim for honoring the Sabbath, kindling the lamps while the day is still great, and in winter lighting the furnace before dark, to avoid desecrating the Sabbath [by kindling fire thereon]. For due welcome to the Sabbath, the women must prepare beautiful candles.

As to games of chance, I entreat my children never to engage in such pastimes. During the leisure of the festival weeks they may play for trifling in kind, and the women may amuse themselves similarly on New Moons, but never for money. In their relation to women, my sons must behave continentally, avoiding mixed bathing and mixed dancing and all frivolous conversation, while my daughters ought not to speak much with strangers nor jest nor dance with them. They ought to be always at home, and not be gadding about. They should not stand at the door, watching whatever passes. I ask, I command, that the daughters of my house be never without work to do, for idleness leads first to boredom, then to sin. But let them spin, or cook, or sew.

I earnestly beg my children to be tolerant and humble to all, as I was throughout my life. Should cause for dissension present itself, be slow to accept the quarrel; seek peace and pursue it with all the vigor at your command. Even if you suffer loss thereby, forbear and forgive, for God has many ways of feeding and sustaining His creatures. To the slanderer do not retaliate with counterattack; and though it be proper to rebut false accusation, yet is it most desirable to set an example of reticence. You yourselves must avoid uttering any slander, for so will you win affection. In trade be true, never grasping at what belongs to another. For by avoiding these wrongs—scandal, falsehood, money-grubbing—men will surely find tranquillity and affection. And against all evils, silence is the best safeguard.

Now, my sons and daughters, eat and drink only what is necessary, as our good parents did, refraining from heavy meals, and holding the gross liver in detestation. The regular adoption of such economy in food leads to economy in expenditure generally, with a consequent reluctance to pursue after wealth, but the acquisition of a contented spirit, simplicity in diet, and many good results. Concerning such a well-ordered life the text says: "The righteous eateth to the satisfaction of his desire." Our teachers have said: "Methods in expenditure are half a sufficiency." Nevertheless, accustom yourselves and your wives, your sons and your daughters, to wear nice and clean clothes, that God and man may love and honor you. In this direction do not exercise too strict a parsimony. But on no account adopt foreign fashions in dress. After the manner of your fathers order your attire, and let your clothes be broad without buckles attached.

Be on your guard concerning vows, and cautious as to promise. The breach of one's undertakings leads to many lapses. Do not get into the habit of exclaiming "Gott!," but speak always of the "Creator, blessed be He"; and in all that you propose to do, today or tomorrow, add the proviso, "If the Lord wills, I shall do this thing." Thus remember God's part in your life.

Whatever happiness befall you, be it in monetary fortune or in the birth of children, be it some signal deliverances or any other of the many blessings which may come to you, be not stolidly unappreciative like dumb cattle that utter no word of gratitude. But offer praises to the Rock who has befriended you, saying: "O give thanks unto the Lord, for He is good, for His mercy endureth forever. Blessed art Thou, O Lord, who art good and dispenseth good."

Besides thanking God for His bounties at the moment they

occur, also in your regular prayers let the memory of these personal favors prompt your hearts to special fervor during the utterance of the communal thanks. When words of gratitude are used in the liturgy, pause to reflect in silence on the goodness of God to you that day. And when ye make the response: "May Thy great Name be blessed," call to mind your own personal experience of the divine favor.

Be very particular to keep your house clean and tidy. I was always scrupulous on this point, for every injurious condition, and sickness and poverty, are to be found in foul dwellings. Be careful over the benedictions; accept no divine gift without paying back the Giver's part; and His part is man's grateful acknowledgment.

Every one of these good qualities becomes habitual with him who studies the Torah; for that study indeed leads to the formation of a noble character. Therefore, happy is he who toils in the Law! For this gracious toil fix daily times, of long or short duration, or it is the best of all works that a man can do. Week by week read at least the set portion with the commentary of Rashi. And when your prayer is ended day by day, turn ever to the word of God, in fulfilment of the Psalmist's injunction, "passing from strength to strength."

And O, my sons and daughters, keep yourselves far from the snare of frivolous conversation, which begins in tribulation and ends in destruction. Nor be ye found in the company of these light talkers. Judge ye rather every man charitably and use your best efforts to detect an honorable explanation of conduct however suspicious. Try to persuade yourselves that it was your neighbor's zeal for some good end that led him to the conduct you deplore. This is the meaning of the exhortation: "In righteousness shalt thou judge thy neighbor. " To sum up, the fewer one's idle words the less one's risk of slander, lying, flattery—all of them, things held in utter detestation by God.

On holidays and festivals and Sabbaths seek to make happy the poor, the unfortunate, widows and orphans, who should always be guests at your tables; their joyous entertainment is a religious duty. Let me repeat my warning against gossip and scandal. And as ye speak no scandal, so listen to none, for if there were none received there would be no bearers of slanderous tales; therefore, the reception and credit of slander is as serious an offense as the originating of it. The less you say, the less cause you give for animosity, while in the multitude of words thee wanteth not transgression.

Always be of those who see and are not seen, who hear and are not heard. Accept no invitation to banquets, except to such as are held for religious reasons: at wedding and at meals prepared for mourners, at gatherings to celebrate entry into the covenant of Abraham, or at assemblies in honor of the wise. Games of chance, for money stakes, such as dicing, must be avoided. And as I have already warned you about that, again let me urge you to show forbearance and humility to all men, to ignore abuses levelled at you, but the indignant refutation of charges against your moral character is fully justifiable.

Be of the first ten in Synagogue, rising betimes for the purpose. Pray steadily with the congregation, giving due value to every letter and word, seeing that there are in the Shema 248 words, corresponding to the 248 limbs in the human body. Be careful too to let the prayer for redemption be followed immediately by the eighteen benedictions. Do not talk during service, but listen to the precentor, and respond, "Amen" at the proper time.

After the morning prayer, read the Chapter about the Mannah, the passages associated with it, and the eleven verses, with due attention to clear enunciation. Then recite a Psalm in lieu of a reading in the Torah; though it were well not to omit the latter passing, as I said above, from strength to strength, from prayer to the Bible, before turning to worldly pursuits. Or if ye can perform some act of loving-kindness, it is accounted as equal to the study of the Law.

I beg of you, my sons and daughters, my wife, and all the congregation, that no funeral oration be spoken in my honor. Do not carry my body on a bier but in a coach. Wash me clean, comb my hair, trim my nails, as I was wont to do in my lifetime, so that I may go clean to my eternal rest, as I went

clean to Synagogue every Sabbath day. If the ordinary officials dislike the duty, let adequate payment be made to some
poor man who shall render this service carefully and not
perfunctorily.

At a distance of thirty cubits from the grave, they shall set
my coffin on the ground, and drag me to the grave by a rope
attached to the coffin. Every four cubits they shall stand and
wait awhile, doing this in all seven times, so that I may find
atonement for my sins. Put me aside in the ground at the right
hand of my fathers, and if the space be a little narrow, I am
sure that he loves me well enough to make room for me by his
side. If this be altogether impossible, put me on his left, or near
my grandmother, Yuta. Should this also be impractical, let me
be buried by the side of my daughter.

Anne Frank (1929-1945)

Anne Frank, a Dutch teenager, became famous posthumously for her diary-journal written in an Amsterdam attic while hiding from the Nazis with her family and four other Jews. Discovered after she died in Bergen-Belsen, a concentration camp, it has been published in numerous languages, produced as a play on most of the world's leading stages, and made into a popular motion picture. In both its written and dramatic form Anne Frank's diary-journal is cherished for its poignancy, psychological insight, and literary talent. Written between June 14, 1942 and August 1, 1944, the diary-journal records in unpretentious yet beautiful language the reactions of each of the members of the trapped group. The young girl's optimism, yearning for freedom, and love of others has had so deep an emotional impact on millions of people that she has become a symbol of the wonderful Jewish children the world lost in the Holocaust.

Wednesday, 29, December, 1943

Dear Kitty,

I was very unhappy again last evening. Granny and Lies came into my mind. Granny, oh, darling Granny, how little we understood of what she suffered, or how sweet she was. And besides all this, she knew a terrible secret which she carefully kept to herself the whole time.[1] How faithful and good Granny always was; she would never have let one of us down. Whatever it was, however naughty I had been, Granny always stuck up for me.

Granny, did you love me or didn't you understand me either? I don't know. No one ever talked about themselves to Granny. How lonely Granny must have been, how lonely in spite of us! A person can be lonely even if he is loved by many people, because he is still not the "One and Only" to anyone.

And Lies, is she still alive? What is she doing? Oh, God, protect her and bring her back to us. Lies, I see in you all the time what my lot might have been. I keep seeing myself in your place. Why then should I often be unhappy over what happens here? Shouldn't I always be glad, contented, and happy, except when I think about her and her companions in distress? I am selfish and cowardly. Why do I always dream and think of the most terrible things—my fear makes me want to scream out loud sometimes. Because still, in spite of everything, I have not enough faith in God. He has given me so much—which I certainly do not deserve—and I still do so much that is wrong every day. If you think of your fellow creatures, then you only want to cry, you could really cry the whole day long. The only thing to do is to pray that God will perform a miracle and save some of them. And I hope that I am doing that enough.

Yours, Anne

---

[1] A severe internal disease.

Glückel of Hameln (1646-1724)

The charming reminiscences of the life and times of Glückel of Hameln are today given the title of *Memoirs*. Glückel herself is so modest as to write that she does not deserve an autobiography. Even so, her *Memoirs* shed much light on a world shaken by the Thirty Years War, massacres of Jews in 1648 and 1649, and the messianic fiasco of Sabbatai Zevi.

To assuage her loneliness as a widow and to inculcate her husband's ethics into the hearts of her children, Glückel tells us that she began the *Memoirs* in 1691. (She was to complete seven "books," parts of them copied out for her by her children.) Glückel held a simple faith in God's providence, describing humbly and with stoic equanimity her own vicissitudes as wife and widow, rich and poor. Writing in the Judeo-German of the time, she quotes from the Bible, Talmud, and Siddur (prayer book) and fills her pages with Hebraisms.

Glückel vividly pictures not only her own personality but also the appearance and character of many of the personages with whom she came into contact. She makes clear many different aspects of German-Jewish life, telling of private and public affairs with innumerable details of human interest, as when narrating how merchants combined business with

213

matchmaking. No wonder scholars regard Glückel's *Memoirs* as an invaluable resource.

Zipporah's Wedding

When my eldest child, my daughter Zipporah, was nearly twelve years of age, Reb Loeb, the son of Reb Anshel of Amsterdam, broached a match with Kessmann, the son of Reb Elia Cleve. My husband, of blessed memory, left six weeks earlier than usual on his half-yearly visit to Amsterdam and wrote to the matchmaker to meet him there to see what could be done. At that time there was a war in progress,[1] and Elia Cleve and his family were forced to move from Cleve to Amsterdam. On my husband's arrival in that town, rumor spread that he was about to ally himself by marriage with Reb Elia. This was on Post day when people read their letters on the Bourse. Many disputed the tale and there was much wagering, for Elia Cleve was a very wealthy man worth 100,000 or more Reichstaler. My husband was then still quite a young man, just beginning to get on nicely in business, and there was a houseful of young children, God protect them. What God proposes must indeed come to pass, however much people may dislike it. Is it not proclaimed in Heaven forty days before birth that this man's son shall wed that man's daughter?

So it came to pass that my husband joined himself through marriage with the wealthy Elia Cleve, our daughter's dowry being settled at 2,200 Reichstaler in Dutch money. The date of the marriage was fixed for eighteen months later, at Cleve; my husband to pay one hundred Reichstaler towards the wedding expenses.

When the time of the wedding drew very near, we left for Cleve—my husband, I with a babe at the breast, the bride Zipporah, Rabbi Meyer of Klaus who is now rabbi in Fried-

---

[1]   Louis XIV's war against Holland, 1672.

burg, our man-servant Fine Shmuel and a maid—quite a handsome retinue. In company with Mordecai Cohen, Meyer Ilius and Aaron Todliche we went from Altona by boat. I cannot describe the jolly and merriment of our journey. In joy and happiness we arrived at Amsterdam three weeks before the wedding. We stayed with Reb Loeb Hamburger, whom I have already mentioned, and spent more than twelve ducats every week. But we did not mind this as during this time my husband, of blessed memory, did some business and earned more than half the dowry.

Fourteen days before the wedding, with music and hilarity, a company of twenty, we travelled to Cleve and were there received with great honor. Reb Elia Cleve's house was really like a king's palace, handsomely furnished in every way—like a lord's mansion. We had no rest all day from eminent and distinguished visitors who came to see the bride. In truth my daughter was really beautiful and had no equal. There was a great excitement in preparation for the wedding.

At that time Prince Frederick[2] was in Cleve. The senior prince, the Elector, was alive, and Frederick was yet a lad little more than thirteen. Soon after, the Elector died and Frederick became Elector in his place. Prince Maurice[3] and his court, too, were there. Their curiosity was aroused and they made it known that they wished to be present at the wedding. It may easily be imagined what preparations Reb Elia Cleve made for such distinguished guests.

On the wedding day, soon after the marriage ceremony, there was a collation of all kinds of the finest sweetnesses, foreign wines and fruits out of season. How can one describe all the excitement! How all the thoughts of Reb Elia Cleve and his family were taken up with the reception and accommodation of the visitors! There was not even time to produce and count the dowries, as is the custom at such times. So we put our dowry and Reb Elia his dowry into a bag and sealed it, to be counted after the wedding.

When we stood all together under the canopy with the bride

---

[2]   Later Elector of Brandenberg, and in 1701 King Frederick I of Prussia.
[3]   Prince of Nassau.

and bridegroom we found that in the great excitement the Ketubah had not been drawn up! What was to be done? All the distinguished guests and the young Prince stood about waiting to see the ceremony under the canopy. Rabbi Meyer advised that the bridegroom might appoint a surety who would undertake that the ketubah would be written directly after the ceremony. In the meantime we were to continue with the marriage. And so it was, the rabbi reading the ketubah from a book.

After the ceremony all the distinguished guests were led into the great hall, the walls of which were lined with gilded leather. A long table covered with regal delicacies stood in the center, each guest being served in order of rank. My son Mordecai was then about five years old; there was no more beautiful child in the whole world and we had dressed him neatly and prettily. The courtiers nearly swallowed him for admiration, especially the Prince who held his hand the whole time. After the courtiers and other guests had consumed the confects and enjoyed the wine, the table was cleared and removed. Masked dancers entered and presented different poses quite nicely and suitably to the entertainment. They ended with the Dutch Dance. It was all very splendidly done.

Among the guests there were also many Portuguese [Jews], one of whom was a jeweler of the name of Mocatti who had with him a beautiful little golden watch set in diamonds, worth 500 Reichstaler. Reb Elia asked Mocatti for the little watch, desiring to present it to the young Prince. But a good friend, standing close by, said to him. "Why should you do this? To give such an expensive present to the young Prince? It is not as if he were the Elector." But, as I have already mentioned, the Elector died soon after, and the young prince, he is still Elector, succeeded him. Thereafter whenever Elia Cleve met the friend who prevented him giving the present, he would throw it up angrily at him. And in truth, if Elia Cleve had given the present the Prince would never have forgotten it, for great people never forget such things. Well, why cry for what has gone?

The young Prince, Prince Maurice, and all the courtiers enjoyed themselves and left fully satisfied. For a hundred years no Jew had had such high honor. The wedding-day ended in joy and gladness.

Jehudah Halevi (c. 1080-c. 1140)

A skillful poet famous for religious hymns and songs of Zion, Jehudah Halevi also made his mark in *Al Kusari*. Originally written in Arabic and then translated into Hebrew, *The Kusari* was inspired by an exchange of letters between Ibn Shapnet, the great Jewish statesman of Spain, and Joseph, the last king of Kusaria, a Tartar nation whose rulers had adopted Judaism.

In *The Kusari* Jehudah Halevi utilized the legendary story of the conversion of the Kusars in 749 C.E. A Rabbi, Christian, and Moslem hold a dialogue on the virtues of the religion of each, after which King Bulan chooses Judaism. Jehudah Halevi's purpose is to defend traditional Judaism against the inroads of secular philosophy, particularly the rational speculations of the Greeks. He maintains that trying to reconcile Judaism with reason is futile because the Bible, which is super-rational, depends on revelation. The Jewish people, to use Halevi's phraseology, are the heart of world society, purifying and distributing lifeblood to the nations. In the Diaspora, the life of individuals and of the nation is incomplete, but the sufferings of exile will cleanse the Jews of sin and prepare them for restoration, which will occur as soon as the Jews again settle in Israel. Afterward, the Jews will bring redemption and salvation to all the other peoples of the world.

In the course of his argument, Halevi takes up many problems, among them free will, God's providence, and anthropomorphisms in the Bible. Some passages in *The Kusari* on the nature of Hebrew elucidate aspects of grammar and phonetics.

The Kusari

The Christian replied: I believe that all things were created, that God is eternal, and that he created the whole world in six days, and that all men are descended firstly from Adam, and secondly from Noah, to whom they are accordingly related. God provides for all his creatures, but entertains special relations towards man: with him is wrath, mercy, and favour; he speaks with his prophets and his saints: he appears and reveals himself to them, dwelling amongst those that please him. I believe in general all that is written in the law, and all the traditions of the children of Israel, facts which it is impossible to doubt since they are so fully known, so imperishable, and were so loudly proclaimed before a great multitude. Then (afterwards), however, the Godhead was incarnate, and took flesh in the womb of a virgin, one of the noblest women in Israel, who bore him in semblance human, in mystery divine—in semblance a prophet, in mystery God. This was the Messiah, called the Son of God, and this is the mystery of Father, Son and Holy Ghost, although when we proclaim the Trinity it is really the Unity only which we believe. I believe further that the Messiah dwelt amongst Israel for their glory, so long as they adhered to the idea of the Godhead (manifest in him), but that at last they rebelled against him and crucified him. From that time till now, the wrath of God had continued against the multitude of the rebellious, but (His) grace has been upon every one of those who followed the Messiah, as well as upon the nations which have followed them, and to which we belong. We are not, indeed, descendants of the family of Israel, but we are worthier than they are to bear their name, because we have followed the Messiah, and the twelve apostles who represent the twelve tribes. A great number of Israelites followed the Twelve: these formed the nucleus of the Christian people, and well did they deserve the rank and title of Israel's sons. We have become powerful in different lands: and all nations are invited to attach themselves to this creed, and enjoined to glorify the Messiah and His cross. Our laws and customs are derived partly from the commandments of the Apostle Simon (Peter), partly from the Torah, which we read, and the truth of which is beyond question: for the Gospel itself relates what the Messiah said:—I came not to destroy one title of the law of Moses, but to confirm and explain it.

The king replied: To argue on this subject is quite useless; for reason rejects most of what thou hast said. Only when the evidence and proof of a fact is so manifest to all that every man, from utter inability to confute it, is bound to accord belief, can reason come in to explain any part of it which may appear strange. In fact this is the method pursued by scientific men for explaining the wonderful occurrences of nature which, so long as they are simply related without having been seen, they ignore; but after having examined them, they express a definite opinion and try to assign their causes, either in the stars or in the winds, inasmuch as the evidence for them cannot be denied. Moreover, the words are new to me; and as I have not been trained up in them, I am disinclined to accept them without a thorough investigation.

The king called next a learned Mohammedan to enquire concerning the belief and practices of Mohammedanism. His answer was as follows: We affirm the unity and eternity of God, the creation of the world, and the descent of the whole human race from Adam and from Noah. We deny in general the corporeality of God, endeavoring to explain any difficulty which may here meet us by saying that the expression which occasions it is only metaphorical or approximately true. We are bound to confess that the Koran is the Word of God: for the Koran is in itself a miracle, inasmuch as no man could compose such a book as it is, or even a single chapter of it, and we are therefore of course compelled to accept it even for its own sake. I believe further that our prophet is the last of the prophets, that he annulled all the laws in existence before him, and that he invites all nations to attach themselves to Islam. The recompense of the obedient will be that in Paradise his soul will return to his body, and that there he will live in the midst of delights, with plenty to eat and drink, and every other pleasure he may desire; the punishment of the rebellious will be the condemnation to dwell after death in a fire where his pains will never cease.

The King of the Khazars answered: one who undertakes to guide a man in the right way concerning the knowledge of God, and to convince him of what he denies, namely that God had held intercourse with flesh, can only do so successfully by the help of irrefragable evidences: only thus I repeat, could one who doubts be persuaded that God had held intercourse with flesh. If your book is a miracle because it is written in Arabic, it certainly cannot be regarded as such by a foreigner like myself: if read to me, it makes no other impression upon me than any other book in the same language.

The Mohammedan replied:—Miracles were indeed wrought by the Prophet, but they are not given as areas on for accepting his law.

The Khazar said:—A man can only be led to believe that God entertains relations with flesh through some miracle by which the nature of a thing is changed, and in which he may be enabled to perceive that the change could only have been caused by him who created all things out of nothing: moreover, this change must have been seen by a multitude, and not known merely from traditions and tales: and it must have been submitted to a searching examination, else it might be accounted for by the power of the imaginations or by collusion. These great principles, viz., that God who has created both this world and the next, the angels, the heavens and the light, entertains relations with man, who is a piece of impure clay, that he speaks with him and answers his requests and wishes, might be believed on the evidence of miracles (but in no other way).

The learned Mohammedan answered:—Is not our book

filled with narratives respecting Moses and the children of Israel? No one is able to deny what God did unto Pharaoh; how he divided the sea, and saved those whom he loved but drowned those with whom he was wroth; how he gave them manna and quails by the space of 40 years, and spoke with Moses upon Sinai; how he made the sun stand still for Joshua, and helped him against the giants. Neither again, is it possible to deny what he did at the time of the deluge, and how he destroyed the people of Lot.* All this is sufficiently clear, and there can be no suspicion of the operation of imagination or of collusion.

The King of the Khazars then said:—There can be no longer any doubt that I must enquire of the Jews, who are the remnant of the ancient Israelites: for I see that all the proofs for the existence of God's law upon earth are derived ultimately from them. He accordingly called a learned Jew and questioned him about the principles of his faith.

---

* The inhabitants of Sodom and Gomorrah are called by Mohammedan writers "the people of Lot."

Maimonides (Moses Ben Maimon)
(1135-1205)

"From Moses to Moses, there was none like Moses" is a frequently quoted epigram in which there is much truth. Titanic figures, both men had an influence deep and lasting. Their achievements mark off milestones of human progress. Appearing in an era of brutish superstition, each man advocated faith regulated by reason. And by emancipating the human mind, each Moses led the Jews to freedom.

A polymath and the greatest Jewish philosopher of the Middle Ages, Moses Ben Maimon was called Rambam (Rabbenu Moishe Ben Maimon) by Jews, Maimonides by Christians. Today, he is famous worldwide as Maimonides. Born in Cordova, he fled from Spain and persecution, wandering through Morocco and Palestine, settling at last in Egypt. There he practiced medicine, becoming in time personal physician to the Sultan and to the *Nagid* (head) of Egyptian Jewry.

Although born in the medieval period, Maimonides was a renaissance man of indefatigable industry with an encyclopedic mind that encompassed the Bible, the Talmud, astronomy, ethics, mathematics, medicine, and philosophy. His first major work was a treatise on the Calendar, his second an elucidation of logic, his third a commentary on the *Mishnah*. Then came his masterpiece, *Mishneh Torah*, and finally the *Guide for the Perplexed*. He also wrote numerous Responsa accepted as legally authoritative by Jews all over the world.

The *Mishneh Torah* and *Guide for the Perplexed* were immediately controversial. Whole communities split into factions for and against. Some Jewish opponents denounced the volumes to the Inquisition, which burned many copies in the 1230s. After a century of fierce debate, Jews accepted the work of Maimonides as authoritative. Both volumes became universally popular and remain so today.

In the *Mishneh Torah*, Maimonides attempted to codify the law according to subject matter rather than to the winding sequence of Talmudic discussion. He writes that his hope is for an arrangement so systematic "that the entire Oral Law will be clearly ordered for everyone, without question and answer, without differences of opinion." Concise and logical, Maimonides is excellent at classification, skillfully subsuming subordinate subject matter under appropriate rubrics. He divided the entire labyrinthine mass of the Talmud into fourteen distinctly demarcated and readily followed parts. So clear, so practical is the *Mishneh Torah* that it became the model, if not the basis, for later codes.

In *Guide for the Perplexed*, written in the form of letters to a disciple, Maimonides states that his aim is to help those who cannot harmonize reason and religion, Aristotelian philsophy and Rabbinic Judaism. But he is interested neither in compromise nor in building a bridge from Athens to Jerusalem. The Torah, he argues, is not to be taken literally. Its language carries moral, philosopical, and spiritual meanings often expressed in allegory or symbol. Medieval churchmen, such as Aquinas and Duns Scotus, admired Maimonides and applied some of his methods to smoothing out inconsistencies of Roman Catholic theology.

Precepts

Mishneh Torah

Chapter II.

1. Teachers of young children are to be appointed in each province, district and town. If a city has made no provision for the education of the young, its inhabitants are placed under a

ban, till such teachers have been engaged. And if they persistently neglect this duty, the city is excommunicated, for the world is only maintained by the breath of school children.

2. Children are to be sent to school at the age of six or seven years, according to the strength of the individual child and its physical development. But no child is to be sent to school under six years of age. The teacher may chastise his pupils to inspire them with awe. But he must not do so in a cruel manner or in a vindictive spirit. Accordingly, he must not strike them with whips or sticks, but only use a small strap. He is to teach them the whole day and part of the night, so as to train them to study by day and by night. And there is to be no holiday except on the eve of the Sabbath or festival, towards the close of the day, and on festivals. On Sabbaths, pupils are not taught a new lesson, but they repeat what they had already learnt previously, even if only once. Pupils must not be interrupted at their studies, even for the re-building of the Temple.

3. A teacher who leaves the children and goes out (when he should be teaching them), or does other work while he is with them, or teaches lazily, falls under the ban "Cursed be he that doeth the work of the Lord with a slack hand" (Jer. 48:10). Hence, it is not proper to appoint any one as teacher unless he is God-fearing and well versed in reading and in grammar.

4. An unmarried man should not keep school for the young because the mothers come to see their children. Nor should a woman keep school, because the fathers come to see them.

5. Twenty-five children may be put in the charge of one teacher. If the number in the class exceeds twenty-five but is not more than forty, he should have an assistant to help with the instruction. If there are more than forty, two teachers must be appointed.

6. A child may be transferred from one teacher to another who is more competent in reading or grammar, only however, if both teacher and the pupil live in the same town and are not separated by a river. But we must not take the child to school in another town nor even across a river in the same town, unless it is spanned by a firm bridge, not likely soon to collapse.

7. If one of the residents in an alley or even in a court wishes to open a school, his neighbors cannot prevent him. Nor can a teacher, already established, object to another teacher opening a school next door to him, either for new pupils or even with the intention of drawing away pupils from the existing school, for it is said, "The Lord was pleased for His righteousness sake, to make the Torah great and glorious" [Is. 42:21].

Thirteen Principles of Faith (Ani Ma'amin)

The Thirteen Principles of Faith composed by Moses Maimonides appears in two forms in the Siddur; the poetic version in the *Yigdal* and the prose in the mourning service, as a supplemental addition.

Although many of his contemporaries, as well as many who came after him, did not endorse the Thirteen Principles, there have been thousands and thousands of adherents who subscribe to the creed without question. During the Holocaust many pious Jews went to their death chanting the *Ani Ma'amin*: "I believe with complete faith."

The Thirteen Principles of Faith

1. I believe with complete faith that the Creator, blessed be He, is both the Creator and Guide of all His creations, and that He alone has made, does make and will make all things.

2. I believe with complete faith that the Creator, blessed be His name, is One and that there is no other Unity that can be compared and that He alone is our God, past, present, and future.

3. I believe with complete faith that the Creator, blessed be His name, is not corporal, and that He is free from all bodily substance, and that He has not any form at all.

4. I believe with complete faith that the Creator, blessed be His name, is the first as well as the last.

5. I believe with complete faith that to the Creator, blessed be His name, and only to Him, is it fitting to pray and to no other beside Him should we pray.

6. I believe with complete faith that all the words of the prophets are true.

7. I believe with complete faith that the prophecy of our teacher Moses, peace unto him, was true, and that he was foremost of the prophets, both of those who came before and those who came after him.

8. I believe with complete faith that the entire Torah which we now have in our possession is the very same given to Moses our teacher, peace be unto him.

9. I believe with complete faith that the Torah will not be altered and that there will never be another one from the Creator, blessed be His name.

10. I believe with complete faith that the Creator, blessed be His Name, knows all the actions of mankind and all their thoughts, as is said, " It is He that formed the hearts of all of them and is mindful of their actions."

11. I believe with complete faith that the Creator, blessed be His name, rewards those who obey His commandments and punishes those who go against His commandments.

12. I believe with complete faith in the coming of the Messiah, and even though He delay, still will I daily await his coming.

13. I believe with complete faith that there will be a revival of the dead at the time when it will be the will of the Creator, blessed be His name and exalted His renown throughout all time.

(Tr. L. L.)

Moses Mendelsohn (1729-1786)

One of the tragic ironies of modern Jewish history is that many who called themselves followers of Moses Mendelsohn were ready to sacrifice Jewish tradition and religion for emancipation. Rather than try to rehabilitate Jewish life and bring about a renaissance of Jewish culture, Mendelsohn's goal, they sought escape from anything Jewish. Others misunderstood Mendelsohn's views as implying the repudiation of Judaism although he made absolutely clear his unequivocal advocacy of Jewish law and tradition, carrying his Jewishness openly and with dignity—as the great German playwright Lessing showed in *Nathan the Wise*. Even the name Mendelsohn took proclaims his Jewishness: his father's name was Mendel, hence Mendelsohn.

Frequently termed the German Socrates and the Father of the Jewish Enlightenment Movement—he attained remarkable proficiency in philosophy, mathematics, literature, and languages—Mendelsohn sought to use his fame and popularity for the betterment of the Jewish people. He fought hard for Jewish emancipation, arguing strongly for separation of church and state, and waged an uncompromising assault against those Christians hostile to Jews and Judaism. He sought not so much to reform as

228

to renovate. He attempted to get the Jews to remedy their ills themselves by adjusting their ways and customs to changing circumstances, particularly by increasing their knowledge of secular subjects. Mendelsohn translated the Pentateuch into German, appending to it a Hebrew commentary by himself and others for a dual purpose: to help speed the spread of modern culture among Jews by inspiring them to exchange Yiddish for German, and to reveal the beauty of Hebrew and evoke a renaissance of the language.

In *Jerusalem* (1783) Mendelsohn argued that all faiths are good so long as they lead people to good behavior. Especially critical of dogmas he writes that he values religion for its ethical and moral principles, considering that religion best which is most tolerant and which encompasses the entire human race in love. Viewing Judaism as an amalgam of reason and law, he calls it an ideal religion whose precepts are judged by deeds in observance of God's commandments.

Convictions

The Ideal Government

"Which form of government is the best?" is a question which has hitherto been answered in many different ways, seemingly all equally correct. The fact, however, is: it is too indefinite a question, nearly as much as as another of the same sort in medicine, viz., "Which kind of food is wholesomest?" Every constitution, every climate, every age, sex, profession, etc., requires a different answer. And so does our politico-philosophical problem. For every people, for every stage of civilization at which that people has arrived, another form of government may be the best. Many despotically-ruled nations would feel very miserable were they left to govern themselves; and so would high-spirited republicans if subjected to a monarch. Nay, many a nation, as improvements, general habits and principles undergo changes in it, will change also its form of government, and, in the course of ages, run the whole round from anarchy to absolutism in all their shades and modifications, and yet be found to have all along chosen the form of government which was best for them under existing circumstances.

But under every circumstance, and with every proviso, I think it an unerring standard of a good government, the more there is under it, wrought by morality and persuasions, and accordingly, the more the people are governed by education itself. In other words, the more opportunity there is given the citizen to see evidently that he foregoes some of his rights for the public good only; that he sacrifices part of his own interest to beneficence only; and that therefore he gains on the one side as much by acts of beneficence as on the other, he loses by sacrifices. Nay, that by sacrificing he even profits in inward happiness, because it enhances the merit and dignity of the action, and, therefore, also increases the true perfection of the beneficent himself. So it is, for instance, not advisable for the state to charge itself with all offices of philanthropy, not even the distributing of charity excepted, and convert them into public establishments. Man feels his own worth when he is acting liberally; when it is obvious to him that by his gift the alleviates the distress of a fellow-creature; that is, when he gives because he *pleases*; but when he gives because he *must*, he feels only his fetters.

It ought, therefore, to be the chief endeavor of the state to govern mankind by morals and persuasions. Now there is no other way of improving men's principles, and by means of them also their morals, but conviction. Laws will not alter persuasions. Arbitrary punishments or rewards generate no maxims, nor do they improve morals. Fear and hope are no criterions of truth. Knowledge, reasoning, convictions: they alone bring forth principles which, through credit and example, may pass into manner.

The Office of Religion

Religion must step in to assist the state, and the church become the supporter of civil happiness. It behooves her to convince the people, in the most emphatic manner, of the truth of noble sentiments and persuasions; to show them that the duties to man are also duties to God, the transgressing of which is itself the greatest misery; that serving one's country is true religion; probity and justice the commandment of God; charity His most holy will; and that a right knowledge of the Creator will not let misanthropy harbor long in the creature's heart. To teach this is the office, duty, and vocation of the Church; to preach it, the office, duty, and vocation of her ministers. How could it ever have entered men's thoughts to let the Church teach and her ministers preach quite the reverse?

But when the characters of a people, the stage of civilization at which it has arrived, a population swelled along with its national prosperity, multiplied relations and alliances, over-grown luxury, and other causes render it impossible to govern it by persuasions only, the state has recourse to public institutions, compulsory laws, punishments of crime, and reward of virtue. If a citizen will not come forward in the defense of the country from an inward feeling of his duty, let him be either allured by rewards or compelled by force. If people have no longer a sense of the intrinsic value of justice; if they no longer acknowledge that uprightness of life and dealing is true happiness, let injustice be corrected; let fraud be punished.

In this manner, it is true, the state gains the object of society only by half. External motives do not render him happy on whom they do nevertheless act. He who escheweth fraud from love and honesty is far happier than he who only dreads the arbitrary penalty which the state attaches to fraud; but to his fellow-man it is of little consequence from what motives evil-doing is refrained, or by what means his rights and property are secured to him. The country is defended all the same, whether the citizen fight for it from patriotism, or from fear of positive punishment; although the citizen himself is happy in the former case, and unhappy in the latter. If the internal happiness of society cannot be entirely preserved, at last external peace and security must, at any rate, be enforced.

Accordingly, the state is, if need be, contented with dead works with services without spirit, with consonance of action without consonance of thought. Even he who thinks nothing of laws must do as the law bids, when once it has been sanctioned. The individual citizen may be allowed the privilege of judging of the laws, but not that of acting up to his judgment; for, as a member of society, he was obliged to surrender that right, because without such surrender a social compact would be a chimera. Not so religion!

Religion knows of no action without persuasion, of no work without spirit, of no consonance of acting without consonance of thought. Religious observances without religious thoughts are ideal boys' play and no worship; this, as such, must, therefore, proceed from the spirit, and can neither be purchased by rewards nor enforced by punishments. But from civil actions also religion withdraws its auspices, so far as they are not produced by principle but by authority. Nor has the state to expect any further co-operation of religion when it cannot act otherwise than by rewards and punishments; for when that is the case, the duties toward God cease to be of any consideration; and the relations between man and his creator have no effect. All the help religion can then lend the state consists in teaching and comforting. It instills, by its divine lessons, into the citizen, principles tending to public utility; and, with its superhuman consolation, supports the malefactor doomed to die for the public good.

Church vs. State

There appears an essential difference between the state and religion. The state dictates and coerces; religion teaches and persuades. The state enacts laws; religion gives commandments. the state is armed with physical force, and makes use of it need be; the force of religion is love and benevolence. The former renounces the undutiful, and thrusts him out; the latter receives him in its bosom, and yet, in the last moments of his present life, tries, not quite unavailingly, to instruct, or, at least, to console him. In one word: civil society, as a moral entity, may have compulsory rights, nay, was actually invested with them by the social compact; religious society lays no claim to it; nor can all the compacts in the world confer it on it. The state possesses perfect rights; the church only imperfect rights....

Of Human Progress

In respect to the human race at large, you do not perceive a constant progress of improvement that looks as if approaching nearer and nearer to perfection. On the contrary, we see the human race, as a whole, subject to slight side swings; and it never yet made some steps forward but what it did, soon after, slide back again into its previous station, with double the celerity. Most nations of the earth pass many ages in the same degree of civilization, in the same crepusculous light, which appears much too dim to our spoiled eyes. Now and then, a particle of the grand mass will kindle, become a bright star, and run through an orbit which, now after a longer, now after a shorter period, brings it back again to its standstill, or sets it down at no great distance from it. Man goes on; but mankind is constantly swinging to and fro, within fixed boundaries; but, considered as a whole, retains, at all periods to time, about the same degree of morality, the same quality of religion and irreligion, of virtue and vice, of happiness and misery; the same result, when the same is taken into account against the same; of all the good and evil as much as was required for the transit of individual man, in order that they might be trained here on earth, and approach as near to perfection as was allotted and appointed to every one of them.

On Freedom of Conscience

Brethren, if it be genuine piety you are aiming against at, let us not feign uniformity when variety is, evidently, the design and end of Providence. None of us feels and thinks exactly alike with his fellow-man; then, wherefore impose upon one another by deceiving words? We are, alas, prone enough to do so, in our ordinary transactions, in our general conversation, comparatively of no material importance; but wherefore also in things involving our spiritual and temporal welfare, and constituting the whole purpose of our creation? God has not stamped on every man a peculiar countenance for nothing: why, then, should we, in the most solemn concerns of life, render ourselves unknown to one another, by disguise? Is not this resisting Providence so far as with us lies? Is it not frustrating the designs of creation, if it were possible, and purposely acting against our vocation and destiny, both in this life and that to come?

Regents of the earth, if an insignificant fellow-inhabitant of it may be allowed to life up his voice unto ye, O listen not to the counselors who, in smooth words, would misguide you to so promiscuous an undertaking. They are either blind themselves and cannot see the enemy of mankind lurking in ambush, or they want to blind you. If you hearken to them, our brightest jewel, freedom of consciousness, is lost. For your happiness' sake, and for ours, religious union is not toleration; it is diametically opposite to it. For your happiness' sake, and for ours, lend not your powerful authority to the converting into a law any *immutable truth*, without which civil happiness may very well subsist; to the forming into a public ordinance any theological thesis, of no importance to the state. Be strict as to the life and conduct of men; make that amenable to a tribunal of wise laws; and leave thinking and speaking to us, just as it was given us, as an unalienable heirloom; as we were invested with it, as an unalterable right, by our universal father.

If, perhaps, the connection of privilege with opinion be too prescriptive, and the time has not yet arrived to do away with it altogether, at least endeavor to mitigate, as lies with you, its deleterious influence, and to put wise bounds to prejudices now grown too superannuated;* at least pave, for happier posterity, the way to that height of civilization, to that universal forbearance amongst men, after which reason is still panting in vain. Reward and punish no doctrine; hold out no allurement or bribe for the adoption of theological opinions. Let everyone who does not disturb public happiness, who is obedient to the civil government, who acts righteously toward you, and toward his fellow-countrymen, be allowed to speak

---

* We regret to hear also the Congress of the United States (1783) harp on the old string, by talking of an established religion.

as he thinks, to pray to God after his own fashion, or after that of his forefathers, and to seek eternal salvation where he thinks he may find it. Suffer no one to be a searcher of hearts, and a judge of opinions in your states; suffer no one to assume a right which the Omniscient has reserved to himself. *"As long as we are rendering unto Ceasar the things which are Caesar's, render ye, yourselves, unto God the things which are God's. Love truth! Love peace!"*

Responsa

Responsa (in Hebrew *she'alot u-t'shubot*, question and answers) is a Latin term for written replies of rabbinic authorites to questions posed by individuals and communities on all aspects of Jewish life and law from the time of the Geonim (c. 550-c. 1050). Queries at first came to Babylonian academies from nearby areas. Then people in distant lands and succeeding centuries turned to the Geonim (*Gaon* is Hebrew for "excellence," applied by extension to the rector of an academy) for answers. The Geonim were careful to cite Talmudic references for their decisions and to present their own ideas in refutation of possible objections, and so the Responsa often came to be the equivalent of scholarly treatises. Like the Talmud itself, they are technical, discursive, complicated.

Because of the vicissitudes of Jewish history, it became necessary time and again to reinterpret Halakhic concepts, precepts, and practices for which the Talmud has no exact parallel. With the decline of Babylonian academies in the eleventh century, Jews addressed queries to rabbinic authorities in Europe and elsewhere rather than submit problems to non-Jewish courts. After World War II survivors of the Holocaust, men as well as women, inquired as to the status of wives forced into whoredom by the Nazis. Modern technology causes many Halakhic problems, such as determination of paternity in cases of artificial insemination.

Thus, over the centuries after the closing of the Talmud the Responsa became the chief mechanism for the development of Jewish law in accordance with changes in society and the emergence of new conditions of life. For years the Responsa often ended with the formal "thus is the correct practice" or "thus is the final decision," although answers by rabbinic authorities have historically been considered advisory opinions rather than binding decisions.

But the *Responsa* are also invaluable as a primary historical source, for in them are revealed not only the economic, political, and social conditions of the Jews in all the centuries and countries of their long history but also their ideas, feelings, and beliefs.

Rabbenu Gershom Ben Judah (960-1040)

A Rabbi's Livelihood

Question:

As for your question which is as follows: "Reuben" had a *maarufia* [a customer who was his alone] with certain priests for many years.

This Reuben was a scholar. He taught Torah to the public without pay. His students, becoming aware of the profit that he made through his *maarufia*, trespassed into it, to his loss. [They sought to take these private customers away from him.] Complaint was made against the students and the community forced them, by ban and decree, to break off all contact with the *maarufia*. But the question that was in doubt was whether they [the community] had the right to exclude the rest of the people who were not his disciples [from trespassing into this business].

Answer:

From your question it is possible to infer that in your locality you do not have the general custom of *maarufia*. [In those localities where the custom prevailed, there would have been no question of anyone trespassing on anyody else's *maarufia*]. Since you do not have that custom in your community, no one can compel the community to allow him (Reuben) to keep this business to himself.

Rab Huna said in the Talmud [B.B. 21b]: "If one who lives in a gateway and sets up a mill and another one comes into that gateway and sets one up by his side, the law is that he can be prevented from doing so, for the first one can say to him, "You are cutting off my livelihood." Yet though Huna said that the law is not according to him because they [the other scholars] raised the following objection to him [in the same Talmudic passage]: "If a man establishes a store beside the store of his fellow, etc," and in that discussion traced the dispute to earlier scholars and concluded that it was Simon ben Gamaliel who said originally that one can prevent even one's neighbor [from opening a competitive store next door]; nevertheless the law in that earlier dispute is not according to Simon ben Gamaliel, but according to the preceding scholar who said that one cannot prevent the competitor from opening the store. (Thus the law is in general that you cannot prevent a competing neighbor from opening a store next to yours.)

Nevertheless [although that is the law], it applies only in localities where they do not have the custom of allowing a man to have a monopoly; but in places where they do have the custom he may prevent a competitor from opening the store, since everything depends upon the customs of the province.

Furthermore, the right of free competitions applies to men in general, but not to a scholar who engages in the Torah and in the affairs of Heaven. It is proper to give such a person special status in order that he may not be distracted from his study. For Rabbi Nahman said [ibid, 22a] that you may not prevent peddlers from opening a stall. Even the citizens of a city where the peddlers are strangers may not prevent them, since Ezra the Scribe arranged for peddlers to travel from city to city (the Talmud says Ezra arranged it so that the daughters of Israel might be able to buy ornaments). The peddlers may not be prevented from travelling about, but they can be prevented from establishing a settled business [next to a store that already exists. This applies to ordinary peddlers], but if the travelling merchant is a scholar, then he is permitted to establish even a fixed [competing] business.

Also we are told [ibid] that Rab Dimi of Nahardea brought a shipment of dried grapes to Mahusa by ship and the exilarch said to Rab: "If Rab Dimi is a scholar, give him a monopoly." Further it is said [Yoma 72b] Rabbi Yohanan compared two verses: Make for thyself an ark of wood [Ex. 25:10 (i.e., that Moses should make the Ark of the Covenant himself)]. But another verse [Deut. 10:1] says: Let them make an ark of acacia wood [here using the plural, the verse indicates that the people should make it for Moses]. This proves [said Rabbi Yohanan] that the people of a city are commanded to do a scholar's work for him. Therefore Rabbi Yohanan concludes as follows: How do we describe a scholar? One whose townsmen are commanded to do his [secular] work for him; which means that the scholar is one who neglects his own secular affairs and engages in the affairs of Heaven.

For all these reasons we can conclude that the community is in duty bound to make a special arrangement for this scholar whose work is the work of Heaven and who teaches the Torah in public without pay. They must make arrangements so that he should not be disturbed from his studies. They should decree against the entire community (not only against his own pupils, who owe him a special debt) that they must abstain from interfering with his *maarufia*. They will receive a reward for this and enjoy a long life. As it is written [Prov. 3:18]: It is a tree of life for those who take hold of it and those who support it are happy.

Isaac Alfasi (1013-1103)

Contract with a Teacher

Question:

Reuben and his wife and sons originally dwelt in eastern France, many days' journey from Spain.

He [Reuben] left his wife and his sons in their native place and was content to wander through the communities in the land of Spain. He came to a certain province [in Spain] and preached in public. When five of the leaders of the community met him, they urged him to bring his wife and his sons to that province and dwell among them [i.e., to become their teacher]. But Reuben hesitated because his wife was far away [and the expense of bringing his family would be great]. But they continued to try and persuade him, and he ultimately agreed. They contracted with him, by formal contract.

They agreed to give him 24 gold pieces, maravedis, every year for a term of three years; and he agreed to read before them *Halakah* [i.e., some legal compendium or the *Talmud*], the *Mishnah* and Scriptures, to expound the weekly portion, and to do whatever else they agreed upon, in writing, and in the presence of witnesses. Reuben further agreed formally that he and his wife and his sons would come to the community, by the festival of Sukkot. When the time fixed upon came, he arrived and they welcomed him joyously. Some of them said: Let us begin by studying the *Mishnah*, others said: let us begin by studying the *Talmud*. Finally they all agreed [on the course of study]: they began with the tractate *Berakhot* ["Blessings," the first tractate of the *Talmud*], which they would study for four days out of the seven; on the fifth day, Scriptures; on the sixth day, interpretations of the weekly portion.

[It was customary to study the weekly portion on Friday, to be prepared for the public reading of it the next day in the synagogue.] But after that, one of them, Issakhar, quarreled with his neighbor and said to him, "I cannot understand the profound *Halakhah* and I do not want it." And instead [of four full days of *Talmud*], he suggested, let there be read out to them [to the class] three lines of *Talmud* and then three lines of *Mishnah*. But his companions said, "we do not want that " [scaling down our course of study]. There upon Issakhar arose and said, "I do not desire to read [i.e., to study] and I will not pay my share." Thereupon Reuben [the teacher] answered and said, "I have a formalized written contract in my hands, and witnesses. I may do no other than fulfill what is in my contract and what I had agreed upon with you."

Answer:

We studied this question and investigated all the conditions set forth in it. We see that they are strong and valid and that it is obligatory upon you to fulfill all the conditions that you made between you. As for Issakhar, who changed his mind and does not wish to fulfill the conditions which he agreed to together with his fellows, he has not done right. He is obligated to give Reuben all that he has taken upon himself as his part of the pay. If [when he has paid his share] he wishes to sit and study on the conditions that he had made, then all is well. If not, he has no complaint against Reuben, for note that he, Reuben, did not present an obstacle [to the fulfillment of the contract].

Now, although we learn in the *Mishnah*: "He who hires workmen and they deceive one another [as to wages, etc.] they have against each other nothing but murmurings." [i.e., they have no legal recourse, except that they can grumble about it. Of course, each of them, the workmen or the employer, is free to abandon the contract. In other words, under these circumstances, the contract can be voided. But there can be no suit. All they have against each other are complaints.]

But where does this apply [i.e., that they can void the agreement if they feel they have been misled]? It applies only when the workmen have not yet begun their work, but if they have already begun to work, the employer cannot withdraw from the arrangement. As we learn: "where does this apply [that they can do no more than complain and withdraw], only where the workmen have not gone down to work?"

"If, for example, the donkey-drivers have started out, but did not find the grain [which they were to transport], or the farm-laborers went out and found the field wet [so that they could not work], then he must pay them their wages." So here in the case of this Reuben [the teacher], if they had changed their mind before he had transplanted his family, they would be able to do so. Since, however, he has brought them from their native place and spent his money to bring them and furthermore, has actually begun his new employment, now they can no longer retract and are in duty bound to pay him according to all the conditions.

And, in fact, even if he had not yet gone [to fetch his family], since he has the contract they are no longer permitted to change their minds, as it is said [Zeph. 3:13]: "The remnant of Israel will not do wrong nor speak falsehood, nor will deception be found in their mouth." [This verse is frequently quoted in the legal literature when an appeal is made to conscience and decency, beyond the strict requirements of the Law]. Of course, the court cannot rely merely upon their words; but if it is explained [to a court] that he has already gone [to his native town] and sold his chattels and spent money because of them, they are not permitted to deceive him, but are in duty bound to fulfill all the conditions that they had made with him.

As for Issakhar, if they wish, they can do him a kindness, provided Reuben agrees with them [they might make a special arrangement for Issakhar]. This would be doing a great kindness, since they are not in duty bound to go beyond the law by setting aside a special time for him alone. Also, Reuben is not in duty bound to teach him individually, for he had only contracted to teach all of them together, but not to teach one separately. Therefore, if Issakhar wished to sit and learn, let him sit and learn. If not, let him give his share of the pay for the teaching.

Baruch Spinoza (1632-1677)

One of the world's great philosophers, Spinoza was a descendant of Portuguese Marranos, and he openly returned to Judaism in Holland. (Marrano, probably meaning "damned" or "swine," was a Spanish term for a Jew who accepted Christianity through coercion.) Although its sources are teachings of various medieval Jewish thinkers and its system parallels those of other Jewish savants, Spinoza's philosophy in its main tenets is antagonistic to the fundamental principles of Judaism. And so he was formally excommunicated by the Sephardic community in 1656 for, among other heresies, casting doubt on the integrity of the Biblical texts. After wandering from city to city he settled in the Hague, where he ground lenses for a living.

Spinoza's philosophy is complex and highly technical. Much of it is contained in the posthumously published *Ethics*, where he holds that there is but one substance in the universe. God is nature and nature is God. The world is identical with the deity, whose two fundamental attributes are mental and physical. Thus, Spinoza advocates a form of monism, identifying mind and matter, finite and infinite, as manifestations of one universal.

243

The iron law of necessity is preeminent: cause and effect reign supreme and freedom of the will is a chimera.

Spinoza's *Tractus Theologico-Politic* examines prophecy, miracles, composition of the Old Testament, and a host of other subjects with the avowed purpose of defending freedom of thought except in connection with morality, in which area religion, he thought, should make the rules. Underlying these themes is Spinoza's desire to vindicate himself in regard to his excommunication by asserting that the Judaism of his time was not the Judaism of Moses and that the Jewish religion should be expressed not in ritual but in moral deeds.

In his initiation of modern Bible criticism, his exposition of pantheism, and his treatment of cause and effect, as well as in many other areas, Spinoza profoundly influenced the course of Western, especially German, philosophy.

The God of Man's Making

God is, and acts solely by the necessity of His own nature. He is the free cause of all things. All things are God, and so depend on Him, and without Him they could neither exist nor be conceived; lastly, all things are predetermined by God, not through His free will or absolute wish, but from the very nature of God or infinite power.

Yet there remain not a few misconceptions, which might and may prove very grave hindrances to the understanding of the concatenation of things. I have thought it worthwhile to bring these misconceptions before the bar of reason.

All such opinions spring from the notion commonly entertained that all things in nature act as men themselves act, namely, with an end in view. It is accepted as certain that God himself directs all things to a definite goal (for it is said that God made all things for man, and man that he might worship Him). I will, therefore, consider this opinion, asking first, why it obtains general credence, and why all men are naturally so prone to adopt it? Secondly, I will point out its falsity; and, lastly, I will show how it has given rise to prejudices about good and bad, and right and wrong, praise and blame, order and confusion, beauty and ugliness, and the like. However, this is not the place to deduce these misconceptions from the nature of the human mind.

All men are born ignorant of the causes of things, all have the desire to seek for what is useful to them, and they are conscious of such desire. Herefrom it follows, first, that men think themselves free inasmuch as they are conscious of their volitions and desires, and never even dream, in their ignorance, of the causes which have disposed them so to wish and desire. Secondly, that men do all things for an end, namely, for that which is useful to them, and which they seek. Thus it comes to pass that they only look for a knowledge of the final causes of events, and when these are learned, they are content, as having no cause for further doubt. If they cannot learn such causes from external sources, they are compelled to turn to considering themselves, and reflecting what end would have induced them personally to bring about the given event, and thus they necessarily judge other natures by their own. Further, as they find in themselves and outside themselves many means which assist them not a little in their search for what is useful, for instance, eyes for seeing, teeth for chewing, herbs and animals for yielding food, the sun for giving light, the sea for breeding fish, etc., they come to look on the whole of nature as a means for obtaining such conveniences. Now as they are aware that they found these conveniences and did not make them, they think they have causes for believing that some other being has made them for their use.

As they look upon things as means, they cannot believe them to be self-created; but, judging from the means which they are accustomed to prepare for themselves, they are bound to believe in some ruler or rulers of the universe endowed with human freedom, who have arranged and adapted everything for human use. They are bound to estimate the nature of such rulers (having no information on the subject) in accordance with their own nature, and therefore they assert that the gods ordained everything for the use of man, in order to bind man to themselves and obtain from him the highest honor.

Hence also it follows that everyone thought out for himself, according to his abilities, a different way of worshipping God, so that God might love him more than his fellows, and direct the whole course of nature for the satisfaction of his blind cupidity and insatiable avarice. Thus the prejudice developed into superstition, and took deep root in the human mind; and for this reason everyone strove most zealously to understand and explain the final causes of things; but in their endeavor to show that nature does nothing in vain, i.e., nothing which is useless to man, they only seem to have demonstrated that nature, the gods, and men are all made together.

Consider, I pray you, the result: among the many helps of nature they were bound to find some hindrances, such as storms, earthquakes, diseases, etc.: so they declared that such things happen because the gods are angry at some wrong done them by men, or at some fault committed in their worship. Experience day by day protested and showed by infinite examples that good and evil fortunes fall to the lot of pious and impious alike; still they would not abandon their inveterate prejudice, for it was more easy for them to class such contradictions among other unknown things of whose use they were ignorant, and thus to retain their actual and innate condition of ignorance, than to destroy the whole fabric of their reasoning and start fresh.

They therefore laid down as an axiom, that God's judgments far transcend human understanding. Such a doctrine might well have sufficed to conceal the truth from the human race for all eternity, if mathematics had not furnished another standard of verity in considering solely the essence and properties of figures without regard to their final causes. There are other reasons (which I need not mention here) besides mathematics, which might have caused men's minds to be directed to these general prejudices, and have led them to the knowlege of the truth.

I have now explained my first point. There is no need to show at length that *nature has no particular goal in view, and final causes are mere human figments*. However, I will add a few remarks in order to overthrow the doctrine of a final cause utterly.

This doctrine does away with the perfection of God: for, if God acts for an object, He necessarily desires something which He lacks. Certainly, theologians and metaphysicians draw a distinction between the object of want and the object of assimilation; still, they confess that God made all things for the sake of Himself, not for the sake of creation. They are unable to point to anything prior to creation, except God Himself, as an object for which God should act, and are therefore driven to admit (as they clearly must), that God lacked those things for whose attainment He created means, and further that He desired them.

We must not omit to notice that the followers of this doctrine, anxious to display their talent in assigning final causes, have imported a new method of argument in proof of their theory—namely, a reduction, not to the impossible, but to ignorance; thus showing that they have no other method of exhibiting their doctrine. For example, if a stone falls from a roof onto someone's head, and kills him, they will demonstrate by their new method that the stone fell in order to kill the man; for, if it had not by God's will fallen with that object, how could so many circumstances (and there are often many concurrent circumstances) have all happened together by chance? Perhaps you will answer that the event is due to the facts that the wind was blowing, and the man was walking that way. "But why," they will insist, "was the wind blowing, and why was the man at the very time walking that way?"

If you again answer, that the wind had then sprung up because the sea had begun to be agitated the day before, the weather being previously calm, and that the man had been invited by a friend, they will again insist: "But why was the sea agitated, and why was the man invited at that time?" So they will pursue their questions from cause to cause, till at last you take refuge in the will of God—in other words, the sanctuary of ignorance. So, again when they survey the frame of the human body, they are amazed; and being ignorant of the causes of so great a work of art, conclude that it has been fashioned, not mechanically, but by divine and supernatural skill, and has been so put together that one part shall not hurt another.

Hence anyone who seeks for the true causes of miracles, and strives to understand natural phenomena as an intelligent being, and not to gaze at them like a fool, is set down and denounced as an impious heretic by those whom the masses adore as the interpreters of nature and the gods. Such persons know that, with the removal of ignorance, the wonder which forms their only available means for proving and preserving their authority would vanish also. But I now quit this subject, and pass on to my third point.

After men persuaded themselves that everything which is created is created for their sake, they were bound to consider as the chief quality in everything that which is most useful to themselves, and to account those things the best of all which have the most beneficial effect on mankind. Further, they were bound to form abstract notions for the explanation of the nature of things, such as goodness, badness, order, confusion, warmth, cold, beauty, deformity, and so on; and from the belief that they are free agents arose the further notions, praise and blame, sin and merit.

Everything which conduces to health and the worship of God they have called good, everything which hinders these objects they have styled bad; and inasmuch as those who do not understand the nature of things do not verify phenomena in any way, but merely imagine them after a fashion, and mistake their imagination for understanding, such persons firmly believe that there is an order in things, being really ignorant both of things and their own nature.

When phenomena are of such a kind that the impression they make on our senses requires little effort of imagination, and can consequently be easily remembered, we say that they are well-ordered; if the contary, that they are ill-ordered or confused. Further, as things which are easily imagined are more pleasing to us, men prefer order to confusion—as though there were any order in nature, except in relation to our imagination—and say that God has created all things in order; thus, without knowing it, attributing imagination to God, unless, indeed, they would have it that God foresaw human imagination, and arranged everything so that it would be most easily imagined.

If this be their theory, they would not, perhaps, be daunted by the fact that we find an infinite number of phenomena, far surpassing our imagination, and very many others which confound its weakness.

The other abstract notions are nothing but modes of imagining, in which the imagination is differently affected, though they are considered by the ignorant as the chief attributes of things, inasmuch as they believe that everything was created for the sake of themselves; and, according as they are affected by it, style it good or bad, healthy or rotten and corrupt. For instance, if the motion which objects we see communicate to our nerves be conducive to health, the objects causing it are styled beautiful; if a contrary motion be excited, they are styled ugly.

Things which are perceived through our senses of smell are styled fragrant or fetid; if through our taste, sweet or bitter, full-flavored or insipid; if through our touch, hard or soft, rough or smooth, etc.

Whatsoever affects our ears is said to give rise to noise, sound, or harmony. In this last case, there are men lunatic enough to believe that even God Himself takes pleasure in harmony; and philosophers are not lacking who have persuaded themselves that the motion of the heavenly bodies gives rise to harmony—all of which instances sufficiently show that everyone judges of things according to the state of his brain, or rather mistakes for things the forms of his imagination. We need no longer wonder that there have arisen all the controversies we have witnessed, and finally skepticism: for, although human bodies in many respects agree, yet in very many others they differ; so that what seems good to one seems bad to another; what is pleasing to one displeases another, and so on.

The Zohar

The Zohar (Hebrew for brightness, splendor), about whose composition little is known, remains the most popular exposition of Jewish mysticism, The Hasidim consider it sacred, and among world Jewry it is still the third most influential book after the Bible and the *Talmud* despite the undeniable fact that it has been as harmful as beneficial to Jews. Perhaps the Spanish *Kabbalist* (*Kabbala* being Hebrew for received or traditional lore, a term applied to mystics) Moses de Leon wrote it, utilizing ancient material. More probably it is a compilation of the old and new by many writers. Certainly de Leon first brought it to public attention in Spain at the end of the thirteenth century. He attributed authorship to Simeon ben Yohai, who flourished in the second century, to invoke the sanctity of age and the authority of a miracle-working rabbi.

The Zohar is an ambiguous, contradictory, paradoxical volume that confuses the sublime with the ridiculous. Like the *Talmud* it is a huge work with a unity stemming from its aims and teachings; yet it is difficult in organization because it too proceeds often by free association. *The Zohar* borrows terms, phrases, and ideas from science and philosophy; yet it relies on revelation from the spirit world for proof. It was obviously aimed at glorifying Judaism at a time in which Jews were wretched pariahs; yet Christian theologians of that and later eras insist it "proves" the "truths" of Christianity. It affirms the supreme worth of Judaism; yet, like the paganism of old, it relies on astrology, prophecy, and the use of numbers for magical purposes in hope of penetrating the Divine Radiance and influencing the course of world events. *The Zohar*, as its title indicates, glows with a splendor inherent in Judaism: the belief that any individual Jew can influence the destiny of the universe by becoming a better person. Yet it is marred by superstition, obscurantism, and magic.

Most of *The Zohar* is in the form of a mystical commentary on sections of the Pentateuch and portions of Writings (Song of Songs, Ruth, Lamentations, etc.). The language—Aramaic with some Hebrew—is exotic, enigmatic, and highly pictorial. From the opening lines, which quote Daniel 12:3 ("Those who are wise shine as the brightness [*Zohar*] of the firmament"), light and color are particularly utilized in innumerable ways for symbolic description. Homilies, parables, allegories, myths, and exegeses abound because [*The Zohar*] regards the Torah as an outer cloak under which lies the true body of Divine Wisdom. Often lofty in concept but fantastic in assertion, poetic in insight but superstitious in acceptance of the irrational, exalted in love of God and man but interested in demonology, *The Zohar* has been highly praised by romantics and bitterly denounced by rationalists.

Jonah

In the story of Jonah we have an allegory of the whole of a man's career in this world. Jonah descending into the ship is symbolic of man's soul that descends into this world to enter into his body. Why is he called Jonah [lit. aggrieved]? Because as soon as he becomes partner with the body in this world he finds himself full of vexation. Man, then, is in the world as in a ship that is traversing the great ocean and is like to be broken, as it says, "so that the ship was like to be broken." [Jonah 1:4].

Furthermore, man in this world commits sins, imagining that he can flee from the presence of his Master, who takes no notice of this world. The Almighty then rouses a furious tempest; to wit, man's doom, which constantly stands before the Holy One, blessed be He, and demands his punishment. It is this which assails the ship and calls to mind man's sins that it may seize him; and the man is thus caught by the tempest and is struck down by illness, just as Jonah "went down into the innermost part of the ship; and he lay, and was fast asleep."

Although the man is thus prostrated, his soul does not exert itself to return to his Master in order to make good his omissions. So "the shipmaster came to him," to wit, the good prompter, who is the general steersman, "and said unto him: What meanest thou that thou sleepest? Arise, call upon thy God, etc.; it is not a time to sleep, as they are about to take thee up to be tried for all that thou hast done in this world. Repent of thy sins. Reflect on these things and return to thy Master.

"Was it thine occupation," wherein thou wast occupied in this world; and make confession concerning it before the Master; "and whence comest thou"; to wit, from a fetid drop, and so be not thou arrogant before him. "What is thy country"—reflect that from earth thou wast created and to earth thou wilt return; "and of what people art thou"; that is, reflect whether thou canst rely on merits of thy forbears to protect thee.

When they bring him to judgment before the Heavenly Tribunal, that tempest, that is none other than the judgment doom which raged against him, demands from the King the punishment of all the King's prisoners, and then all the King's counsellors appear before Him one by one, and the Tribunal is set up. Some plead in defense of the accused, others against him. Should the man be found guilty, as in the case of Jonah, then "the men rowed hard to bring it to the land, but they could not"; so those who plead on his behalf find points in his favor and strive to restore him to his world, but they cannot; "for the sea grew more and more tempestuous against them", the prosecution storms and rages against him, and convicting him of his sins, prevails against his defenders.

Then three appointed messengers descend upon the man; one of them makes a record of all the good deeds and the misdeeds that he has performed in this world; one casts up the reckoning of his days; and the third is the one who has accompanied the man from the time when he was in his mother's womb. As already said, the doom summons is not appeased until "they took up Jonah," until they take him from the house to the place of burial. Then proclamation is made concerning him. If he was a righteous man, it runs: Render honour to the King's image! "He entereth into peace, they rest in their beds, each one that walketh in his righteousness" [Isa. 57:2].

But when a wicked man dies, the proclamation runs: Woe to that man. It would have been better for him had he never been born! Regarding such a man it is written, "and they cast him forth into the sea, and the sea ceased from its raging," that is, only after they have placed him in the grave; and so "Jonah was in the belly of the fish," which is identified with "the belly of the underworld [*sheol*]," as is proved by the passage, "Out of the belly of the underworld [*sheol*] cried I."

"Three days and three nights"; these are the three days that a man lies in his grave before his belly splits open. After three days it ejects the putrid matter on his face, saying: "Take back what thou gavest me; thou didst eat and drink all day and never didst thou give anything to the poor; all thy days were like feasts and holiday, whilst the poor remained hungry without partaking of any of thy food. Take back what thou gavest me."

In regard to this it is written: "and I will spread dung upon your faces," etc. [Malachi 2:3]. Again, after the lapses of three days, the man receives chastisement in each organ—in his eyes, his hands, and his feet. This continues for thirty days, during which time the soul and the body are chastised together. The soul therefore remains all that time on earth below, not ascending to her place, like a woman remaining apart all the days of her impurity.

After that the soul ascends whilst the body is being decomposed in the earth, where it will lie until the time when the Holy One, blessed be He will awaken the dead. A voice will then resound through the graves, proclaiming: "Awake and sing, ye that dwell in the dust, for thy dew is as the dew of light, and the earth shall cast forth the dead [*rephaim*]" [Isa. 26:19]. That will come to pass when the Angel of Death will depart from the world, as it is written: "He will destroy death for ever, and the Lord God will wipe away tears from off all faces; and the reproach of his people will he take away from off all the earth" [Ibid, 25:8].

It is of that occasion that it is written: "And the Lord spoke unto the fish, and it vomited out Jonah upon the dry land"; for as soon as that voice will resound among the graves they will all cast out the dead bodies that they contain. The term *rephaim* [the dead] being akin to the root, *rapha* [healing], indicates that the dead will be restored to their former physical condition. But, you may say, is it not written elsewhere, "the *rephaim* will not rise" [Ibid, 27:14]? The truth is that all the dead will be restored to their former state whilst in the graves, but some of them will rise and others will not. Happy is the portion of Israel, of whom it is written, "My dead bodies shall arise" [Ibid, 27:19].

Thus in the narrative of that fish we find words of healing for the whole world. As soon as it swallowed Jonah it died, but after three days was restored to life and vomited him forth. In a similar way, the Land of Israel will in the future first be stirred to new life, and afterwards "the earth will cast forth the dead."

Said R. Simeon: "Alas for the man who regards the Torah as a book of mere tales and everyday matters! If that were so, we, even we, could compose a torah dealing with everyday affairs, and of even greater excellence. Nay, even the princes of the world possess books of greater worth which we could use as a model for composing some such torah. The Torah, however, contains in all its words supernatural truths and sublime mysteries.

"Observe the perfect balancing of the upper and the lower worlds. Israel here below is balanced by the angels on high, of whom it says: "Who makest thy angels into winds" [Ps. 104:4]. For the angels in descending on earth put on themselves earthly garments, as otherwise they could not stay in this world, nor could the world endure them. Now, if thus it is with the angels how much more so must it be with the Torah—the Torah that created them, that created all the worlds and is the means by which these are sustained. Thus, had the Torah not clothed herself in garments of this world the world could not endure it.

"The stories of the Torah are thus only her outer garments, and whoever looks upon that garment as being the Torah itself, woe to that such a one will have no portion in the next world. David thus said: 'Open thou mine eyes, that I may behold wondrous things out of Thy law' [Ps. 119:18], to wit the things that are beneath the garment. Observe this. The garments worn by a man are the most visible part of him, and senseless people looking at the man do not seem to see more in him than the garments. But in truth the pride of the garments is the body of the man, and the pride of the body is the soul.

"Similarly, the Torah has a body made up of the precepts of the Torah, called *gufe torah* [bodies, main principles of the Torah], and that body is enveloped in garments made up of worldly narrations. The senseless people only see the garment, the mere narrations; those who are somewhat wiser penetrate as far as the body. But the really wise, the servants of the most high King, those who stood on Mount Sinai, penetrate right through to the soul, the root principle of all, namely, to the real Torah. In the future the same are destined to penetrate even to the supersoul (soul of the soul) of the Torah.

"Observe that in a similar way in the supernatural world there is garment, body, soul, and supersoul. The heavens and their hosts are the outer garment, the Community of Israel is the body which receives the soul, to wit, the 'Glory of Israel'; and the supersoul is the Ancient Holy One. All these are interlocked within each other.

"Woe to the sinners who consider the Torah as mere worldly tales, who only see its outer garment; happy are the righteous who fix their gaze on the Torah proper. Wine cannot be kept save in a jar; so the Torah needs an outer garment. These are the stories and narratives; but we must penetrate beyond."

Fiction

Narrative writing occurs in every period of Jewish history. The Bible contains stories apparently written as separate works and fitted to the text later on by redactors. In the Talmudic era, tales were composed for didactic and exegetic purposes. In medieval times, fiction in the form of short stories became an independent literary form although largely based on Arabic originals, Biblical narratives, and Haggadic anecdotes. Collections of stories were published in book form, with distinctions between fact and fiction not always clear. Translations and Jewish versions of medieval tales, such as the Arthurian legends, became popular. Later, the Hasidim enthusiastically told stories of their leaders, in the process adding to the vast store of Jewish legends.

Yiddish, primarily a mixture of German and Hebrew although it contains a sprinkling of other languages, became a literary medium late in the medieval era. Aimed at women,

Yiddish tales at first were based on German romances. Sentimental, verbose, and moralistic, the stories were nevertheless popular. Then masters such as Mendele and Sholem Asch demonstrated the power and aesthetic value of Yiddish fiction. Today, Israeli stories and novels written in Hebrew rank with the best in the contemporary world.

Yiddish developed during the Middle Ages among the Jews of Central and Eastern Europe. Although varying dialects of Yiddish evolved with different accents, the essential elements (German, Hebrew, Old French, Old Italian, Slavic) were the same. Because Hebrew letters were used for English, Jews throughout the world could communicate in writing with each other and be confident of full understanding.

A folk language, Yiddish was employed in everyday affairs whereas Hebrew, the holy tongue, was reserved for religious matters. The first major works in Yiddish were contemporaneous with the beginnings of vernacular literature in France, Germany, and Italy. But violent prejudice against Jews and frequent uprootings and expulsions prevented further development of Yiddish literature until almost the end of the eighteenth century, when Jewish writers again were able to look outside the shtetl for literary models. Yiddish was regarded merely as a medium for light reading or for didactic material aimed at women who had no knowledge of Hebrew. Not until the turn of this century did writings in Yiddish win high esteem. As late as 1888 many Jewish leaders agreed with A. L. Gordon, who chastised Sholem Aleichem for writing in Yiddish: "It is a bridge of shame of the driven wanderer, and I have always considered it the duty of every educated Jew to see to it that the dialect should gradually disappear from our midst."

Affectionately referred to even today as the Mamaloshen (mother tongue), Yiddish has charm, fluidity, spontaneity, and warmth. But the Holocaust incinerated the geographical heartland of Yiddish, and cultural assimilation elsewhere in the Diaspora brought with it virtual abandonment by the vast majority of Jews.

Shmuel Yosef Agnon (1888-1970)

The first writer of fiction in Hebrew to receive the Nobel Prize for Literature, Agnon was all his life a traditional Jew in the full sense of the word. Born with the surname Czazkes in Buczacz, Galicia, (in Southern Poland, then part of the Austro-Hungarian Empire), he was given a deeply religious upbringing. Having been steeped as a youngster in the Bible, Talmud, Midrash, and other Jewish classics, as an adult he immersed himself in Jewish lore—both ancient and modern. Agnon emigrated to Israel in 1909, where, except for the years 1912-23 spent in Germany, he lived for the rest of his life.

Agnon achieved immediate success with "Agunot," his first story published in Israel, from which he took his pen name. *Agunah* (plural *agunot*) in Hebrew refers to a wife who, although her husband has disappeared, cannot remarry because there is no conclusive evidence of his death. The central theme in Agnon's writings, as his choice of name implies, is the plight of the modern Jew. Displaced and in exile, he is homeless, alone, alienated. Like an *agunah*, the Jew is the victim of irreparable separation. Agnon's story "Soil for the Land of Israel" pictures the Diaspora Jew who, disassociated from Eretz Yisrael and the traditional community, is forced to live in a hostile world.

Agnon views the modern world as without the spiritual cohesiveness and moral grandeur of the past, so that ethical life does not seem to matter anymore. Because traditional Jewish life and modern secular culture are in direct opposition, Agnon seeks a new existence while he longs for a way of living that was but will be no more. His Galician novel, *In the Heart of the Seas*, tells a miracle-studded tale of pious Hasidim. *A Guest for the Night* portrays the moral and material degradation of the shtetl and implies that Eretz Yisrael is the last possible place of refuge for spirituality in the twentieth century.

Agnon's style—sensitive, supple, lucid, yet, intricately allegoric, metaphoric, and allusive—is a harmonious mosaic of thirty centuries of Hebrew writings. Even as a word conveys a contemporary significance in an Agnon story it can retain echoes of connotations, feelings, and experiences from recent centuries, the medieval era, and ancient times that add depth and breadth to Agnon's themes and motifs. Perhaps because Agnon seeks the flavor of old Jewish tales, quaint and rambling and poetic in his writing yet modern in the use of irony and symbolic patterns, his style remains peaceful and lyrical—the obsolete locutions and archaic diction from different works over many centuries having been creatively absorbed in it.

Agnon's dozen or so volumes of short stories, novellas, and novels have already become classics. His fiction has a wide range, including folklore, psychological studies, social satire, and parables. Paradoxically, by concentrating on the minutest of details, Agnon focuses on the universal. Even so, while he reveals he conceals, so that every object and every action are themselves and yet other things as well. Reality becomes myth, and myth becomes reality. Agnon has originated in modern Hebrew literature, if not a new genre, certainly a unique way of telling a story, thus enabling a reader to perceive its insights and at the very same time appreciate its artistry.

The Rejuvenating Years

In Jerusalem I was the guest of a man who honored me, prepared a feast for me, and seated me next to his father at the head of the table. The old man took pleasure at every dish that was served, saying: "Enjoy it, for it is grown in Israel and is even mentioned in the Mishnah." I was happy to be with such distinguished, God-fearing people. "My friends," I said, "you are blessed. I too am blessed to be able to sit with you—men of good deeds. At every dish that is placed before you, you remember where it is mentioned in the writings of the rabbis.

At every precept you observe, you recall its source in our laws. Of this the *Ethics of Our Fathers* says: 'It is as if they had eaten from the table of the Creator.' "

After we ate and drank, the old man took his cup and said grace in a clear, pleasant voice. Both the man and his voice pleased me. I saw that he knew how to make the blessing and that it was becoming in him to bless. I noticed also a custom of his. As he blessed the land he poured water into his cup of wine in tribute to the strength of Israel's vintage. Rejoicing I said, "Blessed is the land in which no matter where a man turns, he learns Torah and good manners."

When he reached the part of the grace which reads, "the good and beneficent," I heard him say: "May the All-Merciful bless my father." I said to myself: I had compared him with the pious and with men of good deeds, but after hearing what he just said, I see that he doesn't even know what almost everybody does. I thought that he knew how to say grace, and that it became him to say it, but now I see that he does not even understand the meaning of the words—as if an old man of seventy has a father living and can say of him, "May the All-Merciful bless my father." He is but an ignoramus who doesn't know the meaning of the words, and since "May the All-Merciful bless my father" is printed in the prayer-book, he recites it. Woe unto him who blesses his father at the time he lies in Gehenna, punished because of his son! For anyone who leaves behind him an ignorant son, though he deserves Paradise, is thrown into Gehenna and punished because he did not teach his son Torah.

As the old man finished saying the blessing after meals another man entered. He was spry and erect. He had the face of a young man and a black beard was about his face in a sort of semicircle. He wore a velvet hat and a white coat that reached well below his calves. A broad sash was folded again and again about his waist, and a velvet cloak, green as the leaf of a leek, covered his coat. His hands were thrust behind the sash. His stockings were white and his legs had leather slippers. He was so light on his feet that his slippers seemed to chase but could not catch him. At the sight of the man, the company rose in his honor. But not everyone's manner of rising was the same. The old man's son half-stood, half-sat. But the old man rose with respect, and after he had completed the grace he left his seat and offered it to the newcomer. The guest said: "Sit down, my son, sit down."

But the old man continued standing in reverence, took a pinch of snuff so that he should be able to stand (for tobacco relieves fatigue) and patiently waited for the guest to sit down. The guest seated himself in the chair, removed the pillow, and in a tender voice said: "The generations are weaker, the body is frailer, and strength is ebbing. A man sitting in a chair now has to have pillows and cushions. I remember that we used to sit on rocks and no one ever complained to his friend, 'The seats are hard!' "

Then the newcomer asked, "Is there anything to eat?" And they brought him black bread, olives, onions, and a cup of water. I thought: How strange! The table is full of all good things and he asks, Is there anything to eat? They themselves feast on white bread and drink the choice wines of the land and they give him black bread and water.

He stretched out his hand and lifted the black bread with joy and blessed it with a happiness that I had not seen even at the tables of dukes and princes when they sat before delicate meats and the finest wines. He ate with such joy that I myself longed to eat again; and they stood before him with awe and respect like people who pay homage to a great man who has come to sit with them.

What are you doing? I thought. If he is so important to you, why didn't you share your food with him? Haven't you had the best of everything? You are the sons of Abraham, sitting in the place of Abraham, and yet your deeds are not the deeds of Abraham. Our father Abraham slaughtered three oxen for three men, and it is not said that he ate as much as a crumb that day. But my heart spoke up to defend them. I said to my heart, What! Can you find good in their actions? Yes, it answered and said: Blessed is Israel, that they live in the Land of Israel, and that they are greater than the rest of Israel in

Torah, good deeds and in observance of the Law. Even the poorest among them deprives himself of food, and takes what is meant for his own mouth to give to a poor man. If so, why didn't they offer him what they themselves ate? Because that man is a righteous man and checks his pleasure and eats nothing too much, for while the Creator's Temple is in ruins, should his own table have delicacies?

But my mind and heart did not agree. For the man was eating heartily, did not sigh while eating, and said nothing to ennoble the meal with anything spiritual. In fact, he was enjoying himself. He joked and called the old man, "My son." If he is so pious, I thought, why does he joke? Didn't our scholars, may their memories be blessed, compare the table to an altar? I turned to the old man—the father of the man who had invited me—and said: "With your permission, I'd like to say something."

"Say it," he said.

"I am surprised," I said, "that an old man like you stands before a younger man. Thank God that we are in Jerusalem and not among the sages of Athens. Or perhaps we have become worthy of the times of the Messiah as described in the Tractate *Sotah*: 'When the Messiah comes, the aged will stand before the young.'

They began to laugh and I said: "You are laughing at me."

"God forbid," they answered.

I said: "You laugh at me and say, God forbid, we're not laughing at you, but in spite of that my heart tells me that you do nothing wrong. However, what shall I do, if my eyes and heart do not agree?"

Said the old man: "Will you become angry at me if I tell you something from the Torah?"

"Manners precede Torah," I said, "and what is more, respect your elders is in the Torah."

"He *is* an old man," he said, "and hasn't the Torah commanded us, 'Honor thy father'? If another old man had come, I would also have risen out of respect for him and said, 'Sit down, if you please.' And since he *is* my father, why should I not rise in respect and give him my place?"

I was completely astonished when my host—the old man's son—added: "I see that you didn't know that he is my grandfather. Now that you know that he is my father's father, say that we act as we should and according to the precepts."

"You are right," I said, "but I should like to ask a question I wanted to ask before but did not."

"What is it?" he asked.

"The respect you give him," I said, " is no doubt according to law. However, you ate all sorts of delicacies and drank old wine but have given your grandfather no delicacies and no wine, and only black bread, olives, onions, and water. Would you call that respectful?"

The father of the old man spread out his hands and clapped them together, saying: "My son, my son, you too make the same mistake that others make. You think that eating good things is good for you! It is only a punishment. Just as when a sick man is fed all sorts of delicacies and cannot enjoy them. He eats this and wants that. His soul is empty and his face is greenish. But a healthy man eats and drinks water, enjoys it and is happy. His soul is full and his face shines, and the healthier his body is, the more he despises delicacies and longs for simple foods."

I was astonished and stared at this grandfather who was a youth compared to his own son and thought: Can there be a father who looks younger than his son?

Then the father of the old man said: "How weak have the generations become and how frail is the world! A man of Israel who is not as twisted as a ram's horn and doesn't groan, whose limbs do not tremble and whose bones do not shake, whose hands and feet are perfect, and who is the master of his own body—even though he is older than ten elders they don't believe his age. But the early generations are not like the later ones. The first generations settled in Israel because of sorrow and toil, because of wanderings and persecutions, because of need and lack of food. But they praised the Name, saying, 'How happy and blessed are we that we pray morning and night in Jerusalem, that we sit before You in Jerusalem and learn Torah in Jerusalem.' And because they were content with their lot and with their living and did not rebel against suffering, their faces gleam and their bodies are of iron, their strength keeps increasing and they live long lives.

"But the later generations toil and never have enough. If they lack but one of all the earth's pleasures, they immediately get so angry that their bodies look rusty. One day they want to go here, another day there; one day to the north, another day south. Comes a wind and they groan, Oh, our legs are tottering. Comes the sun and they soon complain, Oh, our teeth are melting. Woe to us that we are here and have gone from there. If we were there we could have put ice on our heads and covered ourselves with snow. And they don't realize that the land of Israel is better than all other lands, for here every city has its own climate: something that other countries do not have. And Jerusalem is superior to them all, for here you have every climate. In every quarter of Jerusalem you will find a different kind of air, because since the destruction of the Temple the earth has grown smaller.

"Heaven forbid that I should disparage the later generations and give them a bad name. Worthy of their lot are all they who live in the Land. For everyone who dwells in Israel is called righteous even though at first glance he is not righteous. For if he were not righteous, the earth would spew him out, as it is written: 'And the land spat forth its inhabitants.' But since it hasn't ejected him, he is righteous, though he may be in the grip of wickedness. Listen, I will tell you a secret. The Holy One, blessed be He, knew that His children wanted to be in His palace, but since they were so few, He gave them the strength to stand up to robbers and troops, evil men and beasts."

I said, "Blessed is He who gave His palace to His watchmen. Blessed are you who are worthy, and blessed is the Eternal Who made you worthy." At that moment I had learned seven things from him. I learned why the old man had said, "May the All-Merciful bless my father." Because his father was alive. And I learned why they ate delicacies and drank wine, and gave him only plain food and water. Because delicacies are a punishment, but a healthy man eats in his hunger and drinks water in his thirst. I learned also why the father of the old man looked like a youth. For he was of the first generation, men of great strength who risked their lives and asked for nothing but shelter in His holy courtyard; and He gave them the strength to withstand all. And I learned why the later generations are weak and weary. Because they find no satisfaction in their residence in Israel. I learned, too, why one feels all the world's climates in Israel. Because the earth has grown smaller. And I learned that everyone who lives in Israel is called righteous, even though he be in the grip of wickedness.

The grandfather ate his bread with joy and his face lit up. He drank water from a clay jug, washed his fingers, and said the grace after meals with a cheerful voice. Such is the voice of the elders of Jerusalem in praising and thanking His name for even a crumb that He gives them. Anyone who has not heard the voice of the elders of Jerusalem saying grace has never heard the voice of gratitude.

But lo and behold! When he came to "may the All-Merciful," he shut his eyes and gently said, "may the All-Merciful bless my father." I was dumbfounded and thought: he looks like a scholar but prays like an ignoramus; he blesses but doesn't know whom he is blessing. As if this old man has grown old and who has grown-up grandsons can have a father living?

However, since he is an old man, I thought, ending his days in Jerusalem, I will sit with him. Perhaps I shall learn something from him. I waited until he had completed saying grace. After he had finished, I said: "I should like to ask a question but I am afraid it will trouble you."

"My son," he said, "if you ask well, why are you afraid of troubling me?"

I then said: "I know that you are one of the elders of Jerusalem. I should like to hear about everything that has happened in Jerusalem. Perhaps you remember some of the events that took place."

His face lit up immediately and he said: "Like the slave who was lucky enough to stop at the king's palace and gets his greatest joy out of describing all the wonders that his eyes have seen and what his ears have heard within the palace walls. Blessed is the Creator whose mercies are many in Israel! Though they have sinned against Him, He opens the gates of Jerusalem for them; as it is written, 'Enter His gates with thanksgiving.' If it were not for that verse in the Torah we never would have dared picture Him as a man who draws people into this house." And he began telling me stories about the pious men who had been in Jerusalem. In their day no one else was seen in Israel. And so he went on, and his talk was spiced with Scripture and Mishnah, with law and lore.

I said to myself: I will ask him why he said, May the All-Merciful bless my father. For since when is a grace a memorial prayer? But because he was describing things I longed to hear, I did not interrupt him for fear that he would leap from subject to subject and from incident to incident. And there is nothing harder on the ear than that. In the midst of his talking, he came to an important point but couldn't explain it clearly. "This happened ninety years ago," he said. "I was three at the time and was riding on my father's shoulders. My father slapped my face, saying, 'You don't deserve the slap, but I want you to remember that you were here. You don't know what you are seeing now, but in the future you will remember and rejoice.' If you want to hear more about it, ask my father and he will tell you."

"Excuse me," I said, "please repeat what you have just said. I don't think I heard you well."

He answered: "You will have to ask my father about this; he remembers and rejoices in the telling."

At that moment I thought: how right was Solomon when he said: "Let not your mouth be hasty!" No sooner did I question his saying grace as a memorial prayer than he tells me his father is alive. I then told him about my own work that takes me from one part of Jerusalem to another.

He said: "Even if you had eagle's wings you could not catch him."

"Why?" I asked.

"Every day after prayers," he replied, "my father goes from one end of Jerusalem to the other in order to fulfill what is written: 'Turn about Zion and go round her.' By the time you reach one place, he is at another. When you reach Mount Scopus he is at the Mount of Olives. By the time you reach the Mount of Olives he is at the Tower of David. When you reach the Tower of David, he is at the graves of the Small Sanhedrin. And when you are at the Small Sanhedrin he has reached the Great Sanhedrin. We should like to go with him, but what can we do if there is not enough strength in us? If so, how can we fulfill the verse: 'Turn about Zion and go round about her; count her towers'? Come, let us recount the greatness of Jerusalem whom the Holy One, blessed be He, returned to Israel despite the fact that He had entrusted it to other nations."

As we were talking, another man entered. His beard was long and his earlocks were curled. His eyes were like two doves and his face was shining like the Gates of the East. A smile never left his lips. His appearance was that of a king, but his clothes were as simple as those of plain people. At the sound of his feet, they all rose. But not everyone's manner of rising was alike. The old man who had been talking to me rose in reverence, not like his son who half stood, half sat, and who at length wasn't able to stand on his legs. The grandfather drew himself up straight as a snake and bowed his head gently, not like his son whose head dropped after eating.

The newcomer entered and greeted them. "Welcome," they answered. They brought him a jug of water, a cotton towel, and an earthen dish. He rolled up his sleeves and took the dish, ready to wash his hands and eat his breakfast. Seeing that his hands were dusty, he lifted them saying: "These hands that have been graced by the dust of the Holy Land, should I shake them free of this dust?"

"Father," they asked, "Why is today different? Every day you come early and today you have come so late."

He said: "My sons, on my way I reached a place below Jerusalem where a man was plowing in a field. I thought: I will help him. Not only today, but every single day from now on I will plow and hoe and weed with him until the earth brings forth bread and I will eat my own bread like a babe who thrives at its mother's breasts." The old man saw that his words surprised us and he added: "Do you think that I have forgotten the day of death? By your lives, I have already prepared a grave at the Mount of Olives, higher than the rest of the graves, facing the site of the Temple. There I have left a flask of olive oil for the time when I give up my soul and you place my bones in my grave." He spread his hands from the top of his head to the ground, measuring his length. "I have prepared a grave," he said, "according to my own height, not a short one where they bend a dead man's legs under him, but a grave to fit me." He spread his finger on the muscle of his left forearm and pinched the spot where the phylactery is placed, saying: "Fortunate are you, my body, that you will be buried in Jerusalem! The place where you have been worthy of living, you are worthy of living there upon your death." As he spoke, the old man saw me and said: "Peace unto you."

"And unto you, peace," I answered.

He said: "A new face!"

I bowed my head humbly and said: "A new face that likes the old."

Then his son, grandson and great-grandson stood up and indicating me said to him: "He wants to hear the stories of old times from you, for he loves Jerusalem."

His face lit up immediately and he said: "Ask, my son, ask."

Seeing his friendly face, I began asking questions and he answered me. I asked and he answered. And about every occurrence and every event, though it happened fifty, seventy, eighty, even ninety years ago, he said, "I have seen it with my own eyes, may I live to see the Redeemer; I have heard it with my own ears, may I live to hear the Messiah's trumpet." He said this even for incidents that took place three and four generations ago, almost as if the Holy One, blessed be He, unfolded the generations before him like a notebook. I asked him how old he was.

"Do you begrudge me my long years?" he asked.

"May the Lord lengthen your days," I said, "to see the bounty of Jerusalem till your one hundred and twentieth year. Out of the depths of my love and affection have I asked you."

"I am ninety," he said.

"Permit me to say something."

"Speak," he said.

"Then there are two wonders here," I said.

"What are they?" he asked.

"I have never seen a son the senior of his father," I answered, "for your son says he is ninety-three and, what is more, of everything that you have related you say, 'I witnessed it,' even though it took place more than ninety years ago. If so, there are things of which you say 'I saw them,' and you weren't even born!"

The old man smiled, smoothed his beard and said to me: "My son, know that I have spoken the truth and, God forbid, no lie passed my lips."

Then I said, "With your permission, I will say that there is yet a third wonder here."

"Blessed is the Eternal," he said: "blessed is He who conducts His world in wisdom and order! But, if you have come to seek wonders, there is nothing that is not a wonder. Is there a greater wonder than that you and I are living? But listen and you will know that I have spoken truthfully."

"Respected elder, please continue," I said.

"My son," he said, "Why shouldn't I tell you? It is no secret. When I came to Israel I was twenty-seven, and I have lived here ninety years. But I swear to you by Him who rested His glory in Jerusalem that all the years I lived outside the Land are as nothing in my eyes. Therefore I say I am ninety."

Hearing this, I stood up, moved and shaken. I took his hand in mine and lifted my eyes to heaven and blessed Him with all my heart and said: "May the Lord fulfill your years until one hundred and twenty."

He too lifted his eyes heavenward and answered, "Amen," to the blessing. "Amen. So be His will."

Blessed is the Eternal who portions out life to all living creatures! For the sake of Jerusalem my blessing was accepted by Him, and the man remained among the living until his one hundred and twenty years in the Land of Israel were completed. And he passed on at a ripe old age, and as was his strength in days gone by, so was it at the hour of his departing. He really could have lived longer, but out of respect for our teacher Moses, may he rest in peace—as it is written, and Moses was one hundred and twenty years old at the time of his death—he gave up his life and took it upon himself to leave the world and go to his final rest, sound in body and limb and perfect in his senses. And following his bier were his son and grandson and great-grandson, sons of the third and fourth generation, all distinguished elders—even the youngest of them older than your grandfather.

From the day he prepared his grave until the day he died, that area was filled with many graves, for everyone desires burial in the Land of Israel, because the dead of Israel come to life first in the days of Messiah. When they came to bury the old man they feared they would find no room. Suddenly the flask of olive oil that he had left closed in his grave opened and its fragrance spread. There they buried him: in the choicest of graves, opposite the site of the Temple. The earth, worthy of him during his lifetime, was worthy that he lie in it at death like a babe nestled in its mother's bosom, until the fulfillment of the verse: "Lo, on the hills are the feet of the Herald and death is forever destroyed."

(Tr. Curt Leviant)

Sholem Asch (1880-1966)

The first novelist in Yiddish to win world renown, with his works translated into almost all modern languages, Sholem Asch remains the most widely read Yiddish novelist of the twentieth century. This is so despite his trilogy of Christological novels which continue to antagonize Jewish public opinion.

Asch was born in Kutno, Poland, where he received a traditional education as well as an introduction to the secular culture of modern Europe, and lived in the United States during World War I. He returned to the U.S. in 1938 and emigrated to Israel in 1955. He began as a Hebrew writer but soon turned to Yiddish in order to reach a wide audience.

Asch's first stories were as melancholy as romantic. Then came *Dos Shtetl*, portraying with love and sympathetic understanding the inner beauty and poetic charm of the small Jewish towns in Eastern Europe, placid and innocent, stabilized by tradition and hallowed by piety. *America* depicts the Golden Land realistically as a country characterized by rugged individualism, heartless materialism, and disappearing Jewishness. Not well enough known is *Kiddush Ha-Shem* (*Sanctification of God*), a masterpiece depicting Jewish sacrifical heroism during the brutal pogroms of the seventeenth century.

Asch wrote other excellent novels idealizing and glorifying Jewish mores and the unbreakable will of the Jewish people. But his Christology novels beginning with The *Nazarene*, in which he sought to reconcile Judaism with Christianity, came at the very moment of Hitler's early triumphs. Jews everywhere bitterly condemned the novels and derogated the author as an apostate. After World War II Asch settled in Israel, where he again glorified Judaism and Jews, this time in the novel *Moses*.

The most prolific of all writers in Yiddish, Asch composed short stories, dramas, and novels. More important, his novels have entered the mainstream of Western culture—bringing to Christians as well as Jews the knowledge that Yiddish literature contains works of the first rank, replete with a timeless, quintessentially Jewish literary quality: esthetic beauty infused with moral grandeur.

Moses

Horeb was not a lofty mountain; it did not measure up to the towering masses about it, reaching into the heavens. The approach to the plateau which crowned it was made by a series of steep, cascading terraces; it was not one of the copper-ore mountains, but sandstone throughout, and its clefts sprouted desert shrubs and spare cactus. Surrounded by the monstrous peaks which thrust their savage bulk into the skies, it made an impression of tranquillity, modesty, and retirement.

Moses stood at the foot of the hill and lifted his eyes in awe and reverence, seeking a sign from Jehovah. There was nothing to be seen and nothing disturbed the somber and oppressive silence. No vision appeared on the heights, and no leaf or shrub or cactus stirred.

Moses lifted his arms and called out in supplication:

"God of Abraham, Isaac, and Jacob, hearken to my voice. All things have happened according to the word Thou gavest our fathers, and Thou has fulfilled the promise Thou gavest me on this spot. Thou has freed the Bnai Israel from bondage, Thou didst give them bread in their need, and water to drink.

Now I have brought them to Thy hill, that they may receive the commandment and the law as Thou didst tell me in this place, Thou God of faithfulness and truth."

In the tremendous silence the prayer clamored and vibrated across the arches of the hills and died down slowly.

Then he heard a voice calling from the height, the voice which had sounded from the burning bush:

"Thus shalt thou speak to the house of Jacob, and this say to the children of Israel. Ye have seen what I have done to the Egyptians, and how I have carried you on eagles' wings and brought you to Me. And now, if you will hearken to My voice and observe the covenant with Me, you shall be peculiarly My own among all the nations, for Mine is all the earth. And you will be unto Me a kingdom of priests and a holy people. These are the words which thou shalt speak to the children of Israel."

Joyously Moses returned to the encampment. He assembled the elders and rehearsed before them the word of God, as he had been bidden:

"Of all the peoples of the world, which are all His, Jehovah desires to choose us as His peculiar people, a people of priests, a people of holiness, so that we may be an example to the other nations. We, the chosen people, are the first to acknowledge the one living God, and to take His law as the rule of our life, so that the world may see what is just and what is unjust, and from us learn the way to God. Will you take upon yourselves the yoke of this doctrine? Will you submit to the laws which God will give you, to be His holy people according to His desire?"

"We will accept all that God desires, we will obey all His words," answered the elders with one voice.

And Moses went on:

"Not for yourselves alone do you consent to obey God's commandments, but for your children, and your children's children; for not with you alone does He make the covenant, but with all who are with us today, and with all who are not with us today."

"We accept the covenant with God for our children and for our children's children, for all who are with us today and for all who are not with us today," answered the elders of Israel.

It was only then that Moses issued, in the name of God, the instructions concerning the mighty event which was to occur three days hence at Sinai, so that the people might know how to conduct itself and how to hold itself in readiness.

During this period the men and women were to abstain from each other. They were to sanctify themselves, and to wash their garments. For on the third day Jehovah Himself would descend upon the mountain in the eyes of the whole people.

So the children of Israel set about the preparation. Singly and in groups they came to the edge of the streams and washed their garments in the water cascading from the hills. But not their garments alone did they purify; it was as though the living waters were rushing through their souls, cleansing them of the stains of slavery in preparation for the third day. They knew now that the holy mountain would, on that third day, be fire from base to summit, and that they would not dare to approach it; man or beast that drew near it would be utterly consumed. And already they trembled at the thought of Jehovah's dread appearance, and they talked in low tones among themselves of the frightful experience which confronted them.

"They say Jehovah will bring forth not only a new order of the world, but a new creation. He will enfold all creation in His laws and commandment; the sun will shine, the earth will give forth its fruits, and the springs their water, in accordance with the order of His Torah—His law. A like portion will be given all men, no matter whether they sow a large field or a small; the harvest will be the same—even as it is with the bread which He causes to rain down from Heaven," said humbly and trustingly an ancient elder, his eyes shining in his sunburned face.

"They say He will restore the order of the world as it was in the six days of the creation. Man will not have to plow and sow; the trees will give their fruit untended, as it was in the garden of Eden when Adam and Eve lived there and had not yet sinned," said a second Hebrew, a long, lean haggard figure, all skin and bones, with deep-set, dreamy eyes.

Thus they spoke among a learned group, steeped in the

tradition of the tribe of Judah. Elsewhere the talk had a very different stamp.

"Who knows what burdensome decrees He will issue! Even before He reveals Himself on the mountain He already forbids us our wives. What will He do after? Perhaps He will forbid us entirely to multiply, perhaps He will want us to be like the angels," complained a burly, broad-boned son of the tribe of Dan, with a thick tangled beard and a vast, hairy chest.

"Hast thou an alternative? Our forefathers sold us unto Jehovah as slaves. For when Father Abraham made the covenant with Him, he delivered us unto Him, with our wives and children, for evermore to do His will."

"But are we not His slaves? Does he not feed us on His heavenly bread, and open up springs of water for us? And what does He desire of us? Have you not heard what Moses said, that if we only do His will, we shall become His children?"

"But why does he not give His doctrine, His teaching, His Torah to the angels in heaven? They do not need wives, and they need not eat or drink. They can live on His presence alone," insisted the Danite, waving his might arms excitedly.

"Scorpions in thy mouth and snakes in thine eyes, because thou blasphemest thy God; thy end will be as bitter as that of Pharaoh or of Amalek. Hast thou forgotten the rod of Moses?"

"Today I may still talk; tomorrow, perhaps, I shall not be able to. Let me pour my heart out, then. Three days without a wife! And who knows what's to follow!"

In Korah's circle, too, they talked of the great event.

"The way of the world is this: first a people conquers a land, then it settles therein; later it sets forth the laws and commandments according to the manners of the life of those that dwelt there. But with us it is all topside-turfwise: before we have conquered the land which God has promised us, before we have so much as set foot in it, we are already given the laws whereby we shall live in it," said the sagacious Korah.

"Moses says that it is indeed the whole purpose of our liberation. Not for our own sakes did God redeem us, but that we might be the servants of His law. It is for the sake of the Torah that He brought us out of Egypt. That is, not for us, and not because of the promise He gave the forefathers, but for the laws and commandments which He has prepared for the land. We, and our wives, and our children are nothing! And the law, the Torah is everything. Pharaoh held us as slaves in Egypt that we might build Pithom and Rameses; and Moses leads us into Canaan that we may be the slaves of the law which he is to give us," said Dathan.

"Law or no law—I only want to see him bring us into the land of milk and honey which we were promised. Thus far he has brought us not into a fruitful land, but into a stony wilderness."

"Did not God help Joshua to overcome the Amalekites?" asked a bystander.

"Who is Amalek? A rotten branch. But let him measure himself against the mighty cedars of Lebanon, against the Canaanites, the Hittites, the Moabites."

"As he conquered Amalek, so he will conquer all the enemies of God, of Israel and of Moses...."

The new overseers of the people saw to the separation of the men from the women. They divided the families. The women and the younger children remained in the encampment, while the men and the older boys spent the night outside, on the rocky plateau. The next day Moses led them, in their shining garb, to Mount Horeb, and let them pass the second night in its neighborhood. The men and the older boys he placed on one side of the hill, the women with little ones on the other. It was the first time that the men and women had been separated from each other.

A great change had come over the countenance and bearing of this people. The three months of freedom in the wilderness had taken the cringing look out of their eyes, which were now the clear and open eyes of freemen. The ashen-gray, pulpy skin which had made their faces the faces of slaves had become firm and bronzed. Their limbs were no longer heavy and listless; they had taken on liveliness, energy, and elasticity. Black, curly beards adorned the faces of the men, and their heads were covered with mighty shocks of hair; and two long curls, the token of the Bnai Israel, hung down over their cheeks, one from each temple. More than one hairy chest was decorated with a golden stomacher brought from Egypt, or stripped from a dead warrior, Egyptian or Amalekite. With their finger rings and earrings, the emblems of freemen, with the precious Egyptian linens thrown over their shoulders, they looked, these slaves of yesterday, like a great assembly of one of the indigenous desert tribes.

No less striking was the appearance of the women. Their bodies were swathed in rich stuffs and multicolored robes; they were adorned with earrings, nose rings, and neckbands; with hair new-washed and shining eyes they stood erect, freed not only from the yoke of the Pharaoh, but from that inner yoke which had oppressed their souls—row upon row of them, a fresh-plowed virgin field ready to receive the seed of God.

That night, as they rested in the enclosed circle of the hills, they already felt a vault settling over them—an arch composed of innumerable wings, of eagles or of angels. They were being drawn into the orbit of a new authority, they were being sundered from their surroundings; it was as if they were finding themselves in a vast sanctuary, of which the mountains were the walls; and they were unable to move from the spot. When the depths above them began to whiten, they saw a ponderous mass of clouds suspended over their heads; the sun did not emerge to disturb the brooding twilight; the summit of the mountain was enveloped by a black cloud which emitted coils of smoke, as though the mountain were standing over an abyss of fire. But they saw no fire; they saw only the smoke which, as it ascended, formed layer upon layer above the cloud. Now and again lightning flashes split the thickening gloom, played for an instant in the rolling smoke, and were extinguished. Thunder followed on every flash, reverberating with tremendous echoes. Then a ram's horn was heard, pealing ever more loudly.

A shudder passed through the hosts. But Moses commanded them to draw nearer. With beating hearts they crept toward the base; the clouds closed over them, and they were commanded to halt.

The smoke poured more and more heavily from the upper levels and the ram's trumpet pealed more and more loudly.

Moses called up the mountainside:

"Jehovah! Jehovah!"

And a voice was heard answering down the slopes:

"Moses! Moses!"

Then the people saw Moses ascending into the thickest part of the cloud, ascending into it, and vanishing. After a brief interval he emerged and spoke to the priests who stood in the front; and he warned even them not to set foot on the mountain. He that did so would surely perish, for Jehovah Himself was now there.

The lightning and the thunder stopped; the ram's trumpet was heard no more. Intense silence fell from the skies and settled on all the earth. No leaf rustled anywhere, no bird lifted itself into the air. Nothing stirred on the ground or in the space above it; it was as if all creation had been petrified. And the terror which seized the assembled host in this stillness was greater than the terror which had been inspired in them by the lightnings, the thunder, and the trumpet peals.

Then a single voice was heard ringing out from the midst of the enveloped mountain:

"I am Jehovah, thy God, who brought thee forth from Egypt, out of the house of bondage."

The voice beat against the encircling summits and was dashed back into the valley; it was heard reverberating in the infinite distance, carried on the waves of the air, then brought back again by the dying echoes. So it sounded over the whole world, carried everywhere, across the deserts and seas and mountains.

And once again it was lifted:

"Thou shalt have no other god before Me...."

Again it pealed over the hills and through space, dwindling slowly into a vibrating like the strings of a harp.

"Thou shalt not make unto thee any graven image....
Thou shalt not take the name of Jehovah thy God in vain....
Remember the Sabbath day to keep it holy....
Honor thy father and thy mother....
Thou shalt not murder....
Thou shalt not commit adultery....
Thou shalt not steal.....
Thou shalt not bear false witness against thy neighbor....
Thou shalt not covet thy neighbor's house...."

A long time passed before the voice of God sounded out the ten commandments from the smoking mountain. An interval ensued after each commandment. The voice waited until each commandment had been carried throughout the world and had reached every people; for the words were uttered not for one people alone, and not for one age, but for all peoples and for all generations until the end of time. And the ten commandments were a renewal of the act of creation; inasmuch as man and all else that lives issued from the first act of creation, so the continuation of life depends on the second act of creation, the giving of the law. And just as the first act of creation made a division between chaos and order, so the second act of creation made division between good and evil, between right and wrong. From this day forth there would be a center of reference, a line of conduct, a standard whereby to measure good and evil in all the corners of the earth, for all men and for all generations until the coming of the great day of God.

Lion Feuchtwanger (1884-1958)

The son of a prosperous manufacturer, Lion Feuchtwanger was born in Munich. After years of study elsewhere, he returned to Munich and received the degree of Doctor of Philosophy from the university there. He achieved instantaneous worldwide fame with publication of *The Jew Suss* (made into a film in England) and *The Ugly Duchess*, in which he applied touches of modern psychology to the historical romance. A later novel, *The Oppermans*, about a German-Jewish family, lampooned the Nazis. The liberal and humane sentiments in these and other novels and plays of Feuchtwanger stem from his pacifism and left-wing politics. For a time he edited a journal in Moscow. Later, after having been interned in France, he emigrated to the United States and died in Los Angeles.

Kabbalists

I

He crouched lower, and declaimed, in an obscure, unpleasantly broken and rumbling voice, half chanting, verses from the secret revelations. Skin, flesh, bones, and blood vessels are a garment, a shell and not the man himself. But the mysteries of the highest wisdom are in the organization of the human body. As in the firmament enclosing the earth there are stars and constellations which interpret deep and hidden mysteries, so there are on the skin of our bodies lines and wrinkles and symbols and signs, and they are the stars and constellations of the body, and they have their mystery, and the wise read and interpret them.

Come and behold! The spirit chisels the countenance, and the wise man recognizes it. When the spirits and souls of the upper world take shape, they have their form and their certain outline, which later mirrors itself in the faces of men.

II

By the lake of Tiberias the Master of the Kabbala, Rabbi Isaac Luria, walked with his favourite pupil, Hayyim Vital Calabrese. The men drank out of the Fountain of Miriam, fared out on the Lake. The Master spoke of his wisdom. The Spirit brooded over the waters; the skiff stood still. It was still a marvel that it did not sink, for heavy with the lives of millions was the Rabbi and his word.

Back to the Fountain of Miriam the men returned again. And again they drank. Then suddenly the fountain changed its course. It formed a bow in the air, with two vertical rays, a cross ray above them. Into the bow strode the Rabbi to be a third vertical ray. So out of him and the Fountain came the character Shin, the beginning of the most exalted of the names of God, Shaddai. And the character waxed, and spanned itself over the lake, and spanned itself over the world.

When the pupil Hayyim Vital returned out of his trance the fountain flowed as before, but the Rabbi Isaac Luria was no longer there.

But this middle column in the sacred character was the only thing he had written down of his learning. For the words of his wisdom fell from his lips and were like snow. They were there, they were white and glittered and were cooling; but no one could catch hold of them. So his wisdom fell from his mouth and no one could lay hold upon it. The Rabbi did not write it down and did not even suffer that others should write it. Because what is written is changed, and becomes the death of the spoken word. Therefore, even the Scriptures are not the word of God, but a mask and a distortion, what wood is to the living tree. Only in the mouth of the wise does it rise up and live.

Yet after the Rabbi had gone, his pupil could not refrain from setting down his wisdom on paper in the vain and lying symbols of the written word. And he wrote the Book of the Tree of Life, and he wrote the Book of the Metamorphoses of the Soul.

Oh, how wise had been the Master in that he had not soiled his knowledge with the written word, in that he had not twisted his wisdom, by means of the evil magic of letters! Elias, the prophet, had appeared to him by day, Simon ben Jochai by night. The language of birds had been revealed to him, of trees, of fire, of stone. The souls of the buried he could see and the souls of the living when on Sabbath Eve they soared to Paradise; also he could decipher the souls of men on their brows, draw them to him, speak with them, and then release them again to return to their places. The Kabbala had opened itself widely before him, so that the bodies of things were like glass to him: he saw in One, body, spirit and soul; air, water and earth were full of voices and shapes, he saw God's shuttle weaving the world, the angels came and held discourse with him. He knew that over all there was mystery, but for him mystery opened its eyes, fawned on him like an obedient dog. Marvels bloomed on his way. The Tree of the Kabbala entered into him and broke through him, its roots were deep in the bowels of the earth, its crest in Heaven fanned the countenance of God.

But oh, how this wisdom was changed in the books of his pupil! In wild confusion foolishness and wisdom sprouted from them. False prophets and Messiahs grew out of the characters; magic and thaumaturgy, wonders and miracles and harlotry and ostentation and falseness flowed from them into the world. The pallid countenance of Simon ben Jochai looked out of these characters, and in the thicket of his silvery beard lay snared and destroyed myriads of saints and holy men; and out of the symbols of these books gleamed naked and impudent the breasts of Lilith, and at her nipples hung lisping and babbling and with drunken senses the children of lust and of power.

And this is one passage from the secret wisdom of Rabbi Isaac Luria Ashkinasi:

"It may happen that in one human body more than one soul may suffer a new incarnation, and that at one time two, yea several souls, may unite themselves by means of this body in a new earthly fate. It may be that the one is balsam, the other poison; it may be that the one is an animal's, the other a priest's or devoted anchorite's. Now they are confined in one place, belonging to one body as the right and the left hand. They interpenetrate, they bite into each other, they impregnate each other, they flow into each other like water. But though ever brushing each other, recreating each other, always this union is the means by which one soul aids another, that the guilt might be expiated on whose account they suffer the new incarnation."

These are a few sentences from the secret wisdom of the Rabbi Isaac Luria, the eagle of Kabbalists, who was born in Jerusalem, for seven years mortified himself, alone, on the banks of the Nile, brought back his wisdom of Galilee and performed miracles among the people, never defiled his wisdom with writing and paper, and mysteriously vanished on the Lake of Tiberias in the thirty-eighth year of his life.

Theodor Herzl (1860-1904)

Founder of political Zionism, the World Zionist Organization, and the Zionist Congress, Herzl was born to an assimilated family in Budapest, where he was educated in the spirit of German-Jewish enlightenment. He studied law in Vienna, but became a highly successful journalist and playwright. The Dreyfus Affair (1895) galvanized him into seeking an immediate, practical solution to the plight of the Jewish people. Obsessed by an idea which in his diary he first referred to as "a work of infinite grandeur, a mighty dream," he ended by writing *Der Judenstaat* (*The Jewish State*, 1896), which aroused the opposition of many Jewish leaders by proposing the establishment under international auspices of an independent Jewish nation. Nevertheless, within a few years Herzl had awakened world Jewry to the real possiblity of creating a Jewish state and in so doing inspired a new and proud era of Jewish history.

For almost twenty centuries the Jews had been scattered over the globe in diverse communities speaking different languages. During the eighteenth and nineteenth centuries invidious distinctions were made between the "Jewish" Jews of Russia and the acculturated Jews of western Europe. But

Herzl insisted in a sentence of *Der Judenstaat* that would become famous: "We are a people—one people."

Despite his lack of familiarity with Jewish history and culture, Herzl analyzed the "Jewish problem" clearly and profoundly. As a result of a visit to Palestine, he wrote *Altneueland* (*Old-New Land*, 1902), a novel depicting a modern state in the ancient homeland. The novel's last words, "If you will it, it is no fairy tale," became the slogan of Zionists worldwide. Even as many of Herzl's prophecies have come true, so many of his ideas have been adopted by the planners of Israel today.

Utterly devoted to the Zionist cause, Herzl spent all his time and personal funds on it until overwork, anxiety because of lack of concrete achievement, and incessant struggling with Jews as well as non-Jews wore him out. Herzl succumbed to pneumonia at the early age of forty-four. After World War II, in accord with the desire expressed in his will, his remains were brought to Jerusalem, where, as a result of a resolution by the Knesset, they were reinterred in an imposing setting on Mt. Herzl.

Old-New Land

Kingscourt and Friedrich spent several days in the ancient homeland of the Jews.

Jaffa, the port of entry, made a most unpleasant impression on them. Although in a favored situation geographically, on a headland overlooking the blue Mediterranean, Jaffa was pathetically shabby. Landing in the poorly equipped harbor was quite a feat. And walking in the filthy, uncared-for alleys of the town, which stank to high heaven, was an introduction to every sort of Oriental wretchedness. Apprehensive Jews, miserable Turks, bedraggled Arabs loitered like lazy beggars bereft of hope. Kingscourt and Freidrich found breathing difficult amid the appalling stench, as of rotting food and moulding graves.

Hurrying away, Kingscourt and Friedrich boarded an antiquated train of the primitive little railway line to Jerusalem. As in Jaffa, so outside the town: the land was desolate, a victim of neglect, with much sand and marsh and few fields. The train chugged past blackened Arab villages where naked children played in the dust. In the distance were the hills of

Judea, once clothed with forests. Now, the train climbed up bare and soilless rocky wastes except for a very few cultivated terraces.

"If this is our homeland," groaned Friedrich, "then it has been brought just as low as we Jews."

Kingscourt agreed. "It surely is dreadful. Abominable, in fact, but something could be done by way of afforestation. What this land needs are water and shade. With half a million firs newly planted, it could have an undreamed-of future."

"And who is to supply the water and shade?"

"You Jews, damn it all!"

It was a fine night when the little train reached Jerusalem.

"Devil take me! This is gorgeous!" bellowed Kingscourt. Making the cabdriver stop, he told the hotel porter who had met them at the station, "You, stay up there and tell that fool cabby to go slow behind us while we walk a bit. What's this valley called?"

"The Valley of Jehoshofat, sir."

"Devil take me! So there is such a thing outside the Bible. And I thought it just a story. Here is where Jesus walked. What do you say to that, Friedrich? Oh, I forgot. But you must feel something, too."

"Jerusalem!" was all Friedrich, his voice quivering with emotion, could say. Could he explain how these hitherto unknown walls had so stirred his heart and mind? Was it the memory of almost forgotten words heard long ago in childhood? Bits of prayer his father had whispered? A picture of the Seder touched his soul and a Hebrew sentence he hardly remembered rose into his consciousness, *"Leshanah habah be Yerushalayim"* (next year in Jerusalem). He saw himself as a little boy walking side by side with his father to synagogue. But now his faith, youth, and father were all dead, although he stood before the walls of Jerusalem, magically beautiful under the moon. Hot tears stung his eyes. He stopped, unable to control himself, as the tears wet his cheeks.

Kingscourt saw. Swallowing a "Devil take me," he got behind Friedrich so as not to disturb him and signaled the driver to stop.

Friedrich sighed, came out of his revery, and apologized in embarrassment. "Forgive me for making you wait. It was such an odd feeling. I don't know what came over me."

Kingscourt took his young companion's arm and said in what for him was a gentle tone, "Do you know, Friedrich Lowenberg, I'm beginning to like you."

And so in the moonlight, the two, Christian and Jew, went up arm in arm to Jerusalem, the Holy City.

But in the raw light of day Jerusalem was much less attractive. The narrow, airless streets stank. What with people in rags—beggars, cripples, starving children—crowding the cramped passageways, everything appeared tawdry. Scolding women and screaming shopkeepers added to the general feeling of sleaziness. The once royal City of David had sunk into the depths of degradation.

Kingscourt and Friedrich toured the famous places and ruins, coming at last to a wretched alley flanked by the Wailing Wall. The disgusting sight of beggars ostentatiously muttering prayers shocked them.

"Here you see, Mr. Kingscourt," said Friedrich, "that our nation has died a thousand deaths. Nothing could be deader than the Jewish people. Nothing remains of the Jewish State but fragments of the Temple Wall. No matter how deep I pierce into my unconscious, I do not detect anything in common with these degenerates—exploiters of our mourning for a vanished nation."

Friedrich had spoken aloud, not thinking that he could be understood by the wailing beggars or even the dragomen all around them. But there was a third man in European clothing like Kingscourt and himself who at once addressed them in good German although with a Slavic accent.

"Sir, by your words you are apparently Jewish—or at least of Jewish descent."

"That is so," admitted Friedrich, somewhat taken aback.

"Then you will permit me to rectify the mistakes you made a moment ago. More remains of the Jewish nation than the Temple stones and these wretched specimens of humanity who, for sure, are not practicing an admirable trade. Today, you should not judge the Jewish nation by its poor or its rich."

"I am not a plutocrat, said Friedrich defensively.

"I see what you are, a stranger to your people. If you were to visit us in Russia, you would perceive that a Jewish nation still exists. Out of love for our past and belief in the future, we have a living tradition. The best, the most accomplished of Russian Jewry have remained faithful to the Jewish nation. We have no desire to join another. We are what our ancestors were."

"Good for you!" cried Kingscourt.

Shrugging, Friedrich politiely said a few words to the Russian Jew in parting. When Friedrich and Kingscourt looked back from the end of the narrow alley they glimpsed him standing at the Wall, deep in prayer.

While dining that night at the English hotel where they had rooms, they saw the Russian Jew with a young lady, evidently his daughter. They met later in the lobby and casually resumed the morning's conversation.

The Russian Jew introduced himself as Dr. Eichenstamm. "And this is my daughter, like me an opthalmologist."

"What," exclaimed Kingscourt, "this young lady is a doctor!"

"Yes. Sasha studied with me and in Paris. She is my assistant."

Dr. Eichenstamm stroked his long gray beard. "We did not come here for pleasure," he said. "We are studying eye diseases. Because of the filth and the slovenly way of life, there are many such. Everything, including the people, is neglected, impoverished, decayed, ruined. Yet the land itself is unspoiled."

"I don't see what's so good about it," said Friedrich.

"It is not a fable. It is the truth!" said Dr. Eichenstamm. "The land only needs men to be true to it once again."

Sasha turned to her father. "Why not suggest that the gentlemen visit our settlements?"

"Settlements?" said Friedrich.

"Jewish settlements. Something else you have never heard of, Mr. Lowenberg. Yet they are among the most remarkable accomplishments in modern Jewish history. In several cities of Europe and America an association has been founded. Called 'Lovers of Zion,' the members aim to set up villages to help Jews become a nation of farmers once more in our own country. Some philanthropists have contributed money.

Already there are several such villages. The old, old soil is again bearing fruit. You should see these settlements before leaving Palestine. How about it, Mr. Lowenberg?"

Friedrich quickly agreed. Next day the Eichenstamms joined Friedrich and Kingscourt on a trip to the Mount of Olives. Near the top they passed an imposing residence belonging to an Englishwoman.

"You can easily build a modern house on this ancient soil," said Dr. Eichenstamm. "What a marvelous idea to live up here. This is one of my dreams, too."

"Or we might build an eye hospital here," smiled Sasha.

Atop the mountain, they looked at the city and its hills and at the range of rock-strewn mountains all the way down to the Dead Sea.

Friedrich became thoughtful. "Jerusalem must have been beautiful. Maybe that's why our ancestors could never forget it. Maybe that's why they always hoped to return."

Eichenstamm was ecstatic. "It reminds me of Rome. On these hills another great city could be built, a truly marvelous one. Think how the view from here would be then. Better than from the Gianiculo. If only my old eyes could see such a sight!"

"Not us," said Sasha wistfully. "We shall not live to see it."

Kingscourt said nothing despite his amazement at hearing such fantastic sentiments. Later, alone with Friedrich, he remarked, "What an odd pair, that father and daughter, so practical and yet so idealistic. I've never met Jews like them."

Next morning, after saying good-bye to the Russians, Kingscourt and Friedrich took their advice and drove to see the settlements. Rishon-le-Zion and Rehovot were like oases in the midst of barren wastes. Industrious and skillful hands had brought life back to the dead soil. They saw productive fields, extensive vineyards and well-tended orange groves.

The Mayor of Rehovot informed Kingscourt and Friedrich: "What you see is no more than ten to fifteen years old. Our movement received its first impetus with the Russian pogroms of the eighties. But some settlements deserve higher praise than ours. The founders of Katra, for example, were intellectual, professionals who put aside their books for hard manual labor. Out of the whole world, educated farmers exist only here—scholars tilling the fields."

"Extraordinary!" cried Kingscourt. But his amazement grew even greater when the Mayor of Rehovot asked the young farmers to perform an Arabic "capriccio" on horseback. The youths mounted in a bound, galloped into the fields, executed several caracoles quickly, and turned around and around with loud huzzahs. Tossing rifles and caps into the air, they caught them at full speed and galloped back in formation, singing a Hebrew song.

Kingscourt's enthusiasm was boundless. "Devil take me! These youngsters ride like fiends. If my great-grandfather had cavalrymen like these to ride to the attack at Rossbach...."

Friedrich, however, was not much interested in these earthy athletic activities with their animated high-jinks. He was happy to return to Jaffa and the yacht ready to weigh anchor. On a fine afternoon in late December, they left Palestine's sunny coast and sailed west to Port Said, remaining two days before moving on through the Suez Canal. They reached the Red Sea on New Year's Eve, with Friedrich sunk deep in still another round of depression.

After sunset Kingscourt summoned him on deck. "Tonight we'll celebrate, son! Bottles of champagne are cooling right now. And look at the menu."

"What's so special, Mr. Kingscourt, about tonight?"

"Man, don't you know? It's the last day of the year. If dates have any meaning, this one certainly has."

"Not for us," said Friedrich heavily. "We've begun to live outside time, haven't we?"

"Well, true, if you put it that way. Nevertheless, this is a special date. At midnight we'll sink time into the sea, the Red Sea. When this idiotic era in which we've been condemned to live is over, we'll try to imagine something great. Meanwhile, I'll have a refreshing bowl of punch brewed for us. A good drink is the best thing in this worst of all possible worlds."

The wine was excellent. And the cook did his best. Kingscourt, who drank about three times as much as Friedrich, remained more or less clearheaded. But Friedrich felt foggy and heard Kingscourt's words as if in a dream.

As the clock struck midnight, Kingscourt bellowed, "Here's the New Year. Time, die a dishonorable death. A toast to your demise. What were you but blood, shame and progress. Drink up, son. You isolated contemporary, drink up!"

"I can't," muttered Friedrich.

"Product of a weak-kneed generation! Stand on tiptoe and look here, especially here, at the sea where your old Moses executed his greatest act. The Jews went through dryshod—at low tide of course. And that fool of a Pharaoh let himself get caught by the turn of the tide. Not supernatural at all. That's just what is so impressive. The means were crude, but Moses saw what could be done with them. Think of what a primitive time it was. Then imagine what your old Moses carried off. What would he say if he were to come alive and see all of today's marvels—railroad, telephone, telegraph, and all the machines, such as this yacht with its propellers and electric search-light. He'd understand nothing. For three days, I guess, you would have to explain and explain. Then, trust him, he'd know all. And you know what he would do? He'd laugh his head off at the silly irony. All this progress is pearls before swine because mankind doesn't know what to make of it. If you look at human beings as individuals, you will think they are wicked. Look at the whole bunch together and you will see they're plain stupid. Incredibly stupid! The world has never before been so wealthy, and never before has there been such poverty. People, millions of them, starve or nearly starve while wheat rots or is tossed away. That's all right with me, son, because the more the better. Every bit helps. There'll be fewer deceivers and traitors, fewer ungrateful, lying wretches."

Friedrich's tongue was sluggish, but he managed to get out, "Don't you think people would act better if they lived better?"

"No, I don't! If I did, I'd stay right with them, not wander off to some desert island. I'd advise them how to become better. There's no need to wait one hundred and fifty years nor for the millennium. On this very day, with all the knowledge available, the human race could begin to improve its lot. There's no need of a philosopher's stone, no need of a balloon in the sky. Whatever's needed to make a better life is right here on earth. And do you realize who can show the way? *You Jews*! Because your conditions are so wretched, you've nothing to lose. You could erect a pilot plant for the whole human race over where we've just come from, a new land on old soil. *OLD NEW LAND!*"

But Friedrich heard Kingscourt's words in a dream. Friedrich had fallen asleep and, in his imagination, was sailing through the Red Sea into the future.

(Tr. A.F.B.)

Mendele Mokher Sefarim (c. 1836-1917)

After some ten years of writing in Hebrew, S. J. Abramowitsch turned to Yiddish to reach the Jewish masses. He used the pseudonym of Mendele Mokher Sefarim (Hebrew for Mendele the Bookseller) in order not to harm his literary reputation, for the literate of his day looked down on Yiddish as the vernacular of the uneducated. Chosen for its symbolic value (the bookseller served as a link between communities and as a purveyor of knowledge), the pseudonym became—as was to happen with Sholem Aleichem—the only name by which the author is known.

Born in Lithuania, Mendele traveled much, coming into contact with all kinds of people and finally settling in the Ukraine. Like Dickens, he was interested in character and milieu. Mendele was a realist who relied on his memory for exact particulars so that his fiction in all its rich detail covers only the period from about 1850 to 1880. At first merciless in satire and ironic observation, at the end Mendele turned to a gentler humor and a memorializing that was less harsh.

Influenced by the Haskalah (Hebrew for enlightenment) into believing that education brings freedom and enlightenment, Mendele tried to get

294

Jews to look at their problems and defects and correct them. Although fiction, his work is valuable as historiography as well as art. His is the most complete picture of nineteenth century Jewish life in Eastern Europe. Because of Mendele, life in the shtetl, despite the destruction of the Yiddish heartland by the Nazis, lives on. He consciously tried to portray Jewish life in all its variegated aspects, providing little plot but including, especially in his early years, much realistic description as well as sharp satire of an impractical people and their stagnating ways. An allegory, *The Nag*, compares the Jewish people in abject poverty, oppressed and humiliated, with an old, haggard mare driven to exhaustion. *Journeys of Benjamin the Third*, a travesty of Jewish travel writers, satirizes the impracticality and social impotence of the Jews, mocking their gross ignorance of life and circumscribed horizons.

Called the "Grandfather of Yiddish literature" by Sholem Aleichem, Mendele was in a real sense the father of both the Yiddish and the Hebrew novel. Seeking a precise, realistic, and natural prose, Mendele abandoned the hitherto popular Biblical style and created out of the Talmud and other rabbinic writings a prose style that not only made modern Hebrew fiction possible, but also continues to be a dominant influence. Although primarily a Yiddish writer, Mendele translated his major works into Hebrew—filing, polishing, and rewriting his stories to capture the exact word and apt image. His descriptions of nature are undoubted masterpieces.

The Nag

This is Mendele the book peddler speaking. Glory be to the Creator! For, after His creation of all this enormous universe, He took counsel with His host of heavenly angels and did create a universe-in-little—by which you may take to mean man, who is justly called *olam katan* (a microcosm), since man, if you look at him closely, combines in himself all species of creatures and creations. You will find in him all possible wild beasts, as well as all the different breeds of cattle. You will find in him the lizard, the leech, the Spanish fly, the Prussian cockroach, and, to top it all off, a devil and a werewolf, a clown, a Jew-baiter, and many another uncanny foe of man and scourge of God. You will see, as well, among these universes-in-little all sorts of amazing sights. Here's a tomcat, for instance, playing with a baby mouse; here's a polecat making its way into a hencoop and sinking its teeth into the necks of the poor little fowl; here's a monkey mimicking and mocking everyone in sight; here's a dog standing up on its hind legs and wagging its tail for anybody who throws it a crust; here's a spider leading a fly astray, enmeshing it, strangling it, and sucking all the juices out of it; here are midges, overtaking a passer-by and humming all sorts of secrets in his ears: here are thousand of things no less amazing.

However, that's not all what I'm leading up to.

Glory to the Holy Name (I have said), Who contemplates in silence all that is going on in this universe-in-little and still does not give it the quietus, and puts off His wrath, and tolerates trangressions, and evinces not a little mercy toward man the imperfect. In short, I was about to tell you, at this point, of a certain great favor bestowed upon me right after He had, at first, chastised me just a little.

My little nag, kind master, is no more. My faithful horse, who passed all the days of her life in righteous toil, who served me faithfully and truly, who could have given pointers in topography to the natives of all the tiny hamlets and cross-roads settlements, who was a remarkable connoisseur of little wayside inns, who had, in my company, crisscrossed almost all the pales of Israel, who was personally known to almost all of our orthodox communities—my poor nag departed this life one fine day, as a matter of fact it was on Lag Baomer, in the town of Glupsk [Foolstown]. It is painful to give the reason; poverty, however, is no disgrace: the poor little thing simply passed away from starvation. Her daily fodder consisted of chopped straw, and only on rare occasions would there fall to her lot a few dry crusts of bread that I had bought from beggars who wandered about with sacks over their shoulders. Ah, woe to the horse that falls into the hands of a peddler of Jewish books! A wanderer, she wanders without end and in all probability labors more than her fellow creatures who draw wares more choice than ours and yet she is supposed to exist on practically nothing. A Jewish bookman lives all his life on virtually the same footing, and, one might say, he himself, with his wife and children, dies from hunger ten times a day....

However, that's still not what I'm leading up to.

The Lord (I have said) sent me a visitation. I was left without a horse, had nothing with which to buy another, and yet I had to get to the fairs in time. As you can see, I was up against it.

And there I was, sitting all by myself in the House of Prayer, in low spirits, when suddenly a friend of mine walked in, headed straight for me, and asked:

"Reb Mendele, would you like to buy a nag, maybe?"

"I'd buy it with pleasure," I answered with a sigh, "but where would I get the money?"

"Bah!" said he, "That's no trouble at all. You won't have to pay a copper of spot cash. It's quite possible they'll lend you a little something besides. Never fear, they know you're an honest man."

"In that case," I said, "I am most willing to buy your nag right now, without any further beating around the bush. Well, let's go, if you please—we'll have a look at her."

"Why, there's no need of putting yourself out, actually. I have the nag right here with me...."

"What do you mean, you have it here with you?" I voiced my astonishment.

"Why, right here—inside my coat." my friend smiled.

"Are you laughing at me or what?" I asked in vexation. "Look for someone else to make fun of—I don't find your little jokes at all entertaining right now."

"God forbid! I'm not joking at all," said my friend, and took from under his coat a whole stack of papers. "You see, Reb Mendele, all this belongs to a certain gentleman, a good friend of mine—you'll find his name right here on his stories. And it is one of these tales that bears the title, *The Nag*. The man who wrote it is, at present—and may this never be said of you!—he is...well, how am I to put it to you? He has bees in his bonnet, as the saying goes, but just the same, we who are his good friends would very much like to see his stories in print, as is fit and proper. To whom else were we to turn in this matter but to you, Reb Mendele, who enjoys such well-earned prestige in our region? We are asking you to go through these stories quite thoroughly and put them in shape. We rely upon you in this. You can go right ahead and print *The Nag*. We'll talk over the terms later, and I can assure you that you won't be out anything. If you need some money right now, why, we won't quibble over a small amount. Well, now, do you want to do it, Reb Mendele?"

"Do I? What a question, really! I want to with all my heart," I answered, and almost launched into a dance, so overjoyed was I.

I attended to my affairs and, full of zeal, tackled *The Nag*. I spared no labor and did my work properly.

And now, gentlemen, just a word or two concerning *The Nag*.

The Nag is written in a high-flown manner, after the fashion in which the ancients wrote. Each man will understand it in his own way and in keeping with this common sense. For honest folk who don't go grabbing at the stars in the sky, it will be simply a fairy tale. Those who look deeper may find in it a reflection of all of us who are sinners. Take me, now—I have seen in the nag all our little Jewish souls and have grasped the secret of why they exist in this world. I'm ready to wager that, in turning the pages of this book, many of us—each according to his nature—will exclaim vehemently: "Why, this is aimed at our Nusen Reb Heikes—" "—at our Zalaman Yukele Reb Moteles—" "—at Hershke Reb Abeles." Still others will declare: "He has discovered the secret of our poorbox collections, of our benevolent city fathers and all our lovely ways," and so on and on.

That's the sort of problem I posed to the Rabbinical judiciary in the town of Glupsk and to all the bigwigs in the vicinity. "As you know," I told them, "at the time I put out *The Tax*, I promised the public a sequel. It was more than a promise. It was a vow. Tell me, my dear sirs, what's the proper, lawful thing to do now? I am publishing *The Nag*. May I consider that I have fulfilled my promise concerning a sequel to *The Tax*?"

Well, they certainly pondered, and then pondered some more. They scratched and scratched behind their ears and, at last, came to a decision. "Yes, Reb Mendele," they answered, "after due deliberation, we do hereby release you from your vow. Let *The Nag* be considered the equivalent of your having kept your word, as if you had turned out the second part of *The Tax* and everything appertaining thereto. The thing isn't so bad, really, and after all, you've appealed to almost every taste."

How many thanks, then, should I render to the All Highest! Had I acquired *The Nag* just so, without any deposit toward the purchase of a horse, it would have been well. Had I acquired it with a small deposit, but it did not serve as a substitute for the second part of *The Tax*, and had the Rabbinical judiciary not absolved me of my vow without scratching behing their ears, that, too, would have been well. And even if they had scratched, but had given no reason for doing so, even then everything would have been well.

And therefore I should render thanks to the All Highest over and over again, because *The Nag* did have something of *The Tax* about it, and because the Rabbinical judiciary had released me from my vow, and because they did scratch themselves most horrendously as they gave me absolution, and because I know why they scratched themselves and understand that *The Nag* is worth scratching oneself behind the ear about...by way of redemption for all our transgressions.

That, gentlemen, is precisely what I wanted to say right out in my brief foreword. Whatever I have in mind is on the tip of my tongue.

Humbly,
Mendele the Book Peddler

Written the first day of the month
of Elul, in a cart laden with books,
on the road between the town of Glupsk
and Teterevka (Grouseville).

The Sabbath of the Poor

Six days in the week Shmulik the rag-picker lives like a dog. But on the eve of the Sabbath all is changed in his house. The walls are whitewashed, the house is cleaned; a new cloth shines on the table, and the rich and yellow bread, a joy to the eyes, rests thereon. The candles burn in their copper candlesticks, burnished for the Sabbath; and a smell of good food goes out of the oven, where the dishes are covered. All week long the mother of the house has been black as coal; to-day her face is resplendent, a white kerchief is tied on her head, and a spirit of grace has breathed upon her. The little girls, with bare feet, have come back from the bath; their hair is coiled in tresses; they linger in the corners of the room; by their faces it may be seen that they are waiting, joyous hearted, for those whom they love.

"*Gut Shabbos*," says Shmulik, as he enters; and he looks with love on his wife and his children, and his face beams. "*Gut Shabbos*," says Moishele, his son, loudly, as he too enters hurriedly, like one who is full of good tidings, and eager to spread them. And to and fro in the house the father and the son go, singing, with pleasant voices, the *Shalom Aleichem* songs that greet the invisible angels that come into every Jewish house when the father returns from the house of prayer on the eve of the Sabbath.

The rag-picker is no longer a dog; to-day he has a new soul. It is *Shabbos*, and Shmulik is the son of a king. He says the *Kiddush* over the wine, and he sits down at the table. His wife is on his right, and his children are around them. They dip their spoons into the dish, to take a little soup, a piece of meat, a fragment of fish, or barley, or of the other good things that they know nothing of during the week. The children carry these dainties to their lips with their five fingers, so that they may lose nothing of them. They eat carefully, as attentive to their food as the squirrel at the top of a tree, when he crunches a nut between his teeth and all his mind and body are concentrated on the act....

Now Shmulik clears his throat and begins to intone a song of the Sabbath, "Beautiful and holy is the Sabbath day. And. his voice becomes stronger as he goes on to the *Ma Yafit*, and sings of the weary who find rest, and of the wild river Sambatyon, which is tumultuous six days of the week, and on the seventh rests from its rage: "Sambatyon, Sambatyon, wild with haste every day." Sambatyon...is not Sambatyon Israel? All week long Israel runs from place to place. When the Sabbath day comes he pauses and rests; and on the eve of the Sabbath there is no more sadness and no more sighing.

Isaac Leib Peretz (1851-1915)

Peretz was born in Zamosc, Poland, where he received a secular as well as a religious education in the tradition of Eastern European Jews. After studying Russian jurisprudence, he practiced law until 1877. But his liberal views got him into trouble with the Czarist government, which compelled him to abandon his profession. From 1891 to the time of his death he worked as an official in the department of burial sites of the Jewish community of Warsaw. During his years as an attorney, Peretz wrote little. Later, although only a minor government official, he singlehandedly made Warsaw a literary Mecca for Jews, himself encouraging many beginning writers.

A man of many contradictions, Peretz opposed Zionism but sought a Jewish national renaissance, wrote in Yiddish but called it jargon, termed Hebrew the true national language but referred to attempts to revive it as silly, championed as a socialist freedom of thought but glorified rabbis whom he attacked for stereotyping ideas, strove to break the chain of tradition in Judaism but idealized religious life in the shtetl.

Often referred to as the "Father of Yiddish Literature," Peretz began as a Polish and Hebrew writer. To reach the Jewish masses, he turned to Yiddish

302

and in his forties became a master of the short story, although he was almost as skillful in drama, poetry, and the essay. Many of his stories satirize religious petrification and social hypocrisy. Some picture the disarray of Jewish society and evoke the pain and confusion of historical changes the people did not comprehend. Other stories, even more poignant, take as heroes the common Jew who suffered hardship with messianic hope. Although Bontzie Shwayg, the protagonist of his most popular story, is mistreated on earth, in heaven he joins the revered. In the volume *Hasidic Tales*, Peretz treats the religious ecstasy of the Hasidim as an attempt to free Jews from the artificial constraints of a stereotyped religion by transmuting ordinary experiences into lofty spiritual events, ethically righteous, that make of Judaism an exciting, joyous experience.

The Rabbi of Nemirov

Round about the Penitential days, shortly before the New Year, when Jews the world over pray for the remission of sins and for a happy year to come—round about those days, early in the morning, the Rabbi of Nemirov was wont to disappear. Simply vanish!

He was nowhere to be seen; neither in the synagogue, nor in the study-rooms, nor making one in a group at prayer—least of all of course, was he to be found at home. The door of his home stood open, and men and women went in and out at will; nothing was ever stolen from the Rabbi's house. But not a living thing was to be seen there.

Where could the Rabbi be?

Where, indeed, if not in heaven? Busy days, these, for the Rabbi, the days before the New Year. Are there not Jews enough, bless them all, in need of a livelihood, of peace, health, husbands for their daughters? Are there not Jews who want to be good, and would be good if it were not for the Evil Spirit, who looks his thousand eyes into every nook and cranny of the world, tempts and then tells, reports it in heaven that such and such a one has fallen.... And who is to come to the rescue, if not the Rabbi himself?

Everybody understood that.

But once there came into Nemirov a Litvak, a Lithuanian

Jew. He thought otherwise. He laughed at the whole story. You know these Litvaks, enemies of the Hassidim, cold-blooded and exact. It's little enough they care about anything but what's written in black and white, proof positive, and no mistake about it. They want chapter and verse before they believe anything, and their heads are crammed chockful of texts, the whole Talmud by heart. They'll prove to you, beyond the veriest shadow of a glimmer of a doubt that Moses himself, while he lived, couldn't get into heaven: he had to stop ten levels below—the book says so. How then shall the Hassidim mount into heaven? Can you argue with a man like that?

"Well, where do you say the Rabbi goes during those days?" we ask him angrily.

"No business of mine," says he, shrugging his shoulders. And, believe it or not, he made up his mind to get to the bottom of the business—for that's what a Litvak is like.

And that very same evening, soon after prayers, this fellow steals into the Rabbi's bedroom, hides himself under the bed, and...waits. He was ready to wait all night just to find out what became of the Rabbi in the early mornings of those Penitential days.

Anyone else would have dozed off and fallen asleep. A Litvak has a way of getting round it. He kept awake just by repeating in his mind a whole tractate of the Talmud—*Chulin* or *Nedarim*, I don't remember which.

In the early dawn he hears the beadle going the rounds, waking good Jews to Penitential prayers.

But the Rabbi had been awake for something like an hour already, lying there and moaning to himself.

Whosoever has heard the Rabbi of Nemirov when he moans in his affliction knows what burden of grief, of anguish for his people, he bears. No one could hear him, and not weep with him. But the heart of a Litvak is every bit of it iron. He heard, but he lay there, under the bed, while the Rabbi, God be with him, lay on the bed.

Then the Litvak heard how the beds throughout all the

house began to creak, as the household woke from sleep. He heard the murmuring of words, the splash of water, the closing and opening of doors. Then, when the household had departed, the house was silent and dark once more, except where a moonbeam broke through a crack in the shutters....

He confessed afterwards, did the Litvak, that when he found himself alone in the house with the Rabbi, he was seized with fear. He felt a creeping in his skin, and the roots of the hair of his beard tingled and pricked like thousands of needles.

And reason enough, too. Can you imagine it—he alone in the house with the Rabbi, in the early morning, on a day of Penitentials? But a Litvak is a Litvak...he trembled like a caught fish—and endured.

At last the Rabbi, God bless him, began to get up.

He dresses himself first, then he goes to the clothes-closet and takes out a bundle, and out of the bundle tumbles a heap of peasant clothes, a smock, a huge pair of boots, a big fur cap with a leather strap studded with brass buttons.

The Rabbi puts these on, too.

From one of the pockets in the smock there stuck out the end of a thick rope—a peasant's rope.

The Rabbi leaves the room. The Litvak follows.

Going through the kitchen the Rabbi stoops, picks up a hatchet, hides it under his smock and goes on.

The Litvak trembles—and persists!

The dread of those days of judgment, before the beginning of the New Year, lies on the dark streets. Here and there you could hear the cry of Jews at prayer; here and there you heard a moaning from a sickbed at an open window. The Rabbi sticks to the shadows, flits from house to house, the Litvak after him.

The Litvak hears the beating of his own heart keeping measure with the heavy footsteps of the Rabbi. But he persists, follows—and is with the Rabbi when the end of the town is reached.

There's a little forest at the end of the town.

The Rabbi, God bless him, plunges into the forest. Thirty or forty paces within the forest he stops near a young tree, and the Litvak nearly drops with amazement when he sees the Rabbi take out his hatchet and begin to chop at the tree.

And the Rabbi chops steadily at the tree until it begins to give creaks, bend and then cracks. And the Rabbi lets it fall, and begins to chop it up, first into logs, then into chips. He gathers up the chips into a bundle, binds it round with the rope which he takes from his pocket, throws the bundle over his shoulder, shoves the hatchet back under his smock, and begins to walk back to the town.

He stops in one of the poorest alleys at the end of the town, at a broken-down hut, and knocks at the window.

A frightened voice asks from within: "Who's there?" The Litvak recognizes the voice of a sick woman.

"*Jo*," answers the Rabbi, in the accent of a peasant.

"*Kto jo*, who's there?" the same frightened voice asks, in Russian.

"It's I, Vassil," answers the Rabbi, in the same language.

"Which Vassil? I don't know you. What do you want?"

"Wood," answers Vassil, "I've got wood to sell—very cheap, next to nothing...."

He waits for no answer and makes his way into the house.

The Litvak steals after him, and, by the gray light of the dawn looks around the room, broken, poor, unhappy.... A sick woman lies in bed, wrapped in rags, and in her sick voice she says, bitterly: "Buy? What shall I buy, and how? What money have I, a widow and sick."

"I'll give it to you on credit," says Vassil, "six groschen in all."

"And where shall I ever get the money to pay you back?" the sick woman moans.

"Foolish woman," the Rabbi rebukes her, "see, you are a sick woman, and a widow, and I am willing to lend you this wood. I will trust you. I am certain you will pay for it some day. And you have a great and mighty God in heaven, and will not trust Him. You will not trust Him to the extent of *six groschen....*"

"And who will light the fire for me?" she moans again. "I am sick and have not the strength to rise, and my son is away at work."

"I'll light it for you," says the Rabbi.

And the Rabbi bent down to the fireplace, and began to light the fire, and as he arranged the wood he repeated, in a low voice, the first of the Penitential prayers, and when the fire was well lighted he was repeating the second of the Penitential prayers. And he repeated the third of the Penitential prayers when the fire had died down—and he covered the oven....

The Litvak, who had seen everything, remained in Nemirov, became one of the most passionate adherents of the Rabbi of Nemirov.

And later, when the adherents of the Rabbi of Nemirov told how, every year, in the dread Penitential days before the New Year, it was the custom of their Rabbi to leave the earth, and to ascend upward, as high as heaven, the Litvak would add quietly, "And maybe higher, too."

Sholem Aleichem (1859-1916)

Born in the repressive Russia of the Czars, Solomon Rabinowitz tried various occupations open to Jews throughout his lifetime, although he remained first and foremost a writer—taking the *nom de plume* Sholem Aleichem, which means "peace be with you." A traditional Jewish greeting, it should be considered as one name, so that he is never referred to as Aleichem but always as Sholem Aleichem. The pen name is a key to his popularity, for by helping his readers to laugh at themselves and the world around them, he gave them, if not peace of mind, some solace in the face of their suffering.

Beginning as a Hebrew novelist, Sholem Aleichem soon turned to the speech of the masses and forged a literary language out of Yiddish, the Mamaloshen (the mother tongue), which had been regarded as a debased utterance of the folk. A prolific author, Sholem Aleichem wrote some thirty volumes of short stories, novels, and plays—with many others unpublished. He became, to use his own words, "the watchman of Jewish provincial life," portraying the hopes, interests, and worries of hundreds of characters on every level of society and in every occupation. Famous in his own time as creator of the small town, Kasrilevka, symbol of the shtetl, and of Menachem Mendel, a schlemiel who fails in all sorts of ventures but remains indomitable in woe as in joy, Sholem Aleichem is best known today for the character Tevye der Milchiger (Tevye the Milkman) portrayed in the musical *Fiddler on the Roof.*

Often called the Jewish Mark Twain, Sholem Aleichem was, like the ghetto Jews, able to laugh at himself, though with an undercurrent of sadness flowing from a sympathetic understanding of tragic elements basic to Jewish life in the Diaspora. Like Mark Twain, Sholem Aleichem observed people and institutions, not romantically through rose-colored glasses, but accurately through lenses of love. His was a kindly pen. Although frequently relying on satire, he never drew a thoroughly evil character. Nor was he didactic or moralistic although he dealt with poverty, hunger, and pogroms. His style is that of broad comedy, relying for effect on such devices as outlandish names, distorted quotations, ironic situations, and the extensive use of monologues. His heroes are unheroic. Weak, often foolish, they are never wicked. They esteem learning more than wealth, and they treat all Jews as members of one large family.

Sholem Aleichem's is a human comedy, one that rivals those of Trollope, Balzac, Hardy, and Faulkner in scope. In chronicling the rhythms of life in the shtetl (birth and death, youth and age, days of worship and work, home and business) he re-created an entire culture. No wonder he remains the most popular Yiddish writer.

The Passover Guest

"I have a Passover guest for you, Reb Yoneh, such a guest as you never had since you became a householder."

"What sort is he?"

"A real Oriental citron!"

"What does that mean?"

"It means a 'silken Jew,' and personage of distinction. The only thing against him is he doesn't speak our language."

"What does he speak, then?"

"Hebrew."

"Is he from Jerusalem?"

"I don't know where he comes from, but his words are full of a's."

Such was the conversation that took place between my father and the beadle, a day before Passover, and I was wild with curiosity to see the "guest" who didn't understand Yiddish, and who talked with a's. I had already noticed, in synagogue, a strange-looking individual, in a fur cap, and a Turkish robe striped blue, red, and yellow. We boys crowded round him on all sides, and stared, and then caught it hot from the beadle, who said children had no business "to creep into a stranger's face" like that. Prayers over, every one greeted the stranger, and wished him a happy Passover, and he, with a sweet smile on his red cheeks set in a round gray beard, replied to each one, "Shalom! Shalom!" instead of our "Sholom." This "Shalom! Shalom!" of his sent us boys into fits of laughter. The beadle grew very angry, and pursued us with slaps. We eluded him, and stole deviously back to the stranger, listened to his "Shalom! Shalom!," exploded with laughter, and escaped anew from the hands of the beadle.

I am puffed up with pride as I follow my father and his guest to our house, and feel how all my comrades envy me. They stand looking after us, and every now and then I turn my head, and put out my tongue at them. The walk home is silent. When we arrive, my father greets my mother with "a happy Passover!" and the guest nods his head so that his fur cap shakes. "Shalom! Shalom!" he says. I think of my comrades, and hide my head under the table, not to burst out laughing. But I shoot continual glances at the guest, and his appearance pleases me; I like his Turkish robe, striped yellow, red, and blue, his fresh red cheeks set in a curly gray beard, his beautiful black eyes that look out so pleasantly from beneath his bushy eyebrows. And I see that my father is pleased with him, too, that he is delighted with him. My mother looks at him as though he were something more than a man, and no one speaks to him but my father, who offers him the cushioned reclining-seat at the table.

Mother is taken up with the preparations for the Passover meal, and Rikel the maid is helping her. It is only when the time comes for saying Kiddish that my father and the guest hold a Hebrew conversation. I am proud to find that I understand nearly every word of it. Here it is in full.

My father: "Nu?" (That means, "Won't you please say Kiddish?")

The guest: "Nu-nu!" (meaning, "Say it rather yourself!")
My father: "Nu O?"("Why not you?")
The guest: "O nu?" ("Why should I?")
My father: "I O!" ("You first!")
The guest: "O-ai!" ("*You* first!")
My father: "E-o-i!" ("I beg of you to say it!")
The guest: "Ai-o-e!" (I beg of you!")
My father: "Ai-e-o-nu?" ("Why should you refuse?")
The guest: "Oi-o-e-nu-nu!" ("If you insist, then I must.")

And the guest took the cup of wine from my father's hand, and recited a Kiddish. But what a Kiddish! A Kiddish such as we have never heard before, and shall never hear again. First, the Hebrew—all a's. Secondly, the voice, which seemed to come, not out of his beard, but out of the striped Turkish robe. I thought of my comrades, how they would have laughed, what slaps would have rained down, had they been present at that Kiddish.

Being alone, I was able to contain myself. I asked my father the Four Questions, and we all recited the Haggadah together. And I was elated to think that such a guest was ours, and no one else's.

Our sage who wrote that one should not talk at meals (may he forgive me for saying so!) did not know Jewish life. When shall a Jew find time to talk, if not during a meal? Especially at Passover, when there is so much to say before the meal and after it. Rikel the maid handed the water, we washed our hands, repeated the Benediction, Mother helped us to fish, and my father turned up his sleeves, and started a long Hebrew talk with the guest. He began with the first question one Jew asks another:

"What is your name?"

To which the guest replied all in a's and all in one breath:

"Ayak   Bakar Gashal Damas Hanach Vassam Za'am Chafaf Tatzatz."

My father remained with his fork in the air, staring in amazement at the possessor of so long a name. I coughed and looked under the table, and my mother said, "Favele, you should be careful eating fish, or you might be choked with a bone," while she gazed at our guest with awe. She appeared overcome by his name, although unable to understand it. My father, who understood, thought it necessary to explain it to her.

"You see, Ayak Bakar, that is our Alef-Bes inverted. It is apparently their custom to name people after the alphabet."

"Alef-Bes! Alef-Bes!" repeated the guest with the sweet smile on his red cheeks, and his beautiful black eyes rested on us all, including Rikel the maid, in the most friendly fashion.

Having learned his name, my father was anxious to know whence, from what land, he came. I understand this from the names of countries and towns which I caught, and from what my father translated for my mother, giving her a Yiddish version of nearly every phrase. And my mother was quite overcome by every single thing she heard, and Rikel the maid was overcome likewise. And no wonder! It is not every day that a person comes from perhaps two thousand miles away, from a land only to be reached across seven seas and a desert, the desert journey alone requiring forty days and nights. And when you get near to the land, you have to climb a mountain of which the top reaches the clouds, and this is covered with ice, and dreadful winds blow there, so that there is peril of death! But once the mountain is safely climbed and the land is reached, one beholds a terrestrial Eden. Spices, cloves, herbs, and every kind of fruit—apples, pears, and oranges, grapes, dates, and olives, nuts and quantities of figs. And the houses there are all built of deal, and roofed with silver, the furniture is gold (here the guest cast a look at our silver cups, spoons, forks, and knives), and brilliants, pearls, and diamonds bestrew the roads, and no one cares to take the trouble of picking them up, they are of no value there. (He was looking at my mother's diamond earrings, and at the pearls round her white neck.)

"You hear that?" my father asked her, with a happy face.

"I hear," she answered, and added: "Why don't they bring some over here?" They could make money by it. Ask him that, Yoneh!"

My father did so, and translated the answer for my mother's benefit:

"You see, when you arrive there, you may take what you like, but when you leave the country, you must leave everything in it behind, too. And if they shake it out of you no matter what, you are done for."

"What do you mean?" questioned my mother, terrified.

"I mean, they either hang you on a tree, or they stone you with stones."

The more tales our guest told us, the more thrilling they became, and just as we were finishing the dumplings and taking another sip or two of wine, my father inquired to whom the country belonged. Was there a king there? And he was soon translating, with great delight, the following reply:

"The country belongs to the Jews who live there, and who are called Sefardim. And they have a king, also a Jew, and a very pious one, who wears a fur cap, and who is called Joseph ben Joseph. He is the high priest of the Sefardim, and drives out in a gilded carriage, drawn by six fiery horses. And when he enters the synagogue, the Levites meet him with songs."

"There are Levites who sing in your synagogue?" asked my father, wondering, and the answer caused his face to shine with joy.

"What do you think?" he said to my mother. "Our guest tells me that in his country there is a temple, with priests and Levites and an organ."

"Well, and an altar?" questioned my mother, and my father told her:

"He says they have an altar, and sacrifices, he says, and golden vessels—everything just as we used to have it in Jerusalem."

And with these words my father sighs deeply, and my mother, as she looks at him, sighs also, and I cannot understand the reason. Surely we should be proud and glad to think we have such a land, ruled over by a Jewish king and high priest, a land with Levites and an organ with an altar and sacrifices—and bright, sweet thoughts enfold me, and carry me away as on wings to that happy Jewish land where the houses are of pine-wood and roofed with silver, where the furniture is gold, and diamonds and pearls lie scattered in the street. And I feel sure, were I really there, I should know what to do—I should know how to hide things—they would shake nothing out of *me*. I should certainly bring home a lovely present for my mother, diamond earrings and several pearl necklaces. I look at the one mother is wearing, at her earrings, and I feel a great desire to be in that country. And it occurs to me, that after Passover I will travel there with our guest, open my heart to him, tell him the whole truth, and beg him to take me there, if only for a little while. He will certainly do so, he is a very kind and approachable person, he looks at every one, even at Rikel the maid, in such a friendly, such a very friendly way!

So I think, and it seems to me, as I watch our guest, that he has read my thoughts, and that his beautiful black eyes say to me:

"Keep it dark, little friend, wait till after Passover, then we shall manage it!"

I dreamt all night long. I dreamt of a desert, a temple, a high priest, and a tall mountain. I climb the mountain. Diamonds and pearls grow on the trees, and my comrades sit on the boughs, and shake the jewels down onto the ground, whole showers of them, and I stand and gather them, and stuff them into my pockets, and, strange to say, however many I stuff in, there is still room! I stuff and stuff, and still there is room! I put my hand into my pocket, and draw out—not pearls and brilliants, but fruits of all kinds—apples, pears, oranges, olives, dates, nuts, and figs. This makes me very unhappy, and I toss from side to side. Then I dream of the temple. I hear the priests chant, and the Levites sing, and the organ play. I want to go inside and I cannot—Rikel the maid has hold of me, and will not let me go. I beg of her and scream and cry, and again I am very unhappy, and toss from side to side. I wake—and see my father and mother standing there, half dressed, both pale, my father hanging his head, and my mother wringing her hands, and with her soft eyes full of tears, I feel at once that something has gone very wrong, very wrong indeed, but my childish head is incapable of imagining the greatness of the disaster.

The fact is this: our guest from beyond the desert and the seven seas has disappeared, and a lot of things have disappeared with him: all the silver wine-cups, all the silver spoons, knives, and forks: all my mother's ornaments, all the money that happened to be in the house, and also Rikel the maid!

A pang goes through my heart. Not on account of the silver cups, the silver spoons, knives, and forks that have vanished: not on account of mother's ornaments or of the money, still less on account of Rikel the maid, a good riddance! But because of the happy, happy land whose roads were strewn with brilliant, pearls, and diamonds; because of the temple with the priests, Levites, and the organ; because of the altar and the sacrifices; because of all the other beautiful things that have been taken from me, taken, taken, taken!

I turned my face to the wall, and cried quietly to myself.

Elijah the Prophet

It is not good to be an only son, to be fretted over by father and mother—to be the only one left out of seven. Don't stand here. Don't go there. Don't drink that. Don't eat the other. Cover up your throat. Hide your hands, Ah, it is not good—not good at all to be an only son, and a rich man's son into the bargain. My father is a money-changer. He goes about amongst the shopkeepers with a bag of money, changing coppers for silver, and silver for copper. That is why his fingers are always black, and his nails broken. He works very hard. Each day, when he comes home he is tired and broken down. "I have no feet," he complains to mother. "I have no feet, not even the sign of a foot." No feet? It may be. But for that again he has a fine business. Mother is satisfied. So am I. "We shall have a Passover this year, may all the children of Israel have the like, Father in Heaven!"

That's what my mother said, thanking God for the good

Passover. And I also was thankful. But shall we ever live to see it—the same Passover.

Passover has come at last—the dear sweet Passover. I was dressed as befitted the son of a man of wealth—like a young prince. But what was the consequence? I was not allowed to play or run about, lest I catch cold. I must not play with poor children. I was a wealthy man's son. Such nice clothes, and I had not one to show off before. I had a pocketful of nuts, and no one to play with.

It is not good to be an only child, and fretted over—the only one left out of seven, and a wealthy man's son into the bargain.

My father put on his best clothes and went off to the synagogue. Said my mother to me, "Do you know what? Lie down and have a sleep. You will then be able to sit up at the Seder and ask the Four Questions!"

Was I mad? Would I go to sleep before the Seder?

"Remember, you must not sleep at the Seder. If you do, Elijah the Prophet will come with a bag on his shoulders. On the first two nights of Passover, Elijah the Prophet goes about looking for those who have fallen asleep at the Seder and takes them away in his bag." Ha, ha! Will I fall asleep at the Seder? I? Not even to broad daylight. "What happened last year, mother?" "Last year you fell asleep soon after the first blessing." "Why did Elijah the Prophet not come then with his bag?" "Then you were small; now you are big. Tonight you must ask Father the Four Questions. Tonight you must say with Father—'Slaves were we.' Tonight, you must eat with us fish and soup and *matzah* balls. Here is Father, back from the synagogue."

"Good *Yom-tov!*"

"Good *Yom-tov!*"

Thank God, Father made the blessing over wine. I, too. Father drank the cup full of wine. So did I, a cup full, to the very dregs. "See, to the dregs," said Mother to Father. To me she said: "A cup full of wine! You will drop off to sleep." Ha! ha! Will I fall asleep? Not even if we were to sit up all the night, or even to broad daylight. "Well," said my father, "how are you going to ask the Four Questions? How will you recite Haggadah? How will you sing with me—'Slaves were we'?"

My mother never took her eyes off me. She smiled and said: "You will fall asleep—fast asleep." "Oh, Mother, Mother, if you had eighteen heads, you would surely fall asleep, if someone sat opposite you and sang in your ears, 'Fall asleep, fall asleep!'"

Of course I fell asleep.

I fell asleep, and dreamt that my father was already saying, "Pour out Thy wrath." My mother herself got up from the table, and went to open the door to welcome Elijah the Prophet. It would be a fine thing if Elijah the Prophet did come, as my mother had said, with a bag on his shoulders, and if he said to me, "Come, boy." And who else would be to blame for this but my mother, with her "fall asleep." And as I was thinking these thoughts, I heard the creaking of the door. My father stood up and cried, "Blessed art thou who comest in the name of the Eternal." I looked towards the door. Yes, it was he. He came in slowly and so softly that one scarcely heard him. He was a handsome man, Elijah the Prophet, an old man with a long grizzled beard reaching to his knees. His face was yellow and wrinkled, but it was handsome and kindly without end. And his eyes! Oh, what eyes! Kind, soft, joyous, loving, faithful eyes. He was bent in two, and leaned on a big, big stick. He had a bag on his shoulders. And silently, softly, he came straight to me.

"Now, little boy, get into my bag and come." So said the old man to me, but in a kind voice and softly and sweetly.

I asked him, "Where to?" and he replied, "You will see later." I did not want to go, and he said to me again, "Come." And I began to argue with him. "How can I go with you when I am a wealthy man's son, of what great value are you?" Said I, "I am the only child of my father and mother." Said he, "To me, you are not an only child." Said I, "I am fretted over. If they find that I am gone, they will not get over it; they will die, especially my mother." He looked at me, the old man did, very kindly and he said to me, softly and sweetly as before, "If you do not want to die, then come with me. Say good-bye to your father and mother, and come." "But how can I come when I am an only child, the only one left alive out of seven?"

Then he said to me more sternly: "For the last time, little boy. Choose one of the two. Either you say good-bye to your father and mother, and come with me, or you remain here, but fast asleep forever and ever."

Having said these words, he stepped back from me a little and was turning to the door. What was to be done? To go with the old man, God-knows-where and get lost, would mean the death of my father and mother. I am an only child, the only one left alive out of seven. To remain here, and fall asleep forever and ever—that would mean that I myself must die....

I stretched out my hand to him, and with tears in my eyes I said, "Elijah the Prophet, dear, kind, loving, darling Elijah, give me one minute to think." He turned towards me his handsome, yellow, wrinkled old face with its grizzled beard, reaching to his knees, and looked at me with his beautiful, kind, loving, faithful eyes, and he said to me with a smile, "I will give you one minute to decide, my child—but no more than one minute."

I ask you, "What should I have decided to do in that one minute so as to save myself from going with the old man, and also to save myself from falling asleep forever? Well, who can guess?"

Isaac Bashevis Singer (1904-   )

The second Jewish novelist to receive the Nobel Prize for Literature, Singer is quite similar to and yet very different from Agnon, the first Nobel Laureate. Each writes in a language known only to Jews—and a minority of Jews at that—Singer in Yiddish, Agnon in Hebrew. Each pictures the shtetl as a society in disarray. Unlike Agnon, Singer has won wide popularity in translation. Like Agnon, artfully naive and slyly sophisticated, Singer employs the devices of Jewish folk tales by means of which the supernatural is woven into the ways and appearances of reality. Where in Agnon's fiction the results are miracles beneficial to man, in a Singer story the results make up a chain of duality linking the conscious and unconscious, material and spiritual, good and evil in an uneasy tension that defies the assurance of an orderly and harmonious life.

Born in the hamlet of Leoncil, Poland, Singer was educated by his father, a Hassidic rabbi. Under the influence of his older brother I. J. Singer, who became a novelist, Singer wrote fiction as a teenager growing up in Warsaw. In 1926 he became a journalist for Yiddish newspapers. In 1935 he followed his brother to New York City, where he became a regular contributor to *The*

Forward. Despite early recognition by critics and fellow authors such as Saul Bellow, Singer was not well known until *The Family Moskat* (1950), a novel dealing with the breakup of traditional piety in the twentieth century. Since then his novels, short stories, and children's books have been best-sellers in the U.S. and Europe—partially because Singer scrupulously collaborates with his translators to create not so much an exact copy of the Yiddish as a second original that brings the flavor and spirit of the Yiddish into English.

Yiddish readers, imbued with traditional Judaism, its belief in a God of law and logic, and its faith in the moral significance of human behavior, are uneasy about Singer and his stories on sex, the irrational, and a demonic supernatural independent of orthodox theology—even though the boundaries of Singer's literary world are those of the shtetl and of Jewish culture. Perhaps they sense in him the existential feelings of man alienated in an absurd universe. Singer's ambiguity and irony arouse disturbing ideas about human actions being often inaccessible to reason, about law as an unsuitable basis for moral choice, and about logic as an invalid method for understanding the universe.

Singer is concerned with ambiguity, ambivalence, irony, and paradox, not just of style but of what people call reality. *The Magician of Lublin*, a novel, asks: What is truth? What is reality? What is honesty? One answer is that a person acts as if all he sees is objectively real although the scene and its meaning are in part creations of that person's mind. For Singer, this is accurate but too simple. The novel resonates with issues wider than the sequence of events in the plot.

Singer puts the moral element at the center of all his fiction, contrasting wickedness, sensuality, corruption, and deception with goodness, righteousness, spirituality, and probability. Unlike Sholem Asch in *Kiddush Ha-Shem*, Singer portrays Hassidic and Kabbalistic Judaism degenerating into the demonic instead of rising into the Messianic. Singer remakes the real world into an ugly horror to suggest that evil is an emanation of our sinful existence. *Satan in Goray* begins as a factual chronicle of a shtetl, describing events in homes, marketplaces, and synagogues. Gradually, the novel becomes a gothic tale, describing events in the soul and the realm of the supernatural. Some of these events, such as the rape of the female protagonist by a satanic dybbuk, are utterly horrible. The reader, led from one horror to another and guided from the natural to the supernatural, willingly suspends disbelief—almost in terror—as Singer mercilessly leads the way from piety to sin and so to the experience of evil from other-worldly beings. The reader thinks he understands until Singer introduces ambiguity and irony to the point of mystification. The impact of *Satan in Goray*, as with other works of Singer, is disturbing not only because of the demonic, which Singer forces us to take seriously, but also because of his deliberate withholding of explicit meanings.

The Strong Ones

Cheder, too often described as a place where innocent children suffered at the hands of a sloppy, ill-tempered teacher, was not quite that. What was wrong with society was wrong with cheder.

There was one boy with constantly clenched fists who kept looking for a chance to hit someone. Assistant bullies and sycophants surrounded him.

Another boy, for whom it was not practical to use violence, acted the little saint, smiling at everyone, doing favors, and all with an expression that implied immeasurable love. But in his quiet ways he schemed to acquire things, to taste something wonderful for nothing. Pious though he was, he showed friendship for the bully while feigning sympathy for his victims. When his friend the bully decided to give someone a bloody nose, the little saint would run to the victim with a handkerchief while gently admonishing the bully. "You shouldn't have done that...."

There was another boy who was interested only in business, trading a button for a nail, a bit of putty for a pencil, a candy for a roll. He was always losing out on bargains, but in the end he got the best of everyone. Half the cheder was indebted to him, since he lent money on interest. He and the bully had an arrangement whereby anyone who reneged had his hat snatched off.

Then there was the liar who boasted that his family was rich and famous and that Warsaw's elite visited his home. Promising us dates, figs, St. John's bread, and oranges from theoretical weddings and circumcisions and a projected summer vacation, he demanded advance presents from all of us.

Then there was the victim. One day the bully drew blood from him and the next day he gave the bully a present. Smiling with sly submissiveness, the victim indicated another boy who needed a beating.

From my seat in cheder I saw everything, and even though

the bully had punched me, I presented him with neither smiles
nor gifts. I called him an Esau and predicted that his hereafter
would be spent on a bed of nails. He hit me again for that, but I
didn't weaken. I would have nothing to do with the bully, the
priggish saint, the moneylender, or the liar, nor would I pay
them any compliments.

I wasn't making out too well. Most of the cheder boys had
grown hostile, informing against me to the teacher and the
tutor. If they caught me in the street, they said, they'd break
my leg. I recognized the danger. After all, I was too small to
take on the entire cheder.

The trip to cheder each morning was agonizing, but I
couldn't complain to my parents—they had their own troubles. Besides, they'd probably say, "That's what you get for
being different from everyone else...."

There was nothing to do but wait it out. Even the devil had
to weary. God, if He supported truth and justice, must inevita-
bly side with me.

The day came when it seemed to me impossible to go on.
Even the teacher, in that hellish atmosphere, opposed me,
though I knew my Pentateuch. The rebbetzin made malicious
remarks about me. It was as if I were excommunicated.

Then, one day, everything changed. The bully miscalcu-
lated the strength of a new boy, who just happened to hit back.
Then the teacher hurled himself at the bully, who already had
a lump on his head. He was dragged to the whipping bench,
his pants were pulled down, and he was whipped before all of
us. Like Haman, he was punished. When he tried to resume his
reign of terror, he was repulsed in favor of the victor.

The moneylender also met his downfall. The father of one
boy who had paid out too much interest appeared at cheder to
complain. A search of the moneylender's pockets proved so
fruitful that he too was whipped.

The saint's hypocrisy was recognized at last, despite his
whispered secrets and his flatteries.

Then, as if in response to my prayers, the boys began speaking to me once more. The flatterers and the traders offered me
good will and bargains—I don't know why. I might even have

formed a group of my own, but I wasn't inclined that way. There was only one boy whose friendship I wanted, and he was the one I chose. Mendel was a fine, decent person without social ambitions. We studied from the same Pentatuch and walked with our arms about each other. Others, jealous, intrigued against us, but our friendship remained constant. We were like David and Jonathan....

Even after I left cheder, our friendship persisted. I had attended several cheders, and from each one I retained a friend. Occasionally, in the evenings, we would meet near the markets and walk along the sidewalk, talking, making plans. My friends' names were Mendel Besser, Mottel Horowitz, Abraham something-or-other, Boruch-Dovid, and others. More or less their leader, I would tell them things my older brother had told my mother. There was a great feeling of trust among us, until one day I had the impression that they resented me. They grumbled about my bossiness; I had to be demoted a little. They were preparing a revolution and I saw it in their faces. And even though I asked how I had offended them, they behaved like Joseph's brothers and could not answer in a friendly way. They couldn't even look at me directly. What was it they envied? My dreams....I could actually hear them say as I approached them, "Behold this dreamer cometh....Let us slay him and cast him in some pit....Let us sell him to the Ishmaelites...."

It is painful to be among one's brothers when they are jealous. They had been good to me, they praised me, and then they were mean. All at once they grew angry. Turning away as I approached, they whispered....

Friendships with me are not casual; I cannot make new friends easily. I wondered if I had sinned against them, or deceived them. But, if so, why hadn't they told me what was wrong?

I could not recollect having harmed them in any way, nor had I said anything against them. And if someone had slandered me, why should my friends believe it? After all, they were devoted to me.

There was nothing to do but wait it out. My kind has to

become accustomed to loneliness. And when one is alone there is nothing to do but study. I became a diligent scholar. I would spend whole days in the Radzymin study house and then pore over religious works at home. Purchasing and renting books from peddlers, I read constantly. It was summertime and the days were long. Reading a story of three brothers, I imagined that I could write too, and began to cover both sides of a sheet. "Once there was a king who had three sons. One was wise, one foolish, and one merry...." But somehow the story didn't jell.

On another paper I began to draw freakish humans and fantastic beasts. But this too wearied me, and going to the balcony, I looked down the street. Only I was alone. Other boys were running, playing, and talking together. I'll go mad, I thought —there was too much happening in my head all the time. Shouldn't I jump from the balcony? Or spit down on the janitor's cap?

That evening, at the Radzymin study house, a boy approached me, acting as go-between. He spoke tactfully, suggesting that my friends were eager for an understanding but, since I was the minority, it was up to me to make the first move. In short, he suggested that I submit a plea for a truce.

I was infuriated. "It wasn't I who started this," I said. "Why should I be the one to make up?"

"'You'll regret it," he warned.

"Leave!" I commanded.

He left angrily. His job as as trucemaker had been spoiled. But he knew I meant what I said.

Now that they had sent an intermediary, I knew my friends were remorseful. But I would never give in to them.

I grew accustomed to being alone and the days no longer seemed interminable. I studied, wrote, read stories. My brother had brought home a two-volume book called *Crime and Punishment*. Although I didn't really understand it, it fascinated me. Secluded in the bedroom, I read for hours. A student who had killed a crone suffered, starved, and reasoned profoundly. Coming before the prosecutor, he was questioned....It was something like a storybook, but different. Strange and lofty, it reminded me of the Kabala. Who were the authors of books like this, and who could understand them? Now and then a passage was illuminated for me, I understood an episode and became enthralled by the beauty of a new insight.

I was in another world. I forgot about my friends.

At evening services in the Radzymin study house, I was unaware of the men among whom I stood. My mind was wandering, when suddenly the intermediary approached.

"Nothing you have to say can interest me," I said.

"Here's a note," he told me.

It was like a scene from a novel. My friends wrote that they missed me. "We wander about in a daze...." I still remember what they said. Despite this great triumph, I was so immersed in my book that it scarcely seemed important any more that they wanted to make amends. I went out to the courtyard, and there they were. It reminded me of Joseph and his brothers. They had come to Joseph to buy grain, but why had my friends come to me?

Neverthless, they did come, ashamed and somehow afraid. Simon, Levi, Judah....Since I had not become Egypt's ruler, they were not required to bow down to the earth. I had nothing to sell but new dreams.

We talked together late and I spoke of my book. "This is no story book, this is literature...." I said. I created for them a fantastic mélange of incidents and my own thoughts, and infected them with my excitement. Hours passed, They begged me to forgive them, confessed that they had been wrong and never would be angry with me again....

They kept their word.

Only time separated us. The rest was accomplished by the German murderers.

Israel Zangwill* (1864-1926)

More a vignette than a short story, Israel Zangwill's *The Sabbath Breaker* pictures with delicacy of sentiment and spice of wit the life of East European Jews in the shtetl, emphasizing their rituals—making clear how they kept alive the ages-old tradition and how that tradition kept them whole and together.

The Sabbath Breaker

The moment came near for the Polish centenarian grandmother to die. From the doctor's statement it appeared that she had only a bare quarter of an hour to live. Her attack had been sudden, and the grandchildren she loved to scold could not be present.

---

*See page 356 for the headnote on Zangwill

She had already battled through the great wave of pain, and was drifting beyond the boundaries of her earthly refuge. The nurses, forgetting the trouble her querulousness and her overweening dietary scruples had cost them, hung over the bed on which the shrivelled entity lay. They did not know that she was again living through the one great episode of her life.

Nearly forty years back, when already hard upon seventy, she received a letter. It arrived on the eve of Sabbath on a day of rainy summer. It was from her "little boy"—her only boy—who kept a country inn seven-and-thirty miles away, and had a family. She opened the letter with feverish anxiety. Her son—her *Kaddish*—was the apple of her eye. The old woman eagerly perused the Hebrew script, from right to left. Then weakness overcame her and she nearly fell.

Embedded casually enough in the four pages was a passage that stood out for her in letters of blood: "I am not feeling very well lately; the weather is so oppressive and the nights are misty. But it is nothing serious; my digestion is a little out of order, that's all." There were troubles for her in the letter, but she let them fall to the floor unheeded. Panic fear, traveling quicker than the tardy post of those days, had brought rumor of a sudden outbreak of cholera in her son's district. Already alarm for her boy had surged about her heart all day; the letter confirmed her worst apprehension. Even if the first touch of the cholera fiend was not actually on him when he wrote, still he was by his own confession in that condition in which the disease takes easiest grip. By this time he was on a bed of sickness—nay, perhaps on his death-bed, if not dead. Even in those days the little grandmother had lived beyond the common span; she had seen many people die, and knew that the Angel of Death does not always go about his work leisurely. In an epidemic his hands are too full to enable him to devote much attention to each case. Maternal instinct tugged at her headstrings, drawing her towards her boy. The end of the letter seemed impregnated with special omen—"Come and see me soon, dear little mother. I shall be unable to get to you for some time" Yes, she must go at once—who knew but that it would be the last time she would look upon his face?

But then came a terrible thought to give her pause. The Sabbath was just "in"—a moment ago. Driving, riding or any manner of journeying was prohibited during the next twenty-four hours. Frantically she reviewed the situation. Religion permitted the violation of the Sabbath on one condition—if life was to be saved. By no stretch of logic could she delude herself into the belief that her son's recovery hinged upon her presence—nay, analyzing the case with the cruel remorse-lessness of a scrupulous conscience, she saw his very illness was only a plausible hypothesis. No, to go to him now was beyond question to profane the Sabbath.

And yet, beneath all the reasoning, her conviction that he was sick unto death, her resolve to set out at once, never wavered. After an agonizing struggle she compromised. She could not go by cart. That would be to make others work into the bargain, and would moreover involve a financial transaction. She must walk! Sinful as it was to transgress the limit of two thousand yards beyond her village—the distance fixed by rabbinical law—there was no help for it. And of all the forms of traveling, walking was surely the least sinful. The Holy One—blessed be He!—would know she did not mean to work; perhaps in His mercy He would make allowance for an old woman who had never profaned His rest-day before.

And so, that very evening, having made a hasty meal, the little grandmother girded up her loins to walk the seven-and-thirty miles. No staff did she take with her, for to carry such came under the Talmudic definition of work. Neither could she carry an umbrella, though it was a season of rain. Mile after mile she strode briskly on towards that pallid face that lay so far beyond the horizon, and yet ever shone before her eyes like a guiding star. "I am coming, my lamb," she muttered. "The little mother is on the way."

It was a muggy night. The sky, flushed with a weird, hectic glamor, seemed to hang over the earth like a pall. The trees that lined the roadway were shrouded in a draggling vapor. At midnight the mist blotted out the stars. But the little grandmother knew the road ran straight. All night she walked through the forest, fearless as Una, meeting neither man nor beast, though the wolf and the bear haunted its recesses, and snakes lurked in the bushes. But only the innocent squirrels darted across her path. The morning found her spent, and almost lame. But she walked on. Almost half the journey was yet to do.

She had nothing to eat with her; food, too, was an illegal burden, nor could she buy any on the holy day. She said her Sabbath morning prayer, walking, hoping God would forgive the disrespect. The recital gave her partial oblivion of her pains. As she passed through a village the dreadful rumor of cholera was confirmed; it gave wings to her feet for ten minutes, then bodily weakness was stronger than everything else, and she had to lean against the hedges on the outskirts of the village. It was nearly noon. A passing beggar gave her a piece of bread. Fortunately it was unbuttered, so she could eat it with only minor qualms lest it had touched any unclean things. She resumed her journey, but the rest had only made her feet move more painfully and reluctantly. She would have liked to bathe them in a brook, but that, too, was forbidden.... Then the leaden clouds melted into sharp lines of rain which beat into her face, refreshing her for the first few moments but soon wetting her to the skin. The downpour made her sopped garments a heavier burden and reduced the pathway to mud which clogged still further her feeble footsteps. In the teeth of the wind and the driving shower she limped on. A fresh anxiety consumed her now—would she have the strength to hold out? Every moment her pace lessened, she was moving like a snail. And the slower she went, the more vivid grew her prescience of what awaited her at the journey's end. Would she even hear his dying word? Perhaps—terrible thought—she would only be in time to look upon his dead face! Mayhap that was how God would punish her for her desecration of the Holy Day. "Take heart, my lamb!" she wailed. "Do not die yet. The little mother comes."

The rain stopped. The sun came out, hot and fierce, and dried her hands and face, then made them stream again with perspiration. Every inch won was torture now, but the brave feet toiled on. Bruised and swollen and crippled, they toiled on. There was a dying voice—very far off yet, alas!—that called to her, and, as she dragged herself along, she replied: "I am coming, my lamb. Take heart! The little mother is on the way. Courage! I shall look upon thy face, I shall find thee alive!"

Once a wagoner observed her plight and offered her a lift; but she shook her head steadfastly. The endless afternoon wore on—she crawled along the forest way, stumbling every now and then from sheer faintness, and tearing her hands and face in the brambles of the roadside. At last the cruel sun waned, and reeking mists rose from the forest pools. And still the long miles stretched away, and still she plodded on, torpid from over-exhaustion, scarcely conscious, and taking each step only because she had taken the preceding. From time to time her lips mumbled: "Take heart, my lamb! I am coming." The Sabbath was "out" when, broken and bleeding and all but swooning, the little grandmother crawled up to her son's inn on the border of the forest. Her heart was cold with fatal foreboding. There was none of the usual Saturday night litter of Polish peasantry about the door. The sound of many voices weirdly intoning a Hebrew hymn floated out into the night. A man in a caftan opened the door and mechanically raised his forefinger to bid her enter without noise. The little grandmother saw into the room behind. Her daughter-in-law and her grandchildren were seated on the door—the seat of mourners.

"Blessed be the True Judge!" she said, and rent the skirt of her dress. "When did he die?"

"Yesterday, We had to bury him hastily ere the Sabbath came in."

The little grandmother lifted up her quavering voice and joined in the hymn, "I will sing a new song unto Thee, O God: upon a harp of ten strings will I sing praises unto Thee."

The nurses could not understand what sudden inflow of strength and impulse raised the mummified figure into a sitting posture. The little grandmother thrust a shrivelled claw into her peaked, shrunken bosom, and drew out a paper, crumpled and yellow as herself, covered with strange crabbed hieroglyphics whose hue had long since faded. She held it close to her bleared eyes—a beautiful light came into them and illumined the million-puckered face. The lips moved faintly: "I am coming, my lamb!" she mumbled. "Courage! The little mother is on the way. I shall look on thy face. I shall find thee alive."

Folklore

Jewish literature is rich in folklore. Even the most religious books, such as the Bible and the Talmud, contain a good deal of it. Each generation has added its own myths, legends, parables, tall tales, magic stories, fables, romances, anecdotes, homilies, fantasies, songs, witty sayings, proverbs, curses, and jokes to the vast repository of Jewish folklore—and has adapted for Jewish purposes the lore of the *Goyim* (foreigners) in whose midst they dwelt.

Jewish folklore, primarily a spoken performance rather than a literary text, is distinguished by highly moralistic and ethical strains. In the Talmud, for example, the *Haggadah* exists alongside the *Halakhah* with its legal dialectic and provides a leaven for expounding Torah, pointing up a lesson with an illustrative example or making concrete an abstract principle.

Stemming from diverse cultures in many eras, Jewish folklore is amazingly varied in form, theme, motif, mood, idiom. Yet it has a definite unity of purpose. Often witty and ironic, subtle and imaginative, tolerant and gentle, it is almost always moralistic and religious. Again and again, the characters are the pious and the law abiding, the scholars and the sages, the martyrs and the miracle-workers. But there are also fools as well as wise men, rogues as well as righteous men, demons as well as angels.

Each period of Jewish history has produced its own body of folklore. The Middle Ages saw the development of clever animal fables. The shtetl experience resulted in the rich compilations of Sholem Aleichem and anecdotes revolving about Menachem Mendel and Tevye, as well as cycles of tales concerning the men of Chelm, a mythic land where the line between wisdom and foolishness disappears. The Hassidic movement produced miracle stories of righteous heroes, the Tzaddikim. The nineteenth century witnessed the growth of legends about the Rothschilds and Moses Montefiore. In Israel today the old and the new from all over the world mix as the Ashkenazim and the Sephardim re-tell and re-create Jewish folklore in dance, song, and story.

And so Jewish folklore, unique by reason of its ethical content and its long and continuous yet variegated development, continues to reflect Judaic customs, traditions, values, and beliefs in the tender-sad visions of the Jewish people and their God-fearing ways of looking at the world, both the natural and the supernatural.

Berechiah Ben Natronai Ha Nakdan
(c. 1200)

Known in medieval France and England as Benedict le Pointeur for his punctuation of the Bible (*nakdan* is Hebrew for punctuation), Berechiah became famous for his compilation *Mishle Shualim* (Fox Fables) in which he translated earlier tales of Aesop and Marie de France, adding narratives from the Bible, Talmud, and Midrashim. Undoubtedly the main reasons for the popularity of *Mishle Shualim* were the comic effects and allusive nuances Berechiah achieved by capping his tales with quotations or references in Hebrew spoken by a bear, a fish, or other animals unknowingly satirizing foibles of mankind.

A scribe familiar with Jewish writings, Berechiah took his title from the Talmud, which applies the term "fox fables" generically to any short narrative in which animals talk to each other while conveying or reinforcing a truth, precept, or insight. As Jotham's tale of the trees in quest of a king reveals (Judges 9:8-16), fables have long played a significant role in Jewish literary tradition.

Crow & Fox

Great is the Power of Pride even Surpassing Greed

A crow mounted a fig tree, carrying a cheese in his mouth. Under the tree stood a fox, devising and scheming how he might bring the cheese down to earth. He called to the crow: "Stately, handsome, and sweet bird, good and agreeable and lovely, happy is he who is paired with thee. If all the beauties were at thy side their comeliness would not equal thine. If thou shouldest assay to sing songs thou wouldst surpass all birds in music and wouldst be sole perfection, for no flaw is to be found in thee. See whether thy voice matches thy stature and the majesty of thy plummage, for thou art free of fault." The crow said to himself: "I shall let him hear my voice, and he shall heap praise upon praise." So he opened his mouth to raise his voice, whereupon the cheese immediately fell and landed near the head of the fox, who said: "Of the precious things of heaven above this hath come to me from him, that raiseth his voice; no longer will I listen to the sound of song." So he went to his own place after he had obtained his desire of the crow.

This parable is for the proud and haughty and for the flatterers and falsifiers who deceive them with their lies and honeyed words, and extract their wealth which they had secreted in vain and in utter futility. Beware, therefore, of the seducer, and be not swayed by the aspect of his figure and the loftiness of his stature; let him not trap thee with his eyeballs, with his false lips, with his violent hands.

And I plied my poesy and said:

A friend hath fooled me; 'tis easy to befool a fool;
Easier still it is when one makes himself a fool.

Ox, Lion, Ram

Who Hath a Lurking Enemy
Shall Tremble Morning and Evening

An ox saw a lion and ran away, for the lion roared and bellowed and trumpeted after him, and he hid him in a certain pit beneath thick flaxen cordage, where a ram was hidden. His heart's terror made him tremble in fear of the ram. Said the ram to him: "Why art thou afraid? Surely thou and I belong to the same herd." The ox answered: "Every animal I see alive is in my eyes a mighty lion. If I had found thee alone I had not feared thee, but now because of the lion I am confounded and atremble."

The parable is for a man that has an enemy whom he fears always, morning and evening, walking and sitting, rising and lying down. Every man he imagines is his enemy, and says, "Now shall I be pursued"; but it is the sound of a driven leaf that pursues him.

Wolf & Cattle

Whose Feet Are Accustomed to Robbery's Path,
His Eye Will Not Spare Another's Wealth

A wolf who was the king's vizier and a chief made it his goal to destroy all flesh. He robbed and ravaged, plundered and uprooted; all that he found he pierced. And the beasts and the fowl and the cattle upon whose families confusion had been visited went to the lion to complain of him. Said the lion: "Evil it is and rebellious if, as ye say, he hath bared his teeth. Hath he indeed destroyed according as the cry that hath come unto me? I shall judge him, so that he will turn his back from destroying, and shall cast the prey from his teeth."

And he sent word to the wolf: "Come unto me on the morrow. Hearken and obey, delay not." So he came, and the lion addressed him with sternness and said to him: "Wherefore hast thou done so? No more crush the neck of the cattle, nor rend the beasts for prey. Thine own food are such carcasses and mangled bodies of fowl or cattle as thou wilt find dead in the field. But the living thou shalt not lurk after nor hunt down. If thy canst not keep my words, swear to me that thou wilt not eat meat for two full years, to atone for thy sins, which are inscribed and sealed. This is the sentence that I determine for thee." So the wolf swore this matter: that he would not eat flesh for two years from the day he preyed upon any that dwelt among the beasts.

The wolf departed thence and went upon his way, and the lion was left king in his lair. The wolf ate not of any four-legged creature, in keeping with the oath which he swore, unless he found some mangled body or carcass cast out into the field or upon the road.

One day when he was famished he turned this way and that and saw a fat kid, desirable to look upon and good to eat; and he said: "Who can keep the commandment?" Within him his thoughts were at war whether to set his face against the kid, and he said in his heart: "If my lust vanquish me and I again smite a living creature as I have done aforetime, from that day I must count two full years during which I must not eat flesh. This is the thing I swore to the king; but my heart hath devised a way to fulfill mine oath: The days of the year number three hundred and sixty-five; let the opening of my eyes be reckoned a day, and their closing a new night."

And he opened his eyes after that he had shut them tight, and the evening and morning were the first day. So doing he counted two years, and his iniquity was removed and his sin atoned.

Then his eyes turned to the kid of their choice and looked upon him and pierced him; and he said: "Lo, I have made atonement before my food." So he seized the kid by the neck and cut it up and ate it, as was his wont in the beginning. Still

is his arm stretched out against living things, as in days of old
and years gone by.

The parable is for a man wont ever to steal and rob, whose
eye spares not the wealth of others. Their wealth and their toil
he spoils and plunders and if he swears in the presence of all,
his heart will cunningly circumvent his oath and he will
account himself innocent of his curse.

Martin Buber (1878-1965)

Buber found in Hasidism (from the Hebrew for piety, loyalty) not only a direct concern for the individual human being and a felt need to enter into loving relationships with other human beings and with God, but also the goal of maintaining communities in which such relationships can be sustained. Buber studied European Hasidic folklore: miracle stories, parables, moral anecdotes, stories of fervor and faith. From these, he culled material for his *Tales of the Hasidim*, a volume which made known the inner Hasidic world. Buber's interpretive retelling of these tales became part of both Jewish and world culture, with the result that Hasidism has had a vitalizing effect on contemporary theology. Today, Hasidism is centered in New York City and in Israel.

Rooted in Jewish mysticism and influences, particularly by the dualism of the *Kabbalah*, Hasidism embodies a series of contradictions: stressing popular appeal, it combines the arcane with esoteric doctrines; employing the outer forms of religion, it concentrates on inwardness; practicing religious experiences in masses it relies on a chosen individual, the *Tzaddik* (Hebrew for the just or righteous), to mediate between God and man; earthy, even sensual, it aims at joyous union with the world of the spirit beyond physical concerns. Hasidism stresses the here-and-now, as though it would change the future tense of the Bible into the present: "You shall be holy, for I the Lord your God, am holy" (Leviticus 19:1).

The Severe Penance

(*A Hasidic Story*)

The young Rabbi Michael, the "Slotscher," had imposed hard penance on a man who had unwittingly desecrated the Sabbath. For it had happened that the man's cart had broken down, and, though journeying fast, he had not reached the town before the Sabbath had set in.

The man tried with all his might to fulfill the penance imposed upon him, but he soon became aware that his strength was failing and that he was becoming ill, and finally that his mind was weakening. Suddenly he learnt that the Baal Shem was travelling through the country, and that he was stopping at a place near by.

Summoning courage, he went to the Master and besought him to impose penance that would set him free from the one which he had committed. "Take a pound of candles to the prayer-house," said the Baal Shem, "and have them lit for the Sabbath; that shall be thy penance." The man thought that his communication could have been only half heard, and urgently repeated his request. When the Baal Shem still persisted in his mild sentence, the man confided to him what a severe punishment had been inflicted upon him. "Only do as I bid thee," said the Master. "But let Rabbi Michael know that he is to come to the town of Stow where I am keeping the next Sabbath." With a lightened heart the petitioner took his leave.

Rabbi Michael's carriage wheel broke on the way to Stow and he had to proceed on foot. Although he made as much haste as he could, when he entered the town it was already dark, and when he stepped over the Baal Shem's threshold he saw that the Master had risen, goblet in hand, in order to recite the blessing over the wine in preparation for the day of rest. The Master stopped short in what he was doing and said to the man who stood dazed before him: "Good Sabbath, thou man free from sin! Thous hast not tasted the pain of the sinner, and hast never borne within thee his broken heart; thus it came easy to thee to administer harsh penance. Now taste the pain of the sinner! Good Sabbath, you sinner."

Chelm Folktales

Like its counterparts the cities of Gotham in England, Abdera in Greece, and Schildberg in Germany, over the years the real village of Chelm in Poland gained a reputation in folklore as a center of innocent stupidity. The mythic community of Chelm, peopled with simpletons, became the focus of a considerable body of Yiddish folk-humor. According to legend, an angel of the Lord was carrying a bag filled with the souls of the foolish unborn when the bag burst directly over the village of Chelm; thus, the tiny village received more than its just share of foolish souls. The irreverent tales that center about the antics of the Chelmer, the residents of Chelm, show man in his naivete and insouciance. The harshness of Mendele's narratives does not appear here. The stories of Chelm depict an entire community of decent, well-meaning, but befuddled fools trying to cope with the everyday problems of life. The Chelmer, blithely unaware that they themselves are world famous for stupidity, not that other communities never do things the same way they do, pity anyone living outside of Chelm because any other way is the wrong way. These whimsical folktales, as often as not, are a mixture of scorn, understanding, and sympathy that, along with their shtetl settings, irony, and wit, give them a distinctively Jewish flavor.

Legends

As the story goes, an angel was flying over the villages of central Europe, carrying in a large sack the souls of all those that were to be born during the coming year. On one side of the sack, were the foolish souls and on the opposite side were the wise ones. Unfortunately, as the angel passed over the village of Chelm, the angel in confusion emptied only the foolish ones over the city, sprinkling the village with foolish souls, without the leavening of some needed wisdom. And thus there arose the memorable city of Chelm.

It is told that two residents of Chelm were waiting together, strolling on the main promenade that goes through the center of town. One carried an umbrella and the other did not. Suddenly the sun was obscured by dark clouds and it began to shower.

"Quick, my friend," said the umbrella-less Chelmite, "open your umbrella before we are both drenched."

"It will serve no purpose," responded his friend. "No use at all."

"And why is that? Certainly your umbrella should protect us from the rain."

"It will not," said the one, still carrying the closed umbrella, "since the umbrella is broken and filled with holes."

"Then why did you carry that umbrella, since it has no value?"

"Ah," said the one with a twinkle, "that is easy to answer. I did not think it would rain today."

These same two fellows were once engaged in a heated discussion.

The first said, "This is a philosophical problem to which I seek an answer. Do people grow from the feet up or from the head down?"

"Now, indeed," said his friend, "this is a problem and we must find out. Let us go and spend the week in our delightful village of Chelm and investigate the matter. We will return to the synagogue at the end of a week and report our findings."

And so the two friends parted and spent the week observing. At the end of the week, true to their word, both met in the synagogue.

The first exclaimed, "How easy this problem was to solve. I have the answer. All people grow from their feet up."

"And how did you arrive at this erroneous conclusion?" asked the other.

"When my son became bar mitzvah last year I bought him his first pair of long pants. They were so long that they touched the ground. And yet today, they come well above his ankle. So there is your proof that we grow from the feet up."

"Such nonsense!" exclaimed his friend. "You are completely wrong and I can prove it to you by your very own son. Yesterday your teen-aged son was standing with all his classmates in a straight line and I observed all the young people. All at once I saw the truth. They were all the same at the bottom of their feet. But at the tops of their heads they differed greatly in size."

And finally we are told that these very same residents of Chelm entered into a dispute over the relative value of the solar bodies.

Fellow Number One argued that the sun was the most important of all the heavenly bodies. "Look how beautiful the sun is. It shines with such great force and gives light and heat to all those who are fortunate enough to be put out of doors on a bright sunny day."

"No, no, no," said his friend, vehemently shaking his head so that his beard waved to and fro. "The moon is more beautiful and more important. Any fool can see that. I am surprised that you did not come to this conclusion at once."

"And how did you, Friend Simpleton, reach this conclusion?"

"That was simple. After all I have observed that the sun shines only during the day when it is light and no one requires extra sunlight. But at night when it is dark and we could all use a little light when we leave our homes to go to the synagogue or to a neighbor for a cup of tea, then the moon is out when we all need it. So I definitely conclude that the moon is more important."

(Adapted and retold by L.L.)

The Midrash

Called in the plural *Midrashim* but referred to generally under the singular form, the *Midrash* (Hebrew for to seek, examine, interest) makes up an important part of the voluminous corpus of Talmudic literature originally devoted to oral exegesis of the Bible, especially to the Torah, the Five Books of Moses. Composers of the Midrash sought to find new meanings for the Biblical terms in addition to the literal, so that they could be applied to changing life situations while they comfort, exhort, and edify.*

While the entire *Talmud* is replete with Midrashic exposition, the term *Midrash* is usually reserved today for specific exegetical collections that retain the order of verses as they occur in Scripture. Although early collections were compiled at the same time as the *Mishnah* and *Gemarah*, *Midrashic* activity persisted for more than a thousand years, terminating after

---

* Often in *Midrash* a word or phrase of the Bible stimulates the commentator to a word or idea of his own, so that the result is not so much an explanation of a particular text as it is a teaching based on verbal association. No wonder that in the *Midrash* there sometimes appear two (or more) different comments on a single verse of Scripture.

the end of the Gaonic period, about 1200 C.E. The *Midrash* was gradually superseded by the study of theology and mystical reliance on the Kabbalah.

Originating as homilies in the synagogues and the academies, *Midrashim* consisted of inspirational but diverting allegories, anecdotes, aphorisms, fables, legends, myths, parables—each interpreting a Scriptural verse or passage and deriving from the text an ethical principle or lesson. Like the *Talmud*, the *Midrash* consists of both legal or *Halakhic* and sermonic or *Haggadic* writings; unlike the case of the *Talmud*, here the *Haggadic* are by far more numerous. Where *Halakhic Midrashim* appeal to the intellect in interpreting legal points or regulations and expounding practices the rabbinic sages wanted the people to follow, the *Haggadic* address the heart in poetic metaphors that stimulate the imagination and affect the emotions.

Over the centuries, a number of *Midrashic* collections were compiled. *Mechiltah*, an exposition of the Book of Exodus only partially extant, is typical of early creations of the *Tannaim* in Hebrew. The *Midrash Rabbah*, a later collection by the *Amoraim* in Aramaic, contains interpretations of the Five Books of Moses and the five Scrolls (Ecclesiastes, Esther, Lamentations, Ruth, the Song of Songs). To this day, these *Midrashim* and numerous others are read in many synagogues throughout the year, serving as a source of homilies for preaching.

Wisdom

Rabbi Abbahu and Rabbi Hiyya ben Abba came to the same town at the same time. Rabbi Hiyya delivered a scholarly discourse on the Law, while Rabbi Abbahu delivered a Midrashic sermon. Thereupon all the people left Rabbi Hiyya and came to Rabbi Abbahu.

Rabbi Hiyya was greatly discouraged, but his colleague said to him: "I will tell thee a parable. Two men once entered the same town, the one offering for sale precious stones and pearls, the other tinsel. To whom do you think people thronged? Was it not to him who sold the tinsel, seeing that that was what they could afford to buy?"

Sotah, 40a

Let not the simple parable seem trivial in thine eyes, for through it thou acquirest an insight into the complex Law.

Shir ha-Shirim Rabbah, 1,8

On God

Rabbi Akiba said: "Do not act toward the Lord as other nations act toward their gods. They honor them solely when times are good, but when misfortune befalls them, they curse their gods. But you who belong to Israel should offer praise no matter whether the Lord brings you good times or evil."

Mekilta to Shemot, 20:30

The Emperor Hadrian, having returned from conquering the world, called his courtiers and said to them, "Now I demand that you consider me God."

Hearing this, one of them said, "Be pleased then, Sire, to aid me in this hour of need."

"In what way?" asked the Emporer.

"I have a ship becalmed three miles out at sea, and it contains all I possess."

"Very well," Hadrian said. "I will send a fleet to rescue it."

"Why bother to do that?" asked the courtier. "Send merely a little puff of wind."

"But whence am I to get the wind?"

"If you do not know," the courtier retorted, "then how can you be God who created the wind?"

Hadrian went home highly displeased.

Tanhuma Bereshit, 7:10

On the Way of Goodness

The way of goodness is at the outset a thicket of thorns, but after a little distance it emerges into an open plain; while the way of evil is at first a plain, but presently runs into thorns.

Sifre on Deuteronomy, 11:6

Isaiah said, "Sovereign of the Universe, what must a man do to be saved from the doom of hell?" God said to him, "Let him give charity, dividing his bread among the poor, and giving his money to scribes and their students; let him not behave haughtily to his fellow-men; let him busy himself in the Torah and in its commandments; let him live in humility and not speak in pride of spirit. If he humbled himself before all creatures, then will I dwell with him, as it says, 'I dwell with him that is of a humble spirit' (*Isa.* 57:15). I testify that he who has these qualities will inherit the future life; whoever has Torah, good deeds, humility, and fear of heaven, will be saved from doom.   *Pesikta Rabbati,* 198a

Rabbi Levi, in the name of Rabbi Simeon ben Lakish, said: "The gazelle is the animal best beloved of God. When she gives birth to a fawn, God sends an herb to heal her. When she is thirsty, she digs her horns into the ground and moans. God hears her pleas and aids her to find water in the deep pits. When she goes forth to drink, she is at first in terror of the other beasts, but God imbues her with courage. She stamps with her feet and uses her horns. The beasts then flee from her. Why does God love her? Because the gazelle harms no one, and never disturbs the peace."   *Midrash Samuel*

See that thou dost not say: "Inasmuch as I have been despised my comrades shall be despised with me; inasmuch as I have been cursed, my comrades shall be cursed with me."
Rabbi Tanhuma said: "If thou dost this, reflect whom thou dost despise, for it is written: 'In the image of God He made him.' "   *Bereshit Rabbah,* 24:7

There is not absolute good without some evil in its midst.
                                    Tanhuma, Intro., 9

On Forgiving the Enemy

Learn to receive blows, and forgive those who insult you.
                                    Abot d'R. Nathan, 41

Rabbi Abba said in the name of Rabbi Alexandria: "He who hears himself cursed, and is able to stop the curser, yet remains silent, he makes himself a partner with God. Does not God hear how the nations blaspheme Him, yet remain silent?
                                    Midrash Tehillim, 86:1

God loves the persecuted and hates the persecutors.

Pesikta Rabbati, 193b

If others speak ill of you, let the worst they say seem to you trifling. But if you speak ill of others, let each trivial remark seem to you enormous.

If you have done much good, let it be in your own eyes as little, but a small benefit from others should seem to you very great.

If A says to B: "Lend me your scythe," and B refuses, and the next day B says to A: "Lend me your shovel," and A replies "I will not, seeing that you refused to lend me your scythe"—that is revenge [which the Law forbids].

If A says to B, "Lend me your spade," and B refuses, and the next day B says to A, "Lend me your scythe," and A replies, "Here it is, for I am not like you, who would not lend me your spade"—that is bearing a grudge [which is also forbidden].

Sifra, 89b

Who is the bravest hero? He who turns his enemy into a friend. *Abot d'R. Nathan*, 23

On Brotherliness

When the year has been prosperous, people become brotherly toward each other. *Bereshit Rabbah*, 89:4

If a man knows any evidence in favor of the defendant, he is not at liberty to keep silent regarding it, for thus he may become responsible for the man's death. If a man sees another in mortal danger by falling into a river, through an attack by robbers, or some other evil, he is in duty bound not to stand idly by, but must come to the rescue. Moreover, if he sees one man pursuing another to kill or to ravish, he is in duty bound to try and prevent the crime, if need be by taking the life of the pursuer. *Sifre Kędoshim Perek*, 4

It is easy to acquire an enemy, but difficult to acquire a friend. *Yalkit Shimeoni on Pent.*, 845

A man should not say: "I will love the learned and hate the unlearned," but rather shall he say: "I will love them all."

Abot d'R. Nathan, 16

If a man gives to his fellow all the good gifts of the world with a dour countenance, the Scripture regards it as if he had given nothing; but if he receives his fellow cheerfully, the Scripture regards it as if he had given him all the good gifts in the world.

Abot d'R. Nathan, 13

What should be done if one of two wayfarers in the desert has a little water, and the other has none? Were one of them to drink all the water, he would be able to survive, but were they to divide it, both would die. Ben Paturi said they should both drink and die, for it is written: "And thy brother shall live with thee."

Sifra on Vayikra, 25:36

On the Social Conscience

Rabbi Simeon ben Eleazar said: "If a man sits in his place and keeps silent, how can he pursue peace in Israel between man and man? So let him leave his place and roam about in the world, and pursue peace in Israel. Seek peace [not alone] in your own dwelling place, but pursue it everywhere."

Abot d'R. Nathan, 12:26a

It is to the glory of the righteous that, even when they are on the point of death, they do not think of their own affairs, but concern themselves with the needs of the community. Thus when God told Moses that he must die, the latter's first concern was that God should appoint a leader in his place.

Sifre Bamidbar, 138, f. 52a

If the man of learning participates in public affairs, and serves as judge or arbitrator, he gives stability to the land. But if he sits in his home and says to himself: "What have the affairs of society to do with me? Why should I concern myself with the lawsuits of people? Why should I trouble myself with their voices of protest? Let my soul dwell in peace!"—if he does this, he overthrows the world.

When Rabbi Ammi's hour to die was at hand, his nephew found him weeping bitterly. He said: "Uncle and Teacher, why dost thou weep? Is there any Torah which thou hast not learned and taught? Is there any form of kindness which thou hast not practiced? And thou hast never accepted a public offer or sat in judgment."

The Rabbi replied: "It is for this very reason that I weep. I was given the ability to establish justice in Israel, but I never tried to carry it out." *Tanhuma to Mishpatim*

What shall a man do to be of use in the world if he is not inclined by temperament to be a scholar? He should devote time to public affairs and to the public welfare.

Vayikra Rabbah, 25

Tales

The Special Sabbath of David

Rabbi Judah said in the name of Rab, "How do you explain the verse, 'Lord, allow me to know when I shall die and the length of my days; let me know when I shall cease to live!' "

David said to the Holy One, "Lord of the Universe, let me know when I shall die."

God replied, "I have ordained that man shall not know when he is to die."

David pleaded, "And what shall be the length of my days?"

"I have ordained that man shall not know the length of his days."

"Then let me know when I cease to live."

Then God answered, "You shall die on a Sabbath."

David pleaded, "Let me die on the first day of the week."

God said to him, "Your son, Solomon, shall begin ruling on that first day of the week, and the reign of one king may not overlap the reign of another even by a hair's breadth."

"Then," pleaded David, "may I die on Friday?"

God replied, "It is written, 'A day in thy courts is better than a thousand.' Thus, I prefer one day in which you concern yourself with studying Torah to a thousand offerings which your son, Solomon, will bring to the altar."

And so it was that every Sabbath, King David sat and studied Torah until sunset. On that Sabbath when David was supposed to die, the Angel of Death came to him, but could not take him because David was studying Torah and the Angel of Death is powerless as long as a person is fulfilling a commandment of the Lord. The Angel of Death tried resorting to cunning in order to interrupt the King's study of Torah. He went into the garden and shook the trees. David went out to discover the cause of the noise. As soon as he put his foot on the steps, he collapsed and died.

(from Shab. 30a—30b)

(Tr. L. L.)

Scholarship Is the Best Merchandise

This is a story about a scholar who was in a ship with many merchants. They said to that scholar: "Where is your merchandise?" He said to them: "My merchandise is greater than yours." They searched the ship but found nothing that belonged to him. They began to mock him. Pirates fell upon them, looted and took everything in the ship. They landed and entered the city, and they had no bread to eat and no clothes to wear. What did that scholar do? He went to the House of Study, sat down, and expounded. The people of the city came, and when they saw that he was very learned they treated him with great respect, and gave him a proper stipend, as it behooved, in greatness and in honor. The leaders of the community began to walk on his right and on his left and to accompany him. When the merchants saw this, they came to him, and entreated him and said to him: "We beg of you, do us a good deed and recommend us to the people of the city, for you know what we were and what we have lost in the ship. We beg of you, have pity on us, talk to them, even if only about a piece of bread that it be given us to eat, so that we live and die not of hunger." He said to them: "Did I not tell you that my merchandise was greater than yours? Yours is lost and mine remains!"

(Tanh. Mishpatim, par. 2)

Israel Zangwill (1864-1926)

Born in London of parents who had emigrated from Russia, Israel Zang-will achieved worldwide fame as the "Jewish Dickens." While teaching at the Jewish Free School, he became well known by contributing to the Anglo-Jewish press. Commissioned to write a novel by the Jewish Publication Society of America, he produced *Children of the Ghetto* (1892), a humorous but sympathetic portrayal of immigrant Jewish life in London's East End, which achieved great success. Equally applauded works on Jewish themes include *Dreamers of the Ghetto*, with portraits of Disraeli, Heine, Lasalle, and other great figures hurt by the tragedy of Jewish existence in Christian lands; *The King of the Schnorrers*, with hilarious depictions of London Jewry in the eighteenth century; and *The Voice of Jerusalem*, with biting essays on Jewish affairs.

Recruited by Herzl for his fame as a Jewish man of letters, Zangwill became an ardent Zionist, but left the movement and founded the Jewish Territorial Organization (JTO) to provide a haven for oppressed Jews by establishing an independent Jewish community elsewhere than in the land of Israel.

The Master of the Name

A Description of Israel Baal Shem Tov

It was April ere I began to draw near my destination. The roads were still muddy and marshy; but in that happy interval between the winter gray and the summer haze the breath of spring made the world beautiful. The Stri River sparkled, even the ruined castles looked gay, while the pleasure-grounds of the lords of the soil filled the air with sweet scents. One day, as I was approaching a village up a somewhat steep road, a little gray-haired man driving a wagon holding some sacks of flour passed me, whistling cheerfully. We gave each other the "Peace" salutation, knowing ourselves brother Jews, if only for our furred caps and ear curls. Presently, in pity of his beast, I saw him jump down and put his shoulder to the wheel; but he had not made fifty paces when his horse slipped and fell. I hastened up to help him extricate the animal; and before we had succeeded in setting the horse on his four feet again, the driver's cheeriness under difficulties had me feel quite friendly towards him.

"Satan is evidently bent upon disturbing my Passover," said he, "for this is the second time that I have tried to get my Passover flour home. My good wife told me that we had nothing to eat for the festival, so I felt I must give myself a counsel. Out I went with my slaughtering-knife into the villages on the north—no, don't be alarmed, not to kill the inhabitants, but to slaughter their Passover poultry."

"You are a shochet," said I.

"Yes," said he, "among other things. It would be an intolerable profession," he added reflectively, "were it not for the thought that since the poor birds have to be killed, they are better off in my hands. However, as I was saying, I killed enough poultry to buy Passover flour; but before I got it home, the devil sent such a deluge that it was all spoilt. I took my knife again and went out into the southern villages, and now, here am I in another quandary. I only hope I shan't have to kill my horse, too."

"No, I don't think he is damaged," said I.

When I had helped this good-natured little man and his horse to the top of the hill, he invited me to jump into the cart, if my way lay in his direction.

"I am in search of the Baal Shem," I explained.

"Indeed," said he, "he is easily to be found."

"What, do you know the Baal Shem?" I cried excitedly.

He seemed amused at my agitation. His black eyes twinkled. "Why, everybody in these parts knows the Baal Shem," said he.

"How shall I find him, then?" I asked.

He shrugged his shoulders. "You have but to step up into my cart."

"May your strength increase!" I cried gratefully. "You are going in his direction?"

He nodded his head.

I climbed up the wheel and plumped myself down between two flour-sacks. "Is it far?" I asked.

He smiled. "Nay, if it was far I should scarcely have asked you up."

Then we both fell silent. For my part, despite the jolting of the vehicle, the lift was grateful to my spent limbs, and the blue sky and the rustling leaves and the near prospect of at last seeing the Baal Shem contributed to lull me into a pleasant languor. But my torpor was not so deep as that into which my new friend appeared to fall, for though as we approached a village another vehicle dashed towards us, my shouts and the other driver's cries only roused him in time to escape losing a wheel.

"You must have been thinking of a knotty point of Torah (Holy Law)," said I.

"Knotty point," said he, shuddering. "It is Satan who ties those knots."

"Oho," said I, "though a shochet, you do not seem fond of rabbinical learning."

"Where there is much study," he replied tersely, "there is little piety."

At this moment, appositely enough, we passed by the village Bes Ha-midrosh, whence loud sounds of "pilpulistic" (wire-drawn) argument issued. The driver clapped his palms over his ears.

"It is such disputants," he cried with a grimace, "who delay the redemption of Israel from exile."

"How so?" said I.

"Satan induces these rabbis," said he, "to study only those portions of our holy literature on which they can whet their ingenuity. But from all writings which would promote piety and fear of God he keeps them away."

I was delighted and astonished to hear the shochet thus deliver himself, but before I could express my acquiescence, his attention was diverted by a pretty maiden who came along driving a cow.

"What a glorious creature!" said he, while his eyes shone.

"Which?" said I laughingly. "The cow?"

"Both," he retorted, looking back lingeringly.

"I understand now what you mean by pious literature," I said mischieviously: "The Song of Solomon."

He turned on me with strange earnestness, as if not perceiving my irony. "Ay, indeed," he cried, "but when the rabbis do read it, they turn it into a bloodless allegory, Jewish demons as they are! What is the beauty of yonder maiden but an emanation from the Divine? The more beautiful the body, the more shiningly it leads us to the thought of God."

I was much impressed with this odd fellow, whom I perceived to be an original.

He had got me into such sympathy with him—for there was a curious attraction about the man—that I felt somehow that, even if the Baal Shem were an ascetic, I should still gain nothing from it, and that my long journey would have been made in vain, the green pastures and the living waters being still as far off as ever from my droughty soul.

The old man now began to walk with the horse, holding its bridle, and reversing its direction.

"Aren't you jumping up?" I asked.

"We are going up now, instead of down," he said, smiling. "Brody sits high in the seat of the scornful."

A pang of shame traversed my breast. What! I was riding
and this fine old fellow was walking! But ere I could offer to get
down, a new thought increased my confusion. I, who was bent
on finding the Baal Shem, was now off on a side-adventure to
Brody. And yet I was loath to part so soon with my new friend.
And besides, I told myself, Brody was well worth a visit. The
reputation of its Talmudical schools was spread over the
kingdom, and although I shared the old man's repugnance to
them, my curiosity was alert. And even on the Baal Shem's
account I ought to go there. For I remembered now that his
early life had had many associations with the town, and that
it was his wife's birthplace. So I said, "How far is Brody?"

"Ten miles," he said.

"Ten miles!" I repeated in horror.

"Ten miles," he said musingly, "and ten years since I set
foot in Brody." I jumped down. "'Tis I must walk, not you," I
said.

"Nay," said he good-humoredly. "I perceive neither of us
can walk. Those sacks must play Jonah. Out with them."

"No," I said.

"Yes," he insisted, laughingly. "Did I not say Satan was
determined to spoil my Passover? The third time I shall have
better luck perhaps."

I protested against thus causing him so much loss, and
offered to go and find the Baal Shem alone, but he rolled out
the floor-bags, laughing.

"But your wife will be expecting them," I remarked as the
cart proceeded with both of us in our seats.

"She will be expecting me, too," he said, smiling ruefully.
"However, she has faith in God. Never yet have we lacked
food. Surely He who feedeth the ravens—" He broke off with a
sudden thought, leaped down, and ran back.

"What is it?" I said.

I saw him draw out his knife an slip open the sacks. "The
birds shall keep Passover," he called out merrily.

Then he took out a pipe and, begging permission of me,
lighted it. As the smoke curled up, his face became ecstatic.

"I think," he observed musingly, "that God is more pleased

with this incense of mine than with all the prayers of all the rabbis."

This shocked even me, fascinated though I was. Never had I met such a man in all Israel. I shook my head in half-serious reproof. "You are a sinner," I said.

"Nay, is not smoking pleasurable? To enjoy aright aught in God's creation is to praise God. Even so, is not to pray the greatest of all pleasures?"

"To pray?" I repeated wonderingly. "Nay, methinks it is a heavy burden to get through our volumes of prayer."

"A burden!" cried the old man. "A burden to enter into relation with God, to be reabsorbed into the Divine Unity! Whoso does not feel this joy of union—this divine kiss—has not prayed."

"Then have I never prayed," I said.

"Then 'tis you that are the sinner," he retorted, laughing.

His words struck me into a meditative silence. It was toward twilight when we approached the great Talmudical center. To my surprise a vast crowd seemed to be waiting at the gates.

As we came near, we heard the people shouting, and nearer still, made out the sounds. Was it? Yes, I could not be mistaken. "The Baal Shem! The Baal Shem!"

My heart beat violently. What a stroke of luck was this! "The Baal Shem is there?" I cried exultantly.

I peered eagerly towards the gates, striving to make out the figure of the mighty Saint.

The dense mob swayed tumultuously. Some of the people ran towards our cart. Our horse had to come to a standstill. In a trice a dozen hands had unharnessed him. There was an instant of terrible confusion, in which I felt that violence was indeed meditated; then I found our cart being drawn forward as in triumph by contesting hands, while in my ears thundered from a thousand throats, "The Baal Shem! The Baal Shem!" Suddenly, I looked with an incredible suspicion at the old man, smoking imperturbably at my side.

"'Tis indeed a change from Brody," he said, with a laugh that was half a sob.

A faintness blotted out the whole strange scene—the town

gates, the eager faces, the gesticulating figures, the houses. It was the greatest surprise of my life.

Poetry

Jewish poetry reflects Jewish history. *Lemech's Song* (Gen. 4:23) is but one example of many poems in the Old Testament that have roots in remote antiquity. Later on, the prophetic books, often critical of the State, are filled with the kind of poetry Yeats called "truth sung in passion." In the great philosophical drama of Job, the protagonist, even as the Jewish people were doing, questions the nature of good and evil, of reward and punishment—enigmas central to life and living. Other poems in the Bible blend realism and mysticism, rationality and supernaturalism, as in the famous "Voice out of the Whirlwind" (Job 41).

In post-Biblical days, Hebrew poets found outlets for their talents in the Haggadahs, which contains beautiful lyrics, laments, and poetic prayers. Medieval Jewish lyrics were essentially devotional, and this outpouring of the soul found

363

its way into the *piyyutim*, religious poems that often reach the sublime.

Secular poetry developed rapidly in the tenth century, with such themes as the love of Zion and hope for return to the land of ancient promise, as well as nature, love, friendship, and valor. Unfortunately, a good deal of nuance and subtlety of language is lost in the translation of medieval Hebrew poetry. The modern reader must either be content to taste the rare wine from others' lips or else to go back to the original Hebrew versions and sip for himself.

How much of Hebrew poetry has been lost will probably never be known. Some of it has been recovered in unlikely places. Despite appropriation by Christians, *Mo-oz Tzur*, the thirteenth century Jewish hymn known as "Rock of Ages," is chanted in synagogue at Chanukah.

For more than 200 years following Jewish expulsion from Spain, Hebrew poetry lapsed into quiescence. There were attempts to write poems, but results were generally unoriginal, imitative, and sterile. The Hasidic movement and, a century later, the surge of Zionism gave impetus to the creative mind. Just as study of Kabbalah influenced medieval poetry, so too did Hasidism influence poetry in the eighteenth century and afterwards with its insistence that through song man can reach the ineffable. For the Hasidim, the lyric unites the spheres and arranges a unity of elements that bring harmony to the soul. For the Zionists, as for the medieval Jews dreaming of the Khazars, the concept of an independent Jewish state had a galvanizing effect.

A reawakening of ancient themes and the development of new forms characterize the onset of modern Jewish poetry. For the most part poems are rooted in Judaic soil, although many poets go outside the fields of Judaism to draw from foreign strains and to robe them, along with translations, in Jewish garb. Both in Israel and in the Diaspora Jewish poets are striving to add the challenge of new conditions and ideas to traditions and values of old. This creative outpouring, dynamic in its expression of self and people, has produced a renaissance worldwide in scope and universal in attraction.

Hayyim Nachman Bialik (1873-1934)

Acclaimed as the greatest Hebrew poet of modern times, Bialik also earned an eminent reputation as essayist, translator, and short-story writer. Although he lived his best years as a poet in Odessa, Bialik was strongly influenced by the spiritual Zionism of Ahad Ha'am. He, too, hoped that a reborn Israel would serve as a cultural center for world Jewry. Many of Bialik's poems reflect tangible and ideological predicaments of the Jews in his day—pogroms, poverty, assimilation—in much the same way as the essays of Ahad Ha'am. Bialik escaped from Russia after the Communist Revolution and ensuing civil war and lived in Tel Aviv until his death a decade later. He was buried next to his idol, Ahad Ha'am.

For a number of different reasons, one of which was his time-consuming position as literary editor of several periodicals, Bialik wrote few poems during the last twenty years of his life. His prose writings, some of which have become classics, were composed for the most part between 1907 and 1917. They deal with such subjects as Jewish culture, Hebrew literature, language, and style. In "Halakhah and Aggadah," Bialik acts as disciple of Ahad Haam and argues for Jewish cultural continuity and coherence. In "Revealment and Concealment," Bialik pictures the universe almost in the terms of later Existentialist writers as an abyss of inhuman chaos and nothingness, a terrifying conception which mankind has partially concealed behind the veil of language. Bialik compiled an anthology of rabbinic lore, translated *Don Quixote* and *William Tell* into Hebrew, and edited the collected works of Solomon Ibn Gabirol and Moses Ibn Ezra.

Best known as a poet, Bialik is at one and the same time deeply Jewish and universal in appeal. Like Agnon's stories, Bialik's poems record the spiritual crisis of modern man in a world in which religion and tradition have collapsed around him. His rhetoric rages and thunders in awareness of his tragedy as man and Jew. The cycle of furious poems evoked by pogroms of Czarist Russia turns Jewish martyrdom into world calamity. In "Upon the Slaughter" and "I Knew in a Dark Night" he expresses disgust at Jewish passivity and threatens to shake the throne of God if justice is not done. "The City of Slaughter" galvanized Jewish youth to form an army of defense, later to develop into the Haganah, the army of Israel.

If anyone deserves the title of Jewish Poet Laureate it is Bialik. Yet he is not a poet concerned solely with Jewish national self-interest in either a chauvinistic or parochial way. A many-sided figure, he wrote humorous verse, intensely personal love poems of exquisite beauty, ballads and lyrics of all kinds. His language makes use of 3,000 years of Jewish tradition, experience, and lore. A literary vehicle of extraordinary richness, power, and complexity, Bialik's lucid Hebrew reawakened the language and brought it to heights unreached since the Golden Age of Hebrew literature in medieval Spain. Even today, fifty years after his death, poets deliberately imitate his style and unconsciously paraphrase his lines.

Night

I know that this my crying, like the crying
Of owls on ruins in a wilderness,
Wakes neither consolation nor despair.
I know that these my tears are as a cloud
Of barren waters in a desert land,
That my lament, grown old with many years,
Is strengthless in the stony hearts of men.
Still the unhappy heart in vain laments
And seeks in vain to weep itself to rest.

From my pent prison I put forth my head
And call upon the storm and question it,
And search the clouds and with the gloom confer—
When will the darkness and the tempest pass?
When will the whirlwind die and the clouds scatter
And moon and stars break forth again in light?
I search from heaven to earth, from earth to heaven:
No sign, or answer—only storm and night.

Within the womb God consecrated me
To sickness and to poverty and said:
Go forth and find thy vanished destiny.
And among the ways of life buy air to breathe
And steal with craft a beggar's dole of light,
Carry from door to door thy beggar's pack;
Before the wealthy crook the knees for bread....
But I am weary now with wandering:
Ah, God, my God, how long is yet the road?

From the dark womb, like an uncleanliness,
On a heap of gathered foulness I was cast,
Unwashed from filth, with rags for swaddling-clothes,
My mother stretched to me a withered breast
And stilled me with the bitter milk of madness.
And in my heart a viper made its nest
And sucks my blood to render it in poison.
Where can I hide me from its burning fangs?
God! answer me with either life or death.

In the broad sky the light clouds are unraveled
And stars among them are like single pearls.
The wind moves dreamlike in the tranquil darkness
And in the wind still broods the peace of God.
And a faint whisper, like a secret kiss,
Laden with revelation, stirs the grass,
And sleep that heals and comforts fall on earth—
But not on me, the outcast,—not on me.

In the dead night-time I begin my song,
When two alone awake, my pain and I.
Beneath my skin my bones are turned to dust,
My weak eyes fail, for they have wept too long.
Now my song wakens like a bird at dawn,
Her dewy wings beat rain into my heart
And melt the tear-drops on my frozen eyes....
In vain, in vain, for tears alone I know.

Bring me not rain-drops, but a fount of tears,
Tears that will shake the hearts of men with storm;
Then by the ancient mounds of desolation,
By the ruined Temple, by my fathers' graves,
Where the road passes I will take my stand,
And travelers on the road will pity me,
And charity will waken with their pity.
There let men hear thee, O my song, until
Thy tears are ended and my pain is stilled.

(Tr. Maurice Samuel)

The Sabbath Queen

The sun o'er the treetops is no longer seen;
Come, let us go forth to greet Sabbath the Queen!
Behold her descending, the holy and blest,
And with her the angels of peace and of rest.
  Welcome, O Queen, welcome!
  Enter thou, enter, O bride!
Unto you be there peace, ye angels of Peace.

The Sabbath is greeted with song and with praise,
We go slowly homewards, our hearts full of grace.
The table is spread there, the candles give light,
Every nook in the house is shining and bright.
  Sabbath is peace and rest.

Sabbath is peaceful and blest.
Enter in peace, ye angels of Peace.

O pure one, be with us and light with Thy ray
The night and the day, then go on Thy way,
And we do Thee honour with garments most fine,
With songs and with psalms and with three feasts with wine.
   And by sweetest peace,
   And by perfect peace.
Bless us in peace, ye angels of Peace!

The sun in the treetops is no longer seen,
Come forth; we will speed our Sabbath, the Queen,
Go thou in peace, our holy and pure one!
Know that for six days we wait you, our sure one!
   Thus for the coming Sabbath,
   Thus for the coming Sabbath!
Pass forth in peace, ye angels of Peace!

(Tr. I. M. Lask)

Where Are You?

Out of your hiding place, heart of my being,
Come forth, come quickly to my side.
If I may find salvation, come and save me;
Come, be my master and my guide.
Bring back for but a day the stolen boy;
Let me perish in the springtide of my joy.
At your lips let my soul succumb,
Between your breasts let me bury my hours,
As a butterfly droops when night has come,
Among the scented flowers.

Where are you?

Before I had known you, heart of my being,
Your name was atremble on my lips.
At night I tossed sleepless, crushed my pillow,
My flesh dissolved, my heart was in eclipse.
And all day long, in the Talmud scroll,
In a ray of light, in the form of a white cloud,
When thoughts concern me, or when prayers console,
Lifted on joyous visions, in deepest sorrow bowed,
My soul sought one end, one desire knew,
You, you, you.

The City of Slaughter

Arise and go now to the city of slaughter;
Into its courtyard wind thy way;
There with thine own hand touch, and with the eyes of
    thine head,
Behold on tree, on stone, on fence, on mural clay,
The spattered blood and dried brains of the dead.
Proceed thence to the ruins, the split walls reach,
Where wider grows the hollow, and greater grows the breach;
Pass over the shattered hearth, attain the broken wall
Whose burnt and barren brick, whose charred stones reveal
The open mouths of such wounds, that no mending
Shall ever mend, nor healing ever heal.
There will thy feet in feathers sink, and stumble
On wreckage doubly wrecked, scroll heaped on manuscript,
Fragments again fragmented—
Pause not upon this havoc; go thy way.
The perfumes will be wafted from the acacia bud
And half of its blossoms will be feathers,
Whose smell is the smell of blood!
And, spiting thee, strange incense they will bring—
Banish thy loathing—all the beauty of the spring,
The thousand golden arrows of the sun,

Will flash upon thy curse;
The sevenfold rays of broken glass
Over thy sorrow joyously will pass,
For God called up the slaughter and the spring together—
The slayer slew, the blossom burst, and it was sunny weather!
Then wilt thou flee to a yard, observe its mound.
Upon the mound lie two, and both are headless—
A Jew and his hound.
The self-same ax struck both, and both were flung
Unto the self-same heap where swine seek dung;
Tomorrow the rain will wash their mingled blood
Into the runnels, and it will be lost
In rubbish heap, in stagnant pool, in mud.
Its cry will not be heard.
It will descend into the deep, or water the cockle-burr.
And all things will be as they ever were.

Unto the attic mount, upon thy feet and hands;
Behold the shadow of death among the shadows stands.
There in the dismal corner, there in the shadowy nook,
Multitudinous eyes will look
Upon thee from the somber silence—
The spirits of the martyrs are these souls,
Gathered together, at long last,
Beneath these rafters and in these ignoble holes.
The hatchet found them here, and hither do they come
To seal with a last look, as with their final breath,
The agony of their lives, the terror of their death.
Tumbling and stumbling wraiths, they come, and cower
    there.
Their silence whimpers, and it is their eyes which cry
Wherefore, O Lord, and why?
It is a silence only God can bear.
Lift then thine eyes to the roof; there's nothing there,
Save silences that hang from rafters
And brood upon their air:
Question the spider in his lair!
His eyes beheld these things; and with his web he can

A tale unfold horrific to the ear of man:
A tale of cloven belly, feather-filled;
Of nostrils nailed, of skull-bones bashed and spilled;
Of murdered men who from the beams were hung,
And of a babe beside its mother flung,
Its mother speared, the poor chick finding nest
Upon its mother's cold and milkless breast;
Of how a dagger halved an infant's word,
Its *ma* was heard, Its *mama* never heard.

O, even now its eyes from me demand accounting,
For these the tales the spider is recounting,
Tales that do puncture the brain, such tales that sever
Thy body, spirit, soul, from life, forever!
Then wilt thou bid thy spirit—*Hold, enough!*
Stifle the wrath that mounts within thy throat,
Bury these things accursed,
Within the depth of thy heart, before thy heart will burst!
Then wilt thou leave that place, and go thy way—
And lo—
The earth is as it was, the sun still shines:
It is a day like any other day.

Descend then, to the cellars of the town,
There where the virginal daughters of thy folk were fouled,
Where seven heathens flung a woman down,
The daughter in the presence of her mother,
The mother in the presence of her daughter,
Before slaughter, during slaughter, and after slaughter!
Touch with thy hand the cushion stained; touch
The pillow incarnadined:
This is the place the wild ones of the wood, the beasts of the
    field
With bloody axes in their paws compelled thy daughters yield:
Beasted and swined!
Note also, do not fail to note,
In that dark corner, and behind that cask
Crouched husbands, bridegrooms, brothers, peering from the
    cracks,

Watching the sacred bodies struggling underneath
The bestial breath,
Stifled in filth, and swallowing their blood!
Watching from the darkness and its mesh
The lecherous rabble portioning for booty
Their kindred and their flesh!

Crushed in their shame, they saw it all;
They did not stir nor move;
They did not pluck their eyes out; they
Beat not their brains against the wall!
Perhaps, perhaps, each watcher had it in his heart to pray:
A miracle, O Lord—and spare my skin this day!
Those who survived this foulness, who from their blood
    awoke,
Beheld their life polluted, the light of their world gone out—
How did their menfolk bear it, how did they bear this yoke?
They crawled forth from their holes, they fled to the house of
    the Lord,
They offered thanks to Him, the sweet benedictory word.
The *Kohanim* sallied forth, to the Rabbi's house they flitted:
Tell me, O Rabbi, tell, is my own wife permitted?
The matter ends; and nothing more.
And all is as it was before.

Come, now, and I will bring thee to their lairs
The privies, jakes and pigpens where the heirs
Of Hasmoneans lay, with trembling knees,
Concealed and cowering—the sons of the Maccabees!
The seed of saints, the scions of the lions!
Who, crammed by scores in all the sanctuaries of their shame,
So sanctified My name!
It was the flight of mice they fled,
The scurrying of roaches was their flight;
They died like dogs, and they were dead!
And on the next morn, after the terrible night
The son who was not murdered found
The spurned cadaver of his father on the ground.
Now wherefore dost thou weep, O son of man?

Descend into the valley; verdant, there
A garden flourishes, and in the garden
A barn, a shed—it was their abattoir;
There, like a host of vampires, puffed and bloated,
Besotted with blood, swilled from the scattered dead,
The tumbril wheels like scimitars spread—
Their open spokes, like fingers stretched for murder,
Like vampire-mouths their hubs still clotted red.
Enter not now, but when the sun descends
Wrapped in bleeding clouds and girt with flame,
Then open the gate and stealthily do set
Thy foot within the ambiance of horror:
Terror floating near the rafters, terror
Against the walls in darkness hiding,
Terror through the silence sliding.
Didst thou not hear beneath the heap of wheels
A stirring of crushed limbs? Broken and racked
Their bodies move a hub, a spoke
Of the circular yoke;
In death-throes they contort;
In blood disport;
And their last groaning, inarticulate
Rises above thy head,
And it would seem some speechless sorrow,
Sorrow infinite,
Is prisoned in this shed.
It is, it is the Spirit of Anguish!
Much-suffering and tribulation-tried
Which in this house of bondage binds itself.
It will not ever from its pain be pried.
Brief-weary and forspent, a dark Shekhinah
Runs to each nook and cannot find its rest;
Wishes to weep, but weeping does not come;
Would roar; is dumb.
Its head beneath its wing, its wing outspread
Over the shadows of the martyr'd dead,
Its tears in dimness and in silence shed.
And thou, too, son of man, close now the gate behind thee;

Be closed in darkness now, now thine that charnel space;
So tarrying there thou wilt be one with pain and anguish
And wilt fill up with sorrow thine heart for all its days. ·
Then on the day of thine own desolation
A refuge will it seem—
Lying in thee like a curse, a demon's ambush,
The haunting of an evil dream,
O, carrying it in thy heart, across the world's expanse
Thou wouldst proclaim it, speak it out—
But thy lips shall not find its utterance.

Beyond the suburbs go, and reach the burial ground.
Let no man see thy going; attain that place alone,
A place of sainted graves and martyr-stone.
Stand on the fresh-turned soil.
Such silence will take hold of thee, thy heart will fail
With pain and shame, yet I
Will let no tear fall from thine eye.
Though thou wilt long to bellow like the driven ox
That bellows, and before the altar balks,
I will make hard thy heart, yea, I
Will not permit a sigh.
See, see, the slaughtered calves, so smitten and so laid;
Is there a price for their death? How shall that price be paid?
Forgive, ye shamed of the earth, yours is a pauper-Lord!
Poor was He during your life, and poorer still of late.
When to My door you come to ask for your reward,
I'll open wide: See, I am fallen from My high estate.
I grieve for you, My children. My heart is sad for you.
Your dead were vainly dead; and neither I nor you
Know why you died or wherefore, for whom, nor by what laws;
Your deaths are without reason; your lives are without cause.
What says the Shekhinah? In the clouds it hides
In shame, in agony alone abides;
I, too, at night, will venture on the tombs,
Regard the dead and weigh their secret shame,
But never shed a tear, I swear it in My name.
For great is the anguish, great the shame on the brow;

But which of these is greater, son of man, say thou—
Or better keep thy silence, bear witness in My name
To the hour of My sorrow, the moment of My shame.
And when thou dost return
Bring thou the blot of My disgrace upon thy people's head,
And from My suffering do not part,
But set it like a stone within their heart!

Turn, then, to leave the cemetery ground,
And for a moment thy swift eye will pass
Upon the verdant carpet of the grass—
A lovely thing! Fragrant and moist, as it is always at the
    coming of the Spring!
The stubble of death, the growth of tombstones!
Take thou a fistful, flint on the plain
Saying,
"The people is plucked grass; can plucked grass grow again?"
Turn, then, thy gaze from the dead, and I will lead
Thee from the graveyard to thy living brothers,
And thou wilt come, with those of thine own breed,
Into the synagogue, and on a day of fasting,
To hear the cry of their agony,
Their weeping everlasting.
Thy skin will grow cold, the hair on thy skin stand up,
And thou wilt be by fear and trembling tossed;
Thus groans a people which is lost.
Look in their hearts—behold a dreary waste,
Where even vengeance can revive no growth,
And yet upon their lips no mighty malediction
Rises, no blasphemous oath.

Are they not real, their bruises?
Why is their prayer false?
Why, in the day of their trials
Approach me with pious ruses,
Afflict me with denials?
Regard them now, in these their woes:
Ululating, lachrymose,

Crying from their throes,
We have sinned! and *Sinned have we!*—
Self-flagellative with confession's whips.
Their hearts, however, do not believe their lips.
Is it, then, possible for shattered limbs to sin?
Wherefore their cries imploring, their supplicating din?
Speak to them, bid them rage!
Let them against me raise the outraged hand—
Let them demand!
Demand the retribution for the shamed
Of all the centuries and every age!
Let fists be flung like stone
Against the heavens and the Heavenly Throne!

To a Bird

Greetings! Peace to you, returning
Lovely bird, unto my window
From a warmer clime!
How my soul for songs was yearning
When my dwelling you deserted
In the wintertime!

Chirping, singing, dearest birdling,
Tell the wonders of that distant
Land from which you came.
In that fairer, warmer climate
Are the troubles and the trials
Multiplied the same?

Do you bring me friendly greetings
From my brothers there in Zion,
Brothers far yet near?
O the happy! O the blessed!
Do they guess what heavy sorrows
I must suffer here?

Do they know and could they picture
How the many rise against me,
How their hatred swells?
Singing the wonders of the land where
Spring forever dwells.

Does your singing bring me greeting
From the land, its glens and valleys,
Mountain height and cleft?
Has her God compassioned Zion?
Is she still to graves deserted,
Only ruins left?

Tell me, are the Vale of Sharon
And the Hill of Incense flowing
Still with nard and myrrh?
Does the oldest of the forests
Wake from sleep? Is ancient, slumbering
Lebanon astir?

Falls the dew like pearls on Hermon,
From its snowy heights descending,
Tearlike does it fall?
How fare Jordan's shining waters,
How the hills and how the hillocks
And the mountains all?

Has the heavy cloud departed,
Spreading o'er them deathly shadow,
Dark, enshrouding breath?
Singing, chirping, tell me, birdling,
Of the country where my fathers
Found their life, their death.

Have the blossoms that I planted
Not yet withered as I withered?
(Old am I, and wan—

Fruitful days I, too, remember
Like themselves, but now I'm faded.
Now my strength is gone!)

Chirping, singing, whisper, birdling,
Secrets of the shrubs and bushes,
Murmurings of their shoots,
Have they news of mercies coming,
Have they hopes, as Lebanon's humming,
Soon to swing with fruits?

And the laborers, my brothers—
Have not these who sowed with weeping
Reaped with song and psalm?
Oh, that I had wings to fly with,
Fly unto the land where flourish
Almond tree and palm!

I myself, what shall I tell you,
Lovely bird, what stories hope you
From my lips to know?
In this far, cold land, no singing,
Only sighs and lamentation,
Only groans and woe.

Shall I tell my tale of sorrows
Now well known in all the places
Near and far alike,
Those innumerable sorrows
Of the present, or the others
That are yet to strike?

Fly back to your hills and valleys,
Fly back to your forests, happy
That you're leaving me;
For beside me if you linger,
You, too, singer, will be weeping
For my destiny.

Yet all threnodies and moanings
Will not soothe my anguish,
Will no cure provide
I have seared my eyes with weeping,
I have filled with tears the chalice,
And my heart is dried.

Gone all tears, and gone each hinted
Year of messianic tidings,
All is gone but pain;
Yet I bid you, birdling, welcome.
From the warmer climes returning,
Sing your song again.

Uri Zevi Greenberg (1894-1981)

Born in a Galician village in 1894, Uri Zevi Greenberg, also known as Tur Malka, became a permanent resident of Israel in 1924. His poetry records the agony of a bereft people. In 1918 in Lvov, he witnessed Polish pogroms against the Jews, an experience of horror intensified a hundredfold in 1939 when he visited relatives in Poland. He foresaw the Holocaust in which his relatives, parents, and sister among them, were killed.

A prophet-priest of poetry attempting to place Jewish suffering in perspective, Greenberg laments that like a prophet of old his words are spurned and his writings reviled. He calls himself "a man of vision befouled with mud."

Greenberg is uncompromisingly bitter. His writing reflects anguish and anger at a world that indifferently watched the slaughter of six million Jews. His attacks even touch upon God, who becomes in Greenberg's words "guardian of the Jewish cemetery." Yet, despite the corpse-filled imagery of his poetry, Greenberg does not lose faith. Apocalyptic visions transcend the smoke of crematoria: the Messiah "shall surely come."

Greenberg relies for inspiration on the Bible, the Kabbalah, and Jewish mysticism. Delicate and hauntingly poignant, his lyrics convey the idea that the Jew, elected by God, is a holy instrument of divine will. Greenberg holds fast to belief in Messianic redemption and God's promise to restore Jewish sovereignty.

To God in Europe

We are not as dogs among the gentiles: a dog is pitied by them,
fondled by them, sometimes even kissed by a gentile's mouth;
as if he were a pretty baby
of his own flesh and blood, the gentile spoils him
and is forever taking pleasure in him.
And when the dog dies, how the gentile mourns him!

Not like sheep to the slaughter were we brought in trainloads
but rather—
through all the lovely landscapes of Europe—
brought like leprous sheep
to Extermination itself.
Not as they dealt with their sheep did the gentiles deal with
    our bodies;
they did not extract their teeth before they slaughtered them;
nor strip them of their wool as they stripped us of our skins;
nor shove them into the fire to turn their life to ashes;
nor scatter the ashes over sewers and streams;
like this that we have suffered at their hands!
There are none—no other instances.
(All words are shadows of shadows)—
This is the horrifying phrase: No other instances.

No matter how brutal the torture a man will suffer
in a land of the gentiles
the maker of comparisons will compare it thus:
He was tortured like a Jew.
Whatever the fear, whatever the outrage,
how deep the loneliness, how harrowing the sorrow—

no matter how loud the weeping—
the maker of comparisons will say:
This is an instance of the Jewish sort.

What retribution can there be for our disaster?
Its dimensions are a world.
All the culture of the gentile kingdoms at its peak
flows with our blood,
and all its conscience, with our tears....

(Tr. Robert Friend)

Jehudah Halevi (c. 1080-c. 1140)

Often called the greatest medieval Hebrew poet, Jehudah Halevi wrote many lyrics so sublime that they seem to soar. Although his poetry ranges widely, at the center are a joyousness and intoxication with life. Halevi's eighty love poems, marked by a graceful combination of sound and rhythm, follow conventional modes. His secular poems dealing with friendship or eulogies for friends are often stylistically exaggerated, but his contemplations on the inevitability of death, the omnipotence of fate, and personal loss ring true.

Halevi composed many deeply religious lyrics. His 350 *piyyutim* (a *piyyut* is a religious poem included in the prayerbook as an addition to the liturgy) are deeply emotional, expressing the poet's yearning for redemption of his people. In Halevi's finest lyrics, *Songs of the Diaspora* (*Shirei ha-Galut*), strains of Jeremiah, Job, and David appear in anguished lamentations for the Jewish people in exile, separated from God and homeland.

One of the most interesting poetic cycles of the Golden Age of Spain is Halevi's *Poems of Zion* (*Shirei Tsion*), in which he expresses his longing to return to Eretz Yisrael because only there can the individual Jew, indeed the

384

whole Jewish people, have hope. He attempted to fulfill his own commitment to such a return despite arguments by many against his undertaking the perilous journey to the Holy Land. Contrary to the legend of his being killed at the Wailing Wall in Jerusalem, historians think that, after completing only part of his journey, Halevi died in Cairo and was buried there.

A Letter To His Friend Isaac

But yesterday the earth drank like a child
    With eager thirst the autumn rain.
Or like a wistful bride who waits the hour
    Of love's mysterious bliss and pain.
And now the Spring is here with yearning eyes;
    Midst shimmering golden flower-beds,
On meadows carpeted with varied hues,
    In richest raiment clad, she treads.
She weaves a tapestry of bloom o'er all,
    And myriad-eyed young plants upspring,
White, green, or red like lips that to the mouth
    Of the beloved one sweetly cling.
Whence come these radiant tints, these blended beams?
    Here's such a dazzle, such a blaze,
As though earth stole the splendor of the stars,
    Fain to eclipse them with her rays.
Come! go we to the garden with our wine,
    Which scatters sparks of hot desire,
Within our hand 'tis cold, but in our veins
    It flashes clear, it glows like fire.
It bubbles sunnily in earthen jugs.
We catch it in the crystal glass,
    Then wander through cool, shadowy lanes and breathe
    The spicy freshness of the grass.
Whilst we with happy hearts our circuit keep.
    The gladness of the Earth is shown.
She smileth, though the trickling rain-drops weep
    Silently o'er her, one by one.
She loves to feel the tears upon her cheek,

Like a rich veil, with pearls inwove.
Joyous she listens when the swallows chirp,
  And warbles to her mate, the dove.
Blithe as a maiden midst the young green leaves,
  A wreath she'll wind, a fragrant treasure;
All living things in graceful motion leap,
  As dancing to some merry measure.
The morning breezes rustle cordially,
  Love's thirst is sated with the balm they send.
Sweet breathes the myrtle in the frolic wind,
  As though remembering a distant friend.
The myrtle branch now proudly lifted high,
  Now whispering to itself drops low again.
The topmost palm-leaves rapturously stir,
  For all at once they hear the bird's soft strain.
So stirs, so yearns all nature, gayly decked,
  To honor *Isaac* with her best array.
Hear'st thou the word? She cries—I beam with joy,
Because with Isaac I am wed today.

(Tr. Emma Lazarus)

My Heart Is in the East

My heart is in the east, and I in the uttermost west—
How can I find savour in food? How shall it be sweet to
  me?
How shall I render my vows and my bonds, while yet
Zion lieth beneath the fetter of Edom, and I in Arab
  chains?
A light thing would it seem to me to leave all the good
  things of Spain—
Seeing how precious in mine eyes it is to behold the dust
  of the desolate sanctuary.

(Tr. Nina Salaman)

Longing for Jerusalem

O city of the world, with sacred splendor blest,
My spirit yearns to thee from out the far-off West,
A stream of love wells forth when I recall thy day,
Now is thy temple waste, thy glory passed away.
Had I an eagle's wings, straight would I fly to thee,
Moisten thy holy dust with wet cheeks streaming free.

Oh, how I long for thee! Albeit thy King has gone,
Albeit where balm once flowed, the serpent dwells alone.
Could I but kiss thy dust, so would I fain expire,
As sweet as honey then, my passion, my desire!

(Tr. Emma Lazarus)

Love Songs

"See'st thou o'er my shoulders falling,
    Snake-like ringlets waving free?
Have no fear, for they are twisted
    To allure thee unto me."

Thus she spake, the gentle dove,
    Listen to thy plighted love:—
"Ah, how long I wait, until
    Sweetheart cometh back (she said)
Laying his caressing hand
    Underneath my burning head."

(Tr. Emma Lazarus)

Heinrich Heine (1795-1856)

Born in Dusseldorf, Germany, Hayyim (later Heinrich) Heine, the poor relation of a wealthy family, was to feel like an outsider all his life although he became one of the most famous authors of the nineteenth century. Homeless, ambivalent, and divided are the words for Heine. A Jew in Germany, a German in France, a revolutionary among the bourgeoisie, a conservative among the radicals, he was nowhere at home. It is typical of Heine that belief and disbelief mingled with love and hatred in his feelings toward Judaism: he sought God at the very moment he refused to acknowledge His existence. As divided as his inner self, his poetry is emotional yet intellectual, sentimental yet ironic, sweet yet bitter.

Having given up a business career to study law in hope of gaining public office, Heine settled in Berlin, where he brought out his first book of poetry and became famous. Influenced by Moses Mendelsohn, he helped found the "Society for the Culture and Science of Judaism." But in 1825, to help his advancement in the practice of law and to increase the chance for appointment to public office, he converted to Christianity. Later, he expressed regret at the conversion, saying: "I make no secret of my Judaism, to which I have not returned because I never left it." In *Hebrew Melodies* and other works, Heine expresses admiration for Judaism. After the 1830 revolution, pro-French and under official German censure, Heine left Berlin for Paris, where he resumed his career as journalist and poet.

Many of Heine's poems, including "The Lorelei" and "You Are like a Flower," justly famed for melodious sweetness, were set to music by the best composers of the day. But Heine was also a brilliant political satirist, as in *Germany, A Winter's Tale*, which attacked the anti-democratic policies of Metternich.

Donna Clara

In the evening through her garden
Wanders the Alcalde's daughter;
Festal sounds of drum and trumpet
Ring out hither from the castle.

"I am weary of the dances,
Honeyed words of adulation
From the knights who still compare me
To the sun—with dainty phrases.

"Yes, of all things I am weary,
Since I first beheld by moonlight,
Him my cavalier, whose zither
Nightly draws me to my casement.

"As he stands, so slim and daring,
With his flaming eyes that sparkle
From his nobly-pallid features,
Truly he St. George resembles."

Thus went Donna Clara dreaming,
On the ground her eyes were fastened,
Lo! before her
Stood the handsome, knightly stranger.

Pressing hands and whispering passion,
These twain wander in the moonlight.
Gently doth the breeze caress them,
The enchanted roses greet them.

The enchanted roses greet them,
And they glow like love's own heralds;
"Tell me, tell me, my beloved,
Wherefore, all at once thou blushest?"

"Gnats were stinging me, my darling,
And I hate these gnats in summer,
E'en as though they were a rabble
Of vile Jews with long, hooked noses."

"Heed not gnats nor Jews, beloved,"
Spake the knight with fond endearments.
From the almond-tree dropped downward
Myriad snowy flakes of blossoms.

Myriad snowy flakes of blossoms
Shed around them fragrant odors.
"Tell me, tell me, my beloved,
Looks thy heart on me with favor?"

"Yes, I love thee, oh my darling,
And I swear it by our Savior,
Whom the accursed Jews did murder
Long ago with wicked malice."

"Heed thou neither Jews nor Savior,"
Spake the knight with fond endearments;
Far-off waved as in a vision
Gleaming lilies bathed in moonlight.

Gleaming lilies bathed in moonlight
Seemed to watch the stars above them.
"Tell me, tell me, my beloved,
Didst thou not erewhile swear falsely?"

"Naught is false in me, my darling,
E'en as in my bosom floweth
Not a drop of blood that's Moorish,
Neither of foul Jewish current."

"Heed not Moors nor Jews, beloved,"
Spake the knight with fond endearments.
Then towards a grove of myrtles
Leads the Alcade's daughter.

And with love's slight, subtle meshes,
He hath trapped her and entangled;
Brief their words, but long their kisses,
For their hearts are overflowing.

What a melting bridal carol,
Sings the nightingale, the pure one!
How the fire-flies in the grasses
Trip their sparkling, torch-light dances!

In the grove the silence deepens;
Naught is heard save furtive rustling
Of the swaying myrtle branches,
And the breathing of the flowers.

But the sound of drum and trumpet
Burst forth sudden from the castle.
Rudely they awaken Clara,
Pillowed on her lover's bosom.

"Hark, they summon me, my darling,
But before I go, oh tell me,
Tell me what thy precious name is,
Which so closely thou hast hidden."

And the knight, with gentle laughter,
Kissed the fingers of his donna,
Kissed her lips and kissed her forehead,
And at last these words he uttered:

"I, Señorita, your beloved,
Am the son of the respected
Worthy, erudite Grand Rabbi,
Israel of Saragossa!"

(Tr. Emma Lazarus)

Abraham Ibn Ezra (c. 1090-c.1165)

Famous in his own era as poet, philologist, astronomer, and Biblical commentator, Abraham Ibn Ezra spent the first half of his life in Toledo, Spain, wandering during the second half in Europe, Egypt, and perhaps Palestine and producing the bulk of his writing then. As a result, he became the inspiration for Robert Browning's famous poem on old age.

Ibn Ezra wrote both religious and secular poems, often depending on visual effects—as when he wrote a poem in the shape of a tree. He treated such subjects as friendship, nature, love, Jewish nationalism, and man's yearning for communion with God. The last is a frequent element in his *piyyutim*. Several of his religious poems have been incorporated in the traditional Jewish prayer book used during festivals.

Ibn Ezra's reputation today is firmly secured by his Biblical scholarship. Rejecting the allegorical method of interpretation of Maimonides as artificial and external, Ibn Ezra based his Biblical commentary on internal evidence obtained through philology. He was first to demonstrate that the Book of Isaiah is in reality two books, and he also startled his contemporaries by insisting that the Five Books of Moses had been rewritten after the Prophet's death. It can be argued that Abraham Ibn Ezra is a direct forerunner of Higher Criticism because of his textual analysis of the Bible based on sound scientific principles.

When the Morning of Life Had Passed

When the morning of life had passed as a shadow,
And the path of my years was shortened,
Exile called to me: "O thou, that dwellest at ease, arise!"
At the sound of his voice, mine ears tingled;
I arose, with shaken heart,
To go forth, a wanderer—
And my children cried unto God!

But they are the fount of my life—
How shall I exist without them,
And the light of mine eyes be not with me?

Fate has led me to a land
Wherein my mind is bewildered and my thoughts confused—
To a people rude of speech and obscure in word;
Before the insolence of their gaze, my face is cast down.
Oh, when will God call unto me, "Go free!"
That I may escape from them—if only by the skin of my teeth!

The Song of Chess

I will sing a song of battle
Planned in days long passed and over.
Men of skill and science set it
On a plain of eight divisions,
And designed in squares all chequered.
Two camps face each one the other,
And the kings stand by for battle,
And twixt these two is the fighting.
Bent on war the face of each is,
Ever moving or encamping,

Yet no swords are drawn in warfare,
For a war of thoughts their war is.
They are known by signs and tokens
Sealed and written on their bodies;
And a man who sees them, thinketh,
Edomites and Ethiopians
Are these two that fight together.
And the Ethiopian forces
Overspread the field of battle,
And the Edomites pursue them.

First in battle the foot-soldier[1]
Comes to fight upon the highway,
Ever marching straight before him,
But to capture moving sideways,
Straying not from off his pathway,
Neither do his steps go backwards;
He may leap at the beginning
Anywhere within three chequers.
Should he take his steps in battle
Far away unto the eighth row,
Then a Queen to all appearance
He becomes and fights as she does.
And the Queen directs her moving
As she will to any quarter.
Backs the Elephant[2] or advances,
Stands aside as 'twere an ambush;
As the Queen's way, so is his way,
But o'er him she hath advantage,
He stands only in the third rank.
Swift the Horse[3] is in the battle,
Moving on a crooked pathway;
Ways of his are ever crooked;
Mid the Squares, three-form his limit.

---

[1] The pawn.
[2] The Bishop.
[3] The Knight.

Straight the Wind moves o'er the war-path
In the field across or lengthwise,
Ways of crookedness he seeks not,
But straight paths without perverseness.
Turning every way the King goes,
Giving aid unto his subjects;
In his actions he is cautious,
Whether fighting or encamping.
If his foe come to dismay him,
From his place he flees in terror,
Or the Wind[4] can give him refuge.
Sometimes he must flee before him;
Multitudes at times support him;
And all slaughter each the other,
Wasting with great wrath each other.

Mighty men of both the sovereigns
Slaughtered fall, with yet no bloodshed.
Ethiopia sometimes triumphs,
Edom flees away before her;
Now victorious is Edom;
Ethiopia and her sovereign
Are defeated in the battle.

Should a King in the destruction
Fall within the foeman's power,
He is never granted mercy,
Neither refuge nor deliv'rance,
Nor a flight to refuge-city.
Judged by foes, and lacking rescue,
Though not slain he is checkmated.
Hosts about him all are slaughtered,
Giving life for his deliverance.
Quenched and vanished is their glory,
For they see their lord is smitten;
Yet they fight again this battle,
For in death is resurrection.

---

[4]   The Rook.   (Tr. Nina Salaman)

Solomon Ibn Gabirol (1021-1058)

"I am the master and the poem is my servant!" is the assertion of Solomon Ibn Gabirol, the eleventh century Cordova-born poet, who as early as his teens demonstrated an easy command of poetic form and content. Orphaned as a child, Ibn Gabirol came under the protection of the philanthropist and scientist, Jekutheil Ibn Hasan, who recognized the youngster's genius. After Jekuthiel's death, at the age of twenty Ibn Gabirol traveled to Malaga, where Samuel Ibn Nagela became his patron.

Ibn Gabirol's poetry displays fine handling of Hebrew and Arabic idioms as well as a knowledge of Biblical material, Talmudic literature, Midrashic commentary, and mystical writings. Throughout many lyrics of Ibn Gabirol are strains of anguish, loneliness, disillusion. But he can fill a poem with light, good-natured banter, as in "In Praise of Wine." Ibn Gabirol's religious poems are awestruck at the mystery of God's presence. Perhaps the greatest of these is *"Keter Malkhut"* (Crown of the Kingdom), a lyric filled with wonder at and praise of the omnipresence of God.

Many of Ibn Gabirol's poems are scattered in prayer books and anthologies. It is often difficult to definitely identify his work. Although in one poem Ibn Gabirol speaks as having written twenty volumes, only two of his books are extant.

Night

Night, and the heavens beam serene with peace,
Like a pure heart benignly smiles the moon.
Oh, guard thy blessed beauty from mischance,
This I beseech thee in all tender love.
See where the Storm his cloudy mantle spreads,
An ashy curtain covereth the moon.
As if the tempest thirsted for the rain.
The clouds he presses, till they burst in streams.
Heaven wears a dusky raiment, and the moon
Appeareth dead—her tomb is yonder cloud.
And weeping shades come after, like the people
Who mourn with tearful grief a noble queen.
But look! the thunder pierced night's close-linked mail,
His keen-tipped lance of lightning brandishing;
He hovers like a seraph-conqueror.
Dazed by the flaming splendor of his wings,
In rapid flight as in a whirling dance,
The black cloud-ravens hurry scared away.
So, though the powers of darkness chain my soul,
My heart, a hero, chafes and breaks its bonds.

Night-Thoughts

Will night already spread her wings and weave
Her dusky robe about the day's bright form,
Boldly the sun's fair countenance displacing,
And swathe it with her shadow in broad day?
So a green wreath of mist enrings the moon,
Till envious clouds do quite encompass her.
No wind! and yet the slender stem is stirred,
With faint, slight motion as from inward tremor.
Mine eyes are full of grief—who sees me, asks,
"Oh, wherefore dost thou cling unto the ground?"

My friends discourse with sweet and soothing words:
They all are vain, they glide above my head.
I fain would check my tears; would fain enlarge
Unto infinity, my heart—in vain!
Grief presses hard my breast, therefore my tears
Have scarcely dried, ere they again spring forth.
For these are streams no furnace heat may quench,
Nebuchadnezzar's flames may dry them not.
What is the pleasure of the day for me,
If, in its crucible, I must renew
Incessantly the pangs of purifying?
Up, challenge, wrestle, and o'ercome! Be strong!
The late grapes cover all the vine with fruit.
I am not glad, though even the lion's pride
Content itself upon the field's poor grass.
My spirit sins beneath the tide, soars not
With fluttering seamews on the moist, soft strand.
I follow Fortune not, wher'er she lead.
Lord o'er myself, I banish her, compel.
And though her clouds should rain no blessed dew,
Though she withhold the crown, the heart's desire,
Though all deceive, though honey change to gall,
Still I am lord, and will in freedom strive.

Meditations

Forget thine anguish,
  Vexed heart, again.
Why shouldst thou languish,
  With earthly pain?
The husk shall slumber,
  Bedded in clay
Silent and sombre,
  Oblivion's prey!
But, Spirit immortal,

Thou at Death's portal,
    Tremblest with fear.
    If he caress thee,
    Curse thee or bless thee,
    Thou must draw near,
From him the worth of thy works to hear.

    Why full of terror,
    Compassed with error,
    Trouble thy heart,
    For thy mortal part?
    The soul flies home—
    The corpse is dumb.
    Of all thou didst have,
Follows naught to the grave.
    Thou fliest thy nest,
Swift as a bird to thy place of rest.

    What avail grief and fasting,
    Where nothing is lasting?
    Pomp, domination,
    Become tribulation.
    In a health-giving draught,
    A death-dealing shaft.
    Wealth—an illusion,
    Power—a lie,
    Over all, dissolution
    Creeps silent and sly.
    Unto others remain
    The goods thou didst gain
    With infinite pain.

Life is a vine-branch;
    A vintager, Death.
He threatens and lowers
    More nearer with each breath.
Then hasten, arise!
    Seek God, O my soul!

For time quickly flies,
 Still far is the goal.
Vain heart praying dumbly,
 Learn to prize humbly,
 The meanest of fare.
Forget all thy sorrow,
 Behold. Death is there!

 Dove-like lamenting,
 Be full of repenting,
Lift vision supernal
To raptures eternal.
 On ev'ry occasion
 Seek lasting salvation.
Pour thy heart out in weeping,
Whilst others are sleeping.
 Pray to Him when all's still,
 Performing His will
And so shall the angel of peace be thy warden,
And guide there at last to the heavenly garden.

Emma Lazarus (1849-1887)

Millions of immigrants to the United States have been given hope by the compassion-filled sonnet inscribed on the pedestal of the Statue of Liberty in New York Harbor:

> Give me your tired, your poor,
> Your huddled masses yearning to breathe free....
> I lift my lamp beside the golden door.

Emma Lazarus, author of this famous poem, was born in New York City, the descendant of Sephardic Jews who emigrated to America from Portugal in the seventeenth century. She wrote accomplished but conventional poetry in her early years. Later, strongly affected by George Eliot's novel *Daniel Deronda* and accounts of Russian pogroms of the 1880s, Lazarus began to study Hebrew, turning to medieval Hebrew poets for inspiration and publishing translations of the works of Jehudah Halevi, Solomon Ibn Gabirol, and others.

Friend and fellow writer E. C. Stedman persuaded Lazarus to assist relief workers on Ward's Island, where she encountered many Jewish refugees seeking asylum from persecution. Her subsequent writings were given over to Jewish themes. She began to write with fervor and devotion poems in praise of her fellow Jews, and she expressed her pride in belonging to a group which, despite constant oppression, had not merely survived but had significantly contributed to the advancement of humankind. These ideas were expressed in essays and poems in *Century Magazine* and *Songs of a Semite* (1882). She thus became the first avowedly Jewish-American poet to win international literary recognition.

Lazarus, believing that Jewish life would be much more meaningful through the development of Jewish culture in the United States and the rebuilding of Palestine as a Jewish homeland, became a pioneer American Zionist. She expressed these hopes in prose poems collected under the title *By the Waters of Babylon* (1887).

Lazarus died at the age of thirty-eight. Two years later, when her works appeared in a collected edition, her sister expressly forbade inclusion of Jewish material. It was as if the anti-Semitic attacks of an inimical Gentile world and an unsympathetic assimilated Jewish community remained hostile to her goals even after death.

The Banner of the Jew

Wake, Israel, wake! Recall today
   The glorious Maccabean rage,
The sire heroic, hoary-gray;
   His five-fold lion-lineage:
The Wise, the Elect, the Help-of-God,
The Burst-of-Spring, the Avenging Rod.

From Mizpah's mountain side they saw
   Jerusalem's empty streets, her shrine
Laid waste where Greeks profaned the Law,
   With idol and with pagan sign.
Mourners in tattered black were there,
With ashes sprinkled on their hair.

Then from the stony peak there rang
   A blast to ope the graves: down poured
The Maccabean clan, who sang
   Their battle-anthem to the Lord.
Five heroes lead,and following, see,
Ten thousand rush to victory!

Oh, for Jerusalem's trumpet now,
   To blow a blast of shattering power,
To wake the sleepers high and low,
   And rouse them to the urgent hour!
No band for vengeance—but to save,
A million naked swords should wave.

Oh, deem not dead that martial fire,
   Say not the mystic flame is spent!
With Moses' law and David's lyre,
   Your ancient strength remains unbent.
Let but an Ezra rise anew,
To lift the Banner of the Jew!

A rag, a mock at first—ere long,
   When men have bled and women wept,
To guard its precious folds from wrong,
   Even they who shrunk, even they who slept,
Shall leap to bless it and to save.
Strike! for the brave revere the brave!

Gifts

"Oh, World-God, give me Wealth!" the Egyptian cried.
His prayer was granted. High as heaven, behold
Palace and Pyramid; the brimming tide
Of lavish Nile washed all his land with gold.
Armies of slaves toiled ant-wise at his feet;

World-circling traffic roared through mart and street;
His priests were gods; his spice-balmed kings enshrined,
Set death at naught in rock-ribbed charnels deep.
Seek Pharaoh's race-to-day, and ye shall find
Rust and the moth, silence and dusty sleep.

"Oh, World-God, give me Beauty!" cried the Greek.
His prayer was granted. All the earth became
Plastic and vocal to his sense; each peak,
Each grove, each stream, quick with Promethean flame,
Peopled the world with imaged grace and light.
The lyre was his, and his the breathing might
Of the immortal marble; his the play
Of diamond-pointed thought and golden tongue.
Go seek the sunshine-race, ye find to-day
A broken column and a lute unstrung.

"Oh, World-God, give me Power!" the Roman cried.
His prayer was granted. The vast world was chained.
A captive to the chariots of his pride.
The blood of myriad provinces was drained
To feed that fierce, insatiable red heart.
Invulnerably bulwarked every part
With serried legions and with close meshed Code;
Within, the burrowing worm had gnawed its home;
A roofless ruin stands where once abode
Th'imperial race of everlasting Rome.

"Oh, Godhead, give me Truth" the Hebrew cried.
His prayer was granted. He became the slave
Of the Idea, a pilgrim far and wide,
Cursed, hated, spurned, and scourged with none to save.
The Pharaohs knew him, and when Greece beheld,
His wisdom wore the hoary crown of Eld.
Beauty he hath forsworn, and Wealth and Power.
Seek him to-day, and find in every land;
No fire consumes him, neither floods devour;
Immortal through the lamp within his hand.

The Feast of Lights

Kindle the taper like the steadfast star,
Ablaze on evening's forehead o'er the earth,
And add each night a luster till afar
  An eightfold splendor shine above the hearth.
Clash, Israel, the cymbals, touch the lyre,
  Blow the brass trumpet and the harsh-tongued horn;
Chant psalms of victory till the heart takes fire,
  The Maccabean spirit leaps new-born.

Levi Yitzhak of Berditchev (1740-1809)

Levi Yitzhak was a prominent disciple of Baer of Meseriti who was himself an eminent student of the renowned Israel Baal Shem Tov, the founder of the Hasidic movement. Levi Yitzhak is the author of *K'dushat Levi*, a book of homilies that received a good deal of circulation among the Jewish masses in Eastern Europe. He is also known for his many charming and pious folk songs in which he expresses his love for the ordinary people.

Song of Complaint

Good morning to you, Master of the world!
I, Levi Yitzhak, son of Sarah of Berditchev, come to you
    with a complaint about your people, Israel.
What do you want of Israel?

You always say: Command the children of Israel!
You always say: Speak to the children of Israel!
Father of Mercy! Look how many peoples there are in
  the world—
  Persians, Babylonians, Edomites!
What do the Russians say?
  Our Emperor is the Emperor!
What do the Germans say?
  Our State is the State!
What do the English say?
  Our Kingdom is the Kingdom!
But as for me, Levi Yitzhak, son of Sarah of Berditchev,
  I say:
  May His great Name be glorified and sanctified!
And I, Levi Yitzhak, son of Sarah Berditchev, say:
  I shall not go away, nor stir from my place until
  there is an end—
  Until there is an end to our exile
  May His great Name be glorified and sanctified!

(Tr. L. L.)

Rachel (1890-1931)

Rachel Bluestein, who wrote under the pen name of Rachel, was born in Russia, where she studied art. Emigrating to Palestine in 1909, she worked as a common laborer at Rehovot and Kinneret, where she joined Kibbutz Degania. Her awareness of approaching death from tuberculosis is reflected in autobiographical lyrics, elegiac and melancholy in tone, such as "My Dead." Other poems are simple, straightforward celebrations of the countryside of Eretz Yisrael and of the labor-pioneers restoring the land. As with "Kinneret," some have been set to music.

Perhaps

Perhaps these things never happened
And perhaps, too, after the night
I never arose to till the soil
At dawn's first light.

Perhaps, never at harvest time,
Did I raise my voice
In song. When on the wagon filled with wheat
My heart rejoiced.

And perhaps I never bathed
In the stillness of thy stream
Oh Kinneret, My Kinneret
Were you real? Or was it all a dream?

(Tr. L. L.)

Rachel

Her blood flows through me;
Her voice, as well, is mine.
Rachel, Laban's youngest child,
My soul and heart are thine.

I cannot keep my house,
My city does not please,
Since her garments fluttered
In the ancient desert breeze.

Therefore, I shall hold close
To all my chosen ways,
For I know my soul retains
Memories of former days.

(Tr. L. L.)

Isaac Rosenberg (1890-1918)

Born in Bristol, England, and killed in action in France during World War I, Isaac Rosenberg had time to produce only a slim body of work. He was the first English poet after Emma Lazarus, whose works were saturated with Jewish motifs and spirit. Promising as a painter as well as a poet, Rosenberg died too early to develop his talents. Even so, because of his economy of setting and extraordinary images, as evocative today as when he wrote and painted more than sixty-five years ago, his reputation has grown with the years.

The Jew

Moses, from whose loins I sprung,
Lit by a lamp in his blood
Ten immutable rules, a moon
For mutable lampless men.

411

The blonde, the bronze, the ruddy,
With the same heaving blood,
Keep tide to the moon of Moses.
Then why do they sneer at me?

The Destruction of Jerusalem by the Babylonian Hordes

They left their Babylonia bare
Of all its tall men,
Of all proud horses;
They made for Lebanon.

And shadowy sowers went
Before their spears to sow
The fruit whose taste is ash
For Judah's soul to know.

They who bowed to the Bull god
Whose wings roofed Babylon,
Its endless hosts darkened
The bright-heavened Lebanon.

They washed their grime in pools
Where laughing girls forgot
The wiles they used for Solomon.
Sweet laughter! remember not.

Sweet laughter charred in the flame
That clutched the cloud and earth
While Solomon's towers crashed between,
The gird of Babylon's mirth.

Chagrin

Caught still as Absalom,
Surely the air hangs
From the swayless cloud-boughs,
Like hair of Absalom
Caught and hanging still.

From the imagined weight
Of spaces in a sky
Of mute chagrin, my thoughts
Hang like branch-clung hair
To trunks of silence swung,
With the choked soul weighing down
Into thick emptiness.
Christ! end this hanging death,
For endlessness hangs therefrom.

Invisibly—branches break
From invisible trees—
The cloud-woods where we rush,
Our eyes holding so much,
Which we must ride dim ages round
Ere the hands (we dream) can touch.

We ride, we ride, before the morning
The secret roots of the sun to tread,
And suddenly
We are lifted of all we know
And hang from implacable bough.

Nellie Sachs (1891-1970)

Little known outside Germany, where she was born and lived until just before World War II, Nellie Sachs was a co-recipient in 1966 of the Nobel Prize with Agnon. Sachs escaped the Nazis and settled in Sweden, where she continued to write—but with a difference. While her prewar poetry is highly romantic, her postwar poems, influenced by the Holocaust, are heart-rending lyrics of Jewish suffering in the greatest catastrophe ever to befall the Children of Israel. Her visions of the Holocaust, authentic and accurate, stand forth not as memories of a calamitous past but as the horror-filled reality of a dreadful present. Yet *O the Chimneys* (1961) and *In the House of Suffering* (1946) are filled with a steadfast faith, not only in the indestructibility of the Jewish people, but in the significance and importance of their mission.

You Who Looked On

You whose eyes saw the slaying,
Just as a stare at one's back is felt
So too you sense on your bodies
The stares of the dead.

How many dying eyes will observe you
When from its hiding place, you pluck a violet?

How many hands will be lifted in prayer
On the gnarled, martyred branches
Of an old oak tree?
How much memory will grow in the blood
Of the evening sun?

O the unsung cradlesongs
In the turtledove's night-moan—
Many might have plucked stars from the sky,
Now the old well must do this.

You who looked on,
You who lifted no murderous hand,
But did not shake the dust from your longing
You who stopped there, where dust into light
Is transformed.

(Tr. L. L.)

Saul Tchernichovsky (1875-1943)

Like Bialik, who is also almost unknown in the world of letters outside Israel, Tchernichovsky is a great Hebrew poet who deserves a high place in modern literature. Not for him, he said, were the sad, soul-searching, and Galut-weary ways of the Jewish intellectual or the narrowed path and repressed existence of the ghetto Jew. A lover of life, he glorified in the beauty and bounty of the earth. Emphasizing manly vigor and the unconquerable will needed to achieve and embrace the world in its every particular large and small, he responded enthusiastically to the backbreaking efforts of the pioneers rebuilding Israel.

Born in a prosperous village on the border between Crimea and the Ukraine, Tchernichovsky received a secular education supplemented by lessons from private tutors in both Biblical and modern Hebrew. Because of restrictions against Jews in Czarist Russia, he studied medicine at Heidelberg and at Lausanne. After practicing medicine in Russia during the years of war and revolution, he tried for but could not obtain a medical position in Palestine. He did find posts in Germany and elsewhere in Europe, succeeding after nine years in settling in Tel Aviv in 1931.

Tchernichovsky thought of the poet as a seer who discerns unity in the multiple phenomena of the world: the affinity between elements of nature and the connection between humanity's past and present. The sonnet sequence *To the Sun* reveals Tchernichovsky as a pantheist, a lover of nature who would embrace every aspect of existence (although there are lines that indicate Tchernichovsky, in moments of despair, considered himself swallowed up in the violence and immorality of an alien age). He drew subject matter from many eras and different cultures, translating ancient Babylonian epics, Homer, Horace, Shakespeare, Goethe and Longfellow, and adapted them to Hebrew prosody. As a result of this activity and his secular education, the sources for Tchernichovsky's vocabulary and syntax occasionally seem foreign.

Tchernichovsky is often criticized as being a pagan. He rebelled against the moral and didactic motifs of Hebrew poetry, and he studied the pagan roots of many cultures. He viewed them—particularly the ancient Canaanite cults, as the sonnet "My Astarte" implies— as an indication of how free the Jews could have been if not so restricted by Judaism, which he believed had led to decay and weakening of the national will. The poem "Hymn to Apollo" shows his interest in the ancient Greeks stemming from their affirmation of life and love of beauty.

Credo

Laugh at all my dreams, my dearest;
   Laugh, and I repeat anew
That I still believe in man—
   As I still believe in you.

For my soul is not yet sold
   To the golden calf of scorn
And I still believe in man
   And the spirit in him born.

By the passion of his spirit
   Shall his ancient bonds be shed.
Let the soul be given freedom,
   Let the body have its bread!

Laugh, for I believe in friendship,
  And in one I still believe,
One whose heart shall beat with my heart
  And with mine rejoice and grieve.

Let the time be dark with hatred,
  I believe in years beyond
Love at last shall bind the peoples
  In an everlasting bond.

On that day shall my own people
  Rooted in its soil arise,
Shake the yoke from off its shoulders
  And the darkness from its eyes.

Life and love and strength and action
  In their heart and blood shall beat,
And their hopes shall be both heaven
  And the earth beneath their feet.

Then a new song shall be lifted
  To the young, the free, the brave,
And the wreath to crown the singer
  Shall be gathered from my grave.

Before the Statue of Apollo

To thee I come, O long-abandoned god
Of early moons and unremembered days,
To thee, whose reign was in a greener world
Among a race of men divine with youth,
Strong generations of the sons of earth:
To thee, whose right arm broke the bound of heaven
To set on thrones therein thy strongest sons,
Whose proud brows with victorious bays were crowned.

Amongst the gods of old thou wert a god,
Bringing for increase to the mighty earth
A race of demigods, instinct with life,
Strange to the children of the house of pain.
A boy-god, passionate and beautiful.
Whose mastery was over the bright sun
And over the dark mysteries of life,
The golden shadow—treasuries of song,
The music of innumerable seas—
A god of joyousness and fresh delight,
Of vigour and the ecstasy of life.
I am the Jew. Dost thou remember me?
Between us there is enmity forever!
Not all the multitudes of ocean's waters,
Storm-linking continent with continent,
Could fill the dark abyss between us yawning.
The heavens and the boundless wilderness
Were short to bridge the wideness set between
My fathers' children and thy worshippers.
And yet behold me! I have wandered far,
By crooked ways, from those that were before me,
And others after me shall know this path.
But amongst those that will return to thee
I was the first to free my soul that groaned
Beneath the agony of generations;
For a day came I would endure no more,
And on that day my spirit burst its chains
And turned again towards the living earth.
The people and its God have aged together!
Passions which strengthlessness had laid to sleep
Start into sudden life again, and break
Their prison of a hundred generations.
The light of God, the light of God is mine!
My blood is clamorous with desire of life!
My limbs, my nerves, my veins, triumphant shout
For life and sunlight.

                    And I come to thee,

And here before thy pedestal I kneel
Because thy symbol is the burning sun,
I kneel to thee, the noble and the true,
Whose strength is in the fullness of the earth,
Whose will is in the fullness of creation,
Whose throne is on the secret founts of being.
I kneel to life, to beauty and to strength,
I kneel to all the passionate desires
Which they, the dead-in-life, the bloodless ones,
The sick, have stifled in the living God,
The God of wonders of the wilderness,
The God of gods, Who took Canaan with storm
Before they bound Him in phylacteries.

Yehoash (Solomon Bloomgarden)
(1872-1927)

Yehoash, the name by which Yehoash Solomon Bloomgarden is known, is mostly remembered as a translator, although his mature verse written after he was forty—introspective lyrics, nature poems, and mystical ballads—assures him of a place among the finest Yiddish poets.

In 1890 Yehaosh emigrated to the United States from Russia, where he had been born. Contracting tuberculosis in 1900, he spent ten years recuperating in the Denver Sanatorium for Consumptives. There he began what he regarded as his major work, a translation of the Bible. When done it would be the first complete, scholarly, authoritative version in Yiddish. Posthumously published, Yehoash's translation had an impact on Yiddish similar to that of the King James version on English. Yehoash also collaborated with Charles Spivak, his physician in Denver, to publishing a dictionary of Hebrew and Aramaic elements in Yiddish. After leaving the Denver Sanatorium, he returned to New York. Five years later he settled in Rehovot, Palestine, but returned to New York when World War I spread to the Middle East.

In his own poetry Yehoash worked to achieve the classical purity and perfection of rhythm, music, and image he found when translating many of the world's great classics into Yiddish. Even so, his poems convey the deep emotions of a writer who understands as well as feels the struggle and complexities of human existence.

Interested in folklore and fable, Yehoash turned to Aesop, LaFontaine, and his Jewish roots to revive old tales and to re-create half-forgotten legends. His accounts of Hebrew stories are more than retellings: they are portrayals of the human condition. When Zipporah, wife of Moses, tells her father that with the greatest comes isolation, that her husband has become a great leader with the result that she has lost him, it is a portrait not of one period or one figure but of all men in all times.

Many young Yiddish poets of the twentieth century are indebted to Yehoash who wrote lines that compare favorably with the tempo and temper, diction and imagery, compassion and suggestiveness of the best contemporary poets anywhere in the world.

An Old Song

In the blossom-land Japan
Somewhere thus an old song ran:

Said a warrior to a smith
"Hammer me a sword forthwith.
Make the blade
Light as wind on water laid.
Make it long.
As the wheat at harvest song.
Supple, swift
As a snake, without rift,
Full of lightnings, thousand-eyed!
Smooth as silken cloth and thin
As the web that spiders spin.
And merciless as pain, and cold."

"On the hilt what shall be told?"

"On the sword's hilt, my good man,"
Said the warrior of Japan,
"Trace for me
A running lake, a flock of sheep
And one who sings her child to sleep."

(Tr. Marie Syrkin)

Jephthah's Daughter

"And it became a custom in Israel that the daughters of Israel went from year to year to lament for the daughter of Jephthah, the Gileadite, four days in the year."   —*Judges*.

There is a lonely mountain-top,
    A curse upon it lies;
No blade of grass upon it grows,
    No flowers greet the eyes.

But cold, bare cliffs of granite stand,
    Like sentinels of stone,
Year after year, through wind and snow,
    Around a craggy throne.

And on the topmost, coldest peak
    There is a spot of woe—
A little tomb, an old gray tomb,
    Raised centuries ago.

For there within her grave she lies
    Plucked in an evil hour—
The martyred daughter of her race,
    Israel's fairest flower!

There Jephthah's maid forever sleeps—
  The victim that he vowed—
But, four days in the dreary year,
  The loneliness is loud.

And Gilead's mourning daughters
  Up from the valley throng—
The mountain glens reverberate
  With sorrow and with song!

Oh, loud and long and wild they wail
  The light, untimely spent,
And dance upon the mountain top
  A chorale of lament.

And as they dance they seem to see
  Another dancer, too,
And hear, amidst the measure rise,
  The voice of her they rue!

(Tr. Alter Brody)

People

Now fewer mighty ones and less of the many,
But see, the sky brighter and wider,
And still we go linked together, and closer,
Climbing up and up the steps to where
Each of us given his full height
Will push away the ladder
And stand alone, and share!

(Tr. Raphael Rudnick and Joseph Singer)

The Strongest

I'll be the strongest amid you,
Not lightning, stream or mountain blue,
But dew that falling to the earth
   Gives birth.

I'll be the strongest in my hour,
And lofty tree and quiet flower
Will both drink gratefully
   From me.

I'll be the strongest in the land.
I'll be the word that heals, the hand
That unseen and still, as from above,
   Gives love.

(Tr. Marie Syrkin)

Acknowledgments

Agnon, S.Y. *The Rejuvenating Years*. Translated by Curt Leviant. New York: Jewish Frontier, 1930.

Ahad Ha-Am. "Semi-Consolation." Translated by Arthur F. Beringause. *Russian Journal of Zionists* (c. 1904).

Anski, S. *The Dybbuk*. Translated by Joseph Landis. In *The Great Jewish Plays*. Edited by Joseph Landis. New York: Horizon Press, 1972. Reprinted by courtesy of Joseph Landis.

Apocrypha. "The Aphorisms of Jesus Ben Sirach." In *The Complete Bible*. Chicago: University of Chicago Press, 1939.

"Tobit." Arranged and translated from the Greek by Arthur F. Beringause.

Asch, Sholem. *The God of Vengeance*. Translated by Joseph Landis. In *The Great Jewish Plays*. Edited by Joseph Landis. New York: Horizon Press, 1972. Reprinted by courtesy of Joseph Landis.

Moses. New York: Putnam Publishing Group, 1958. Reprinted by courtesy of Moses Asch.

Berechiah Ben Natronai Ha Nakdan. *Fables of a Jewish Aesop.* Translated by Moses Hadas. New York: Columbia University Press, 1966.

Bialik, H.N. "The City of Slaughter" and "To a Bird." In *Selected Poems.* Edited by I. Efros. New York: Bloch Publishing Company, 1952.

"Night." Translated by Maurice Samuel. In *Selected Poems of Bialik.* New York: Palestine Press, 1927.

"The Sabbath Queen." Translated by I. Lask. In *A Golden Treasury of Jewish Literature.* Edited by Leo Schwarz. New York: Holt Rinehart, 1937. Reprinted with the permission of Leo Schwarz.

"Where Are You?" Translated by Emma Lazarus. In *The Poems of Emma Lazarus.* New York: Houghton-Mifflin, 1888.

"Book of Job." In *The Holy Scriptures.* Philadelphia: Jewish Publication Society, 1917. Copyrighted by and used through the courtesy of The Jewish Publication Society of America.

"Book of Ruth." In *The Holy Scriptures.* Philadelphia: Jewish Publication Society, 1917. Copyrighted by and used through the courtesy of The Jewish Publication Society of America.

Buber, Martin. Excerpted from *I and Thou.* Translated and with an Introduction by Walter Kaufmann. Translation copyright © 1970 Charles Scribner's Sons; Introduction copyright © 1970 Walter Kaufmann. Reprinted by permission of Charles Scribner's Sons.

Caro, Joseph. *Jewish Code of Jurisprudence.* Translated by J.L. Kadushin. New Rochelle, N.Y.: 1923.

Chelm Folktales. Based on oral folktales. Adapted and arranged by Leo Lieberman.

Einstein, Albert. *Out of My Later Years.* New York: Philosophical Library, 1956. Copyright by the Estate of Albert Einstein.

Eldad ha-Dani. *The Travels of Eldad the Danite.* In *Post-Biblical Hebrew Literature.* Translated by Benzion Halper. Philadelphia: Jewish Publication Society, 1930. Copyrighted by and used through the courtesy of The Jewish Publication Society of America.

Eliezer of Maience. "Testament of Eliezer of Maience." In *Ethical Wills*. Edited by Israel Abrahams. Philadelphia: Jewish Publication Society, 1948. Copyrighted by and used through the courtesy of The Jewish Publication Society of America.

Feuchtwanger, Lion. *Power*. New York: Viking Press, 1950. Reprinted by permission of Marta Feuchtwanger, Dr. H.C.

Frank, Anne. *The Diary of a Young Girl*. New York: Doubleday & Company, 1952. Copyright 1952 by Otto H. Frank. Reprinted by permission of Doubleday & Company, Inc.

Glückel of Hameln. "Zipporah's Wedding." In *Memoirs*. Translated by Ben-Zion Lask. In *A Golden Treasury of Jewish Literature*. Edited by Leo Schwarz. New York: Holt Rinehart, 1937. Reprinted with permission of Leo Schwarz.

Greenberg, Uri Zevi. "To God in Europe." In *Modern Hebrew Poetry: A Bilingual Anthology*. Edited and translated by Ruth Finer Mintz. Berkeley, Calif.: University of California Press, 1966. Originally published by the University of California Press; reprinted by permission of The Regents of the University of California.

Halevi, Jehudah. *The Kusari*. In *Miscellany of Hebrew Literature*. Vol. I. London: Trübner & Company, 1872.
"A Letter to His Friend, Isaac," "Longing for Jerusalem," and "Love Songs." Translated by Emma Lazarus. In *The Poems of Emma Lazarus*. New York: Houghton-Mifflin, 1888.
"My Heart Is in the East." Translated by Nina Salaman. In *Apples and Honey*, by Nina Salaman. New York: Doubleday, Page & Company, 1922.

Heine, Heinrich. "Donna Clara." Translated by Emma Lazarus. In *The Poems of Emma Lazarus*. New York: Houghton-Mifflin, 1888.

Herzl, Theodor. *Old-New Land*. Leipzig: H. Selman, Nachfolger, 1902. Translated and adapted from German by Arthur F. Beringause.

Hirschbein, Peretz. *Green Fields*. Translated by Joseph Landis. In *The Great Jewish Plays*. Edited by Joseph Landis. New York: Horizon Press, 1972. Reprinted by courtesy of Joseph Landis.

"Hymn of the Initiants." Excerpt from *The Dead Sea Scriptures*. Translated and edited by Theodor H. Gaster. New York: Doubleday & Company, 1956. Copyright © 1956, 1976 by Theodor H. Gaster. Reprinted by permission of Doubleday & Company, Inc.

Ibn Ezra, Abraham. "The Song of Chess." Translated by Nina Salaman. In *Apples and Honey*, by Nina Salaman. New York: Doubleday, Page & Company, 1922.

"When the Morning of Life Had Passed." In *Selected Verses of Abraham Ibn Ezra*. Translated by Solis-Cohen. Philadelphia: Jewish Publication Society, 1934. Copyrighted by and used through the courtesy of The Jewish Publication Society of America.

Ibn Gabirol, Solomon. "Meditations," "Night," and "Night-Thoughts." Translated by Emma Lazarus. In *The Poems of Emma Lazarus*. New York: Houghton-Mifflin, 1888.

Ibn Pakuda, Bahya ben Joseph. *Duties of the Heart*. Vol. II. Translated by M. Hyamson. New York: Philip Feldheim, 1925.

Josephus. *The Jewish War*. Freely translated from 19th century Hebrew version by Leo Lieberman.

Lazarus, Emma. "The Banner of the Jew." In *By the Waters of Babylon*. 1887.

"The Feast of Lights" and "Gifts." In *The Poems of Emma Lazarus*. New York: Houghton-Mifflin, 1888.

Leivick, H. *The Golem*. Translated by Joseph Landis. In *The Great Jewish Plays*. Edited by Joseph Landis. New York: Horizon Press, 1972. Reprinted by courtesy of Joseph Landis.

Levi Yitzhak of Berdichev. "Song of Complaint." Translated from the Yiddish by Leo Lieberman.

Maimonides (Moses Ben Maimon). "Precepts." In *Guide for the Perplexed*. Translated by M. Friedlander. New York: E.P. Dutton & Company, 1910.

"Thirteen Principles of Faith." Translated from 12th century Hebrew text by Leo Lieberman.

Mendele Mokher Sefarim. "The Nag." Translated by Moshe Spiegel. New York: Beechurst Press.
"The Sabbath of the Poor." Translated by Maurice Samuel. In Jewish Anthology. Edited by E. Fleg. New York: Harcourt, Brace & Company, 1925.

Midrash. Excerpts freely translated, adapted, and edited by Leo Lieberman and Arthur F. Beringause. Based on *Babylonian Talmud*, 1483 edition, Soncino, Italy.

Mishna. "Pirke Avot." In *The Mishnah*. Translated by Herbert Danby. Oxford: Oxford University Press, 1933.

Moses Mendelsohn. "Conviction." In *Post-Biblical Hebrew Literature*. Translated by Benzion Halper. Philadelphia: Jewish Publication Society, 1930. Copyrighted by and used through the courtesy of The Jewish Publication Society of America.

Paltiel, Ahimaaz ben-. *Chronicle of Ahimaaz*. Edited by M. Salzman. New York: Columbia University Press, 1924.

Peretz, Isaac Leib. "The Rabbi of Nemirov." Translated by Maurice Samuel. In *Jewish Anthology*. Edited by E. Fleg. New York: Harcourt, Brace & Company, 1925.

Philo. "On the Confusion of Tongues." Reprinted by permission of the publishers and The Loeb Classical Library from "On the Confusion of Tongues" by Philo, translated by F.H. Colson and G.H. Whitaker. Cambridge, Mass.: Harvard University Press, 1932.
"On the Unchangeableness of God." Reprinted by permission of the publishers and The Loeb Classical Library from "On the Unchangeableness of God" by Philo, translated by F.H. Colson and G.H. Whitaker. Cambridge, Mass.: Harvard University Press, 1932.

Pinsky, David. *King David and His Wives*. Translated by Joseph Landis. In *The Great Jewish Plays*. Edited by Joseph Landis. New York: Horizon Press, 1972. Reprinted by courtesy of Joseph Landis.

Rachel. *Poems*. Translated from Hebrew (c. 1925) by Leo Lieberman.

Responsa. *A Treasury of Responsa*. Translated and edited by S. Freehof. Philadelphia: Jewish Publication Society, 1963. Copyrighted by and used through the courtesy of The Jewish Publication Society of America.

Rosenberg, Isaac. *Poems*. Edited by Gordon Bottomley. London: Heineman, 1922.

Sachs, Nellie. "Ihr Zuschauenden." From *O the Chimneys*. New York: Farrar, Straus and Giroux, Inc., 1967. Copyright © 1967 by Farrar, Straus and Giroux, Inc. Reprinted by permission of Farrar, Straus and Giroux, Inc. Newly translated from German by Leo Lieberman.

Sholem Aleichem. "Elijah the Prophet" and "The Passover Guest." In *Yiddish Tales*. Translated by Helena Frank. Philadelphia: Jewish Publication Society, 1912.

Singer, Isaac Bashevis. "The Strong Ones." In *A Day of Pleasure*. New York: Farrar, Straus, and Giroux, Inc., 1963. Copyright © 1963, 1965, 1966, 1969 by Isaac Bashevis Singer. Reprinted by permission of Farrar, Straus, and Giroux, Inc.

Spinoza, Baruch. "The God of Man's Making." In *The Road To Inner Freedom*. Edited by Dagobert D. Runes. New York: Philosophical Library, 1957.

Tchernichovsky, Saul. *Tchernichovsky and His Poetry*. Edited and translated by Maurice Samuel. London: L.U. Snowman, 1929.

Yahoash (Solomon Bloomgarden). "Jephthah's Daughter," translated by Alter Brody. "An Old Song," translated by Marie Syrkin. "People," translated by Raphael Rodnick and Joseph Singer. "The Strongest," translated by Marie Syrkin. In *The Feet of the Messenger*. Philadelphia: Jewish Publication Society, 1923.

Zangwill, Israel. "The Master of the Name." In *Jewish Literature since the Bible*. Book Two. Edited by Feuer and Eisenberg. Cincinnati: Union of American Hebrew Congregations, 1941.

"The Sabbath-Breaker." In *Ghetto Comedies*. Philadelphia: Jewish Publication Society, 1907.

The Zohar. "Jonah." In *The Zohar*. Translated by Harry Sperling and Maurice Simon. London: Soncino Press, 1984. With permission from Soncino Press.